Freud, Dora, and Vienna 1900

Freud, Dora, and Vienna 1900

HANNAH S. DECKER

THE FREE PRESS
A Division of Macmillan, Inc.
NEW YORK
Maxwell Macmillan Canada
TORONTO
Maxwell Macmillan International
NEW YORK   OXFORD   SINGAPORE   SYDNEY

The Free Press
A Division of Macmillan, Inc.
866 Third Avenue, New York, N. Y. 10022

Maxwell Macmillan Canada, Inc.
1200 Eglinton Avenue East
Suite 200
Don Mills, Ontario M3C 3N1

Macmillan, Inc. is part of the Maxwell Communication Group of Companies.

First Free Press Paperback Edition 1992

Printed in the United States of America

printing number

1 2 3 4 5 6 7 8 9 10

Library of Congress Cataloging-in-Publication Data
Decker, Hannah S.
  Freud, Dora, and Vienna 1900 / Hannah S. Decker.
    p.   cm.
  Includes bibliographical references and index.
  ISBN 0-02-907212-3
  1. Hysteria—Case studies. 2. Psychoanalysis—Case studies. 3. Bauer, Ida, 1882–1945. 4. Freud, Sigmund, 1856–1939. 5. Jews, Austrian—Social life and customs. 6. Vienna (Austria)—Social life and customs. I. Title.
RC532.D39   1990
616.85'24'0092—dc20
[B]   90–40039
                                                       CIP

Grateful acknowledgment is made to the following for permission to reprint previously published material:

Sigmund Freud Copyrights, The Institute of Psycho-Analysis, and The Hogarth Press for permission to quote from *The Standard Edition of the Complete Psychological Works of Sigmund Freud* translated and edited by James Strachey.

From *Sigmund Freud: Collected Papers, Volume III,* authorized translation by Alix and James Strachey. Published by arrangement with The Hogarth Press, Ltd., and the Institute of Psycho-Analysis, London. Reprinted by permission of Basic Books, Inc., Publishers, New York.

Permission granted for the U.S. territory by Atrium Press Ltd., London, and for non-U.S. English-speaking territories by Cassell Publishers Ltd., London, to quote from Stefan Zweig, *The World of Yesterday.*

Material from *The Letters of Sigmund Freud, 1873–1938,* edited by Ernst L. Freud, is reproduced by permission of A. W. Freud et al., by arrangement with Sigmund Freud Copyrights, Colchester.

Material reprinted from *The Jews of Vienna, 1867–1914: Assimilation and Identity* by Marsha L. Rozenblit by permission of the State University of New York Press.

Material reprinted by permission of the publishers from *The Complete Letters of Sigmund Freud to Wilhelm Fliess 1887–1904,* translated and edited by Jeffrey Moussaieff Masson, Harvard University Press, Copyright © 1985 and under the Bern Convention Sigmund Freud Copyrights Ltd., Copyright © 1985 Jeffrey Moussaieff Masson for translation and editorial matter.

Material from *Last Waltz in Vienna: The Rise and Destruction of a Family, 1842–1942* by George Clare. Copyright © 1980 by Verlag Ullstein GmbH. Reprinted by permission of Henry Holt and Company, Inc., and Macmillan London Ltd.

Journal of the American Psychoanalytic Association

Journal of Social History

*To the memory of Samuel Shulman
and for Eugenia Foss Hertzman*

Contents

Preface

Sigmund Freud's story of "Dora," an adolescent girl he treated in his early years as a psychoanalyst, has compelled all who have read it. Drily titled "Fragment of an Analysis of a Case of Hysteria," the name gives little hint of what awaits the reader. For almost a century, psychoanalysts have valued the case history as a pioneering vehicle in theory and technique and have pointed with pride to Freud's courage in publishing a case in which he had badly stumbled. In the past two decades, feminists have read the case from a new vantage point and found that both Freud's treatment and the circumstances of Dora's life buttress their contentions about the sexism inherent in modern Western culture. Now, as a historian, I have sought to mine Freud's text as one would a rich lode, following its many glimmering veins so that his young patient emerges as an historical figure in her own right.

Although the "Fragment" is above all the story of a turn-of-the-century, upper-middle-class Viennese-Jewish family, it provides other insights as well. One meets the medicine practiced one hundred years ago, glimpses late-Victorian attitudes toward women, grasps the significance to Freud of an intensive encounter with a patient, and ponders the origins of "hysteria," an illness already described in an Egyptian papyrus four thousand years ago. From any perspective, one is drawn to Dora's story—a tale of love, betrayal, and what might have been.

Readers who are at home with the text of the "Fragment" will find that I have made certain alterations. One is in Dora's ages. Almost every time Freud states Dora's age, she was actually a year younger. At all times I have been guided by her actual date of birth, November 1, 1882, and have calculated accordingly. The second change I have made is with certain words or phrases of the Strachey English translation. Usually, I have remained content to use the standard translation, but at times I have substituted my own where I believe it is more accurate.

In writing this book, I am indebted to a number of individuals. I owe special gratitude to Peter Loewenberg for introducing me to Dora's family history and to Albrecht Hirschmüller for making available to me pertinent records of the Vienna Jewish Community (Israelitische Kultusgemeinde Wien.) For a wide variety of other information and advice, I want very much to thank Harold P. Blum, Ruth Decker, Talya Fishman, Susan Friesell, Frank L. Holt, Edward D. Joseph, Steven H. Mintz, Constance A. Moore, Erika Nielsen, Gertrud B. Pickar, Claus Reschke, Brian J. Schulman, Noel T. Taylor, and Edwin C. Wood.

I am grateful for the administrative support at the University of Houston, in particular that of James H. Pickering and James W. Pipkin of the College of Humanities and Fine Arts. I wish to thank the university's Research Committee for awarding me two grants-in-aid that facilitated the initial phases of my project. Many staff members of the M. D. Anderson Library at the University were unusually helpful, and I could not have managed without the able services of the Inter-Library Loan Department. And I must add a special note of thanks to two reference librarians: John E. Fadell and Margaret E. Culbertson.

I have been fortunate in having the enthusiastic and extensive advice of several friends and colleagues, chiefly Jeffry Adelman, Linda Auwers, Peter Gay, and James H. Jones. They have saved me from many mistakes and unbalanced emphases, and I will always be grateful for their interest and suggestions. Yet ultimately the book is mine, and I am responsible for its final form.

I derive great pleasure from thanking my editor, Joyce Seltzer; I cannot imagine the book as it is without her encouragement and tutelage. She brings to her work a valuable combination of insight and experience.

Above all, I am moved to acknowledge the creativity and knowledge of my husband, Norman Decker, who has been my intellectual companion in this venture as in so many others. He is my constant anchor in times of trouble as well as triumph, and he alone knows what I owe him.

Prologue: Enter Dora

In 1900 Sigmund Freud treated an eighteen-year-old middle-class Jewish girl for a mysterious cough and loss of voice. He gave his patient the name Dora. At the turn of the century, girls and women—seemingly more so than men—often exhibited physical symptoms without discernible causes. These girls and women were designated as suffering from "hysteria," a hoary name that does little more than announce that the illness was considered feminine: *Hysteria* comes from the ancient Greek word for uterus.

Since both the specific symptoms and the incidence of the malady have changed throughout time, hysteria must be understood in the widest possible psychological as well as social contexts. Freud's tale of Dora, which begins when she was six, provides the opportunity to do just that. Dora was a bright, physically active girl whose parents had become estranged, leaving her unusually close to her ailing father. She became his nurse, a frequent occupation for a nineteenth-century daughter. Dora's father, a hard-driving, self-made textile manufacturer, was as enterprising in manipulating his family and friends as he was his workers. Her mother, cold and withdrawn, sought control over family members through an angry obsession with housecleaning. Thus was set the unhappy personal stage on which Dora came to womanhood.

But the familial milieu was not Dora's only burden. The imperial splendor of fin-de-siècle Vienna was for her a hostile world. As a girl and a woman, she was enveloped by the prevalent misogyny, which, through much of contemporary science and art as well as social conventions, denigrated femaleness. In a medical atmosphere unfriendly to hysterical sufferers, she was considered scheming and devious. Before she came to Freud she had already endured a series of painful and ineffective electrical and hydropathic treatments.

1

In an economically and politically transitional society at odds with itself, Dora was also maligned as a Jew. Vienna's virulent anti-Semitism made her feel both inferior and frustrated. She had failed to achieve the acceptance she had thought would be hers by assimilation into the wider world. Although one need not be Jewish to develop hysterical symptoms, in Dora's case, her Jewishness intensified the feelings of powerlessness and repressed anger that place a human being at risk for hysteria. Historically, hysteria has appeared prominently among groups—such as slaves, soldiers, and servants—who feel they have little control over their lives.

In this multifaceted disease, biology also plays a role. For Dora to develop and retain her strange, intractable physical symptoms, she had to possess the tendency to express her emotional distress in somatic ways.

The case was made to order for Freud. For well over a decade, he had been treating girls and women for hysteria, first with electrotherapy and hypnosis and then—more successfully—with psychotherapy. He had honed the latter method so finely that he had even given it a distinctive name: *psychoanalysis.* He was confident of his ability to deal with Dora's symptoms and labeled her complaints as the most ordinary types of hysterical illness. Writing to a friend, he bragged that the case "has smoothly opened to the existing collection of picklocks." Freud became so pleased with the progress he was making in explaining Dora's symptoms that he was shocked when she abruptly quit the treatment after eleven weeks, giving him but one day's warning.

What had gone wrong? As diverse as the causes of Dora's hysteria was the baggage—personal as well as professional—that the middle-aged Freud brought to a seemingly straightforward case. No psychoanalytic encounter is simple, bringing together, as it does, the lives of both therapist and patient in an intense relationship. And in Dora's case, the therapy was complicated by the newness of the psychoanalytic method.

Not until Dora left the treatment did Freud realize that the analysis had been adversely affected by his failure to discern Dora's transfer of angry feelings onto him. And not until a decade had passed did he become aware that his bombardment of her with sexual interpretations had been premature. Freud never consciously realized the extent to which Dora— "in the first bloom of youth"—had aroused him sexually and that her independent spirit had irked him. But the very name he coined for her, it will be seen, reflected his frustration and irritation.

Freud briefly saw Dora for the last time a year and a half after their first encounter. Yet their lives remained intertwined, first when Dora's brother personally consulted him and later when one of Freud's followers fleetingly treated her—then a woman of forty—for new symptoms. In the end Freud and Dora shared a common destiny in the wake of the Nazis' 1938 invasion of Vienna.

Dora's story began before she ever met Freud, first in the treatment rooms of other neurologists and, even earlier, in the checkered legacy of her Bohemian-Jewish ancestry.

1

"In Spite of Her Reluctance"

One day early in October 1900, Philipp Bauer, a prosperous man of forty-seven, walked out of his apartment house on the Liechtensteinstrasse in Vienna's Ninth District. He turned left, continued on the street, and turned left again when he reached the Berggasse. This took him slightly downhill in the direction of the Danube Canal, and after two blocks he entered an apartment house at Number 19 and turned left to the ground-floor office of Dr. Sigmund Freud. After a brief time in the waiting room, he was called into the doctor's consulting room.

This was not Bauer's first visit. Dr. Freud specialized in neurology and psychotherapy and had treated Bauer for syphilitic symptoms several years earlier. Then, in 1898, Bauer had brought to Freud his fifteen-year-old daughter, Dora, who had been suffering for a long time from a chronic cough, loss of voice, and severe hoarseness. But Dora was tired of seeing physicians who, she invariably found, could not help her. Although Freud proposed treating her with entirely novel methods, she was adamant that she would not begin yet another round of fruitless appointments and refused any treatment.

But now Bauer was returning to arrange an appointment for his daughter. A few weeks shy of eighteen, Dora was no more eager to see Freud than she had been at fifteen, but this time her father would not tolerate her objections. The issue was no longer just a mysterious cough and loss of voice but two wearying years of depression and irritability, recently capped by a suicide note and a fainting episode. Her parents were alarmed, and so Dora, "in spite of her reluctance," as Freud later wrote, was forced to begin the "psychological treatment" he had proposed earlier.[1]

Dora's imperfect health stretched back to childhood. In addition to the usual children's diseases, she had had a series of physical problems from the age of six or seven, when she began to wet her bed. The enuresis had stopped shortly before her eighth birthday but had soon been replaced by a shortness of breath and the now-familiar cough and loss of voice. After a while they too went away. But at twelve, she began to suffer from migraines and the cough returned, this time to remain stubbornly throughout her adolescence. A typical attack usually began with a complete loss of voice and then lasted from three to five weeks, the aphonia meliorating into hoarseness. Doctors could find no evidence of disease or indeed anything physically awry that might be responsible for the symptoms, and no medical treatments had ever helped.

Although Dora's headaches gradually remitted over a span of four years, physical problems continued to plague her. In addition to the chronic cough and hoarseness, she "frequently suffered from gastric pains," constipation, and a vaginal discharge she referred to as a "catarrh." Her menstrual periods were very irregular, sometimes accompanied by "violent pains." At sixteen she was struck by a high fever and right-sided abdominal pain, which was diagnosed as an attack of appendicitis. When she recovered she found herself unable to walk normally and dragged her right foot. Climbing stairs was particularly difficult for a number of months, and even during the time she saw Freud her foot occasionally dragged.

As Freud remembered her, Dora had had several "natural gifts." She was "a girl of intelligent and engaging looks [and] intellectual precocity," yet "she was a source of heavy trials for her parents"—depressed, dissatisfied with herself, unfriendly toward her father, and on "very bad terms" with her mother. She had few if any friends and avoided social occasions. She complained of fatigue and lack of concentration. When she was not ill or feeling out of sorts, she went to art exhibitions, attended lectures for women, and studied on her own.

What Dora suffered from was no mystery to physicians of the day. She, like numerous other women, was afflicted with "hysteria"—a condition manifested by a variety of physical and emotional problems, unaccompanied by any discernible organic changes. Her symptoms were hardly unique; doctors saw their like all the time: shortness of breath, cough, loss of voice, headaches, abdominal pains, depression, social withdrawal, and ennui. Her illness lacked any of the dramatic features that made for one of the more "interesting" cases: numbness of a bodily area, contractures or paralyses of the limbs, exquisite hypersensitivities, inability to walk, partial or full blindness, unremitting pain, amnesias. Even when she was eight, her family doctor had pronounced an attack of dyspnea—difficulty in breathing—to be of "nervous" origin, and within six months the condition had passed. When Freud first saw her, he immediately diagnosed her as "merely a case of *'petite hystérie'* . . . not upon the whole . . . worth recording."

Although in the nineteenth century Dora's condition was not hard to identify, its cause was mysterious. And since hysteria was so rife, its etiology sparked intense speculation and sometimes bitter disagreement among medical men. Explanations of hysteria had a long history. Various ancient Greek philosophers and physicians, including Plato, had argued that the uterus (*hystera*) is an independent entity within a woman's body. Teleologically oriented, these thinkers concluded that the uterus had an ardent desire to create children.[2] If the womb remained empty for too long after its owner's puberty, it became unhappy and angry and began to travel throughout the body. In its wanderings it pressed against various bodily organs, creating "hysterical"—that is, uterus-related—symptoms. So, when a woman felt as if she could not breathe, it was because the uterus was in the throat or was compressing the bronchial tubes. If a woman was lethargic or fainted often, it was because the uterus was impinging on the blood vessels going to the brain. The womb, in its meanderings, might bump up against the heart; this caused palpitations. When the uterus pressed on the liver, it created stomach pain.

The uterine theory of hysteria persisted for many centuries and was still strong in the eighteenth century. But by the end of the nineteenth century, most physicians no longer accepted this notion. They recognized that hysteria existed in men and young children as well and knew, therefore, that it had to have some other etiology. Physicians generally thought that hysterical sufferers had a hereditary, or at least a constitutional, predisposition to the illness. As proof they pointed to its recurrence in families. German and English experts often declared that it was more frequent among "Latin" peoples than among "Anglo-Saxons." Jews and Poles were said to exhibit a high frequency. But after postulating a hereditary taint, physicians then singled out a wide array of factors as the actual instigating agents. A typical list of "occasional causes," compiled by Charles Féré, a world-famous French psychiatrist, included earthquake, lightning, excitation of any of the sense organs, fever, general disease or infection, diabetes, lead poisoning, alcoholism, hemorrhage, diarrhea, overwork, too much sexual activity, excessive physical or mental labor, fatigue, poverty, and imprisonment.[3]

While upholding the underlying factor of hereditary predisposition, some physicians considered hysteria to be the result of an unfortunate or misspent life. Thus hysteria in children could be caused by parental maltreatment (especially that of stepmothers, in one physician's experience) or nursemaids' cruelties. The idle and overgratified life of the rich could be as responsible as the poverty, grief, and anxiety of the poor.[4]

Such explanations notwithstanding, the ideas associating hysteria with essential femaleness never disappeared, not only because they were an ancient staple but because more women than men came to doctors' offices with hysterical symptoms. This circumstance aroused comment but not controversy. It stimulated such clinical observations as: "Hysteria is generally more intense during menstruation, pregnancy, and lactation."[5] It stirred general pronouncements that "nearly all women are said to be somewhat hysterical."[6] And often it provoked eloquent disquisitions on the nature of women. The very makeup of a woman, what the London physician Samuel Wilks called her "organisation," meant that her system was vulnerable to hysteria. Most men could better endure the stresses that in women produced hysteria: "If a man have undergone great bodily fatigue, and his mind have been at the same time harassed, so that exhaustion of his nervous system results, he may be thrown into a state very like that of an hysterical woman."[7] Women easily fell into the hysterical state when they were not doing the work that "especially belong[s] to them such as the rearing of children, domestic avocations, and the like. . . . Superfluous energies . . . having no outlet . . . the whole system becomes disordered, and . . . hysteric symptoms ensue."[8]

Of all women adolescent girls were most at risk, and it was thought that the particular form their illness assumed rendered them dangerous to their families and to society at large. " 'From twelve or fourteen to eighteen or twenty is that period of life to which the tide of natural affection runs the lowest [and] girls . . . are harder and more selfish till the master passion takes them.' . . . The whole nervous system, including the mental and moral nature, becomes so perverted that no circumstance of the most extraordinary kind may not then happen. . . . The behaviour is like that of one possessed of a devil." Dr. Wilks considered a hysterical adolescent girl capable of committing arson or murdering a child.[9]

Thus, doctors often regarded hysterical sufferers with deep suspicion and sometimes with frank hostility. These attitudes influenced treatment in flagrant as well as in subtle ways.[10]

Before Dora began seeing Freud, the doctors to whom she had been brought had diagnosed her as suffering from a nervous complaint and had treated her with the standard methods used for hysterical symptoms. A very wide variety of treatments existed, as is usual when the causes of any illness are essentially unknown. Freud recorded that Dora's previous treatments had included the direct application of electricity to her vocal cords, and hydrotherapy. It is almost certain that she had also received electrical stimuli to other parts of her body, as well as a gamut of routinely prescribed drugs.

Treatment by electric current was much in vogue at the end of the nineteenth century and in the early decades of the twentieth. For about fifty years it was regarded as the most scientifically advanced of all the therapies for hysteria, reflecting the status of electricity as the wonder phenomenon of the nineteenth century.[11] The discoveries of Luigi Galvani in 1786 and Alessandro Volta in 1800 had established that electricity could be chemically generated, and, in honor of Galvani, such electric current was called galvanism. In 1831 Michael Faraday discovered that electricity could be produced by a moving magnet, and "faradism" was born. Believing that an important "life process" with curative benefits had been found, physicians began to apply galvanism and faradism to muscles and other organs. A metal implement was placed on the patient, and rapid shocks were administered.[12] Elaborate electrotherapeutic regimes, with precise instructions for their implementation, were formulated by neurologists and began to be published in the 1860s.[13]

When Freud had first opened his private neurological practice in the spring of 1886, he invested precious florins from a "small, rapidly dwindling supply of cash"[14] in expensive electrical equipment and instruments and followed the procedures specified in the *Handbook of Electrotherapy* by the distinguished German neurologist, Wilhelm Erb.[15] Freud became disillusioned with his ambiguous results within two years and dropped electrotherapy in favor of hypnotic suggestion. But most neurologists retained their faith in electrical regimes, even if not every patient was helped by them.

Dora, definitely diagnosed by 1894 as having hysterical symptoms and with the money to spend on the best treatment, was a clear candidate for electrotherapy. Her neurologists generally agreed that the soundest therapeutic results came from local application of electricity directly to the site of the diseased part. Yet, in cases of "general neurosis or constitutional disease," it was thought advisable to use general faradization or galvanization.[16] Since Dora suffered from "a general disturbance of the nervous system" as well as from specific, localized dysfunctions, she received both systemic and localized treatments.[17]

The initial electrotherapeutic approach may well have been general faradization because it was usually less traumatic than localized treatments and less dangerous than general galvanization (which posed a danger to the central nervous system.) For a session of faradization, Dora would have taken off most of her clothes, perhaps putting on a lightweight gown. Then she sat on a chair and her bare feet were placed on a large, flat, well-moistened electrode or in a basin filled with lukewarm water, either of which was connected to the negative pole of a magnetic coil. The positive pole, for contact with the body, was either a round, sponge-covered electrode two to three inches in diameter or the physician's own moist hand. In the latter case, the therapist held the electrode in one hand, allowed the current to pass through his body, and touched the patient with his free "electrical hand." The "electrical hand" was recommended for "sensitive persons," since in this way the physician could better control the intensity of the current.

For ten to twenty minutes, depending on Dora's reactions, an electrical current would have been applied in varying strengths to her body, beginning with the forehead and proceeding to the temples, the top of her head, the back of her head and neck, and then slowly up and down the spinal column, stopping for longer intervals at "special points." The entire neck would be faradized separately to stimulate its nerves and muscles before the electrode would be applied all over the chest, especially around the heart, and to the abdomen. Here the doctor moved slowly in order to be sure the intestines and abdominal muscles contracted. There would be visible and palpable waves of intestinal contraction (peristalsis) and audible gurgling.[18] "Finally, the muscles and skin of the back and all lower extremities were vigorously stimulated . . . the electrode . . . forcibly drawn over all these parts . . . with such a strong current that active muscular contractions develop[ed] everywhere."[19]

Patients' reactions to general faradization were variable. Many felt refreshed, their symptoms temporarily gone. But others developed dizziness, nausea, trembling, and feelings of faintness. Some defecated as a result of the intestinal contractions. Certain patients had a delayed reaction, so that one or two days later they complained of muscle pain, increased nervousness, headache, and insomnia. Varying with the frequency of treatments, their duration over time, and individual vulnerabilities, minor electrical burns were inflicted, affecting the patient's skin at the sites of application of the electrodes. Patients often felt pricking and burning sensations. Redness of the skin was common, often persisting for hours, and patients developed pimples and welts. After many treatments the skin peeled. Then scabs formed, sometimes leaving small indentations and permanent, pigmented scars after they dropped off.[20] But if a series of treatments was successful, the patient bloomed.

She slept better, ate more, and was no longer troubled by digestive ailments; feelings of weakness dissipated, her head pains disappeared, and nervousness and depression were considerably diminished.

Perhaps Dora did experience some of these improvements after her course of general faradization, but the therapy was of no avail as far as her specific symptoms were concerned. One of Dora's most persistent and disabling conditions was her aphonia; an attack sometimes lasted for weeks. At such times she could speak only in a whisper. Doctors knew exactly what the physical problem was, although not at all why it existed, there being no observable pathology to explain it. On inspection the larynx appeared normal, yet the adductor (tensor) muscles were partially paralyzed, causing the vocal cords to remain separated. When the hysterical sufferer attempted to speak, no sound emerged because the cords did not come together. The remarkable thing—and this was why the loss of voice was undoubtedly hysterical—was that the adductors came together during coughing, and the cords moved freely while the patient was breathing.[21]

Dora's neurologists would have been more comfortable if they could have identified a central nervous system defect that caused the aphonia. But since they were "entirely in the dark with regard to the site of the lesion," they considered it appropriate by default to apply either faradic or galvanic current directly to the nerves and muscles of the larynx.[22] The goal was to cause muscle contractions. Accompanied by the physician's suggestion that the procedure would be curative, faradic or galvanic shocks to the larynx caused many patients to regain their voices.[23]

As a chronic sufferer, Dora probably came for localized treatments two to four times a week. If Erb's advice was followed, she received a series of treatments lasting two to six months, or as long as there seemed some assurance that the sessions were helping or might be expected to do so. Then, after a series was complete, an equal period was spent trying alternate cures: baths, a change of climate, massage. In "obstinate cases," this regimen could go on for years, depending on "external circumstances [and] the pecuniary condition of the patient."[24]

The mildest local electrotherapy for hysterical aphonia was the stimulation of the larynx and its nerves through the skin. One electrode was placed on the neck, and one was moved along the larynx and trachea, evoking involuntary swallowing. If this superficial stimulation failed, a curved implement with an electrode at its tip was inserted into the throat and pharyngeal cavity. Current was then applied directly to the superior laryngeal nerve and the six laryngeal muscles. Only a skilled and determined practitioner could attempt this treatment, since it met "with the greatest difficulties. . . . Each application was followed by gagging, vomiting, temporary aphonia, hoarseness, pain in the neck, etc." A variant of this procedure was the use of the "faradic moxa." Somehow the "electrical brush" was passed into the throat cavity, and the membrane covering the larynx was stroked as faradic current flowed through the wire bristles. The faradic brush produced "violent counterirritation [and was] very painful." Erb said that this method often had "brilliant results" and told of a doctor who had reported recoveries after one session.[25]

Electricity was also the treatment of choice for Dora's chronic cough. Hysterical cough was wearyingly common—it had been the presenting complaint in 1880 of Anna O., Josef Breuer's famous patient. Its description was unvarying from manual to manual: a harsh, loud, monotonous bleat or bark, with a hollow, metallic quality, repeated in the same key for hours during the day without any expectoration.[26]

Unlike aphonia, cough could not be handled by applying electricity directly to an organ, so it was always treated cutaneously. Erb described his cure of a case of "nervous cough" in a girl of twelve, the identical age at which Dora had first manifested the symptom. He used galvanization, transversely through the larynx and from the neck to the larynx, producing the usual involuntary swallowing. The improvement was startling.[27]

Besides loss of voice and chronic cough, Dora told Freud she also suffered from gastric pains and constipation and had in the past been plagued by migraines. The neurologists Dora saw in her early adolescence would have treated these complaints also either with general faradization or galvanization for the overall hysterical condition or with local applications of electricity. In the case of her headaches, it is unlikely that the electrotherapy would have been responsible for their disappearance, because the "nervous" headache of hysteria was widely known to be among the most difficult symptoms to treat. Sometimes—unaccountably—results were "brilliant," but usually one had to be prepared to continue the treatments for months or years to get a permanent effect. While there were no special repercussions from local faradization to the head, there were "definite effects" from galvanization: vertigo, feelings of dullness and confusion, fainting, nausea, and vomiting.[28]

For stomach and intestinal pains associated with hysteria, the prognosis with the use of electricity was mixed.[29] However, for chronic constipation, the outlook was bright; here faradization over sites close to the intestines was "an admirable agent." The current had to be strong enough to produce vigorous contractions of the abdominal muscles. Each treatment lasted from three to ten minutes and was usually followed by defecation. Erb suggested two modifications if results were not obtained by intestinal faradization alone. One was to precede the use of faradism by a few minutes of galvanic current. The second, "to secure more vigorous action," was to take the electrode normally placed on the lumbar vertebrae and put it into the patient's rectum. Ordinarily, electrotherapy for constipation was followed by gradual improvement, so that the patient came to depend less and less on purgatives.[30]

Although physicians invested their money in the latest electrical apparatus, and their time and thought in its utilization, the realists readily admitted the unpredictable nature of electrotherapy. The great Erb, who made his living and his reputation from the therapeutic use of electricity, described the situation candidly: "[Hysteria], with its innumerable symptoms and its variable course, is a frequent object of electro-therapeutics, despite numerous and often surprising failures. On the whole, hysteria resists electrical treatment as obstinately as it does all other measures."[31] Erb did not discuss an unintended by-product, but it manifested itself in Dora, whose ailments did not respond to electrotherapy: Repeated experiences with the unpleasant procedures caused her to lose confidence in the abilities of physicians.

Dora had no better luck with hydrotherapy, a treatment as respectable, if not as modern, as electrotherapy and for some physicians still their first choice for treating nervous complaints. The use of water was prompted by the same theory as the use of electricity—the goal was to shock the system or the affected part. Cold water, therefore, was deemed the best. This was put poetically by Charles Féré: "The vascular reactions which [cold water] produces constitute a veritable gymnastics of the skin."[32] Elaborate facilities and trained attendants were necessary to carry out the various precisely described maneuvers.[33]

Experts recommended above all the general douche—a jet of water to the body; the force of the water was considered as efficacious as its temperature. Brief bursts of water at forty-five degrees Fahrenheit were given for fifteen seconds, or bursts of water at fifty degrees for twenty to thirty seconds.[34] If the patient could not tolerate the cold water or its pressure, then the "Scotch" douche was tried. Warm water (100 degrees Fahrenheit) was sprinkled on the patient for as little as one-half minute to as long as three minutes. Then, when the patient was felt to be ready, the cold-water jet was introduced. There was also the transition douche, starting with warm water and gradually lowering the temperature to cold. Simple immersion in water was not a frequent hydropathic method because it lacked the therapeutic "percussion."[35] Physicians who did not have access to adequate douche facilities could have patients wrapped in cold, wet sheets. Here the goal was to produce sedation through rubbing the patient's body in the sheets. After a time the sheets became warm and the patient relaxed.[36]

We have no way of knowing which of these hydrotherapeutic procedures were used on Dora, but we do know they proved as useless as the faradization. And, if Dora had received any of the standard medicines for nervous complaints, they had had no lasting effect—nor were they usually intended to. By the end of the nineteenth century most physicians were aware that the age-old remedies had limited symptomatic value and that some—such as opium and its derivatives—could be addicting. Doctors continued to prescribe them, however, but stressed their auxiliary and temporary efficacy. Those most frequently advised were various bromides, which were cardiac and cerebral depressants; asafetida, a venerable nostrum whose smell was supposed to drive the womb back where it belonged; valerian, which could act both as a gastrointestinal soother and as a "nerve stimulant"; oil of lavender, a sedative by virtue of its pleasant smell; strychnine, a spinal cord irritant; and quinine, which not only reduced fevers but was regarded as a tonic for debility and exhaustion.[37]

By the time she was fifteen, after three years of various conventional treatments, Dora routinely refused her parents' suggestions to try new specialists. As Freud observed, she "had developed into a mature young woman of very independent judgement who had grown accustomed to laugh at the efforts of doctors, and in the end to renounce their help entirely." In a milieu where at least superficial recognition of medical and parental authority was the norm, Dora managed in many respects to keep her elders at bay. Thus, she had rejected the idea of seeing Freud the first time her father brought her to him in the early summer of 1898. It had been only after overcoming the most strenuous resistance, invoking all his authority, that Philipp Bauer finally compelled his daughter to see Freud two years later, just before her eighteenth birthday.

2

"The Purely Human and Social Circumstances"

Dora, Freud's pseudonym for Ida Bauer, was born in Vienna on November 1, 1882, in an apartment at Berggasse 32, only a few doors away from the building where she was later to visit Freud. Her birth was assisted, as was customary, by a midwife, one Anna Eichenthal. Her father, Philipp Bauer, was twenty-nine, and her mother, Katharina (born Gerber), was twenty; both were Jewish. Dora was her parents' second child.[1]

The Bauers had only recently moved to the Berggasse, and their new quarters were evidence of an increase in material well-being and status. Just fourteen months earlier, Dora's brother, Otto, had been born in a house on the other side of the Danube Canal, in the Leopoldstadt (Second) District, an area largely filled with slum dwellings in which lived poor Jews, many newly arrived in the capital from the provinces. But the Berggasse was in the Alsergrund (Ninth) District, a respectable, middle-class area close to Vienna's fashionable center. The Bauers' star was in the ascendant. Philipp Bauer, although residing in Vienna, had been born in Bohemia and owned textile mills there, in the northwestern reaches of the Austro-Hungarian Empire, an area today part of Czechoslovakia.

Dora's family was representative of many hundreds of Bohemian Jews who had emigrated to Vienna in the latter decades of the nineteenth century. Dora's father, his older brother, and his younger sister were all born in the small market town of Pollerskirchen (today Úsobí), near the Moravian border. It is highly likely that Dora's grandparents, Jakob and Babette Bauer, moved their family from Pollerskirchen to Vienna in the late 1850s or in the 1860s. Dora's mother was born in the mountain town

14

of Königinhof (today Dvůr Králové in north central Czechoslovakia, about twenty-five miles from the Polish border). Most likely Katharina Gerber's family came to Vienna in the 1860s or perhaps a bit later.

Although characterized by cruel social and economic injustices that readily slipped into extremes of murder and massacre, the history of the Jews in Bohemia was not one of unbroken misery. Its particular curse was eternal uncertainty. Frequent expulsions were usually followed by some limited permission to resettle, and life would once more resume, but never with ordinary surety. The legacy bequeathed to Philipp and Katharina Bauer and their two children by centuries of state-decreed inferiority, familial upheaval, and spasms of dubious quiet was the trauma of hopes raised only to be brutally dashed. This pattern appeared yet again once the Jews were formally emancipated, and it colored the background of Freud and Dora's encounter.

The result of many generations' precarious existence was an inherent sense of vulnerability. Although this psychological state accurately reflected their history, it led to the Jews readily agreeing with anti-Semitic explanations of why they were more disposed to neurosis than the non-Jewish population.[2] Evidence of the Jews' belief in their own "hereditary taint" is rife, appearing in such places as the 1894 medical textbook by Hermann Oppenheim, the well-known German-Jewish neurologist; the private letters of Theodor Gomperz, the famous Austrian-Jewish classical philologist; and in the discussions of the Vienna Psychoanalytic Society, whose membership was mainly Jewish.[3] Yet the reasons Jews gave for their supposedly more frequent neuroses were far from the heart of the matter and merely echoed modish intellectual sentiments. In keeping with the Darwinian and anthropological emphases of the time, they discussed their vulnerability in terms of centuries of "inbreeding." Or, taking refuge with—generally anti-Semitic—critics of modernity, they pointed to the Jewish obsession with money or their high-strung, "overly civilized" nature, stemming from generations of "cosmopolitan" living.

However, if nineteenth-century Jews felt themselves weaker and more susceptible to life's risks—and certainly this was not true physically, Jews having a lower mortality rate than that of the surrounding peoples[4]—such notions had to come in part from the sense of imminent danger Jewish parents continued to transmit, in countless small ways, to their children. It is a convergent conclusion of modern psychological, sociological, and historical literature that ethnic discrimination and the stresses of acculturation are sources of mental ill health,[5] and experimental studies have buttressed this view.[6]

In the opening pages of his report on Dora's treatment, Freud wrote that psychoanalysts "are obliged to pay as much attention in [their] case histories to the purely human and social circumstances of [their] patients as to the somatic data and the symptoms of the disorder." Dora's story must be told within the broader framework of Bohemian and Viennese Jewish history.

———

From the time of their first settlement in the eleventh century until the end of the eighteenth century, the Jews in Bohemia were a people apart from the rest of the population. Dependent on the good will of both local and national rulers, as well as on the stability of political and economic conditions, the Jews found their lives to be hallmarked by unpredictability.

In late medieval and early modern times, when conditions were favorable, the Jews would establish a community life, speak Czech like their neighbors, engage in a wide variety of occupations, and regard Bohemia patriotically as their homeland.[7] But then social or economic upheaval would create a climate that fostered repeated atrocities, and Jews would never know when arrests, pillaging of property, extraordinary taxes, large ransoms, massacres, and expulsions would be the order of the day. As soon as unrest abated or a generous ruler appeared, Jews would once again settle, fall into a rhythm of ordinary life, and raise their hopes for the maintenance of their gains. Each time they were mistaken. The Crusades, the decay of feudalism, the emergence of capitalism, Protestant-Catholic religious tensions, the conclusion of the Thirty Years' War (during which their financial help had been welcomed)—all called a halt to Jewish expectations of a predictable existence. The worst psychological damage did not result from inevitable restrictions and special taxes but from the physical attacks and repeated expulsions, often capricious or sudden, that violated the continuity of family life and the pursuit of a livelihood.

By the seventeenth century, Jews had entered numerous crafts and trades.[8] In particular, those in the provinces worked as leasers of distilleries, potasheries, and tanneries. It is likely that Dora's mother's ancestors for a time pursued the latter trade, since *Gerber* means "tanner" in German. Dora's father's family name, *Bauer,* means "peasant" or "farmer," indicating an ancestral rural occupation.[9] A 1724 census found 41,000 Jews in Bohemia, widespread both in Prague and the countryside. The village of Pollerskirchen, where four generations later Philipp Bauer was born, had nine Jewish families, and the town of Nachod, where he came to own a textile mill, had sixty.[10]

In the eighteenth century, however, a program of deliberate population curtailment began.[11] In 1726 the Familiants Law effectively disrupted family life by stringently limiting the number of Jews who could legally marry and have families. Among legally recognized Jews, only the eldest son could marry, after the age of twenty-four and then only on the death of his father. If children other than the oldest son wanted to marry legally, they had to leave the country, which many did. Thus one effect of the new law was yet another expulsion.[12] By forcing many Jews to marry secretly, the Familiants Law created a whole group of illegal Jews. The children of these marriages were considered illegitimate and bore their mothers' names. Moreover, the large number of illegal Jews could not settle anywhere permanently. Forever outside the law, they could not pursue any trade or livelihood and survived by begging. In thirty years' time, the Jewish population in Bohemia fell by one-quarter.[13]

The lives of the legal Bohemian Jews took a sharp and ultimately decisive turn in the closing years of the eighteenth century with the accession of a new emperor, Joseph II. In his policies toward the Jews, Joseph was motivated partly by enlightened notions of combating prejudice and discrimination but mainly by his desire "to render the members of the Jewish nation more useful for the State." He believed there had to be wide-ranging changes in the Jews' education, language, and occupations. Moreover, to further the Jews' integration into society, some of the humiliating laws to which they were subject had to be abolished. These goals were subsumed in the decrees of the Edict of Tolerance of 1782.[14]

Jews were invited to join the wider world, at least in part, but only on condition that they relinquish much of their Jewish heritage. Henceforth, Jewish schoolchildren had to take the same German and secular courses as their Christian neighbors. A German education became the prerequisite for becoming a rabbi or even for a man to marry. In daily life business, legal, and communal records could no longer be kept in the usual Hebrew or Yiddish but had to be written in German.[15]

Some social integration became feasible. High schools and universities were now open to Jewish boys, who upon graduation could engage in certain professions. Prescriptions for distinctive clothing and appearance were nullified, Jews could go outdoors during Christian festivals, and the "body tax," (*Leibmaut*), levied on both livestock and Jews entering city gates, was abolished for Jews (although a tax with another name in the same amount was thereupon demanded of them.) In return for the lifting of these restrictions and of those on livelihood, Jews had to serve in the army. This was a truly revolutionary step in Europe and upset conservative circles and the military as much as it did the Jews. Jewish communities also had to relinquish their autonomous jurisdiction in many legal and financial matters.[16]

As they were commanded to move into the German cultural sphere, Bohemian Jews were invited to join the Christian economic world.[17] Few Jews turned to agriculture because they had had little tradition or experience of farming since early medieval times,[18] and at first only a few families combined enough wealth with the desire for assimilation to send a son to a university. But Jews welcomed the opportunity to learn new crafts and become artisans, something many had always desired but found beyond their grasp because of their frequent expulsions or the monopoly of the Christian guilds. Nevertheless, the weight of historic restrictions was heavy and guild resistance was strong, so Jews entered new fields only slowly.[19]

Since the Habsburg edicts came on the eve of European industrialization, certain Jews availed themselves of the opportunity to become entrepreneurs, especially in textile production. At some time in the nineteenth century, Dora's ancestors became part of this group, having begun their ascent as small traders or agents—occupations a step above peddling.[20]

Joseph II's edict turned the Bohemian Jews in a direction that eventually marked them off as different from most other Jews in the Habsburg Empire. As the use of Hebrew became limited to religious services and observances, and as Jewish children received more of a German than a Hebrew education, Jewish consciousness and life-style underwent a process of attrition. Indeed, to Germanize the Jews and integrate them into the Austrian state had been part of Joseph II's goals. Significantly, his ideas had fallen on fertile ground, for there was at the same time a Jewish Enlightenment (*Haskalah*), which shared some of Joseph's secularizing and modernizing aims.[21]

The result in the nineteenth century was an increasingly assimilated Jewry, separated from their traditions more and earlier than most Central European Jews. Bohemian Jews gradually abandoned Orthodox beliefs and practices, either for Reform Judaism or no Judaism at all. Jewish families were proud to be "progressive," and some no longer attached *mezuzot* containing an excerpt of Scripture to their doorframes.[22] By midcentury, Prague, an ancient center of Jewish learning, displayed little of its Jewish religious and cultural traditions, although many Jews lived there.[23] The Bohemian Jews who moved to Vienna found an atmosphere that only heightened their German acculturation. By the time Dora was born in 1882, her parents observed no other Jewish practice than registering her birth with the Viennese Jewish community.

Yet the old pattern—of the Jews raising their expectations only to be disappointed—reasserted itself. Bohemian Jews steadily grew less religious and increasingly regarded themselves as Germanic, but the Austrian state did not reward them with acceptance. In the first half of the nineteenth century, the Familiants Law remained in effect,[24] Jews were still confined to their old ghettos and areas of residence, and the state even returned to the pre-Josephine policy of restricting occupations. If a secret wedding became known to the authorities, they compelled the rabbi to grant a divorce and took the children from their parents. In court the Jews had to swear a special and humiliating oath.[25]

Taxation was both heavy and harassing. Illegal or newly moved Jewish families could enter into a legal existence only if they paid large fees. Legal families who wished to leave Bohemia had to pay a steep sum to compensate the treasury for the loss of a taxpaying family. The heaviest taxes Jews paid were their "tolerance" tax and those on property, family, and kosher meat. This last levy meant that poor families generally did without meat. There were also additional taxes on marriage, place of residence, and candles used for Sabbath and holiday events. The entire Jewish community was held responsible for an individual's taxes; if a person was late in paying, the police threatened to close the synagogues. Synagogues and cemeteries themselves were subject to special taxes. Whether legal Jews were personally religious or not, they could not escape these taxes because they had to belong to the Jewish community.[26] It is clear from these Austrian regulations, effective well into the modern era, that the National Socialists did not invent all their measures against the Jews.

The legal situation of the Bohemian Jews finally began to improve in the 1840s and 1850s, and with the broad constitutional changes of 1867 and 1868, they were at last emancipated.[27] Their lives changed dramatically. They now paid only the same taxes as everyone else. They were free to move about as well as to settle wherever in the empire they chose. They could buy all forms of real estate. There were no more illegal Jews who had constantly to fear sudden arrest or expulsion. Whoever wanted to could get married and have legitimate children. A Jew in court took the same oath as other citizens. Jewish men entered the legal, notary, and teaching professions. The schools were under state rather than church guardianship.

The Bohemian Jews' newly attained equality was indeed splendid, although marred by a difficulty many temporarily overcame. During the years that the Jews had been adopting the German language and German culture, the Bohemian Czechs had begun to challenge the four-hundred-year dominance of the German Habsburgs over their land. The Czechs' nationalist spirit took concrete as well as violent form in the revolutionary events of 1848. By this date the Jewish-German cultural nexus was well-nigh solidified, and whatever was lacking was supplied in 1867, when the Jews were emancipated by a Germanic emperor and administration. The Jews' loyalty to the Habsburgs became virtually unshakable.[28]

The Jews' link to the imperial regime was strengthened by their admiration of the German cultural world. The university in Prague was German; a Czech university there was not formed until 1882. The German language was the official language of the ruling classes, while Czech was the language of a peasant culture, the language of the village instead of that of the city. Moreover, their secular education in Joseph II's German primary schools had taught the Jews to regard Germanic traditions in a superior light. The Jews were clearly seeking to move into the German cultural and social world, and it was obvious that most looked on traditional Czech rural life as backward. Jews in the surrounding countryside, for example, would travel to Königinhof, where Dora's mother had lived as a child, to attend functions sponsored by the "League of Germans," an action whose significance did not escape the local Czechs.[29]

Thus, as Czech enmity against all things German erupted, it spilled over onto the Jews, resulting in anti-Jewish riots and beatings of individual Jews. To the extent that Czech nationalist ambitions remained unfulfilled, and to the extent that the Jews were granted rights, Czech animosity was stimulated all the more. Each time the Jews' legal situation was improved in the years from 1848 through 1867, Czech bitterness led to serious Jew-baiting and attacks on Jewish homes and workplaces. The Jews were seen as accomplices of the dominant Germans or as allies of the ruling classes. After the Czechs won the right to have schools in their native tongue, they became particularly irked by the presence in their communities of the Jewish German-language schools, a persistent reminder of foreign hegemony and lack of national self-determination.[30] Moreover, as the decades passed, the growing Czech resentment against Jews, especially in the countryside, manifested itself in economic discrimination against Jewish tradesmen and businessmen, eventually becoming a formal movement in the 1890s.

Many Bohemian Jews dealt with the violence, general hostility, and economic hardship by leaving rural areas and migrating to nearby towns and cities, to Vienna, or, in some cases, to the United States. It was in these years that both sets of Dora's grandparents moved to the Austrian capital. Freud's parents, in the neighboring Czech province of Moravia, where there also was anti-Jewish agitation, left home in 1859 and settled in Vienna in 1860; Freud was four years old at the time.[31]

Unlike the Freuds, Dora's family continued to have strong Czech connections. Although the Bauers resided mainly in Vienna and Meran (now Merano), in the South Tyrol, as Dora was growing up, they were constantly affected by the political and social situation in Bohemia; their livelihood depended on their factories there. Katharina Bauer went back to visit her hometown with her young children, Philipp frequently traveled to his mills on business, and Otto attended a secondary school (though, naturally, a German one) in a Bohemian town. For a brief period, shortly before Dora's psychoanalysis, the whole family even returned to live there.

The Bauers', Gerbers', and Freuds' migration to Vienna was typical of the reactions of many Czech Jews, who moved from their rural environment as soon as the law said they could. "Like birds suddenly released from their cages, many Jews . . . fled the narrow, stifling and filthy Jewish quarters of their hometowns."[32] Jews' emigration from the countryside to towns was also part of the larger nineteenth-century Western movement of populations from agrarian areas to industrialized ones. For the Jews, however, such a move was especially radical since the cities where they settled had previously been legally closed to them; they thus assumed a high visibility, inevitably arousing the attention of the indigenous citizens.

The growth of the Jewish population in Vienna was a remarkable phenomenon. Before 1848, except for a very select group of 197 rich families, Jews were forbidden to reside in the capital.[33] Even these privileged families were there only because they provided important commercial services. They were formally designated as "tolerated" and required to pay a huge annual fee to the government. Deemed a "colony" and not a "community," they were enjoined from having a synagogue before 1826. Despite their wealth, they were subject to many of the same restrictions as the Bohemian Jews. So-called alien Jews were permitted, on payment of a fee, to enter the city for a period of from two weeks to two months to conduct business, and Jewish men were allowed to attend the university. Many endeavored to stay on illegally, and for this reason there was a special police office, the Judenamt, devoted to supervising all Jewish activities. Even a wedding ceremony was not legal unless a policeman had witnessed it. Every official notice to a Jew was addressed to "the Jew so-and-so."[34]

By circumventing the law and bribing the officials of the Judenamt, approximately ten to twelve thousand illegal aliens arranged to stay on in the city for years.[35] Some were actually quite well-to-do. Nevertheless they could only maintain their presence by registering with the police as servants to the tolerated families.[36] This duplicity had a degrading effect on all, for the tolerated, when so inclined, extorted exorbitant sums of hush money from their "servants." The Jewish offices and "communities" created by the Nazis were not the first to set Jew against Jew.

The revolution of 1848 opened the gates of Vienna to the Jews, and after 1860 their growth was explosive. When Freud's family arrived in the capital, Jews were only 1.3 percent of the total population. Thirty years later, when Dora became Freud's patient in 1900, the Jews were almost 9 percent of the population. The entire population of Vienna (which enlarged its boundaries in 1890) quadrupled between 1857 (476,220) and 1910 (2,020,309), but the Jewish residents multiplied twenty-eight times (from 6,217 to 175,318).[37] In the 1860s, when the Freuds and the Bauers arrived, the Jewish community in Vienna grew half as much again each year. By the turn of the century, approximately 45 percent of all Viennese were native born, but only 20 percent of the Jews had been born in Vienna.[38] In 1910 Vienna was the largest Jewish city in Europe after Warsaw and Budapest, both of which had unusually high Jewish populations of about 25 percent.

The Jews in the Czech lands of Bohemia and Moravia were the first to take advantage of the freedom to settle in Vienna, and the Bohemian Jews were, on the whole, the richest of all the groups of Jewish immigrants that kept pouring into the city decade after decade. After the Czech Jews came the Hungarians, and then those from the "inexhaustible reservoir" of the poor in Galicia—the so-called Eastern Jews.[39] Most of the newcomers settled in the Leopoldstadt because that had been the site of the seventeenth-century Jewish ghetto (*Judenstadt*) before the great expulsion of 1670.[40] Moreover, their arrival there was made easy because the Leopoldstadt was the terminus of the Northern Railway, which provided cheap, rapid transportation. In 1880 half of all the Jews in Vienna lived in the Second District. By 1900, although Jews were only 9 percent of the total population, they made up 33 percent of the Leopoldstadt.[41]

The Leopoldstadt was the most populous of several suburban districts spread around the historic Inner City (*Altstadt*) and became part of Vienna only in 1861. Located on the other side of the Danube Canal, it was a mixed residential and business area. It had apartment houses that varied from grand to slum, commercial districts, fish shops on floats in the water, various types of diversions, and a large prison. Wooden bridges

linked it with the city proper. It was renowned for its entertainment
facilities, which included two dance halls, a theater, and, above all, the
Prater. This was a two-thousand-acre park encircled by the Danube that
attracted all ages from every class and group of society. In the Freuds' and
Bauers' day, one could watch the deer herd, go to the racetrack, or take
an excursion boat on the Danube. At a restaurant in the Prater, when
Freud was eleven or twelve, a wandering poet predicted to him and his
parents that he would be a cabinet minister. One end of the park was
known as the "people's Prater"—"*Wurstel* [sausage] *Prater*"—because it
offered entertainment for the masses. It was a gigantic permanent fair
with a circus, sideshows, dance bands, booths, cafés, the world's largest
ferris wheel, bowling greens, and fireworks at night. Goethe's Mephis-
topheles had compared a witches' Sabbath to the Prater.[42]

Many of the poor, both Jewish and non-Jewish, flocking to Vienna in
the second half of the nineteenth century, got off the train in the
Leopoldstadt and found rooms right in the district. They often had the
address of a friend or relative and began by staying with that person or in
nearby quarters. Although the Freuds seem to have been subtenants of
one of Freud's relatives in the Third District when they arrived in 1860,
they soon moved to the Leopoldstadt.[43] Many of the immigrant men found
work in the Prater as hawkers. Others became peddlers, clothes dealers,
and small tradesmen.

Even when well-off Jews made their way to the city, they were likely
to live first in the Leopoldstadt because many other Jews lived there, and,
until about 1885, it contained several fine neighborhoods. Physician and
author Arthur Schnitzler (1862–1931), for example—whose father, also a
physician, had a fashionable practice—was born there in 1862 on the
Praterstrasse (then the Jägerzeile), a stately boulevard that led to the
Prater gardens. Theodor Herzl's family moved there in 1878, and in 1879
the street was on the route of the procession in honor of the emperor's
twenty-fifth wedding anniversary.[44] The Leopoldgasse, in the northwestern part of the Leopoldstadt, away from the central slum, was also a
good street, if not as splendid as the Praterstrasse. Dora's brother, Otto,
was born on the Leopoldgasse, and her uncle Karl (her father's older
brother) continued to live there after Dora's family had moved across the
river to the Ninth District.[45]

But the rich and middle classes lived in the same neighborhoods as
the poor, just on different streets and in different houses. Regardless of
the Bauers' exact status when they moved across the river to the
Alsergrund, they were acutely conscious of exactly what they were
leaving behind.

The slums of the Leopoldstadt were as bad as the worst in any Western city 100 years ago. Families of six to ten people regularly lived in one-room apartments, and there were instances of four families sharing a room. Privacy was unknown, and children commonly shared their parents' beds, even while the parents had sexual relations. Toilets and water faucets were in the hallways and might serve as many as a hundred people. Bathing, under such circumstances, occurred infrequently. Freud's sister Anna related how, when they were little children, two strong men brought a large wooden tub with kegs of hot and cold water into the kitchen twice a month and came back the next day to remove them. When the children got older, Freud's mother took them to the municipal baths. Poor Jews with few possessions moved often from one apartment to another. Freud's parents moved six times in fifteen years. Freud told his biographer, Ernest Jones, that his childhood from three to seven (1859–63) contained "hard times and [was] not worth remembering."[46]

In leaving the Leopoldstadt for the Alsergrund in 1881 or 1882, the Bauers were proclaiming themselves part of the new, rising Jewish middle class. By 1900 Jews formed 20 percent of the population of the Ninth District and were most attracted to its southeastern portion, which bordered on Vienna's recent architectural addition, the five-mile-long, splendid Ringstrasse. Half of the Alsergrund's Jews "clustered . . . compactly" on eleven streets, including the Berggasse, where the Bauers lived for a while and to which Freud relocated his practice and family in 1891.[47] From the Berggasse it was a short walk to the Ring, on which Freud took his daily constitutional. Freud was typical of the Jewish professional men who concentrated in the Alsergrund, which was also close to the university.[48]

Jews moving into the Alsergrund, or into the elite buildings in the Inner City, were conscious of the exciting new world that appeared in the *Gründerjahre*—the years of expansion after 1867, when a new constitution went into effect for Austria-Hungary. The guilds everywhere lost their privileges. Between 1867 and 1874, 682 new companies were founded, including 443 new banks.[49] The government encouraged these developments by chartering joint-stock companies, thus fostering and blessing the institutions of capitalism.[50]

A visible symbol of the empire's and, particularly, Vienna's belated entry into the constitutional and economic life of the nineteenth century was the handsome Ringstrasse. As early as 1857 the emperor had announced plans to tear down the walls of the Inner City. In place of the ancient barriers, eight majestic boulevards would now encircle the Altstadt, together with a quay on the section that touched the Danube Canal. The Ringstrasse officially opened in 1865, although further construction continued alongside and nearby. Art, politics, and commerce were served by an opera house, stock exchange, twin-towered church, law courts, museums, parliament building, city hall, and theater; there was also an enlargement of the ancient Habsburg palace compound and grounds. Restoration of old monuments accompanied new buildings for business. There were public parks and grand statuary. For Jews streaming into the city, the razing of the medieval gates and the building of imposing structures dedicated to law, Western culture, and commerce were symbolic of their own release from the ghetto and their hopes for equality and opportunity. No one who aspired to a better life could escape the mood. Adolf Hitler, who moved to Vienna in 1907 to seek artistic success and recognition, later recalled that "the entire Ringstrasse affected me like a fairy tale out of the *Arabian Nights.*"[51]

Jewish participation in the *Gründerjahre* was considerable. In Bohemia Jews were especially important in developing textile centers. It was in Warnsdorf (today Varnsdorf), close to Reichenberg (Liberec), that members of the Bauer family (and perhaps also the Gerbers) built up one of their very successful factories.[52] In Vienna Jews dominated the wholesale export trade and were prominent in establishing factories for furniture, leather goods, cottons, silks, woolens, and chocolate. They pioneered in producing ready-made clothing, in processing foods, and in opening department stores. Young Jewish men applied to the university in record numbers and eagerly entered the professions. Most outstanding was the Jews' leadership of the main Viennese banks; 80 percent of the key positions were held by them. Since Jews also played a large part in Czech banking at the time, it is fair to say that they presided over the banking industry in Austria.[53]

Perhaps the main reason for the capitalist quickening was the fact that the imperial government was under the administration of the Progressive party, a liberal group that had dragged Austria into the nineteenth century by championing constitutional government, a centralized state, economic freedom, full religious toleration, and secular authority over education and marriage. In addition they sought to impose the supremacy of the German-speaking Austrians. As there was only a small number of middle-class Austrians to whom these German nationalists could turn for political support, they sought middle-class Jewish votes. Assimilated, German-speaking Jews, sharing the liberals' centralizing and anticlerical sentiments and grateful for the new constitutional order, were happy to give their loyalty.[54]

When Dora's father and Freud were boys in the 1850s and 1860s, there were great hopes among the Germanized Jews that liberalism would emancipate the Jews, offer them full equality, and enable them to become totally integrated into the surrounding society. Freud recalled his own optimism in 1867 or 1868: "Those were . . . the cheerful hopes of the days of the '*Bürger*' Ministry . . . My father had brought home portraits of these middle-class professional men . . . and we had illuminated the house in their honour. There had even been some Jews among them. So henceforth every industrious Jewish schoolboy carried a Cabinet Minister's portfolio in his satchel," including Freud himself.[55] He had planned to study law and have a political career until diverted to science during his senior year in high school by a moving speech on nature.[56]

The Jews' economic ascent was matched by an intellectual flowering and a cultural influence which Jews had achieved nowhere since the days of Moorish Spain. Jewish boys went to the *Gymnasien* and the university in record numbers. In 1880, when Jews were 10 percent of the Viennese population, Jewish students comprised almost 40 percent of the medical school at the University of Vienna and almost 25 percent of the law school. In 1890, when Jews were not quite 9 percent of the city's population, Jews were one-third of the entire student body of the university and almost one-quarter of the students at the Vienna Technical College.[57]

Although many Jewish men entered the professions, they represented neither the Jews' most common occupations nor their major new pursuits. Between 1870 and 1910, 40 percent of the men were self-employed merchants, a very traditional Jewish occupation. But 25 percent became salaried clerks, salesmen, or managers in commercial and industrial enterprises, and this constituted a radical break with the past for the men, their wives, and their children.[58] Yet as far as the general public was concerned, the business positions had a low profile. What the Viennese citizens could not avoid noticing were the new professional men, 11 percent of the Jews, conspicuous by their activity as doctors, lawyers, teachers, engineers, journalists, actors, singers, and musicians.

Of all the professions, assimilated Viennese Jews most completely dominated journalism, a highly vocal and public pursuit. The organ par excellence of the liberals and "the only Austrian newspaper of world renown" was the *Neue Freie Presse,* founded in 1864, in the days of ascending liberal dominance and Jewish optimism.[59] The main publisher and editor of the *Presse* was Moritz Benedikt, a converted Jew married to a gentile woman.[60] Benedikt was one of the emperor's few close friends and one of the pillars of the imperial Austrian establishment, which he faithfully—some would say blindly—defended. He also spoke for the empire's leading financial and industrial interests. In spite of its comparatively small circulation (35,000–40,000), the *Presse* held an authoritative position in the German-speaking world because of its glittering roster of contributors: Anatole France, Zola, Ibsen, Strindberg, and Shaw. The editor of the literary supplement of the *Presse* was Theodor Herzl, who tortuously traversed the path from conspicuous assimilationist to founder of Zionism—modern Jewish political nationalism.

The *Presse* was widely read by middle-class Jews not only in Vienna but in Bohemia. "There were people in the provinces who added underneath their engraved names on their visiting cards, 'Subscriber to the *Neue Freie Presse.*'" An irreverent joke made the rounds about the assimilated, Jewish readership: "They do not keep the dietary laws, they do not keep the Sabbath. They keep the *Neue Freie Presse.*"[61]

One of Vienna's most distinctive journalists, Karl Kraus (1874–1936), was Jewish.[62] Kraus was "the sarcastic, even vitriolic" editor of his own periodical, *Die Fackel* (The Torch). He owed his renown in part to his caricaturing everyone and everything; he took aim at his fellow Jews as well as the manifold institutions of imperial Austria. *Die Fackel* was read by thousands in Vienna and elsewhere; Freud was an appreciative reader until Kraus added psychoanalysis to his collection of targets.

Jews were never more than 10 percent of the Viennese population. Yet because of their *embourgeoisement* in large numbers, and the tiny indigenous middle class, they set the tone for Viennese cultural and intellectual life. "Jews provided the patronage, the audience, and by press criticism the canons of taste. They provided also the creators: Arthur Schnitzler, Stefan Zweig, Franz Werfel . . . Gustav Mahler." In addition, Jewish actors were the stars of the municipal theater.[63]

The Jews attached themselves to cultural and intellectual activities with the same optimism and hope they had brought to their capitalist participation. It seemed to them that many opportunities lay open to become a part of the Austrian secular world. While there certainly was anti-Semitism in high places—the Archduke Franz Ferdinand being a prominent example—the emperor himself took an unambiguous stance against any formal and official display of anti-Jewish sentiments.[64] As Jews once again raised their hopes for a normal civil life, they felt that this time they would not be disappointed.

The deep cultural integration and Westernization of the Jews displayed itself in their changed attitudes toward religion and Judaism, most of which were well in place even before Dora was born. As an adolescent of eighteen, Freud recognized that Jewish observances no longer had meaning for him because they were not bound up with his everyday life. He wrote to a high school friend: "Our festivals have outlived our dogma, like the funeral meal has outlived the dead. . . . [When] we children of the world [eat], we no longer think, like the pious, that we have done a good deed; rather we are simply conscious of having a good dish."[65]

In various ways Viennese Jews dropped or drastically modified centuries-old religious practices. In 1881, for example, Otto Bauer had a ritual circumcision, but a decade later, Herzl's son was not circumcised. When Arthur Schnitzler was thirteen, the prescribed age for a bar mitzvah, there was no special ceremony. His well-to-do family, with a nod toward tradition, however, showered him with "exceptionally numerous and handsome presents . . . the classics, handsomely bound, a gold watch, and a few ducats" were among the gifts. Freud also had no bar mitzvah, but his parents could not afford expensive mementos. There were forty-two synagogues and temples in Vienna in 1900, yet they were full only four times a year: the first two days of Rosh Hashanah (New Year), Yom Kippur (the Day of Atonement), and the emperor's birthday, a national holiday. As a result Viennese Jews were often dubbed "four-day Jews." Franz Kafka, regretting his own minimal Jewishness, called them "top-hat Jews."[66] Kafka's uneasiness exemplifies the psychological strain assimilation imposed upon Westernized Jews like the Bauers, even if they were not consciously aware of the effects imposed by the flight from their traditions.

Experiencing little connection with their parents' or grandparents' Judaism, Viennese Jews felt free to adopt popular Christian celebrations. While Dora was being treated by Freud, she told him about a gift she had been sent for Christmas. We can assume with virtual certainty that the Bauers not only exchanged Christmas presents, but celebrated the holiday with all the attendant traditional festivities, excluding only church services. This was quite the norm among assimilated Viennese Jews. Martin Freud, Freud's oldest son, only seven years younger than Dora, recalled that "we were brought up without any traces of the Jewish ritual. Our festivals were Christmas, with presents under a candle-lit tree, and Easter, with gaily painted Easter eggs." He wrote candidly about his family, "alienated from Jewish religion and Jewish rites," and told an amusing story of his marriage day when, for the first time in his life, he entered a synagogue. He kept taking his hat off, as a Christian would in a church, and kept wondering why the men with him kept clapping it back on his head.[67]

Nor did the assimilated Jews want to be reminded of the culture they had put behind them. They felt nothing in common with those who had emigrated from Galicia, in the eastern portion of the empire (today part of Poland.) By their dress, speech, and religious habits, these Eastern Jews (*Ostjuden*), were distinctly non-Western and certainly not Germanic, as the Bohemian and Viennese Jews had come to consider themselves. Socially the Viennese, Bohemian, Moravian, and Hungarian Jews traveled in the same circles, married each other, and avoided the Galicians.

Their identity as German Austrians was quite important to the assimilated Jews. Through such a role, they saw themselves as merging even further with Christian society. Many Jews were attracted by a pan-Germanism they saw as leading to a union of German Austria and the recently unified German Empire, a new state in which Jews as Germans would not only find acceptance but could play a significant role.[68]

German nationalism in Vienna found passionate support among the university students, and many of the important student leaders of the nationalist movement were Jews.[69] Although never a prominent nationalist, Freud was an early one. At the end of his high school days, he wrote a friend still living in Moravia that he wished they could be "journeymen imbued with Christian-German fervor" instead of "prosaic" Jews. When he entered the university in 1873, he joined the nationalistic German society, Leseverein der deutschen Studenten Wiens and remained a member until the government dissolved the society in 1878. He retained his wish for German dominance for many years and, in his forties, interpreted a dream to indicate "a desire, probably dating back to my student days, that the German language might be better tolerated in Prague."[70]

The liberal press, reflecting Jewish opinion, spoke out for the superiority of German culture and took a strong German nationalist stance.[71] Thus, when Theodor Herzl deserted German nationalism for Jewish nationalism, Jewish liberal journalists were outraged, for if Herzl was right about the need for a separate Jewish state, then so were the anti-Semites who had argued all along that the Jews were a foreign people, living as parasites off the native population. (And indeed, the anti-Semitic press gave credence to the liberals' analysis by being the only papers that supported Herzl's idea.) Stronger than outrage was Moritz Benedikt's reaction. Benedikt never allowed a single word about Zionism to be printed in the *Neue Freie Presse* until Herzl's death, when he permitted in the obituary a one-sentence acknowledgment of his former editor's decade-long devotion to establishing a Jewish national state.[72]

It was not only the liberal press that reacted negatively to Herzl's Zionism, however. Most assimilated Jews saw no logic in a plan that challenged or denigrated their newfound secular status. This was the position that Dora eventually took. Stefan Zweig recalled the "general astonishment and annoyance of the bourgeois Jewish circles of Vienna" at the publication of Herzl's *The Jewish State (Der Judenstaat)* in 1896. It was labeled "this piece of nonsense, this obtuse tract." Five hundred Austro-Hungarian Jewish communities petitioned the emperor to outlaw Zionism as a godless movement. Martin Freud, then an early adolescent, remembered that before World War I the Jews he knew were either incredulous or ignorant about Herzl. "Emigrate? Who dreamed of leaving beautiful Austria, where they flourished under the protection of a benign and powerful Emperor?"[73] The assimilated Jews passed off Zionism with condescending humor. Several witticisms made the rounds of café and literary circles: "Have you heard? Herzl plans to evacuate us to a new chain of cafés in Argentina!" or "I'm all in favor of a Jewish state, as long as they appoint me ambassador to Vienna." Or finally: "We Jews have waited two thousand years for the Jewish state, and it had to happen to me?"[74]

Zionism was vociferously attacked by those Jews who were content with their present and satisfied that it was leading to an even better future. The majority regarded German nationalism or pan-Germanism as their road to a more integral assimilation. But some Jews, especially intellectuals, found another avenue to assimilation: They became socialists. These Jews, including Dora's brother, were against Zionism for the same reason as their German nationalist cousins: Zionism erred in emphasizing the differences between Jews and non-Jews rather than concentrating (as did both nationalism and socialism) on the similarities. The socialists argued that socialism would lead to the disappearance of national distinctions and of differences between gentiles and Jews because all were artificial divisions due to capitalism. The death of capitalism would mark the completion of the assimilating process already underway.

Austrian socialism attracted many talented Jews.[75] Dora's uncle, Karl Bauer, although a factory owner like her father, was very sympathetic to socialist ideas and passed on his interest to Dora's brother, Otto. In addition to being an expression of the yearning for total assimilation, the extraordinary Jewish interest in socialism was prompted by a wide range of factors. These included the Jews' belief that social justice could be secured on earth; youthful idealism and rejection of bourgeois materialism, both lasting into adulthood; searching for an alternate ideology or a new identity to replace the lost Jewish one; reacting to anti-Semitism and social exclusion; and being a conduit for Jewish self-hatred.[76] Some of these motivations indeed operated within the Bauer family. In the six decades of Dora's lifespan, the Bauers' involvement here, as in so many other spheres, was prototypical of the experiences and concerns of Austrian Jews.

A decade before Dora was born, Heinrich Graetz (1817–91), the great Jewish historian, had ended his eleven-volume *History of the Jewish People* with contentment: "Happier than any of my predecessors, I may conclude my history with the joyous feeling that in the civilized world the Jewish tribe has found at last not only justice and freedom but also a certain recognition. It now finally has unlimited freedom to develop its talents, not due to [gentile] mercy but as a right acquired through thousandfold suffering."[77] By the time Dora came to consult Freud, however, it was becoming clear that there were limits to assimilation and that the Jews had raised their hopes once more in vain.

Regardless of their integrationist desires, the acculturated and assimilated Jews of Vienna "continued to exist as a self-consciously distinct group."[78] Jews associated primarily, if not exclusively, with other Jews. Martin Freud remembers that "rich and poor . . . in one way we all remained Jewish: we moved in Jewish circles, our friends were Jews, our doctor, our lawyer were Jews. If one was in business one's partner was Jewish, one read a newspaper that was written and directed by Jews, and went for holidays to places where Jews were in the majority. . . . My mother was very hospitable, but I can hardly remember a non-Jewish person among the many guests at our home [until my father became internationally recognized.]"[79] His father's activities certainly confirm the son's memories. Freud played cards (Tarok) every Saturday evening with other Jewish physicians and for several years was an actively participating member in the first Viennese lodge of B'nai B'rith, the international Jewish men's organization. And for the first few years, all the men who gathered in Freud's apartment to discuss psychoanalysis were Jewish.[80] When Theodor Herzl published his far-reaching plan for a Jewish nation-state, he argued that assimilation had failed: "The ghetto continues to exist within."[81]

At the turn of the century, the significance of this social fact was only partly realized. Moments of uneasiness and pessimism came, but most Jews pushed these disquieting feelings aside. They knew that the empire was ruled by a monarch who did not lend sanction to anti-Semites. They reminded themselves of the number of Jews who had been ennobled. They looked around and saw the material well-being in which so many

Jews lived, as never before. Judging by their own secure business positions as well as by the number of Jewish students at the University of Vienna, it seemed that the future of their children was assured. Still, the Jews of Vienna did not greet the new century with the same raised hopes they had felt a generation earlier.

One discomfiting change was their liberal champions' loss of political power, both in Vienna and in the country at large. The liberals had risen to power out of the defeats of the Austrian army in 1859 and 1866, rather than as a result of their inherent strength or political mandate. Only because traditional groups had been discredited did the liberals get a chance to govern. And then, while they held sway, they did not succeed in broadening and cementing their power base by an alliance with the still-influential aristocracy. Instead, they teetered in government, with their only support coming from the indigenous, native middle class and the Jews. Nationally they held on to their parliamentary majority by denying the franchise to the peasants and the urban artisans and workers, as well as to the Czechs and Slavs who agitated for national self-determination.[82] In Viennese municipal politics, suffrage was restricted to the well-to-do, and the workers' needs and interests were mostly ignored.[83]

Events inevitably overtook the weak and divided liberals, when on Friday, May 9, 1873, just eight days after the Vienna World's Fair opened, the stock market crashed, ruining thousands and initiating a severe and lengthy depression. The liberals and their allies, the Jews, were blamed for leading the country into a speculative mania that had ended in a stagnant economy and widespread unemployment. The crash and depression not only "discredited liberalism and destroyed the popular faith in its precepts," but created a climate in which widespread anti-Semitism could thrive.[84] Antiliberal interest groups began to organize at the same time the lower classes were given the vote, spelling the political ruin of the liberals in the 1880s and 1890s.

Resistance to liberal rule coalesced on three broad fronts. Small shopkeepers and urban artisans, with some aristocrats, came together to form the Christian Social party. Most of these men felt financially insecure in the face of modern economic trends. They loathed capitalism both practically and ideologically and became increasingly German exclusivists (pan-Germanists); they also hated Jews not only on traditional grounds but because they were associated with liberals. Further, the Slavic nationalities formed very aggressive movements and parties and pressed for extreme decentralization, if not outright autonomy, within the empire. Slav federalism, with its feudal and clerical undertones, boded ill for the future of Jewish civil rights, which had been gained under a strong, central

Habsburg government. Last, certain middle-class intellectuals—Dora's brother was one—joined with urban labor to work for democracy and socialism. While the socialists were not "for" anti-Semitism, they were against any comprehensive pro-Jewish policy, so-called "philo-Semitism." Most Jews stood by helplessly and watched these movements mature, their hopes for acceptance by the gentile majority plummeting once again.[85]

Historical accounts of the era frequently refer to the feelings of approaching doom that underlay the superficial air of gaiety and insouciance in fin-de-siècle Vienna. But usually these histories do not state clearly enough the extent to which pessimism about the future reflected the despair of the Jews and the liberals, as they saw the disintegration of their deeply held aspirations.

Even though the liberals became increasingly impotent, the Jews loyally continued to proclaim their German-liberal adherence. The liberals were the party of religious toleration and equality before the law, and the Jews remained grateful to them for the many opportunities these principles had created. Adolf Jellinek, the chief rabbi of Vienna from 1865 to 1893, reminded the Jews in 1883 that they "could not forget that it was the central parliament . . . that voted for the Bill of Rights [in 1867]."[86] Philipp Bauer is described by Otto's biographer as a man who, early in the twentieth century, still had liberal sympathies.[87] Some Jews even supported extreme German nationalist groups well into the 1880s, thinking that the racism avowed by these groups was a passing feature that would soon disappear. The Jews also maintained their loyalty to the Habsburgs, whom they saw as benevolent, although the governments serving the dynasty began to include some of the Jews' traditional enemies: clericals, aristocrats, and the most conservative of the Slavs, Poles, and Czechs. But the elderly emperor's personal, steadfast policy of toleration toward all ethnic groups in his domains carried more weight for the Jews than the ominous composition of his new administrations.[88]

Concurrent with the liberals' disintegration a new kind of anti-Jewish sentiment arose. In 1879 it even received a new name, "anti-Semitism," a term that came to be used not only by the Jews' detractors—one of them coined it—but by the Jews themselves.[89] Anti-Semitism was different from the traditional abhorrence and suspicion of Jews, although it built on old religious and social foundations. The new hatred was fueled by fears of and anger toward Jewish economic competition as well as by discomfort with urban, technological life, symbolized by the activities of the recently emancipated Jews. Anti-Semitism was rationalized as being "scientific"; that is, it was based on modern racial concepts.[90] Newly enfranchised voters found in the Jews easily available scapegoats on whom to heap their grievances. Anti-Semitism, in turn, was manipulated by rulers and politicians to get votes or manage the mass electorates coming into being in the late nineteenth century. Everywhere, political parties constructed anti-Semitic platforms. The phenomenon of "political anti-Semitism" was developing.[91]

The year that, more than any other, marked the emergence of public, defiant anti-Semitism in Vienna was 1882, the same year Dora was born. For many months, the artisans and shopkeepers of Vienna had been gathering in small groups to talk over their desire for a voice in the political and economic affairs of Vienna and the surrounding region, known as Lower Austria. Vienna was not industrialized, and its manufacturing was mainly in the hands of handcraftmen, who produced "fancy goods"— jewelry, leather products, objets d'art, millinery. These Viennese artisans reacted with anger and some desperation when faced with the lack of guild protection, encroachment by industrialization, depression following the 1873 crash, and, finally, competition from newly arrived Jews who peddled whatever and whenever they could. Traditionally anti-Jewish, the artisans now held the Jews responsible for the dislocations inflicted by the modern world.

Moreover, an unending stream of Eastern Jews (*Ostjuden*)—either Austria's own, seeking relief from the grinding poverty of Galicia, or Russia's, fleeing for their lives from a czar set on destroying them—fired the native Viennese lower classes to action. By their language, dress, and distinctive customs, the new immigrants were highly visible on the streets of Vienna, and "the growth of the Jewish population of Vienna [40,000 in 1869; 113,500 in 1890] lent exaggerated emphasis to the impression of Jewish omnipotence."[92]

In 1882 the artisans' groups amalgamated, forming the Austrian Reform Association (Österreichischer Reformverein), which became the main organ of Viennese anti-Semitism.[93] Speeches at meetings of the Reform Association were highly inflammatory. At one rally in March 1882, the speaker urged the hundreds of workmen to "violence against the [Jewish] capitalists." The meeting became rowdy, fights broke out, and furniture and beer glasses were smashed.[94]

Not long afterward the association passed a resolution calling for laws to wipe out the Jews' emancipation and reinstate all the old legal restrictions on Jewish life. In conjunction with this resolution, sixty thousand posters with vulgar and offensive anti-Semitic jingles were plastered throughout Vienna by Reform Association members. In the Third District—where Freud's family had first lived after their arrival in

Vienna—the association opened a coffeehouse stocked with anti-Semitic newspapers and books and advertised it as the "first anti-Semitic reading room." The printers and distributors involved in these ventures were arrested and placed on trial, but juries refused to convict them. By the time Dora was born, at the end of 1882, "virtually the whole handicraft worker class had been converted to the idea that anti-Semitism was the answer to all its problems."[95] This was the world Dora entered and lived in her entire life.

Yet one is hard put to decide which was more disquieting to the Jews in 1882: the artisans' organized enmity or the emergence into leadership and influence of a radical and single-minded member of parliament, Georg von Schönerer (1842–1921). "Schönerer was the strongest and most thoroughly consistent anti-Semite that Austria produced." It was he who had incited the artisans to riot in the March 1882 rally. Five years later, he introduced in Parliament the most extreme anti-Semitic bill ever proposed in Austria, seeking to make law the resolution of the Reform Association that had demanded the undoing of the Jews' emancipation.[96]

Schönerer was an ideologue, driven by the intensity of his emotional commitment to a new German order, and he had the inherited wealth necessary to advance his ideas and to support like-minded individuals.[97] He joined the Reform Association in 1882 and helped finance its publicity projects. The same year he founded his own organization, the German National Association. Its goals melded German nationalism, socialism, and economic and racial anti-Semitism.[98] Schönerer was defiant: "We will never accept a Jew as a German just because he speaks the language. . . . Standing as we do on the 'brutal fact of race,' . . . we would rather condone in some cases intermarriage with Slavs and Latins than ever with Jews."[99] In the years Hitler lived in Vienna, Schönerer became one of his heroes, and he later modeled much of National Socialism on Schönerer's program and tactics.

By 1882 Schönerer had fashioned anti-Semitism into a major disruptive force in Austrian political life. Threats, name-calling, character assassination, and physical attacks were integral parts of his political style. He was a continually disruptive influence in Parliament.[100] The deputies heard his invectives against "finance Jews, Northern Railway Jews, Jew peddlers, press Jews, Jew swindlers" so often that debate at a crude level became customary.[101] It is a measure of the latent anti-Jewish feeling in Austria that Schönerer, an obvious fanatic, was influential in setting the tone rather than the established forces turning their backs on him. After his entry onto the public scene, popular pressure began to build on the political parties to incorporate anti-Semitism into their programs.[102]

The year of Dora's birth also marked the first step in the widening of the franchise, a political development that eventually brought down the liberals and lifted the Christian Social party to power. Thus, as the petty bourgeoisie of Vienna began to attend anti-Semitic rallies, they also began to vote.[103] How they would be voting in the future could be gauged by a trial that took place in 1882. A Viennese artisan was charged with inciting a crowd against the Jews. He pleaded not guilty, claiming he had acted in good faith on information that Jews committed ritual murder, which he had gotten from a book written by a priest-professor at the University of Prague.[104] Although the book was based on gross distortions of the Talmud, easily shown to be false, the artisan was acquitted.

The same year there was further proof that the general population still believed the medieval myth that Jews killed children and young adults for religious purposes. This was the trial of a fourteen-year-old Jewish boy accused of ritual murder in Tisza-Eszlar, in southern Hungary; the proceedings excited great interest throughout the empire. The boy was found not guilty but was only completely exonerated a year later when a conspiracy to convict him was revealed.[105] No year since the Jews had been emancipated had been more foreboding to their future than 1882.

From the broad Christian coalition, one group, the Christian Socials, emerged as dominant and formally entered Viennese politics in 1893. The Christian Social party was led by Karl Lueger (1844–1910), a parliamentary deputy whose origins were in the lower middle class. As he opportunistically observed the political lay of the land in Vienna, he moved in the 1880s from the left-wing Democratic party to anti-Semitic and socialist politics. By 1895 his party had a majority of the seats on the Vienna City Council, and its members elected him mayor. For two years the emperor refused to confirm Lueger's election, even though subsequent municipal elections gave the Christian Socials added votes. But by 1897 the emperor's government was dependent on Christian Social votes in the Austrian parliament, and in a deal for their national support, promised to confirm Lueger as mayor of Vienna. Reacting to Lueger's appointment, Freud wrote of "the increasing importance of the effects of the anti-Semitic movement upon our emotional life."[106]

Lueger proved to be a popular mayor, and large numbers of the population were grateful for his modernization and expansion of municipal services. He never implemented his anti-Semitic platform, but the anti-Semitism he and Schönerer had injected into Viennese life remained, reminding Jews at every turn that they were Jewish and that total assimilation, even for those who had been baptized, was virtually impossible. By 1906 the Christian Socials were totally entrenched in Viennese politics, holding 158 of the 165 seats in the City Council.[107]

The Bauers had lived away from Vienna for eleven years. When they returned for good in 1899, they—like the city's other Jewish residents—found the new political anti-Semitism "shocking and perplexing."[108] The Jews had worked hard to assimilate, to fit into secular society, and they now found that their very success in doing so was being held against them. Indeed, non-Jews had begun referring to the participation of the Jews in the business and professional worlds as "the Jewish problem" or "the Jewish question." The Jews' ubiquitous presence as a result of emancipation had upset many in the majority, raising thoughts of the Jews' possible moral or racial threat to the established order. What would the Jewish "influence" do to Austrian life? There was a feeling that a decisive struggle, which would have profound consequences, was taking place in all areas of society.[109]

The Jews pondered their response to their "problematic" status and reacted in a number of ways, none of which corrected the situation. Politically, if they supported the liberal parties, they were accused of being greedy capitalists; if they supported the democratic or socialist parties, they were labeled as troublemaking radicals.[110] The impossibility of a satisfactory Jewish response was vividly remembered by Arthur Schnitzler. A Jew "had the choice of being counted as insensitive, obtrusive and fresh; or of being oversensitive, shy and suffering from feelings of persecution. And even if you managed somehow to conduct yourself so that nothing showed, it was impossible to remain completely untouched; as for instance, a person may not remain unconcerned whose skin has been anesthetized but who has to watch, with his eyes open, how it is scratched by an unclean knife, even cut into until the blood flows."[111] An assimilated Jew could not avoid being pained.

The questioning of the Jewish right to exist freely often took crude forms. But it also expressed itself in polite Christian society as a condemnation of the Jews' "bad manners."[112] Soon Jews, especially youthful ones, were saying the same thing about themselves.[113] Jews began to blame each other for the anti-Semitism that surrounded them. Assimilated Jews blamed Eastern Jews and vice versa. Intellectual Jews were embarrassed by both. Modern Jewish self-hatred raged.[114]

Jews of both Freud's and Dora's generations found their self-concept warped by the all-pervasive anti-Semitism. In his adolescence and twenties, Freud experienced strong embarrassment and shame, leading him to derisive stereotyping. In 1872, when he was sixteen, he spent a summer holiday in his home town of Freiberg, visiting friends of his family. On the train trip back to Vienna, he encountered a Jewish family he found "unpalatable." The father—Freud called him "this Jew"—"talked the same way as I had heard thousands of others talk before. . . . He was cut from the cloth from which fate makes swindlers . . . cunning, mendacious . . . unprincipled and without character. I have enough of this rabble."[115] Eleven years later, while a resident at the Vienna General Hospital, Freud attended the funeral of a friend, Nathan Weiss, who had committed suicide. Weiss's family and friends publicly blamed his death on the family of his new wife. Freud described one censorious funeral orator who "spoke with the powerful voice of the fanatic, with the ardor of the savage, merciless Jew." The reaction of Freud and his medical colleagues was to be "petrified with horror and shame in the presence of the Christians who were among us. It seemed as though we had given them reason to believe that we worship the God of Revenge, not the God of Love."[116]

The satiric journalist Karl Kraus, just eight years older than Dora, expressed his self-hatred primarily with mocking attacks on the heavily Jewish liberal press. In 1899, the same year he renounced Judaism, Kraus founded his own journal, which achieved a wide middle-class circulation partly because there were many Viennese Jews who shared his distaste for Jews who appeared Jewish and attached themselves to Jewish causes. Like Kraus, many Jews who were not socialists subscribed to the Marxist notion that German culture had been unfortunately Judaized. In a memorable phrase on the eve of World War I, he spoke of "the destruction of Austria by Jerusalem."[117]

Kraus explained anti-Semitism as due to the existence of religious Jews and perpetuated by the law of inertia. If Jews were no longer identifiable as Jews, they would not suffer as Jews. Intermarriage and the voluntary token acceptance of the Christian religion would lessen persecution, although even these steps were not sufficient for acceptance. Jews had to discipline themselves to shake off the vestiges of the *"Ghettomensch"* that clung to them, and to do so without discussing it as quietly and inconspicuously as possible.[118] Kraus followed his own advice and became a secret convert to Catholicism in 1911. Although Jews converted in order to marry Christians and occasionally from genuine religious vocation, baptism in order to gain acceptance by the wider society was the choice of hundreds of Viennese Jews who sought thereby to eradicate their hated Jewish identity.

One of these Jews was the disturbed and brilliant Otto Weininger (1880–1903), Dora's contemporary. The son of a Jewish anti-Semite, Weininger secured his doctorate in philosophy by the age of twenty-two, immediately converted to Protestantism, achieved fame for his expanded dissertation, *Sex and Character,* became depressed, and shot himself in the same house where Beethoven had died.[119] Weininger's bestseller was a diatribe against women and Jews. It is highly significant for the linkage it displayed between his self-hatred as a Jew and his misogyny. Weininger argued that a woman is pure sexuality, contaminating a man "in the paroxysm of orgasm." All women are prostitutes, even those who appear otherwise. Men could only elude women by avoiding sexual intercourse, and indeed, Weininger took a vow of sexual abstinence several months before he committed suicide.

Weininger wrote that even the most superior woman was immeasurably below the most debased man, just as Judaism at its highest was immeasurably beneath even degraded Christianity. Judaism was so despicable because it was shot through with femininity. As women lacked souls, so too did Jews. Both were pimps, amoral and lascivious. Both sought to make other human beings suffer guilt. Women and Jews did not think logically, but rather intuitively, by association. Weininger declared his era to be not only the most feminine but the most Jewish of all eras. Jews were even worse than women; Jews were degenerate women.

Weininger killed himself because he felt he could not overcome the woman and the Jew in him.[120] It would, therefore, be simple to dismiss Weininger as an extremist and his book as the outcome of a psychotic depression, if not for the fact that *Sex and Character* was the psychological hit of 1903. It was widely reviewed, hailed by some as a masterpiece, and admired by such Jewish contemporaries as Franz Kafka and Hermann Broch. It was the talk of Vienna for months.[121] The truth is that Weininger had only expressed flamboyantly what many believed: that women were an inferior order of being and that all other inferior groups could be compared with women when one was trying to explain the essence of their deficiencies.

Campaigning against these damaging comparisons, Rosa Mayreder, the Austrian feminist, gave a telling example of its widespread and authoritative existence. "The Germans," she pointed out, "ascribe womanly characteristics to the Slavs—a piece of national assumption expressed by [former German Chancellor] Bismarck . . . in April, 1895. 'I believe [he declared] that we Germans, by God's grace, are fundamentally stronger; I mean, manlier in our character. God has established this dualism, this juxtaposition of manliness and womanliness, in every aspect of creation. . . . It is not my wish to offend the Slavs, but they have many of the feminine advantages—they have grace and cleverness, subtlety and adroitness.'" Therefore, the Germans in Austria, Bismarck advised, should remember that they are the superior race and predominate, "just as in marriage the man ought to predominate."[122]

Consider, then, Dora's state of mind at eighteen. She belonged to the very first generation of Jews to be born to equal legal status after hundreds of years of officially decreed inferiority and familial disruption. But neither the state nor the populace was reconciled to emancipation, and as the years went by Dora encountered more, not less, anti-Jewish sentiment. As a woman, she heard the faint beginnings of cries for female equality, but the hard fact is that the confident voices that preached women's inherent inadequacy drowned out any contradiction. It was the general consensus that women were inferior and the insistent proclamation of anti-Semites that the proof of the Jews' deficiency lay in their exhibition of traits commonly associated with women. Thus did antifeminism and anti-Semitism unite at the turn of the century. A young Jewish woman like Dora could be filled with more self-doubt, and even self-loathing, than a Jewish man.

3

"The Family Circle"

The Bauers were representative of many Bohemian Jews who had emigrated to Vienna and yet, at the same time, were a highly specific constellation. The "dominating figure" of the "family circle," Freud recorded, was Dora's father, Philipp Bauer, a man "in his late forties . . . of not entirely ordinary activity and talents, a large manufacturer in very comfortable circumstances." He held sway "owing to his intelligence and his character as much as to the circumstances of his life." Freud also judged Philipp to be "a man of some perspicacity [and] shrewdness." Philipp himself told Freud about his "obstinacy."

Philipp was the paterfamilias in a patriarchal and authoritarian society. The authority of most men in Austria at the turn of the century rested on the firm ground of tradition, tangibly displayed by the decisive governmental role of the Habsburg emperor and the vitality of the Austrian Civil Code, in force since 1811. The Austrian Empire had the trappings of a constitutional monarchy, but its parliament had no real power. Ministers were appointed and dismissed by the emperor and had no responsibility to the legislature. This national state of affairs was mirrored by the place of the husband in the family. The civil law held that wives had to obey their husband's directions in all matters concerning the household and the children.[1]

Dora's father was a contemporary of Freud, born just three years before him. The two men started life with much in common, and this affinity was, no doubt, understood by them throughout their relationship, which covered more years than just the period when Freud analyzed Dora. Knowing the patterns of interactions among Viennese Jews, it can be assumed that many of the people Freud treated—before psychoanalysis was widely known and attracted diverse patients—were quite similar to the Bauers as well as to Freud himself. Conversely, when Bauer consulted Freud, he could safely assume he was dealing with a physician with whom he had much in common and who understood his general concerns and outlook.

Philipp Bauer, like Freud, spent his early years in the wooded, rolling Czech countryside. He was born August 14, 1853 in the small town of Pollerskirchen in eastern Bohemia, only about 120 miles east of Freud's birthplace in a town of about the same size in Moravia. His parents were Jakob and Babette (born Mautner) Bauer.[2] Pollerskirchen was a small market town in the Bohemian-Moravian hills, where Jews had resided for generations among the Czech Catholics. It was one of twenty-three villages that was part of the broad Humpoletz (Humpolec) Jewish community of about nine to twelve hundred Jews. Only the larger town of Humpoletz, six miles from Pollerskirchen, had a synagogue, a religious school, and a Jewish cemetery.[3]

Pollerskirchen was also part of an area surrounding the Moravian town of Iglau (Jihlava), a region long known for the manufacture of woolen cloth.[4] From the earliest days of industrialization, Jews had played a role in the development of the local woolen industry, probably starting as middlemen between producers and consumers. If the Jewish merchant was successful, he could accumulate enough capital to hire artisans to work for him.[5] Therefore, after Joseph II's Edict of Toleration, a Jew in the area around Iglau might come to own a woolen factory. Evidence of this process was already seen at a Prague industrial exhibition in 1791, where products from the woolen factory of Isaak Liebstein of Pollerskirchen were on display.[6] Either Philipp Bauer's family was involved in some aspect of woolen production while they still lived in Pollerskirchen, or they turned to it after the family arrived in Vienna.[7] It was quite common for a manufacturing concern to be based in Vienna but have its operations in Bohemia, Moravia, or Silesia, where there was an abundance of fuel and raw materials, an extensive transportation system, and the availability of a large, skilled labor force.[8]

Philipp Bauer was the third of four children, having two older brothers, Ludwig (dates unknown) and Karl (1848–1916), and a younger sister, Malvine (1855?–1899).[9] At some point after Philipp's second or third birthday, his parents moved the family to Vienna. A pleasant-looking child, he was, however, slightly handicapped from birth by vision in only one eye.[10] At some time in his young manhood he became infected with syphilis, a not-unusual occurrence in his day. Venereal disease was widespread in Vienna, both among Jews and non-Jews. The author Stefan Zweig, Dora's contemporary, recollected: "There was at that time [an]

element that overshadowed the happiest moments: the fear of infection."
In large cities, 10 to 20 percent of young men like Philipp Bauer had a
sexually transmitted illness. Walking through doctors' neighborhoods,
one could read on every sixth or seventh door: "Specialist for Skin and
Venereal Diseases."[11]

Although the transmission of syphilis occurred mainly because of the
lack of a reliable cure, another factor was at work in the contraction of the
disease by middle-class men: Most of them were not "marriageable" for
at least a decade after they reached puberty. The society in which they
lived did not consider them to be socially responsible until they had
achieved a certain economic position, and this did not usually happen until
they were in their mid- to late twenties. The mores of the day did not allow
premarital sexual relationships with girls or young women of their own
class, and early marriage was unthinkable. So, if they wanted to experience intercourse with a woman while still in their late teens or early
twenties, they turned to a variety of transient encounters with poor
young women or prostitutes.[12] Philipp Bauer fit the middle-class stereotype neatly. He was engaged at twenty-six, married at twenty-eight, and
entered married life with syphilis.[13]

But neither defective vision nor the chronic symptoms of syphilis
held Philipp back from rising out of "poor conditions" into "middle-class
prosperity."[14] Already a businessman, he married a Viennese Jewish girl,
nine years his junior, whose family had also emigrated from eastern
Bohemia. In very short order the newlyweds had two children—Otto,
and fourteen months later, Dora—and moved from Leopoldgasse 6–8 in
the poorer Second District to Berggasse 32 in the more prestigious Ninth
District.

Yet, if the Bauer family was anything like Stefan Zweig's, the move
did not signal a passionate embrace of extravagance. Zweig's father was
also a wealthy industrialist with textile mills in northern Bohemia, but he
remained prudent in using his profits for personal indulgence. "The living
conditions of my family," Zweig recalled, "kept pace only haltingly with
the always rapidly increasing fortune. We gradually acquired small com-
forts, we moved from a smaller to a larger house, in the spring we rented
a carriage for the afternoon, traveled second-class in a sleeping
car. . . . Though he was a millionaire, my father never smoked an impor-
ted cigar."[15] Zweig remembered this steadiness and caution as characteristic of the "good Jewish bourgeoisie" in Vienna at the end of the
nineteenth century. The Bauers' own prudence is confirmed by Otto's
follower, Julius Braunthal, who visited Otto in the same apartment where
the family had lived while Freud was treating Dora. Braunthal described

the home as being "in an unpretentious middle-class, four-storey dwelling house."[16]

There is no doubt that Philipp Bauer exuded the air of a solid citizen. He was successful in his business, exemplified the liberal values of the 1860s, belonged to the Freemasons, and was involved in charitable activities. But there was more to Philipp than the good burgher. His son Otto's colleagues depicted him as full of life, charming, friendly, and intellectually alive. One of them described his appearance as that of "a non-Jewish intellectual in the higher ranks of the civil service."[17] Yet when he was thirty-five, his life was drastically interrupted by tuberculosis, a condition rife throughout all classes in the nineteenth and early twentieth centuries. The decision was made to turn over the active management of the factories to his older brother Karl and move the entire family to Meran (Merano), a town in the Austrian Tyrol—today in northern Italy—widely renowned for tubercular cures.[18] Dora was then six years old. For her the move meant going from a large city and a stable neighborhood to a small town where the middle- and upper-class residents were almost all adult transients with very few children and were ill besides. The move also meant leaving behind grandparents, aunts, uncles, and cousins to whom she was close, especially her Aunt Malvine, her father's younger sister.

Merano is situated in a valley and surrounded by mountains to the north, east, and west, which protect it from the winter cold and rain. This location made it possible for the many tubercular patients to be out, taking the air, most of the year. In the summer, when it grew too warm, the invalids would leave their town hotels and pensions and move to resorts in the surrounding hills. An added health attraction was the regional grapes, which grew in a radioactive soil that supposedly made them and the local wine curative. There was a particular promenade in the town, the Was-sermauer, where the well-dressed, middle-class and wealthy invalids walked and sat during the day and, in the autumn, took the "grape cure"—that is, ate the curative grapes. During the springtime, they took the "whey cure," which consisted of drinking milk coagulated with white wine, strained from the curd, and sweetened with sugar.[19] In the fall and winter they especially congregated in the "winter-garden," the least windy part of the Wassermauer, where an old nunnery blocked the cold air and a band played as they sat crowded together, making conversation or gossiping, while others strolled about. Fairs, market days, and religious holidays drew the local peasantry to town and offered colorful diversions. In the evening the local hotels furnished entertainment, such as a recital by a zither player. Sickness and a comfortable, sometimes even merry, resort life went hand in hand.

The surrounding, hilly countryside provided a serene, rural setting nineteenth-century city dwellers found emotionally uplifting. The healthier patients took day excursions and were charmed by the traditionally dressed peasants, herds of cattle, vineyards, orchards, streams, and medieval ruins. A popular contemporary author, who had accompanied his consumptive wife to Meran, described the area as a "lovely valley . . . a real garden of God's own planting . . . " and judged the "sunshine in the North [to be] only an imitation . . . a kind of silver-gilt, in comparison with the genuine solid, unalloyed gold that is lavished here."[20]

Freud knew Meran well, having passed through many times on vacation. His wife had gone there to rest, and her sister, Minna, often went—and continued into the 1920s—for tubercular treatment.[21] It was very common for middle-class Viennese Jews to go to Meran for holidays or rest cures. Arthur Schnitzler spent several weeks there in 1886, trying to cure an enormous swollen gland in his neck, which may have been tubercular. He records that he took the baths at the Kurhaus, played croquet in the garden of his hotel, and went on many walks and outings.[22]

In the mountains and mild winter climate, Philipp Bauer's condition improved considerably, and the family decided to remain in Meran for the sake of his long-term health and hoped-for cure. At times when he was well enough, Philipp traveled north to his factories. But Philipp's life continued to be afflicted by illness. Four years after the diagnosis of tuberculosis was made, he suffered a detached retina in his one good eye, so that blindness seemed imminent. He lay in a darkened room for weeks until rescued by a seeming miracle. His congenitally "blind" eye began to see as his functioning eye was incapacitated by the retinal detachment. After about three months, his vision was good enough so that he could read and write, and it remained so for the rest of his life. This was a period of great fear for the entire family. It was, wrote Otto as an adult, "the evil time out of my childhood," and he remembered his father's regaining of vision as the "most impressive experience" of his youth.[23] Freud affirms the upset of those days for Dora, who, he wrote "was most tenderly attached" to her father and whose "affection for him was still further increased by the many severe illnesses which he had been through since her sixth year."

Two years after the threat of blindness came a still more serious trauma. Philipp's syphilis entered the tertiary stage, and he suffered a meningeal inflammation that caused some paralysis and mental disturbance.[24] A friend in Meran knew Freud and suggested that Philipp travel to Vienna to see him. By 1894 Freud had a considerable reputation among wealthy Viennese Jews as a neurologist and a treater of nervous complaints.[25] He was even listed in an 1893 Vienna Who's Who, *Das geistige Wien (Intellectual Vienna)*.[26] This early popularity drew on three sources: Freud's contacts in Paris in 1885 with the famous neurologist and hypnotist, Jean-Martin Charcot;[27] the professional backing of Josef Breuer, an internist highly regarded by the rich and important in Vienna; and Freud's reputation as an efficacious user of hypnosis. As Freud himself wrote, he had "the reputation of being a miracle-worker."[28]

Philipp told Freud that he had had an acute syphilitic infection before his marriage, and Freud prescribed an appropriate treatment that caused Philipp's symptoms to remit. Philipp was able to return to his regular life, living in Meran and traveling on business. He even began an affair with a younger, married woman; she was the wife of the friend who had recommended Freud. Five years later, in 1899, he recovered his health sufficiently so that he and his family left the Tyrol, settling briefly in Reichenberg, near one of his plants, before returning to Vienna permanently. There they moved into Liechtensteinstrasse 32 in the Ninth District, three blocks away from the Freuds. Remarkably, despite his illnesses, Philipp remained an active and even zestful man throughout his forties and early fifties, still an impressive figure to Freud and to Otto's colleagues.

Philipp was a hardworking and successful textile manufacturer,[29] typical of the first generation of industrial capitalists whom historians have both praised and maligned. Resourceful, forceful, ambitious, and enterprising, these men created a new era in Western history. By introducing factory employment, they changed forever work habits and family relationships in the working classes. They ushered in new patterns of consumer expectation and spending. Their success—and the competitive, even harsh, ethos it spawned—affected their own family life. Philipp Bauer and men like him were the classical liberals of the nineteenth century. They put in long hours (a twelve- or fourteen-hour day was not unusual), expected their workers to do likewise, and desired no interference or regulation from the government except when—as with a tariff on foreign goods—it suited their ends. They wanted a constitutional state, with free speech, a free press, separation of church and state, but a limited franchise that excluded the poor and uneducated. They tended to live carefully on their profits, plowing back capital into plant and equipment, and were generally unconcerned about the living standards of their employees.

Philipp's factories were in northern Bohemia, one in Warnsdorf (Varnsdorf), right across the border from German Saxony (Dresden is nearby, to the west), and another in Nachod (Náchod), a scant mile or two from today's Polish frontier.[30] Both Warnsdorf and Nachod are in regions where the local populace had been home linen weavers at least since the sixteenth or seventeenth century. In the eighteenth century, Bohemia, which was one of the most westernized regions of the Austrian Empire, began to shift away from agriculture, and the textile industry, with Jewish participation, assumed a particularly dynamic role in industrialization.[31]

By the time Philipp Bauer got involved in the Bohemian textile industry, it was concentrated in large factories controlled by relatively few industrial families, most of whom were Jewish.[32] Nevertheless, there was still room for young, ambitious entrepreneurs. Stefan Zweig might have been describing the Bauers instead of his own family when he wrote:

> [My family's] rise was organically bound up with the general rise of the times. . . . The mechanical weaving looms and spinning machines imported from England brought . . . a tremendous lowering of prices [and] it was the Jewish merchants who were the first in Austria to see the necessity and the advantage of a changeover to industrial production. Usually with but limited capital, they founded the quickly improvised factories, at first run only by water power, which gradually grew into the mighty Bohemian textile industry that dominated all of Austria and the Balkans.[33]

Philipp's Nachod factory was in a Czech-speaking area of Bohemia. Jews had lived in Nachod for hundreds of years, since 1455,[34] and after the Josephine reforms of the 1780s, Jews played a key role in making Nachod a center of the textile industry. Although flax spinning and linen weaving were old crafts in the region, local Jewish entrepreneurs—spurred by the demand for cotton and relying heavily on the new machines designed for its production—made Nachod a center of the cotton industry by the early nineteenth century.[35] Sixteen miles to the west was the smaller town of Königinhof—Dora's mother's birthplace—where weaving also had a tradition, and where, similarly, the Jews developed industrialized cotton weaving.[36]

Philipp's other mill was in Warnsdorf, about a hundred miles northwest of Nachod in a German-speaking tip of Bohemia that juts into Saxony. This was a region where Jews had not, on the whole, settled before emancipation. The plant there may have been a joint venture of Philipp's and his wife's families, since the firm of "Bauer and Gerber" owned cotton-weaving, -dying, and -finishing works in Warnsdorf at the turn of the century.[37]

Twenty-two miles to the southeast of Warnsdorf lay the city of Reichenberg (Liberec), which had developed from an old and prosperous German-speaking weaving town into the center of an industrial district that included Warnsdorf.[38] Before 1860, although they were permitted to trade in the town on weekdays, Jews had not been allowed to live in Reichenberg (a few lived there illegally). The Christian clothmakers of Reichenberg bought raw materials from Jews and frequently had to allow Jewish merchants to distribute the finished products. Among the most numerous and important of these middlemen were the Jewish wool dealers, who eventually helped develop the city's modern textile industry.[39] Many of the industrialists who owned factories in Warnsdorf chose to have their homes in Reichenberg, including Philipp Bauer, who also arranged for his son to leave Meran to finish his secondary education there, hoping that he would then attend the local textile technical college and join the family firm.[40]

Dora was very aware that her energetic, hard-driving father had achieved his gains only by circumventing the resistance of a hostile population. Jews were not welcomed by the majority German population in northwestern Bohemia—the territory soon to become known around the world as the Sudetenland. Even more than the Germans in Vienna, the outnumbered Germans in Bohemia were rabidly nationalistic and anti-Semitic. Jews in Bohemia felt themselves to be German and wanted to support (and ally themselves with) the Bohemian Germans, but the latter would have none of it. There was no place for Germanized Jews in the Czech lands: The Germans rejected the Jews as partners in the domination of Bohemia, and the Czechs treated the Jews as allies of the Germans, who would not help in the struggle against German rule. During the brief time the Bauers lived in Reichenberg in 1899, they were thrust in on themselves and other Jews.[41]

The Jews in Reichenberg were 3.5 percent of the population, and their backgrounds and attitudes were very congenial to those of the Bauers. The Jewish community that had been built up over a generation considered itself liberal and progressive and, to the extent that they were religious, followed the Reform tradition. A Talmud Torah (separate Jewish religious school), founded at first, was later abandoned, and Jewish parents in the city relied on religious instruction in the public schools. The Jewish community also chose not to build a *mikva* (ritual bath), on the grounds that it was "an antiquated institution."[42]

After a few months of living in Reichenberg, the Bauers decided to move back to Vienna, perhaps because Otto was not going to the textile institute but was entering the university. Or perhaps it was because Philipp's mistress had decided to leave Meran and move to the capital.

These were worrisome times for Philipp and his family. His factories' operations were in a constant state of upheaval as a result of nationalist turmoil in Bohemia. Indeed, all Bohemian industry was overcome by a depression that was to last almost a decade, a by-product of "the deep underlying jealousies and antagonisms" between Czech and German nationalists.[43] After years of Czech demands for greater government recognition of Czech nationality, the Austrian minister-president, Count Kasimir Badeni, issued new language ordinances on April 5, 1897, designed to increase the use of Czech in the administration of Bohemia and Moravia. Badeni's action immediately aroused an outpouring of German nationalist countersentiment, and his government continued in crisis through the fall of 1897.[44]

In the face of the breakdown of the political process, Badeni resigned on November 27, 1897. The Germans celebrated openly, inducing a paroxysm of Czech rage.[45] Mark Twain, visiting Austria at the time, wrote of the "three of four days of furious rioting in Prague, followed by the establishing there of martial law; the Jews and Germans were harried and plundered, and their houses destroyed; in other Bohemian towns there was rioting—in some cases the Germans being the rioters, in others the Czechs—and in all cases the Jew had to roast, no matter which side he was on."[46]

The national crisis threw economic life into disarray. Czech workers continually disrupted manufacturing operations. A Bohemian textile manufacturer said that unless one lived in Bohemia, it was impossible to "grasp how seriously this affects industry." Profits and investments collapsed, not to recover until 1905. Ernst von Koerber, the Austrian minister-president from 1900 to 1904, concluded: "The national struggles . . . have paralyzed popular energies from which productive labor could have been expected. . . . At a time when in the whole world the industrial upswing means intensification of effort and unification of forces, with us such forces are rendered lame by nationalist strife."[47]

In the midst of his business worries, Philipp was forced into taking some action about Dora's well-being. Her irritability and general ennui had been dragging on for two years; now, on top of these, came a suicide note and a fainting episode. In Meran or Reichenberg, Philipp might have handled affairs differently. But since Dora was in Vienna, near Freud, Philipp insisted that she go into treatment with this neurologist, who had helped him so greatly six years earlier.

In Vienna Dora was in close contact with her father's relations. As Freud observed—and he knew some of these people personally—"it was from her father's family that [Dora] had derived not only her natural gifts and her intellectual precocity but also the predisposition to her illness." Philipp's oldest brother was Ludwig Bauer, a lawyer. He had a son, Julius, who became a physician and eventually an eminent professor in his field.[48] Philipp's second oldest brother Karl, five years Philipp's senior, had taken over the management of the Bauer factories when Philipp became ill with tuberculosis and was very sympathetic to socialist ideas and goals.[49] He never married, and Freud, who had met him once, labeled him "a hypochondriacal bachelor."[50]

Of all her father's relatives, Dora was closest to Philipp's younger sister, Malvine. When she was twenty-three years old, she married Eduard Friedmann, a twenty-six-year-old goldsmith, who had been born in Hungary. She had children, but the marriage was very unhappy. Freud knew Malvine and wrote that "she gave clear evidence of a severe form of psychoneurosis without any characteristically hysterical symptoms." In her early forties she began to lose weight and died fairly quickly under mysterious circumstances.[51] The cause of death in the community records was vaguely listed as "bronchial catarrh." Dora had been very fond of her aunt; Freud said that ever since Dora had fallen ill, she had modeled herself on this woman.[52] When Dora moved back to Vienna, Malvine had been dead for about a year, but Dora remained close to her daughters.

From her earliest years, Dora lived in the midst of chronic illness, both psychological and physical. Such an environment intruded on every aspect of her life. While she was in treatment with Freud, there had been a Bauer family gathering during the Christmas season. A relative had toasted her father and wished him good health for many years to come. But when Dora had looked at her father, she told Freud, she had seen a tired face that quivered strangely in response to the toast. She had thought to herself: "Poor, sick man. He is trying not to think of the future. Who could tell how long he would live?" This is how Dora thought of the vigorous person described by Freud as "a man of not entirely ordinary activity and talents" and the zestful, charming gentleman Otto's friends and colleagues met when they came to the Bauer apartment in later years.[53]

Dora's fondness for her aunt and concern for her father did not extend to her mother, Katharina, at least not when Dora was eighteen. Freud indicated, quite unambiguously, that "she was on very bad terms with her mother." Yet in spite of Dora's alienation from her mother, she resembled her in many essentials.

Dora's mother was born in 1862 in Königinhof, a small town near the source of the Elbe River, which is a mere mountain stream in eastern Bohemia. As the center of a grain-producing district, Königinhof had breweries and flour mills. Together with Nachod, just sixteen miles to the west, it shared in the regional linen- and cotton-weaving industries. Nevertheless, Königinhof was not on a railroad line. The area was predominantly Czech, and Katharina grew up speaking the language.[54]

Katharina's family origins and move to Vienna are obscure.[55] We know from Freud only that she was engaged at seventeen and married at nineteen. She was not aware that Philipp had syphilis and seems to have found out only many years later when a doctor, called in to treat her husband's detached retina, hinted at a venereal etiology. If Freud was correct about her age at marriage, she was already pregnant. If not, she became pregnant immediately upon marriage, for Otto Bauer was born in September 1881. Five months after the birth of her son, she was again pregnant and gave birth to Dora in November 1882. By the age of twenty, she was the mother of two infants. She often returned with her children to visit her rural small town;[56] she obviously missed her relatives and friends there. When she was still a young woman of twenty-six, Philipp became tubercular, necessitating relocation to Meran. The move seems to have ended Katharina's frequent visits home, thereby depriving her of significant emotional sustenance.

Katharina's life was totally bound up with her family. When her husband traveled on business, she was alone in Meran for weeks at a time with her children, the servants, and whatever friends she might have in a mostly transient population. Now and then visits from relatives punctuated her routine. Katharina could have traveled, because she had the money to do so and servants to look after the house and her children, but one does not get a sense from Freud's case history or from any other source that much of her time was spent away from home. She did, upon occasion, however, go to a spa to seek a cure for her gonorrhea, which gave her chronic abdominal pains and a vaginal discharge.

To understand what it was like for a woman to have gonorrhea before antibiotics were discovered, it is helpful to look at a German physician's discussion of the disease eighty years ago:

> The infection of a woman with gonorrhoea . . . is a disaster. . . . Gonorrhoea selects by preference the internal reproductive organs of woman; upon the extensive mucous membranes of these organs the gonococci find the most favorable conditions for their persistent life. . . . "They grow luxuriantly, like a weed. . . . They induce ulceration, they cause adhesions, and they give rise to sterility. . . . This disease has . . . a miserably depressing effect, and in contradistinction from men, [women] are likely to suffer for many years from intense pains . . . often horribly severe. . . . In most cases they are condemned to a life of depri-

vation and misery—not usually for any fault of their own, since most women are infected by their husbands."[57]

Dora believed, and Freud concurred, that her mother had gotten gonorrhea—which Dora mistook for syphilis—from her father. In this regard, Dora identified with her mother, for she herself had a vaginal discharge, although a nonspecific one, and thought that her father's syphilitic condition meant that she herself was sickly by reason of heredity. Once, during a session with Freud, Dora fell to thinking about a visit she had made with her mother to Franzensbad (Františkovy Lázně), where Katharina had gone for a cure of her venereal disease. At that point Freud became aware that Dora was identifying herself with her mother by copying certain of Katharina's symptoms and mannerisms. The trip to Franzensbad had obviously helped to tie Dora more closely to her mother and provide her with models of female illness and activity. It was then, following her mother's lead, that Dora learned to call her discharge euphemistically a "catarrh."

Franzensbad, although lacking the fame of the nearby spas of Karlsbad (Karlovy Vary) and Marienbad (Mariánské Lázně), was specifically known for its cures for women's disorders and nervous diseases. At the far-western end of Bohemia, in low, forested mountains close to the German border, the spa was very popular among middle-class and wealthy Jewish women. As a matter of fact, all thirty-three spas in western Bohemia attracted large numbers of Jews. They came from Central Europe and Russia and included many Orthodox and Hasidic rabbis who sometimes traveled with substantial entourages. As a result, there was not only a thriving kosher hotel and restaurant industry in the spa towns, but Jews operated many of the first-class hotels, which catered to Jews and non-Jews alike. A Jew coming for the cure—the "season" was from May through September—would find a congenial atmosphere.[58]

But the atmosphere was more than congenial, it was grand. The larger spas were elaborate resorts, with architecturally impressive buildings in early-nineteenth-century Greek Revival or late-nineteenth-century massive beaux arts style. In addition to the villas, hotels, and restaurants, there were fancy shops. Music and theater festivals in season boasted some of the most respected European performers. Every important spa was centered around a splendid, ornate colonnade—a high, arched, roofed gallery to accommodate strollers. Franzensbad's colonnade was of Greek Doric design with suitable classical motifs.[59] As in Meran, resort life and sickness went hand in hand.

The cure routine at Franzensbad was in many ways similar to that at any of the other nearby mineral-spring health resorts. The guests got up between five and six in the morning to visit the particular spring of their choice and be served glasses of water from the spring. Many of them sought the cathartic effect that the waters gave. During the day they would take one or more of the special baths recommended for their condition. Cold springs, mostly with temperatures of fifty to fifty-four degrees Fahrenheit, dominated. Guests at Franzensbad also bathed in one of the many mud and gas baths available, although they could choose an effervescent water bath, carbonic acid bath, electric water bath, electric light bath, or a Russian steam bath.

But the unique attraction of the spa was the marsh baths, touted as beneficial for blood circulation and "functional neuroses" such as chorea, neurasthenia, spinal atrophy, and neuralgias. Franzensbad had iron-bearing, rust-colored peat marshes composed of a thick, spongy mass of decomposed roots and shrubs, saturated with salts from the mineral water. This earth was dug up and allowed to stand in heaps until oxidation had converted the naturally occurring minerals into other forms. Then the earth was dried and ground for a bath, which was dark and sulfuric.[60]

A cure also included a special diet and diversions. Patients came prepared to spend a total of three to six weeks, often dividing their time between two spas. Those who wanted bustling surroundings went first of all to Karlsbad. But for a quiet stay with walks in beautiful public gardens, Franzensbad was preferred, especially for guests with nervous diseases.[61]

It is all the more apparent that Dora's childhood world was heavily shaped by illness. She lived permanently in one health resort, and when she went on a special trip with her mother for a few weeks, she found herself in another. At home in Meran and visiting at Franzensbad, she inevitably overheard the invalids and guests discuss their ailments.

Dora was, of course, especially aware of her mother's gynecological problem and of her attempts to cleanse herself in the special baths. To Katharina, this last was of prime importance, because cleaning—"especially since her husband's illness and the estrangement to which it led"— had increasingly become the ruling passion of her life.

Everyone who ever knew Käthe (as Katharina was known) and wrote about the Bauers had the same thing to say about her: she was so obsessed with cleaning the house that she did it continually. And in spite of the availability of servants, she did most of it herself because "nobody else could fulfil [the task] to her satisfaction." She laid down stringent rules designed to facilitate her goal of a truly spotless home. Family members had to take off their shoes before entering, and on Fridays she wanted everyone out because that was the day of her "thorough cleaning."[62]

To ensure that the public rooms remained clean during the week, she kept them locked, and much else besides. Philipp could not get his cigars from the study (*Herrenzimmer*) unless Käthe unlocked the door for him. While Dora was in treatment, she told Freud about a fight her parents were having because Käthe locked the dining room at night. Philipp objected because the only way in and out of Otto's bedroom was through the dining room.[63] On another evening Philipp had called Dora to bring him his brandy before bedtime, but Dora could not get to it because Käthe alone had the key to the sideboard where it was kept. Dora had asked her mother for the key, but Käthe ignored her until she had repeated her request five times. In their home everything had its precise place. For Christmas, Dora had been sent an album of pictures of a German health resort. When she wanted to show it to some relatives, she first had to go to Käthe to ask where the "storage box for pictures" was.

Freud pungently declared that Käthe presented a case of "housewife's psychosis." She was a caricature of a housewife, "cleaning the house with its furniture and utensils . . . to such an extent as to make it almost impossible to use or enjoy them." One of Otto's followers dubbed Käthe "a literal Puritan [who] strove for total cleanliness." Another, discussing the "mental hardship" she imposed, concluded: "It is clear that a wife and mother, who dwelled under this compulsion, was never in the position of giving her husband or children joy, or indeed, any warmth."[64] Käthe's absorption with soil extended to her own body, and she was daily preoccupied with her constipation and attendant remedies.[65]

The family members reacted variously to Käthe's compulsion. Wishing to avoid enraging his mother, Otto accommodated himself to her routines. At nineteen he did not object to being locked into his bedroom at night. Several years later, a cousin, who dropped by the Vienna apartment on a Friday in mid winter, found to her astonishment that Otto was in his room, engrossed in a book, and wearing his winter coat, hat, and gloves. All the windows were open because the house was getting its thorough airing. She asked Otto, by that time a grown man, why he did not close the windows or demand that they be shut. He replied: "Oh, it's not so awful." In later years, Otto told a friend that his mother had worn herself out scrubbing her house.[66]

Dora and Philipp were much less agreeable and solicitous. They often drove Käthe to despair by refusing to take her orders seriously. Käthe made many efforts to involve her daughter in the housework, but with absolutely no success. By the time Dora—contemptuous and mercilessly critical of her mother—was eighteen, Käthe had almost no influence over her. Later, as a woman of forty, Dora complained to a doctor of her mother's cleaning compulsions and lack of affection for her. She said Käthe's only concern had been her constipation.[67] Philipp also was estranged from his wife and went his own way. Yet it would seem that husband and wife had worked out a *modus vivendi.* Although Philipp argued with Käthe about Otto's being locked in at night, he acquiesced in the arrangement that kept him utterly dependent on her for his cigars and brandy.

Käthe's compulsive acts clearly satisfied some deep impulses within her, which will never be exactly known. Yet certain determinants of her actions are not so hidden. Incessant housekeeping was one outlet for Käthe's wrath, aroused by her forced move to Meran, her gonorrhea, her chronic pain, her husband's infidelity, and her daughter's contempt. Käthe's cleaning was a hostile action, making the house virtually unlivable for her family, and Dora and Philipp clearly perceived it as such. In a life where so much was out of her control, Käthe sought to retain some fragments of power. As mistress of the house, she could lock things (and people) up. Of her own small bailiwick, she could say: "If you live here, you abide by my rules." In this her son acquiesced. Her husband, with his path to autonomy mostly open, supported her to an extent. Dora, in an essentially powerless position, rebelled as much as she could, although retaining strong identifications with her mother.

Dora rebelled, but Otto acquiesced. There is much about Dora's older brother that sheds light on Dora's world and illumines the Bauer family's dynamics. An agreeable child and a brilliant student, Otto was his parents' joy and pride. He was born on September 5, 1881, in the Leopoldstadt and although Philipp and Katharina were already estranged from Judaism, he received a traditional ritual circumcision a week later.[68] His first seven years were spent in Vienna and in the Bohemian country town where his mother had been born. Like both his parents, he became fluent in Czech. When he was fourteen months old, his sister was born, and the two children, so close in age, were raised together and developed a wide variety of intimate bonds. With the brief exception of some adolescent years, their attachment lasted throughout their lives.[69] Dora remembered catching from Otto all his infectious childhood illnesses. She also recalled a scene from early childhood "in which she was sitting on the floor in a corner sucking her left thumb and at the same time tugging with her right hand at the lobe of her brother's ear as he sat quietly beside her."

Until he was six or seven, Otto had wet his bed at night and sometimes even in the daytime. Then, when he stopped, she started, at seven or eight. Both children were precocious, and when they were old enough to receive formal instruction they studied together, until Dora fell ill when she was eight. Up to then Otto "had been the model which her ambitions had striven to follow," and she had evidently succeeded.

Otto was seven when his father became sick with tuberculosis and the family moved to Meran. His life, like Dora's, was affected by illness, and he grew up with, and retained into adulthood, the feeling that sickness in his family was a special burden he carried.[70]

At a very early age Otto showed himself sensitive to complex human relationships. Just ten, he wrote a five-act play, *Napoleon's End,* as a Christmas present for his parents. Among other themes, the drama dealt with the plight of a daughter caught between her husband's and father's rivalry and with the emotions arising from the triangle of a husband, his former wife, and his present wife. The capriciousness of fate also occupied Otto. The play revealed a profound absorption in history and literature for one so young. A cousin, Elsa Foges, remembered Otto as a "boy genius"—and with good reason. His play had crowd scenes mimicking those of Schiller and Shakespeare, and the concluding chorus was in the style of the classic Greek tragedies.[71]

Soon after writing *Napoleon's End* Otto entered *Gymnasium* in Meran.[72] His enrollment in a classical university preparatory school at age eleven was not only a function of his obvious talent but an indication of the changed circumstances and aspirations of Bohemian Jews. In 1848 most parents had sent their sons out into the working world when they turned thirteen. Fifty years later it was usual for Jewish boys to attend institutions of higher learning and to continue to be supported by their parents for a number of years beyond early adolescence.

Gymnasium was only for boys ten to eighteen years of age, so there was no question of Dora's attending one. The difference in the secondary education available to boys and girls at the turn of the century is instructive. In eight years Otto took the required courses in Latin, Greek, German language and literature, history and geography, mathematics, and physics, as well as the electives of French and English. These solid subjects were lightened with some gymnastics, singing, drawing, and penmanship.[73] The core of his education was the classics, eight years of Latin and six years of Greek. This meant he read all the famous Greek and Latin texts in the original—the *Iliad,* the *Odyssey,* the works of Plato and Sophocles and those of Livy, Virgil, Tacitus, Horace, Cicero, Ovid, and Julius Caesar.

Instruction in German language and literature was also dominant—
and very demanding. In his sixth year in secondary school, Otto studied
Middle High German and German literature up to Luther, including the
Nibelungenlied. The next year he advanced to New High German and
literature from Luther to Goethe. In his final year he read modern
German literature. This thorough introduction to German culture assumed the natural superiority of the Germanic tradition, and while the
non-Germanic groups in Austria increasingly objected to such orientation, it was enthusiastically accepted by almost all the Jewish students,
including Otto. This indoctrination stayed with him his entire life and
strongly influenced his career. When, after eight years, he passed his
graduating exam (*Matura*), he was first in his class, as Freud had been a
generation earlier.[74]

For Dora this kind of education did not exist. Girls were not admitted
to *Gymnasien* or even to *Realschulen,* the more recently established and
slightly less prestigious secondary schools, whose curriculum was oriented somewhat toward "modern" and "useful" subjects. Instead Dora
attended a convent school in Meran, where neither the idea of a classical
education nor the notion of intellectual rigor was an issue.[75] If she had
grown up in Vienna, she could have had—assuming her parents' approval—a weak approximation of Otto's secondary schooling. After completing a Viennese *Volksschule* (that is, primary school, the only state-
supported education available to girls), Dora could have attended a *Mäd-
chenlyzeum.* This was a privately sponsored, girls' "higher" school that
offered a six-year program for girls ten to sixteen. The curriculum was
something like a boy's *Realschule.* There was no required Latin or Greek,
but there were modern languages and limited math and science. Electives
included sewing, stenography, typing, and—in some *Lyzeen*—Latin. The
curriculum in German language and literature was strikingly less rigorous
than that offered to Otto. The girls read *William Tell,* wrote compositions
on "The Advantages of Country Life" or "An Unlikely Summer Journey,"
and gave a number of poetry recitals. A graduate of a *Lyzeum* could not
matriculate at the university.[76]

The difference between Dora's and Otto's education had academic,
social, and psychological significance. At the turn of the century, the
graduate of a *Gymnasium* was a member of an elite group. A young man
who got through the college-preparatory course and passed the *Matura*
was enormously well prepared in mythology and ancient literature, had a
sure mastery of diction and syntax, and was adept at rising before an
audience, a result of many years' experience in the oral translations of
texts. With almost all his lectures having relied on classical allusions, the

past to him was immediate and relevant, giving the eighteen- or nineteen-year-old graduate not only a sophisticated interest in the current political and social scene but in many cases an unusual maturity (from our perspective) with which to assess events. Since Austrian society was very hierarchical, passing the *Matura* conferred great distinction. The discipline at the *Gymnasium* was harsh, the fear of failure great, and the *Matura* tough. Once a boy passed his examination, his self-confidence was almost always enhanced.[77]

Otto, on the verge of manhood, was also fluent in four modern languages, had become a habitual cigarette smoker, and had decided to dedicate his life to the socialist cause.[78] What a sharp contrast between Otto at nineteen, looking to the future and possessing the abilities to pursue his goals, and Dora at eighteen, dominated by her illness and despairing of life. Moreover, brother and sister were no longer close; the only obvious thing they now shared was cigarette smoking. It is a situation drastically different from the affinity they displayed in their earliest years.

Otto's interest in socialism was first aroused by his bachelor uncle Karl, who was his favorite relative much the same way her Aunt Malvine was Dora's. Karl Bauer enjoyed spending time with his bright nephew and introduced him very early to socialist literature.[79] But the emotional impulse behind socialism lay elsewhere. Otto told his socialist colleagues that as far back as Meran he had realized that the source of his father's prosperity was the labor of the weavers in the Bauer factories and that only the weavers' work and poverty made it possible for him to dedicate himself to his studies, an opportunity "forever denied" them. This theoretical knowledge had become reality to him when at fourteen he learned that certain fellow students could not go on with their studies but would have to go to work, "while he, without question, would be allowed to study further." Then, when he had lived in Reichenberg while completing high school, he had learned firsthand about the weavers who lived in Warnsdorf, where his father's mill was located.

> Of the 25,000 people . . . in the town, about 20,000 derived their livelihood from the textile industry. In almost every one of the humble cottages which were scattered round the centre of the town there were a couple of weaver's looms, tended by children and old people while the adults went to the mills.
>
> The Warnsdorfers . . . were very poor; a salary of 20 or 24 Kronen [equivalent at that time to four dollars or even slightly less—that is, barely a subsistence wage] for a sixty-hours' week was regarded as a high one. . . . Traces of malnutrition and the effect of work at the loom at an

early age were already visible in [the weavers' children's] pale faces, thin bodies and rickety legs.[80]

Otto was prompted to choose a career that would serve the working classes because he felt "morally obligated" to the workers in their fight against social injustice. In his fifth year of *Gymnasium* he organized some students into a Marxist study club, and at sixteen he began to talk to groups of workers about socialism.[81]

It is obvious that Otto had a deep sympathy with those who suffered and that he felt obligated to secure justice for them. Perhaps Otto saw himself—in spite of his family's wealth and his own considerable intellectual achievement—as a victim of injustice. Life's unfairness began for Otto within his family when he was seven and his father became seriously ill. This prompted the uprooting of the family, the disintegration of his parent's marriage, his mother's unhappiness, his father's infidelity, and his mother's absorption in increasingly drastic cleaning rituals.

But—equally important—injustice also had a wider arena. As a Jew, though never an observant one, Otto was burdened with a marginal position in society. And although Otto and Dora appeared to be inhabiting different worlds, this was not entirely the case. Brother and sister shared the emotional repercussions not only of familial but of social alienation. In Vienna they were surrounded by political anti-Semitism, and in Bohemia they were helplessly caught between the Czechs' animosity toward Jews as part of the ruling Germans and the minority Germans' fierce hatred of Jews as sullying German national purity. Gustav Mahler, born Jewish in Bohemia in 1860 and a convert to Catholicism for the sake of his musical career, felt he was "thrice homeless. As a native of Bohemia in Austria, as an Austrian among Germans, as Jew throughout the world. Everywhere an intruder, nowhere welcome."[82]

Otto's family's wealth and his intellect may actually have increased his feelings of victimization. He was legally an equal citizen in the Austrian Empire, he had all the advantages of money and talent, and yet he was still singled out and even ostracized for being either different or inferior when logic told him he was neither. Otto's decision to make a life within the Socialist party was not unique for someone of his background. A large number of the leaders of Austrian and German social democracy and other serious critics of the capitalist system came from Bohemian-Jewish middle-class families: Victor Adler, Heinrich Braun, Wilhelm Ellenbogen, and Ludo Moritz Hartmann are several prominent examples.[83]

There was also a rebellious aspect to Otto's ardent resolve to serve the workers in his father's factories. Not only did Otto refuse to attend the

Reichenberg Textile Institute after high school, but he pledged himself to liberate the very people on whose labor Philipp Bauer's prosperity and professional identity depended. Nevertheless Otto's oedipal strivings were secondary to the seductive allure of socialism for Jews: the promise of integration into the larger society. To the misery of feeling separate from the Christian majority, to the indignity of not being accepted on equal footing with Christian classmates, to the grievance of brilliance denied its reward by the Imperial Civil Service—to all these, socialism offered a permanent solution.

Although Otto was already advanced in socialist thought and activity before he entered the University of Vienna in 1899, two circumstances at that time intensified his absorption and determination. One was the particular anti-Semitism he encountered. Beginning in the 1860s and 1870s, Austrian university students were strongly influenced by German nationalist and pan-German sentiments and became the loudest protagonists of racial anti-Semitism as a corollary of their nationalism.[84] In the year of Dora's birth, they passed a resolution condemning dueling with a Jew on the grounds that "every son of a Jewish mother . . . is born without honor. . . . Such a person cannot differentiate between what is pure and what is dirty. . . . It is impossible to offend a Jew and therefore no Jew can demand satisfaction for any insult he may have experienced."[85]

By the time Otto entered the university, organized anti-Semitism found continual expression. Not only were Jews totally excluded from the fraternities, but there were anti-Semitic articles in the student newspapers, and the nationalist students had formalized their valuation of Jews as unworthy of giving satisfaction in the 1896 Manifesto of the Waidhofen Association of Militant German Student Organizations.[86] Otto related to Dora and his parents the frequent incidents that disrupted Jewish students' university life. What Dora learned took on special significance for her future. She found out that verbal and physical assaults on individuals in lecture halls, corridors, and laboratories were daily occurrences. Fraternity members broke into lecture halls chanting "*Juden hinaus*" until the Jews finally left the room. In 1905 riots occurred when the nationalist students blocked the university entrance to Jewish students. At times there were even boycotts of the classes of Jewish professors.[87] Jewish students responded by forming their own fraternity in 1883 and some went on to become Jewish nationalists—Zionists.[88]

In this atmosphere and already drawn by socialism, Otto met the Socialist party leader, Victor Adler (1852–1918), a man just a year older than his father. This was the second critical event of Otto's university days because he came to worship Adler,[89] a converted Jew who also had his children baptized (his Jewish wife never converted) and who was repelled by Jews who looked or acted "Jewish." Adler's self-hatred had its theoretical base—which must not be confused with its emotional base—in the Marxist view that historical circumstances had fostered certain Jewish hereditary qualities, thereby turning the Jews into predatory economic competitors. As a result, the Jews had intensified the worst features of capitalism. The Jews were not responsible for what they were, but, nevertheless, their actions had brought about anti-Semitism. A socialist society would do away with the demand for "Jewish" economic qualities and simultaneously hasten the Jews' assimilation into the wider world. Once the Jews lost their unattractive economic side, anti-Semitism would cease to exist. "The last anti-Semite," Adler predicted, "will disappear with the last Jew."[90]

In everyday affairs Adler took a "neutral" stance on the issue of "the Jewish question" and ridiculed the liberals' "philo-Semitism" as identical with the defense of "Jewish" capitalism. He adopted the political tactic of not attacking the Austrian anti-Semitic parties, hoping they would grow strong and crush the liberals. Then the Socialists could emerge as the main opposition party.[91] Otto accepted the Marxist notion that the capitalist world had unfortunately been Judaized and dedicated himself to building a socialist society in which Jews would at last find acceptance.[92]

Otto's studies and the socialist milieu became his life. His involvement with his family lessened, accentuating his tolerant approach to their ways and his penchant not to take sides in disputes. This led to an important disagreement between Dora and himself. While she found Philipp's love affair absolutely unbearable, Otto easily accepted it. When she complained to Otto about it—which was often—he shrugged off her complaints, telling her that, as children, they had no right to criticize their father's behavior. He advised that it was not their business and, if anything, that they should be happy their father had found a woman with whom he could be close, since their mother understood him so little.

Dora did not share her brother's philosophical acceptance of Philipp's affair. How had this become so vital to Dora and why had she diverged so totally on the matter from Otto? Considering her poor relationship with her mother, sympathy with Käthe was not the explanation. The key to Dora's intense reaction is to be found in the special circumstances of her life—in her greater rebelliousness, in the fact that her adolescent idealism was focused in an entirely different direction from her brother's, and in the particular nature of her grievances.

4

"*Merely a Case of* 'Petite Hystérie' "

Dora's psychopathology was constructed on a foundation laid by a willful father and an angry mother and buttressed by a patriarchal society and an anti-Semitic world. Although this base was malignant, it was not enough by itself to entrench the physical symptoms that engulfed Dora nor to induce the depression that caused her spiraling despair. The extent and chronicity of her illnesses also derived their power from the very special friendship of her family with another family in Meran, the Ks. Very early in the psychoanalysis Freud made note of the juxtaposition between Dora's unceasing cough and her equally unceasing wish that her father be done with Mrs. K. Although Freud overlooked the roots of Dora's sickness in the larger world, he was quite correct to hypothesize links connecting Dora's symptoms with both the Ks as well as her father.

―――――

In her early childhood Dora had been unusually active, "a wild creature," Freud reported. She also had two very specific memories concerning sucking. She remembered sucking at the breast of her wet nurse sometime between one and one and a half years of age and sucking her thumb until she was four or five, when her father broke her of the habit. The presence of a wet nurse testifies to her family's solid middle-class status but also raises the question of Käthe's having had some difficulty in breast-feeding, so that a nurse had to be hired.

When Dora was six the Bauers left their Vienna apartment and surrendered their sojourns in the Czech countryside to settle in the

Tyrol, south of Innsbruck. The family's move marked an abrupt change in the rhythm of Dora's life. In Vienna Dora had spent much time visiting relatives and was accustomed to her father's being away frequently on business trips. In Meran there was little social calling, and Philipp now remained at home every day for about two years. Father and daughter drew close. For Dora this new intimacy came at the time in her psychological maturation—what psychoanalysts would later call the oedipal period—when she wished for greater closeness with her father. Philipp's enforced stay at home was a joyous gratification of Dora's desires, although, if she was like most other girls her age, it carried with it the unconscious fear of Käthe's retaliation for Dora's frequent and intense possession of her father.

As for Philipp, he was proudly aware of Dora's intelligence, and, feeling she understood more than her years, he made her his confidante even though she was still a child. Throughout the course of his various illnesses, until Dora was twelve or thirteen, he increased their closeness by allowing only her to perform certain of the lighter tasks of nursing.

A daughter nursing her sick father was an everyday nineteenth-century occurrence. Often, however, it led to the illness of the girl or young woman involved, a situation with which Freud was quite familiar. Anna O., who had been treated with hypnosis in 1881–82 by Freud's friend and mentor, Josef Breuer, was a young woman who developed severe hysterical symptoms while she was nursing her tubercular father. Moreover, in the book Breuer and Freud published together in 1895, *Studies on Hysteria,* Freud had reported on the hysterical illness of Elisabeth von R., who had sickened while caring for a father dying of heart disease. It is true that Dora did not have the total, or often even the main, responsibility of tending to Philipp, yet whatever care she gave had to have a special impact because of her extreme youth.

Discussing Miss von R., Freud wrote in 1895 that "anyone whose mind is taken up by the hundred and one tasks of sick-nursing which follow one another in endless succession over a period of weeks and months will, on the one hand, adopt a habit of suppressing every sign of his own emotion, and on the other, will soon divert his attention away from his own impressions, since he has neither time nor strength to do justice to them. Thus, he will accumulate a mass of impressions which are capable of affect [but] which are not sufficiently perceived. . . . He is creating material for a 'retention hysteria.'"[1]

Modern psychoanalysts have spelled out the potentially harmful dynamics involved. When a daughter tends to her sick father, there is a return of the repressed feelings that originated in early childhood, at the time of the girl's intense romantic attachment to her father. These feelings are reawakened by bodily contacts, normally forbidden but now sanctioned by the nursing. The girl is also exposed to her father's severely regressed behavior, which frightens her because of his loss of dominance and control, as well as his displays of weakness; the father is no longer the adult figure on whom the daughter is sure she can depend. She may also feel angry that the parent is not taking care of her—that instead she is assuming the adult, sacrificial role. The girl often identifies with her father, a common childhood characteristic, but one that now means taking on his symptoms in order to relieve her guilty feelings about her role or to assuage her guilt over her revived romantic-sexual sentiments. It was not without significance that Dora's first hysterical symptom was shortness of breath, a condition she had often observed in her tubercular father. The daughter may also be embittered at being exploited as it becomes clear to her that doing the menial jobs of nursing is a role society has reserved for her and other girls, and that her brother is not expected to devote time, interrupt his routine, or carry out unpleasant chores, all of which are required of her.[2]

Dora's special closeness to her father also burdened her with knowledge that was piecemeal, premature, and pernicious. As early as her tenth year, when her father had the detached retina, Dora concluded (through an overheard conversation) that he had done something "improper" before marriage. When she was twelve, she heard the word "syphilis" mentioned when Philipp returned from his consultation with Freud. On this basis she knew that "her father . . . had fallen ill through leading a loose life, and she assumed that he had handed on his bad health to her by heredity." Therefore she identified with her mother when the two went to Franzensbad to seek a cure for her mother's gonorrhea. It was then Dora began to call her seemingly nonspecific vaginal discharge a "catarrh," the word Käthe used to refer to her gonorrheal discharge.[3] During the psychoanalysis Freud was astonished to learn that Dora at eighteen knew that her father had syphilis; obviously he considered such an awareness highly unusual for an adolescent girl. Freud also speculated that Dora "might . . . have imagined to herself that all men suffered from venereal disease," which they passed on to their wives and children, just as her father had done.[4]

As young as seven or eight, Dora began to exhibit mysterious physical maladies. The first episode was an unusually late onset of bedwetting, which her parents regarded seriously enough to call a doctor. Soon after, Philipp became well enough to leave Meran for the first time in two years and to travel on business. During this time Dora went on an excursion in the mountains and became a little out of breath, a condition that persisted. Again the doctor was called. He diagnosed the dyspnea as a "nervous weakness," said it would pass, and prescribed a tonic. Over the next six months, Dora was made to rest and was carefully watched, and the dyspnea gradually disappeared. But it was only a temporary respite; from that time on she had episodic attacks of shortness of breath, some of them quite severe.

Whatever the precipitating factors—and one of them probably was her separation from her father after many months of closeness—Dora suffered some severe trauma at age eight. Her whole personality changed. Freud interpreted the transformation as a shift from a "masculine" to a "feminine" sexual life. It was at this juncture that Dora began to fall behind Otto in her studies. "It was as though," Freud declared, "she had been a boy up till that moment, and had then become girlish for the first time. She had in truth been a wild creature; but after the 'asthma' she became quiet and well-behaved." Two years later she endured a great fright when her father became temporarily blind.

Another significant development during these early years in Meran was the Bauers' making friends with a handsome young Jewish couple already living there. Freud called them the "Ks" and described Mr. K. as "prepossessing" and Mrs. K. as "beautiful." Mr. K. (whose real name was Hans Zellenka) had been born in Meran, made his living as a commercial agent, and traveled frequently on business.[5] He appears to have been one of the many Jewish small traders who began their upward rise in the nineteenth century by becoming an agent or a manager. It is possible that Mrs. K. had a millinery business. She was often ill and had even spent some time in a sanitarium. Dora eventually noticed that Mrs. K. was well when her husband was away on business and became sick when he returned. The Ks had two young children, one a girl named Klara. She was nine years younger than Dora and had a congenital heart defect.[6] By the time Philipp had his syphilitic attack, six years after the Bauers had moved to Meran, Philipp was close enough to the Ks and trusted them sufficiently that he took Mr. K.'s advice to consult Freud and allowed Mrs. K. to nurse him through this very serious illness. For some reason Käthe pulled away from Philipp at this point and avoided his sickroom.

The period of this illness (about 1894) coincided with two dramatic events in the life of Dora, now twelve. The first was that she got sick again, and much more seriously, suffering from migraine headaches, loss of voice, and a chronic cough. It was at this point that her weary trek from doctor to doctor began. Freud postulated connections between Dora's symptoms and her family's relationship with the Ks, but we must also ponder a link between Philipp's latest illness, Dora's displacement from her six-year reign as Philipp's special nurse, and Dora's own new illness. It appears that Dora was a person who "somatized." Through a mechanism still not clearly understood, she continually expressed emotional upset as physical malfunction. The tendency to somatize is a universal phenomenon that has existed throughout human history. Even today— although less so among educated, Western, urban populations—somatic symptoms are more common than emotional complaints as a way of exhibiting psychological distress.[7]

The second momentous event in Dora's twelfth year was that Philipp and Mrs. K. became lovers. This became obvious for all to see the summer after Philipp's recovery, when Dora was not quite thirteen. The Bauers and the Ks left Meran for the summer to go to a hotel in the cooler nearby mountains, and the two families shared a large suite together. Dora described to Freud the details of what had happened:

> One day Frau K. had announced that she could not keep the bedroom which she had up till then shared with one of her children [probably the chronically frail Klara.] A few days later Dora's father had given up his bedroom, and they had both moved into new rooms—the end rooms, which were only separated by the passage [which] offered . . . security against interruption.
>
> When they had returned to [Meran], her father had visited Frau K. every day at definite hours, while her husband was at his business. Everybody had talked about it and had questioned her about it pointedly. Herr K. himself had often complained bitterly to her mother. . . . When they had all gone for walks together, her father and Frau K. had always known how to manage things so as to be alone with each other. There could be no doubt that she had taken money from him, for she spent more than she could possibly have afforded out of her own purse or her husband's. Dora added that her father had begun to make handsome presents to Frau K., and in order to make these less conspicuous had at the same time become especially liberal towards her mother and herself. And, while previously Frau K. had been an invalid and had even been obliged to spend months in a sanatorium for nervous disorders because she had been unable to walk, she had now become a healthy and lively woman.

The Ks and the Bauers were already close owing to their long-standing friendship. But now Philipp's affair with Mrs. K. had an intensifying effect on Dora's relationships with the various members of the K. family, relationships from which Dora did not emerge unscathed. With Mrs. K., an intimate friendship sprang up, as the young woman and the barely adolescent girl began to spend many hours together. When Dora stayed at the Ks', she and Mrs. K. shared the main bedroom and Mr. K. had to sleep elsewhere. They talked to each other about everything, including Mr. K. Mrs. K. confided in Dora the details and concerns of her married life and asked her advice. When Dora admired some of Mrs. K.'s jewelry, Mrs. K. saw to it that Philipp bought his daughter the same piece. Dora clearly had an adolescent crush on Mrs. K.; she spoke to Freud about Mrs. K.'s "adorable white body." Freud believed this indicated Dora's unconscious homosexual love for Mrs. K. He even stated dogmatically: "These masculine or, more properly speaking, *gynaecophilic* currents of feeling are to be regarded as typical of the unconscious erotic life of hysterical girls."

As Dora matured Mrs. K. became her chief source of sexual knowledge, both through their conversations and by making available to her the current popular literature on sex. Prominent among the books Dora found at the Ks' was the immensely successful and widely read *Physiology of Love* by Paolo Mantegazza (1831–1910), an Italian physician, pioneering anthropologist, parliamentary legislator, and social-scientific crusader. Although little known today, at the end of the nineteenth century Mantegazza was generally regarded as one of the foremost authorities on modern sexual life.[8] In addition to his scientific works, Mantegazza produced an entire row of popular books on passions and emotions, health, sexuality, psychology, the relations between the sexes, and critiques of modern culture.[9] These were immediately translated into several Western languages and reprinted in many editions in the late nineteenth and early twentieth centuries, spanning a period of about sixty years.[10]

The Physiology of Love, which Dora had read by the time she was fifteen, was the first volume of a three-part work—the *Trilogy of Love*—"a course of studies on the love relations of mankind."[11] Mantegazza wrote these books in the romantic-sexual reformist tradition of the day, which was to acknowledge openly the sexual passions and work for their healthy expression through "love." This was variously defined, but Mantegazza himself championed a loving, voluntary premarital chastity as a "sublime virtue" that would replace the common, "vulgar," obligatory variety.[12]

If Dora read only *The Physiology of Love,* she did not receive much of a sex education. Despite the word "physiology" in the title, the book is long on passionate disquisitions, emotional broadsides, and rhapsodies to love and quite short on anything remotely resembling a fact about the body.[13] However, the whole trilogy may have been referred to by the name of its first volume, in which case Dora would have gotten something of an anatomical and functional education from the third volume, *Anthropologi-*

cal Studies in the Sexual Relations of Mankind, which concentrated on sexual aberrations, sexual initiation ceremonies, and mutilation rituals in former times and among modern "savages" and "primitives." If Mrs. K. also owned a copy of Mantegazza's *The Physiology of Woman,* Dora would have had a chance to read about the contemporary hypocrisy of putting a woman on a pedestal: "Modern gallantry [has] little real delicacy of feeling because it exhibits an undertone of contempt [for a] woman [as] the representative of a 'weaker,' inferior sex, and . . . in no way the possessor of any proper individual personal value."[14]

Sex, emotions, women's emancipation, jewelry, as well as daily occurrences were the topics that for months on end bound together Dora and Mrs. K. Dora obviously worshipped Mrs. K., but one naturally wonders how much of Mrs. K.'s attachment was heartfelt and how much sprang from a desire to be on good terms with her lover's daughter.

As Dora turned for friendship and vicarious mothering to Mrs. K., the Ks' two small children turned to Dora. She was eager to take care of them, so much so that it was often said she was like a mother to them. She taught them and went on walks with them; it was Freud's opinion that "she had offered them a complete substitute for the slight interest which their own mother showed in them." For the first three years of Philipp's affair, she would go to look for them when she thought her father might be with Mrs. K., since at those times they would have been sent outside. One cannot but note the close succession of the two adult, care-giving roles that formed such a large part of Dora's childhood: first that of nurse to her father and second that of companion-nursemaid-teacher to the Ks' children, one of whom required special attention.

Dora's interest in the Ks' youngsters pleased Mr. K., and Dora and he found themselves discussing the children when events brought them together, which was often. Moreover, K. began to take a kind and friendly interest in Dora, going on walks with her and buying her small presents. Over the years this interest blossomed so that the small presents became valuable—a finely made jewelry box, an expensive letter case—and frequent: flowers every day whenever K.'s business kept him in Meran. Occasional walks were replaced by K.'s spending all his spare time with Dora. When K. was away traveling, he wrote to her "at length" as well as sending her picture postcards. Among the Ks and the Bauers, only Dora knew when he was expected to arrive back home. Dora's parents seemed to give no special thought to the attention K. was paying their daughter and regarded him simply as a close friend of the family who was taking an avuncular interest in their bright child—just as Karl Bauer did in Otto.

Dora herself had tangled emotions about her relationship with Mr. K. It certainly was pleasant—considering the deficiencies of Meran for a young, intelligent girl as well as the handicaps her fluctuating health imposed on her activities—to have a dependable and attentive walking companion and to receive regular letters and gifts from a man highly regarded by her father. But Dora—and she alone—knew that this entertaining and romantic relationship had a frightening aspect. About a year after K. had begun to spend time with Dora, in the spring of 1896 when Dora was thirteen, he invited her to his place of business on the main square of Meran to join him and his wife in watching a church festival. When Dora arrived she found no one in the office except K.; his wife had stayed at home and all his clerks had left. While he closed the shutters, he asked Dora to wait for him by the door of his office, which was near the staircase leading to the next floor. When he came back to Dora, instead of going out the door, he suddenly pulled her to him and kissed her on the lips. Dora felt "a violent feeling of disgust," wrenched herself free, and rushed out the office door to the staircase and from there to the street door.

Afterward Dora still met Mr. K. as usual, except that, for a while, she made a point of not being alone with him. She also begged off a planned expedition with the Ks that meant she would have been away with them for several days. Her distress at the attempted lovemaking caused her to develop a phobic symptom. For then on she would not walk near a man and a woman who seemed attracted to each other. But she told no one about the kiss until she saw Freud in the fall of 1900, and she and K. never mentioned it to each other. Their friendship continued as before, and she did not reject K.'s letters and gifts.

Dora's relations with the K. family obviously consumed a considerable amount of time and were very important to her. These connections were her main emotional sustenance as she began to mature into a young woman. Her family had ceased to be the source of satisfaction it had been earlier. Her longtime closeness to Otto was temporarily on the wane. Otto's schoolwork had become the major competitor for his attention, and he easily became engrossed in it owing to his intellectual bent and his uncle's encouragement. While Dora was not yet on the bad terms with her mother that late adolescence would bring, she much preferred spending time with Mrs. K. Dora and her father remained attached to each other, but Philipp's business traveling often kept them apart.

Dora's illnesses were the focus of a great deal of attention in these years, time-devouring not only by their very existence but by the fruitless search for cures. The shortness of breath she had acquired at eight continued to come and go, but it was no longer her biggest problem. Since her twelfth year she had suffered from migraine headaches and nervous coughing. At first the two always came on together. The headaches gradually grew rarer until they disappeared, but the cough stubbornly remained. Moreover, after a while, a new symptom began to accompany the onset of the cough, and this Dora found especially troublesome: She completely lost her voice. She would begin to cough uncontrollably— always with the characteristic metallic, harsh hacking—and lose the ability to talk for perhaps ten days or two weeks. Then the aphonia would remit, but the cough would continue for another two or three weeks. The whole episode would generally last three to five weeks, although once an attack had lasted unmercifully for several months.

The doctors Dora consulted about her headaches, cough, and aphonia all agreed that she suffered from a nervous illness. So, for at least a couple of years, Dora spent many hours undergoing their prescribed hydrotherapy and electrotherapy. But these brought no results except their own misery and a rash of side effects. They also built up in Dora a repugnance to treatment, a contempt for doctors, and eventually a decision to eschew all further medical intervention, which her parents did not seriously contest. When Dora was fifteen, in 1898, she accompanied her father to Vienna on their way to a visit to the Ks, who were staying in a summer house in the Alps. She was in the midst of one of her coughing attacks, and at that time saw Freud, probably because her father thought highly of his doctor and pushed her at least to meet the man and talk to him—what could she lose? So it was that Dora met Freud, who summed up her history as "merely a case of *'petite hystérie.'*" Freud proposed psychological treatment; Dora said she would think it over, and then, when the episode passed, she declined on the grounds that she was better.

Dora's mysterious chronic physical afflictions were linked to her ambivalent feelings toward her father and Mr. K. When Dora eventually became Freud's patient, he hypothesized that her hacking cough and loss of voice could be traced back to the earliest days of Mr. K.'s courting of her, when Philipp's affair with Mrs. K. began. Dora had taken Mrs. K.'s pattern of sickness as her model but had reversed the alternation of good and bad health: Dora was ill when K. was absent and well when he came back. When K. "was away, she gave up speaking; speech had lost its value since she could not speak to *him.*" But she could write, and Dora remembered that "in the first days of her attacks of aphonia, 'writing had always come specially easy to her.'" Dora and K. had carried on a correspondence while he was traveling on business, to the extent "that she alone was informed as to the date of his return, and that his arrival took his wife by surprise." Dora's response to K.'s absences also mimicked the pattern that had begun with her development of dyspnea when her father first left Meran when she was eight.

In addition to these psychological factors, the etiology of Dora's hysteria, in common with that of other middle- and upper-middle-class women of the day, had a social component.[15] Hysterical symptoms were physical manifestations of the anger and assertiveness a Victorian woman was encouraged not to demonstrate openly. Since vulnerability was frequently admired as a feminine ideal, women could express their dissatisfactions via physical illness and stay within the confines of appropriate and acceptable feminine behavior.[16]

In a Christian society, middle-class Jewish girls and women felt especially powerless. In addition to the continual negative sentiments they had to bear as women and as Jews, they had to cope with the very real disadvantages that barred their admission to higher education and careers. It is impossible to say whether middle-class Jewish girls and women in Vienna suffered from hysteria more than their Christian counterparts did, but some physicians at the time thought so.[17]

Since women often could not be overtly assertive in Victorian life, they could be passively aggressive. Hysteria gave them indirect power, which they used quite well. Hysterical women could leave relatives, friends, and doctors baffled, annoyed, angry—and impotent either to understand the situation or do anything about it. The angrier others became toward the hysterical female patient, the more she responded in the only way she could, indirectly, with intractable symptoms and increased manipulation of those close to her.[18] Dora could avoid fulfilling conventional household responsibilities and leading a normal social life on the grounds of being sick. Her parents were displeased with her, and she was depressed, but everyone accepted her behavior as the inevitable consequence of a medically diagnosed illness. Yet in striking out against a world she did not like, Dora ultimately lashed out most cruelly against herself.

Dora's aphonia was repeated in the illnesses of thousands of girls and women. Paralysis of the vocal cords was one of the most frequent— perhaps even the most common—of all hysterical paralyses in the nineteenth century.[19] A hysterical paralysis of the vocal cords can be deeply expressive of inner anguish over saying something: words we do not wish someone else to hear or a thought we do not want to admit even to ourselves. Consider that somatization is a universal form of exhibiting psychic distress, that indirectness was a common aspect of Victorian life, and that hysteria both conformed to the feminine ideal and was usable by its victims for many ends. Any number of accumulated resentments and yearnings came together through a physiological mechanism to produce Dora's physical symptoms. We can posit that Dora's loss of voice both silently expressed and prevented her from overtly expressing her unconscious anger at Mr. K.'s leaving her and her father's replacing her with Mrs. K., and that the aphonia carried out society's mandate in denying voice to romantic and sexual fantasies deemed to be either nonexistent or unsuitable.

The explanation of Dora's cough poses a greater challenge, although hysterical cough among women was another very common medical phenomenon. It too could serve as a convenient obstacle to talking. But it might also indicate disgust or the desire to get rid of something. Freud's hypothesis of the genesis of Dora's cough must have startled Dora; it still unsettles readers today.

Six days a week, Dora came to Freud's office and hacked and barked metallically throughout the entire session. As she coughed she repeatedly complained about Philipp's refusal to believe that she had told the truth about yet another advance by Mr. K., and she inveighed tirelessly against Mrs. K. for loving her father only because he was "a man of means" (*ein vermögender Mann,* literally "an able [or capable] man"). Since all these things were occurring simultaneously, Freud began to think they were in some way connected. Having decided that Dora's repeated use of "a man of means"—a man who is capable—concealed the opposite, "a man without means" or one who is impotent, Freud asked Dora if she knew there was more than one way to obtain sexual gratification. She said she did. He then told her that she had an unconscious fantasy of Mrs. K. performing fellatio on her father and was expressing this fantasy "by an irritation in her throat and by coughing."[20]

———

Dora came to womanhood "as the age of Victoria merged into the age of Freud";[21] it was a time of social transition and confusion. The nineteenth century had been an era of rapid change, with spectacular successes and resulting challenges. By the end of the century, the middle class, itself newly configurated, faced unprecedented demands from organized labor, radical political parties, and feminist movements, as well as the scorn of avant-garde intellectuals. Change bred anxiety, as the middle class became uncertain what roles it should follow and what social habits it should retain. One way to tolerate the uneasiness of change is to "hedge [it] with precautions"; so the middle class soothed its distress by applying the balm of traditional behavior.[22]

Thus—at the same time that they were being challenged and broken down, as much from within as from without—repressive early Victorian standards continued to govern all areas of middle-class life. As a result of their rearguard maneuvers to allay anxiety, the bourgeoisie were sucked, usually unaware, into charades of far-reaching proportions, which can only be described as hypocritical.[23] While seeking to appease convention yet satisfy goals they publicly eschewed, the middle class characteristically remained blind to the significance of their actions. They did so to protect themselves. "Evasiveness, cant, prudishness, hypocrisy, were cultural defense mechanisms in a time of upheaval, a search for safety."[24] Nevertheless, the choice—albeit unconscious—not to examine one's actions too closely could wreak tremendous harm on relatives, friends, and those in dependent positions. In Dora's case the repressive conventions under whose dominion she was being reared in the 1890s were many. The sharp-sighted observations of Stefan Zweig, the evocative guide to the folkways of the Viennese bourgeoisie, provide a germane introduction.

Once Dora was old enough to begin to dress publicly as a "lady," she was expected in the daytime not to expose any part of her body other than her face, neck, or hands. At night, in formal evening dress, she might show her upper chest, shoulders, and arms. No circumstances might alter these conditions. For if

> even in the hottest summers young girls should play tennis in clothes that permitted freedom to their legs or with naked arms, [that] would have been scandalous, and when a well-behaved woman crossed her feet in society, custom found this to be horribly improper, because her ankles might be disclosed under the hem of her dress. . . . [At the beach] women made painful progress in heavy [bathing] suits which covered them from top to toe, and in the boarding schools and convents the young girls, in order to forget that they had bodies, were forced to bathe in long, white shirts.[25]

Since the Bauers were a "good family," they set out to supervise Dora to prevent her from acquiring sexual knowledge and to minimize the eventuality that a sexual thought might enter her consciousness. "The possibility of two young people of the same social class, but of different sexes, going on an excursion together without proper supervision was unthinkable; or rather, the first thought would have been that 'something might happen.'"[26] The prescribed upbringing of girls from Dora's class commanded that they not be left alone for a single moment. They were given a governess whose duty it was to see that they did not step out of the house unaccompanied, that they were taken to school, to their dancing lessons, to their music lessons, and brought home in the same manner. Every book which they read was inspected. . . . A young girl of good family was not allowed to have any idea of how the male body was formed or to know how children came into the world, for the angel was to enter into matrimony not only physically untouched but completely "pure" spiritually as well.[27]

Yet the everyday attire of a turn-of-the-century middle-class woman loudly proclaimed the contradictory sexual aims and resulting tensions of the era. Female dress was simultaneously repressive and exhibitionistic, meant both to hide and to display sexuality:

The middle of [a woman's] body was laced into a wasp's shape in a corset of stiff whalebone, blown out like a huge bell from the waist down, the neck closed in up to the chin, legs shrouded to the toes, the hair towering aloft with countless curls, locks, and braids under a majestically swaying monstrosity of a hat, the hands encased in gloves, even on the warmest summer day. . . . Every movement, every gesture, and consequently [a woman's] entire conduct, had to be artificial, unnatural and affected in such a costume. The mere make-up of such a "lady" . . . the putting on and taking off of these robes, was a troublesome procedure. . . . First a countless number of hooks and eyes had to be fastened in the back from waist to neck, and the corset pulled tight with all the strength of the maid in attendance. The long hair was curled, brushed, combed, flattened, piled up, with the aid of a legion of hairpins, barrettes, and combs and with the additional help of a curling iron and curlers, by a hairdresser who called daily. . . . This "moral" era by no means regarded as impermissible the building up of the bosom, the hair, or the use of a bustle for reasons of deception or as an adaptation to the common ideal of beauty. . . . [Moreover while] fashion . . . sought in despair to cover up every trace of naked skin and honest growth, [it was] minutely provocative [in its] revelation of the radical differences between the sexes. [Therefore,] the erotic was necessarily strengthened.[28]

Dora's own life provides a model demonstration of how it was possible to suit convention and yet acquire (in Dora's case) and impart (in her parents') sexual knowledge. Clearly, she received a sex education in spite of attending a convent school and being always surrounded by protective governesses.[29] A pose of public innocence coexisted with private enlightenment. The well-known psychoanalyst, Karen Horney, for example, just three years younger than Dora, acquired a fairly thorough sexual knowledge at sixteen or seventeen from friends, books, and seeing prostitutes on the streets of Hamburg.[30] While treating Dora Freud expressed surprise at her sexual knowledge but simultaneously spoke to her as if she possessed a great deal of it.[31]

Dora's parents themselves operated on two levels. They did many things that indicated they wished to rear their daughter conventionally and to shelter her from exposure to sexuality. Her governesses, for example, were meant to fulfill those goals. But the Bauers allowed Dora intimate contacts with her father when she nursed him, and they spoke indiscreetly in front of her. Then, when Dora was barely out of childhood, she stayed with her mother for several weeks at a spa that attracted women who were seeking a cure for sexual diseases. Beginning in her early adolescence, Dora and Mr. K. were allowed to go about together alone, the two of them (as well as Dora's parents) surely aware, the older Dora got, that this behavior was slightly scandalous, even though K. was a married man and a friend of the family. The Bauers also said nothing about the gifts, the flowers, and the mail K. showered on their daughter.

Dora's last governess exemplified the tension between appearance and reality. A woman in her thirties or forties, she was employed by the Bauers until Dora was seventeen. For the first few years, Dora was on "excellent terms" with her, finding the woman attentive, obliging, and amusing. As expected, she taught Dora and went on walks with her. But now the conventional scenario becomes skewed, or at least its fin-de-siècle double emerges. The governess was "well-read and of advanced views"—after all, she was hired by a family loyal to liberalism—and she imparted to her charge the latest information about "sexual life and similar subjects." She discussed with Dora her personal experience with men, concluding "that all men were frivolous and untrustworthy."[32] The woman was also a felt presence in the family. Early on she recognized that Philipp and Mrs. K. were having an affair and "drew Dora's attention to all the obvious features of their relations." An outspoken individual, "she explained to Dora's mother that it was incompatible with her dignity to tolerate such an intimacy between her husband and another woman."

Dora's governess was obviously playing the two roles the family wanted her to, indeed, the same two roles the family itself played. These dualities were comfortable to all, as long as no one drew attention to the incongruities and hypocrisies involved. So, for example, the governess shared her reading and views with Dora, but cautioned against letting her parents find out. The Bauers had hired a governess to escort their daughter, keep her safe, teach her, and supervise her reading. At the same time they had an awareness, as the years passed, that they had hired a woman of "advanced views" who did not keep her ideas to herself. The worldly governess sensed Dora's parents did not want to be put in a position of making hard choices; Dora abided by the woman's advice to keep their conversations private; and the Bauers remained satisfied about their own rectitude. The circle of unplanned conspiracy was complete.

Mrs. K., was, in essence, a second governess to Dora and filled the same "no questions asked" role. On the surface she was a respectable married woman, a friend of the family who took a motherly interest in Dora. Privately she shared the latest Mantegazza sex manuals "and books of that sort" with her young charge. But this was not discussed outside of the Ks' house, and all remained satisfied they were living the lives expected of them. Freud was very well acquainted with such adaptations. The same year he met Dora, he observed: "In matters of sexuality we are, all of us, the healthy as much as the sick, hypocrites nowadays."[33]

So at least superficially, and sometimes from their depths, girls like Dora radiated

> a secret charm. . . . A sort of mild confusion constantly irritated their conduct . . . In those days one could distinguish at a distance a young girl from a woman who had already known a man, simply by the way she walked. . . . [Young girls] were akin to the exotic delicacy of a hothouse plant cultivated under glass in an artificially over-warmed atmosphere . . . the artfully tended product of a definite education and culture.
>
> And that is how the society of those days wished young girls to be, silly and untaught, well educated and innocent, curious and shy, uncertain and practical, and predisposed to this education without knowledge of the world from the very beginning, to be led and formed by a man in marriage without any will of their own.[34]

This, then, was Dora's milieu until she was fifteen and met Freud briefly, in consultation, in June 1898. Soon after, an event occurred that introduced a new step into the late Victorian waltz whose patterns Dora was learning faithfully to follow.

After leaving Vienna that June, Dora and her father proceeded to the Austrian Alps, to a house near a lake where the Ks were spending the summer. The plan was for Philipp to stay for a few days at a nearby hotel and then return home. While he was in the mountains, Mrs. K. would join him early in the mornings, and the two would go off together on excursions. Dora was to live in the house and remain for several weeks.

At the house Dora immediately noticed some strange goings-on. The Ks' children's governess—"a young girl"—behaved very peculiarly when Mr. K. was present. "She never said good morning to him, never answered his remarks, never handed him anything at table when he asked for it, and in short treated him like thin air. For that matter he was hardly any politer to her." Soon the governess took Dora aside and confided in her. K. had made sexual advances to her—"violent love"—while his wife was out of town and had begged her to yield to him since "he got nothing from his wife." The girl had given in, but now K. no longer cared for her. She was planning to give two weeks' notice but would wait just a bit longer to see if K. might change his mind about her.

A day or two after Dora had heard this story, she and Mr. K. went for a boat trip on the lake and when the boat had docked for a while, began to take a walk. They had not gone far when K. launched into an earnest speech that Dora very quickly realized was the beginning of a sexual proposition. The only actual words she recalled later were: "You know I get nothing out of my wife." As soon as it dawned on her what K. was saying, she slapped his face and rushed away. Her first thought was to get back to the house by walking around the lake. But when she learned it would take her two and a half hours, she abandoned her intention and returned to the boat, which soon left. "K. had [then] come up to her and begged her to forgive him and not to mention the incident. But she had made no reply."[35]

Dora and Mr. K. got back to the house at midday and went their separate ways. Dora proceeded to follow her regular routine and took an afternoon nap. She lay down in the bedroom and fell asleep but suddenly awoke to find K. standing beside her. She asked him "sharply" what he was doing there. "By way of reply," as Dora later told Freud, "he said he was not going to be prevented from coming into his own bedroom when he wanted; besides, there was something he wanted to fetch." Dora now felt threatened but said nothing to anyone, except to ask Mrs. K. if there was a key to the bedroom door. There was, and the next morning Dora used it while getting dressed. But when she went to lock the door again for her afternoon nap, the key was missing. Dora was sure K. had taken it and became determined not to remain in the house once her father had returned to Meran. For the next few mornings, she was afraid that K. would come in while she was dressing in the empty house (Mrs. K. having already left to join Dora's father), and she put on her clothes as quickly as she could. But K. did not bother her.

Nevertheless Dora was so unnerved by her experiences that she had the same dream three nights in a row and continued to have it periodically over the next two years. Freud learned of it because she had it again during the treatment: "A house was on fire. My father was standing beside my bed and woke me up. I dressed quickly. Mother wanted to stop and save her jewel-case; but Father said: 'I refuse to let myself and my two children be burnt for the sake of your jewel-case.' We hurried downstairs, and as soon as I was outside I woke up."

On the day her father was ready to leave the Alps for Meran, Dora suddenly announced, "with the greatest determination," that she was not going to stay after all and would depart with him, which she in fact did, although leaving her father in the dark as to her motives. Once home, Dora received a picture postcard from Mr. K. as if nothing had happened. She pondered her situation for about a week and finally told her mother of K.'s sexual proposal but not about the subsequent events at the Ks' house. Her mother told her father, who then consulted with his older brother Karl, and the two men confronted K. with Dora's accusation the next time they saw him. K. not only emphatically denied making any sexual advances but questioned Dora's mental state. He said he had heard from his wife that Dora was obsessed with sex and spent her time at their house reading Mantegazza's *Physiology of Love* and similar books. "It was most likely, he had added, that she had been over-excited by such reading and had merely 'fancied' the whole scene she had described."

Much to Dora's distress, her father accepted K.'s story and explanation. Philipp decided Dora's account was "a phantasy that [had] forced itself into her mind," clearly implying that he believed his daughter to be in the grip of some mental aberration. Her parents' refusal to believe her, Mr. K.'s lie, and Mrs. K.'s betrayal of their intimate reading and conversations plunged Dora into rumination and despair. Over the next two years, she repeatedly begged her father to break off his friendship with the Ks, but Philipp remained firm in his determination not to, although Dora's suffering was plain to him and frequently upset him, sometimes even moving him to tears. Dora's idealization of her beloved father crumbled. She now believed that "he thought only of his own enjoyment, and . . . had a gift for seeing things in the light which suited him best." When feeling especially embittered over her situation, such as at a time when her father would leave home to be with Mrs. K., she would sink under the weight of the thought that "she had been handed over to Herr K. as the price of his tolerating the relations between her father and his wife." Rage at Philipp would overcome her.

At a time when a cover of propriety was socially crucial, Dora was idealistically and inconveniently insisting that all veils be removed. She had become unwilling to go along with a system that simultaneously offered two levels of truth. The adults around her vigorously fought her efforts at exposure and insisted on continuing the various charades by which the middle class attempted to deal with its anxiety at the end of the nineteenth century. But that is only the first significance—the one pertaining to Dora's era—of the chain of events set in motion by K.'s proposition. The other is the display of the timeless weight of men's rule and of their setting the rules, of their traditional denial to women of an equitable seat at life's table. The fact of male domination is all the more apparent because it is a loving father who imposes his will on a devoted daughter. Philipp had used Dora to facilitate his affair with Mrs. K.—she had become his mistress's baby-sitter and her husband's sexual plaything—and he had denied to Dora the validity of her reality when she complained about K.'s behavior. Dora, as a girl, had been taken advantage of in an age-old manner that transcended nineteenth-century social dilemmas.

It is now clear why Dora, unlike Otto, was obsessed with her father's affair and found the situation intolerable. Part of her misery was due to her father's supplanting her with Mrs. K., his using her as sexual bait for Mr. K., and his betraying her when she made K.'s advances public. But there was more. Like all teenagers, Dora and Otto sought to express their idealism during their adolescence. Otto did so with the encouragement of his socialist uncle, and he was able to find an external mode, outside his family, of addressing the diversity of his grievances and the injustices he had witnessed. Through socialism, Otto had a socially approved outlet for venting complaint, outrage, and rebellion. He could move beyond directing his feelings and behavior solely toward family members and instead direct his emotions toward symbolic objects. Such "sublimation" is a healthy step in maturation and increases psychic well-being.

When Dora sought to deal with her grievances and the injustices she had observed, no one encouraged her.[36] On the contrary she was thwarted, most prominently by prevalent customs and traditions. Moreover, because of these conventional obstacles, because of the sexual harassment of her person, because girls had almost no legitimate, external arena for expression of grievances or rebellion, she never advanced past the point of dealing only with the injustices done to her personally.

Eventually Freud came to categorize women as morally deficient.[37] He theorized that men showed greater altruistic behavior as a result of their ability to resolve their oedipal conflicts more successfully than women. This theory sprang from his preoccupation with instinctual drives and the individual's success or failure to deal with them. Thus, he ended up arguing that women's and men's capacity for justice, altruism, and sublimation was due to psychological developments inherent in each sex.[38] Regardless of the accuracy of Freud's hypothesis, he failed to bring into his formula the fact that a girl was literally forced to confine her interests to self and family by her parents, other adults, and various social institutions and, therefore, lacked a public forum in which to play out adolescent idealistic strivings.[39]

Otto's wish to overthrow capitalism was a thirst for revenge no less angry that Dora's wish to separate her father and Mrs. K.[40] If Dora had been a man she might have found a social channel to express her anger. Nefarious wishes deriving from being raised in a pathological family could find socially acceptable outlets if one were a man but might remain locked up in the family forever if one were a woman.

At the end of summer of 1898, the Ks returned to Meran, and Dora was again forced into close public contact with them. The Bauers and the Ks celebrated Christmas together, as they had for a number of years. In spite of Dora's clear unhappiness over her relationship with both Ks, Mr. K. made her a present of a letter case accompanied by a speech about a possible marriage someday.

Dora did not remain long in Meran. Her favorite aunt, Malvine Bauer Friedmann, had become seriously ill, and Dora made plans to go to Vienna. It is not clear when she actually arrived, but she seems to have been there by February or March of 1899. A few days into her stay she became ill with a high fever and abdominal pains, which were diagnosed as appendicitis. She was treated with cold compresses and recovered uneventfully, except that afterward she found it hard to walk normally and began to drag her right foot. Freud interpreted Dora's abdominal attack as a hysterical realization of a fantasied childbirth, since it had occurred nine months after K.'s sexual proposition and was accompanied by a menstrual period and "violent pains." Malvine died on April 7,[41] but Dora stayed on for a while with her uncle and the two Friedmann girls, who were close to her in age.

In the few months Dora lived in Vienna when she was sixteen, and then again when she moved back to the city permanently before her eighteenth birthday, she began to explore the available cultural and educational activities. These helped to occupy her days and gave her some fulfillment. She attended lectures for women, studied on her own, and visited art galleries, especially the newly begun Secessionist shows, which were heavily supported by well-to-do Viennese Jews.

Dora reentered life in Vienna at a time of feminist ferment and expanding educational opportunities for women.[42] After 1888 the Society for Women's Extended Education (Verein für erweiterte Frauenbildung) tried to get girls admitted to the university and have them embark upon the same careers available to male university graduates. In 1892 the society established a girls' high school, which had a regular *Gymnasium* curriculum for the first six of the usual eight years. Slowly this was expanded: In 1901, the school offered seven of the traditional years and at last, in 1910, all eight years. At the same time, women were finally admitted in 1897, without handicaps, to the Philosophical Faculty of the University and three years later to the Medical Faculty.[43]

In 1893 the feminists Rosa Mayreder (1858–1938), an artist, and Auguste Fickert (1855–1910), a schoolteacher, had founded the General Austrian Women's Association (Allgemeiner österreichischer Frauen-verein), which campaigned for greater rights for women as well as harmony between the sexes based on shared activities.[44] One of the paramount social goals of the feminists, and also of some other contemporary reformers, was to do away with the marriages of adolescent girls to (sometimes much) older men for the sake of financial security, either for the girl or her family. The feminists regarded such marriages as legalized prostitution.[45] Moreover, Austrian civil law fostered the domination and patriarchal authority of husband over wife. A husband could, for example, forbid his wife to take certain jobs, and he alone had the right to decide where the family would live. Custom was a reflection of the legal situation: Freud had chosen both apartments in Vienna for his family without his wife's seeing them first. The husband also had the power to administer his wife's property, unless a legal agreement to the contrary had been arranged. At the turn of the century, reform of the marriage codes was also one of the feminists' main aims.[46]

Dora was both stimulated and discouraged by this atmosphere. Like many other middle-class girls, she resolved not to marry early. Intellectually curious and a reader, she involved herself in as many cultural and academic activities as she could take on but was only too conscious of her limitations. She was too old for the private girls' high schools, and when she tried to work on her own, her inability to concentrate and fatigue—prominent symptoms of her depression—constantly got in the way. She began to attend special lectures but was sometimes too depressed to leave the house. As Otto prepared to attend the university and expand his horizons, Dora's limited educational prospects and social life were painfully apparent.

Nevertheless Dora persevered in her attempts at self-education, one aspect of which were her visits to art exhibitions. Dora's interest in art seems to have been a genuine preoccupation, although it no doubt also represented the conventional middle-class desire to be "cultured." She had visited Dresden, and like any tourist went to the Zwinger, the city's famous art museum. But when a male cousin offered to escort her through the galleries, she declined and went alone, stopping in front of the pictures that appealed to her. She became rapt before Raphael's *Sistine Madonna* (*Sixtina*), lost for two hours in contemplation of the very-young-looking Madonna holding her child.[47] Eventually, she had a dream in which her decision to tour the Zwinger by herself played a role, and Freud argued "that 'pictures' [were] a nodal point in the network of her dream-thoughts." A later museum visit seemed to bear Freud out. At the end of 1900 Dora attended the Eighth Secessionist art show in Vienna. There she saw a painting that also worked its way into her dream, because it reminded her of the woods near the lake where Mr. K. had made his sexual proposition.

The Secessionist exhibitions figured prominently in the cultural life of the Bauers and other middle-class Viennese. Copying the 1892 Munich "secession" of rebellious artists seeking new forms of expression, innovative Viennese artists founded their own Secession (Vereinigung bildender Künstler Österreichs) in April 1897 and presented their first exhibition in March 1898. The emperor soon paid it a visit, having decided to support the modern movement for political motives. He saw it as representative of wider European culture and, therefore, as a weapon that might be used against the particularistic cultural demands of the various clamoring nationalities in the Austrian Empire.[48] Even without the imperial imprimatur, the show was a great success (to everyone's surprise), and 218 of the works displayed were sold. Before the exhibit closed in June, it had had seventy thousand visitors.[49] Within a year, the Secessionist style became fashionable—indeed, for a while, a craze.[50]

One reason for the Secessionists' ascendancy was the support and patronage they immediately enjoyed from the families of Jewish bankers, industrialists, and professionals. Stefan Zweig noted that whereas "in public life [the Jews] exerted only a meager influence . . . immeasurable is the part in Viennese culture the Jewish bourgeoisie took, by their co-operation and promotion. They were the real audience, they filled the theaters and the concerts, they bought the books and the pictures, they visited the exhibitions, and with their more mobile understanding, little hampered by tradition, they were the exponents and champions of all that was new. Practically all the great art collections of the nineteenth century were formed by them, nearly all the artistic attempts were made possible only by them."[51]

We do not know if Dora attended a Secessionist exhibition when she was in Vienna in the spring of 1899, but when she returned in the summer of 1900, the city was caught up in the storm of controversy occasioned by the display of a painting by Gustav Klimt (1862–1918) in the Seventh

Exhibition, which had opened in March. Klimt, formerly an Establishment artist but now the leader of the Secessionists, had been commissioned by the Ministry of Culture and Education in 1894 to design three ceiling paintings for the new University of Vienna. But after 1898 Klimt had radically altered his style, one new feature of which was the sensual portrayal of women with seductively long hair. The first commissioned painting, *Philosophy,* brought down on Klimt "the wrath of both old rationalists and new anti-Semites."[52] Eighty-seven faculty members of the university signed a petition asking the Ministry of Culture to reject it, and in the spring and summer of 1900 "the function of modern art in Vienna was vigorously debated by painters, public, and politicians alike."[53] Attending a Secessionist show became a political as well as an artistic statement.

Her interest piqued by the scandal, Dora went to the next Secessionist Exhibition, the eighth, which ran from November 3 to December 27, although it was devoted mainly to the applied arts, with works of designers from Paris, London, and Glasgow. The show received "great critical acclaim and delighted the Viennese public."[54] It is unknown how many times Dora actually visited it, but we do know that she went the last day of the exhibit as part of a tour of Vienna she gave a cousin who was visiting for the holidays. That night she had a dream in which a painting at the exhibition figured. It was a picture of a thick wood with nymphs in the background and, like the *Sistine Madonna,* it aroused thoughts connected with her experience with Mr. K. at the lake, two and a half years earlier.

At the same time that Dora began to emerge from her relatively sheltered life in Meran, Jews everywhere in the Austrian Empire were being forced to ponder just how secure they actually were in face of the anti-Semitic rioting that continued to erupt periodically after the nationalistic crisis of 1897. The Bauers themselves, just days after Malvine's death in April 1899, were faced with violence sparked by labor troubles in Nachod, where one of their factories was located. Troops from nearby barracks had to be called to end the furious attacks.[55] Although calm was restored, the strife was followed by a boycott of Jewish shops. Simultaneously, in the town of Polna, only eleven miles from Philipp's home village of Pollerskirchen, many months of furious agitation against the Jews, identified as representatives of the ruling Germans, culminated in an irrational outburst. A twenty-two-year-old Jewish vagrant and sometime shoemaker's assistant was accused of ritually murdering a nineteen-year-old Christian seamstress to gather her blood to make Passover *Matzot.*[56] Dora, in her own deep despair and agonizingly conscious of how little control she had over her personal life, was sharply reminded that also as a Jew she could not avoid being capriciously buffeted by the outside world.

On April 1, 1899, the body of Anežka Hrůzová, with her throat cut, was found in a wooded area near the Jewish quarter of Polna. Hrůzová, nineteen, had worked for a dressmaker who lived nearby, and every day she had walked to work from her native village. The medical examiners had declared that although they "found no signs of indecent assault . . . the body of Anežka Hrůzová had been completely bled and that the traces of blood found under the body did not correspond to the amount of blood one would expect to find near the body after a murder of this kind."[57] The man indicted for the crime, Leopold Hilsner, lived with his mother near Hrůzová's employer and frequently walked in the area. He had a distasteful local reputation as a somewhat slow-witted idler on the lookout for women. However, there was no real evidence of his involvement in Hrůzová's murder, and Hilsner denied any knowledge of the crime. Polna, a Czech town of some 5,000, had a Jewish population of 212, most of whom were poor and often unemployed. In 1847 more than 500 Jews had lived there, but the Jewish population had been steadily declining as Jews left because of the endemic anti-Semitism and the desire to find a place where they could make a living.[58]

Hilsner was brought to trial on September 12, 1899, on an indictment that did not formally charge ritual murder but suggestively stated that "under [Hrůzová's] body there was an insignificant pool of blood, no bigger than a hand."[59] A Czech nationalist lawyer, Dr. Karel Baxa (1862–1938), his fees paid by a joint Czech-German committee,[60] offered his aid to the Hrůzová family, and worked to convince the jury that the motive of the killer (or killers) was to get the blood of an innocent Christian girl. On September 16 Hilsner was found guilty of murder and sentenced to death by hanging. Jews throughout Austria were horrified and frightened. Blood libels, ritual murder trials, and resulting massacres of Jews had a continuous history going back to the Middle Ages. Since the founding of the Austro-Hungarian Empire in 1867 there had been several ritual-murder accusations. But this was the first time in the new era that the accused had been actually tried and found guilty.[61] The Jews tried to bring pressure on the imperial government to intervene, but public protest meetings in Vienna and throughout Bohemia, as well as an appeal to the prime minister, had no effect.

But later in 1900, on the argument that the medical evidence was faulty, a new trial was ordered, which took place from October 25 to November 14, 1900, coinciding with the early weeks of Freud's analysis of Dora. The Viennese press, including Kraus's *Die Fackel,* followed the trial closely. Although at the second trial there were no references to ritual murder, Hilsner was again found guilty. Eventually, because of the scantiness of evidence against Hilsner, the emperor was prevailed upon to change the death sentence to one of life imprisonment.

The first trial had been followed by anti-Jewish rioting throughout the Czech lands. Organized massacres—pogroms—like those that occurred in Russia did not take place, but "assaults, demonstrations, window-breaking, boycotting of shops, affronts, and psychological tyranny were . . . daily occurrences." Nachod itself again suffered from "riots and plunder." Many Jews in small rural communities fled their homes forever.[62]

The Hilsner trial attracted anti-Jewish agitators from throughout Europe, and the anti-Semitic European press sent journalists to cover the proceedings. In Vienna, anti-Semitic newspapers attacked viciously, and incendiary speeches against Jews were delivered in Parliament. Coinciding as it did with the Dreyfus Affair, the Hilsner case dispirited and intimidated Austrian Jews.[63] Then, just four months after the verdict against Hilsner, blood libel was raised again in a murder case in Nachod.[64] To the Bauer family, running their factories in Warnsdorf, in the face of continual German anti-Semitism, and in Nachod, where Czech unrest often took an anti-Jewish turn, these were emotionally wrenching times. Moreover, the Vienna the Bauers moved back to in 1900 was governed by a self-proclaimed anti-Semitic mayor, and a majority of the City Council had been elected as openly anti-Jewish. Within the decade, anti-Semitic events were to wreak their cumulative toll on Dora.

Although her life proceeded in outwardly normal patterns, Dora in her sixteenth and seventeenth years was not well, nor were her relations vis-à-vis the rest of the world satisfactory. Again, as when she was eight, she underwent a personality change. She became depressed, irritable, and self-critical. Her lifelong affection for her father disappeared, and her relations with her mother worsened. She kept to herself and complained of being tired and unable to concentrate. Moreover, she ate poorly and had little interest in food. She even lost her fondness for jewelry and stopped wearing any. She began to think about killing herself because she felt she could no longer endure life as it was. Desperate, she wrote a suicide note to her parents. She did not actually attempt to take her life, but left the letter where they could find it. Philipp, aware that Dora's suicidal intentions were not serious, procrastinated in taking any action, although he was severely shaken. But then one day after the two had an argument, Dora lost consciousness, became delirious, and had convulsions. Afterward she remembered nothing of the entire incident. It was at this point that Philipp decided that Dora must see Freud.

One day early in the fall of 1900, Philipp left his apartment in Vienna's Ninth District and walked the two to three blocks to Freud's. When Freud admitted him into the consulting room, Philipp announced he was there on account of his daughter and gave a brief history of the problem, starting with his family's becoming good friends with the Ks in Meran. He recounted how Mrs. K. had nursed him devotedly while he was recovering from his syphilitic attack, thus "earn[ing] a title to his undying gratitude." Philipp described Mr. K.'s kindness to Dora over the years and Dora's affection for the Ks' two little children. Then he told of his and Dora's visit two years earlier to the Ks' summer house by the lake and how Dora had suddenly announced that she was leaving, even though everyone had been expecting her to stay several weeks. The story of Dora's accusation and K.'s denial followed:

> I have no doubt [Philipp concluded], that this incident is responsible for Dora's depression. . . . She keeps pressing me to break off relations with [the Ks]. But that I cannot do. For to begin with, I myself believe that Dora's tale of the man's immoral suggestion is a phantasy . . . ; and besides, I am bound to Frau K. by ties of honourable friendship and I do not wish to cause her pain. The poor woman is most unhappy with her husband, of whom, by the by, I have no very high opinion. She herself has suffered a great deal with her nerves, and I am her only support. With my state of health I need scarcely assure you that there is nothing wrong in our relations. We are just two poor wretches who give one another what comfort we can by an exchange of friendly sympathy. You know already that I get nothing out of my own wife. But Dora, who inherits my obstinacy, cannot be moved from her hatred of the K.'s. She had her last attack after a conversation in which she had again pressed me to break with them. Try to bring her to reason.

5

"I Do Not Know What Kind of Help She Wanted from Me"

Sigmund Freud, to whom Philipp Bauer turned in the fall of 1900, was a neurologist—in German, literally a nerve-doctor *(Nervenarzt)*—as well as the practitioner of a form of psychotherapy that, for the past four years, he had been calling "psychoanalysis."[1] He applied this method to those of his patients afflicted with a neurosis such as hysteria, an obsession, an anxiety condition, or even a specific psychotic symptom like hallucinations. Dora, suffering for years from unexplained physical maladies, appeared to be an ideal candidate for his new method of therapy.

Whenever a patient in psychotherapy takes on a particular importance for his or her psychotherapist, as Dora did for Freud, the reaction of the therapist to the patient—the countertransference—has as much influence on the treatment as does the transference of the patient to the therapist. Extended or intensive psychotherapy can be viewed as encompassing the entire lives of the two people who have come together for the therapeutic journey. To understand Freud's psychoanalysis of Dora, then, it is necessary to know as much about Freud and his world when he was forty-four as it is about Dora and hers when she was eighteen.

Freud was just three years younger than the forty-seven-year-old Philipp Bauer. Indeed, the two men had started life not too dissimilarly. Freud was born in 1856 in the province of Moravia, in Freiberg (today Příbor, Czechoslovakia, close to the Polish border.) The Moravian Jews had been made to conform to the same Germanicizing measures that

87

prevailed in Bohemia, and Freiberg physically was not unlike the Bauers' hometown of Pollerskirchen. Set in wooded, rolling terrain near the source of the Oder River, Freiberg was a Czech country town of fewer than five thousand inhabitants, including about 130 Jews who had to travel to get to a synagogue.[2] The railroad line had bypassed the town in the 1840s, with predictable economic and cultural consequences. The twelve-mile trip by cart to the nearest train station had great significance in an era without radio or telephone.[3] Freud's father made a passable although hardly a good living as a merchant. He bought woolen cloth in Freiberg and its environs, had it dyed and finished locally, and then sent it east to Galicia. From Galicia he got wool, honey, hemp, and tallow, which he sold in Freiberg.[4] The Freud family lived in one rented room above a blacksmith's shop.[5]

Taking advantage of the new opportunities open to Jews, the Freuds left Moravia in 1859 and after a temporary stay in Leipzig, Germany, came to Vienna when Freud was four. They lived in a succession of small apartments in poor neighborhoods, having little steady income. Apparently Freud's father did not start a business when he moved his family to Vienna, and he probably made a living from temporary jobs, perhaps working for other Jewish traders. It is likely also that he had some limited private income. But he found himself in bad straits in the disastrous business climate that followed the stock market crash of 1873, and he had to rely for assistance on his wife's family and two grown sons from a previous marriage, who had settled in England. Freud remembered his childhood years in Vienna with distaste and would not talk about them. In his youth and early manhood he was able to complete his education only with numerous "loans" and outright gifts from relatives, family friends, teachers, and colleagues who recognized his abilities. He himself raised money by writing book reviews, doing translations, and giving lessons. He was ashamed of his father's lack of income and felt keenly his relative poverty.[6]

In the capital Freud's parents furthered the assimilation already begun in Freiberg by dropping Jewish dietary practices and not keeping the Sabbath. They did, however, mark certain celebratory holidays; the children dressed up in costume on Purim, and the family held a seder on Passover. Freud was tutored at home until he was nine, when he entered the *Gymnasium* in the Leopoldstadt neighborhood where the family lived. There he performed brilliantly, ranking first in his class for seven of the eight years' course. He graduated at seventeen in 1873 and entered the University of Vienna with plans to become a physician, having previously considered and discarded careers in law, politics, and the military.

Freud's initial goal was to be a research scientist in neuroanatomy, working at the cutting edge of late-nineteenth-century medicine, and he made some promising discoveries as a medical student. But a paying position in the field was rare, and he had no independent income on which to live or support a family. Thus, when he met his wife-to-be, he decided to train for a private practice as a neurologist. In 1900 this meant treating, among other cases, considerable numbers of neurotic patients; these were considered to have "nervous" illnesses, and "nerves" were the province of the neurologist. So neurologists cared for, usually on an outpatient basis, individuals with neuroses, milder psychoses, and neurological diseases, such as tertiary syphilis. Psychiatrists, sometimes still referred to as "alienists," generally had institutional practices in which they saw hospitalized sufferers of severe mental disorders.

When Freud opened his practice in 1886, at the age of thirty, he found, not surprisingly, that a fair number of his patients had illnesses for which there were no organic causes. Following the lead of the French neurologist Jean-Martin Charcot and of his Viennese internist-friend Josef Breuer, Freud started to hypnotize many of these "nervous" patients, either to get them to recall events they could not remember consciously, or to suggest cures, or both. This brought mixed results, although better ones than he could achieve with electrotherapy, hydrotherapy, or drugs.

With a few years' experience, Freud learned that he could obtain more satisfactory effects by pressing his patients for information while they were awake and having them say aloud whatever came into their minds—the phenomenon known as "free association." Freud began to hypothesize about the cause of his patients' conditions and to evolve a theory—the seduction theory—that ascribed their symptoms to a traumatic sexual assault or precocious sexual stimulation in childhood. Using dreams, he uncovered valuable data about the dreamer's life, as well as hidden feelings and wishes. In addition, although in a sporadic way, Freud began to apply to himself the methods he had developed in treating his patients.

After his father died in 1896, Freud became depressed and anxious and turned to a daily, systematic analysis of his dreams and other everyday occurrences, using the method of free association. A scant year later he reluctantly came to the conclusion, based on his own and his patients' analyses, that applying his seduction theory of neurosis in a ubiquitous way was faulty.[7] While he never gave up the notion that sexual assault on children could play a role in the development of neurosis, he came to believe that what was most basic was the child's unrequited wishes, still alive in all adults, usually on an unconscious basis. Prominent among the child's desires were both the yearning for an exclusive relationship with the parent of the opposite sex and jealousy—even hatred—of the parent of the same sex, though the child's feelings were complicated by simultaneous love and animosity toward both parents. Children's attraction to their parents, Freud believed, existed on a biological substratum; hence his new notion eventually became known as the theory of instinctual infantile sexuality.

It was at this transitional and troubled yet fertile juncture in the development of Freud's thinking that Dora became his patient. He had recently abandoned the seduction theory and just published *The Interpretation of Dreams,* the work he considered the most epochal of his entire career.[8] He had concluded that people distorted their dreams to hide socially or personally unacceptable wishes from themselves, and he spelled out the mechanisms of these distortions. He had also revealed his methods for deciphering dreams so that they would yield their secrets. At the same time Freud was feeling his way toward a coherent theory of human sexuality, although it would be another four and a half years before he published his *Three Essays on the Theory of Sexuality.*[9] Thus in 1900 Freud was at a remarkably creative period, and his letters indicate that he was aware of the lofty significance of his work. Yet, as he surveyed the circumstances of his life, he was repeatedly overwhelmed by feelings of discouragement and deprivation.

In September 1900, the month before Philipp Bauer brought Dora to him, Freud learned that once again, as had happened in each of the past three years, he had been passed over by the Ministry of Education for a promotion from a lecturer (*Privatdozent*) to an associate professor (*ausserordentlicher Professor*).[10] The title was desirable for a physician because it conferred great status, which could be translated into higher fees. Freud's promotion could perhaps have been hastened if he had been willing to use contacts in high places, which he resorted to eventually. Nevertheless, Freud believed he was passed over because he was a Jew, a victim of anti-Semitism, something he viewed with despondence.[11]

The Liberal party, for which Freud's parents had lit up their house, was increasingly foundering, and the Christian Socials had ridden to power on the backs of the new, lower-middle-class voters. With the confirmation of the self-proclaimed anti-Semite and demagogue Karl Lueger as mayor of Vienna, the Jews in Vienna shuddered. Confronting the failure of Austrian society to accept the Jews, Freud joined the Vienna Lodge of B'nai B'rith.[12] For several years he was a very active participant, both in committee service and as a speaker. He later said that although he was not personally religious, he found "the attraction of Jewry and Jews irresistible [because of] a clear consciousness of inner identity, and the safe privacy of a common mental construction."[13] The pervasive anti-Semitism in Vienna weighed heavily on Freud, and he worried about his children's future.[14]

But Freud was not depressed just about the future alone; the present also appeared bleak. In a mood of general pessimism, he was downcast over the reception of *The Interpretation of Dreams,* preoccupied with his own aging, and worried about his small practice and limited income. Fleeing from creative work, he wrote his close friend in Berlin, the physician Wilhelm Fliess, "I give myself over to my fantasies, play chess, read English novels. . . . For two months I have not written a single line of what I have learned or surmised. As soon as I am free of my trade, I live like a pleasure-seeking philistine . . . carefully keeping my attention diverted from the subject on which I work during the day."[15]

Freud had hoped that publication of the dream book would bring enthusiastic and widespread recognition of his genius. The work not only contained momentous discoveries about dreams but also large excerpts from his self-analysis, including painfully gained insights about his relationship with his father.[16] Although the response to *The Interpretation of Dreams* was good, it did not approach Freud's high expectations.[17] He complained hyperbolically that "understanding for [the book] is meager; praise is doled out like alms; to most people it is evidently distasteful [and no one] has an inkling of what is significant in it."[18] For almost a year, even as he began to see Dora, his letters dwelt on what he perceived to be the poor or unthinking reaction to his masterpiece.[19] At times he was tormented by doubts about his talents and the value of his work. This was an "inner crisis" that had left him "deeply impoverished." He told Fliess that if they should meet, his friend would see how much he had aged.

Middle age weighed heavily on Freud. At the New Year in 1900 he felt that "the most interesting thing about . . . the new century . . . for us may be that it contains the dates of our deaths." Life's erstwhile pleasures no longer existed for him: smoking "decent" cigars, sexual intercourse, and contacts with people. Yet he also wrote about his Saturday night cardplaying and his twice-monthly attendance at B'nai B'rith meetings.[20] And regardless of anything he ever said about cigars, they were an addiction he never gave up for long. In truth, the depression was slowly lifting, but it would be many months before it would be gone. April found him with "a mood of equanimity and physical well-being," yet in May his forty-fourth birthday confirmed to him that he was "an old, somewhat shabby Israelite."[21]

"Old," to be sure, was a deliberate exaggeration, but behind the word lay Freud's rueful awareness that his sex life was a waning and sometime affair. This ebbing had begun early. In 1893, after the Freuds had had five children in six years, Sigmund and Martha became abstinent for a prolonged period. After that Anna, their last child, was conceived; she was born in December 1895. From then on, birth control was uppermost in the minds of Freud and his wife. Some combination of abstinence and infrequent marital relations was the only method of contraception Freud considered possible, since he believed coitus interruptus, masturbation, and even the use of condoms unhealthy. An 1897 letter to Fliess hints at Freud's restricted sexuality, and in 1900 he stated outright, "I am done begetting children." Scattered remarks and allusions over the next several years indicate that sex was still alive for the Freuds, but barely. Whether avoidance of children was the only issue at stake is not known. A letter to Freud from Emma Jung, Carl Gustav Jung's wife, in November 1911 recalls a talk between Emma and Freud two months earlier. At that time Freud had confided that his "marriage had long been 'amortized,' now there was nothing more to do except—die."[22]

Along with his midlife retrenchment, Freud brooded about his income. His letters to Fliess chronicle anxiously the startings and stoppings of patients' treatments.[23] At times he was down to three or four sessions a day. The departure of any patient was a financial blow, since many relatives depended on his earnings. At home, besides Freud, were his wife, her sister (who required costly rest cures for tuberculosis), and Freud's six children, aged five to thirteen. In Vienna, in varying degrees of dependence, were his widowed mother, an unmarried sister and brother, and a recently widowed sister with a young child. Even later, when Freud was a world-famous, sought-after physician, he fretted over money, never forgetting his impecunious childhood and young manhood. In 1900, with his economic circumstances still insecure, worries about his income—his self-confessed "fear of poverty"—were a constant preoccupation.[24]

Furthermore, Freud's self-analysis was inadequate to break through certain stubborn resistances, and he imposed frustrating, neurotic restrictions on his activities. Although yearning to visit Rome on a holiday, he was as yet unable to bring himself to set foot there. That journey would finally come a year later when he had at last recognized sufficiently the aggressive and erotic wishes his desire for Rome concealed: defiance of the anti-Semites and love of his mother.[25] Citing as reasons "the uncritical adulation of the very young [and] a secret wish," he had also chosen to give up lecturing at the university.[26] This left him only with an audience of the Jewish men of his B'nai B'rith lodge, friendly and encouraging, but not scientifically involved.

Finally, Freud's passionate and intellectually uplifting relationship with Wilhelm Fliess, which had nourished him for many years, was on the wane.[27] Their separation echoed an already-established pattern of Freud's: breaking with significant men in his life. This time the events were particularly painful because they aroused in Freud memories and feelings associated with the disintegration of his earlier long friendship with Josef Breuer. In addition to their prolific correspondence, Fliess and Freud had a tradition of meeting by themselves once or twice a year in a mutually-agreed-upon city for days of stimulating and sustaining conversations. However, their last meeting, in August 1900, ended in a quarrel, and they never saw each other again, although they continued corresponding for a while.[28] It was not till autumn 1902 that Freud devised an emotional and intellectual replacement for Fliess—the Wednesday Psychological Society, a group of psychoanalytically interested men who met in his home.

Contemplating the future with wariness, feeling professionally unappreciated and isolated, and distastefully confronting the incursions of middle age, Freud was often in low spirits in the fall of 1900. Yet despite his insecurities, Freud would not have appeared less than confident to Dora. His sprawling apartment-office at Berggasse 19 was in a well-kept building. In the apartment "the family lived amid solid Victorian comfort, with their embroidered tablecloths, plush-covered chairs, framed photographic portraits, and . . . oriental rugs."[29] In 1900 Freud's consulting room did not yet hold the plethora of rugs, snapshots, plaques, etchings, statuettes, and ancient objects that filled every available space by World War I, but the collection, especially of antiquities, had already begun. If Freud could not afford originals at first, he bought copies, and gradually the genuine articles—either personal purchases or gifts—crowded out the ersatz.[30]

Regardless of how he envisaged himself, Freud was physically imposing. A brisk walker in the city and indefatigable hiker in the country, he appeared vigorous and energetic. "Though only of medium height—he was about five feet seven inches tall—he stood out in a crowd with his authoritative presence, neatly groomed appearance, and observant eyes."[31] He was always the perfect bourgeois, faultlessly dressed in suit and tie, his mustache and beard trimmed daily by a barber.

Freud's eyes added to his commanding air. One colleague at the start of the century described them as "lustrous [and] scrutinizing." Another found them "beautiful" and "serious," gazing "at man from the depths."[32]

Freud himself believed that looking is a civilized substitute for touching.[33] He was aware that his eyes gave him a distinctive look, for in the same month that he began to treat Dora, he had a dream of "Frau E. L. [who] was sitting beside me; she was turning her whole attention to me and laid her hand on my knee in an intimate manner. I removed her hand unresponsively. She then said: 'But you've always had such beautiful eyes.' "[34] Like everyone else, Dora would have been impressed by this compelling man.

One longs to know exactly what transpired during one of Freud's sessions with Dora or at least the precise way he worked with her. But Freud did not take notes during a session "for fear of shaking [Dora's] confidence and of disturbing his own view of the material under observation."[35] He wrote down only Dora's accounts of the two dreams she related as he recalled her words immediately after she left the room but not the analysis as it unfolded, hour by hour. He condensed the analytic material for reasons of space and even altered its sequence "for the sake of presenting the case in a more connected form." Furthermore, his psychoanalytic technique called for Dora to present her past life and present concerns in a haphazard manner. Freud explained in the "Prefatory Remarks":

> I . . . let the patient himself choose the subject of the day's work, and in that way I start out from whatever surface his unconscious happens to be presenting to his notice at the moment. [Thus] everything that has to do with the clearing-up of a particular symptom emerges piecemeal, woven into various contexts, and distributed over widely separated periods of time. . . . I have as a rule not reproduced the process of interpretation to which the patient's associations and communications had to be subjected, but only the results of that process. Apart from the dreams, therefore, the technique of the analytic work has been revealed in only a very few places.

All we know for certain about Dora's sessions is that when Dora entered treatment with Freud, he told her that his method required her to come six days a week, excluding only Sundays. He instructed her to lie on his couch and close her eyes as an aid in concentration. Lying down and shutting the eyes were techniques left over from Freud's days as an hypnotist. He eventually abandoned the closed eyes but kept the supine position as helpful to the patient's ability to associate freely.[36] In spite of Freud's assertions that he "let the patient . . . choose the subject," he was not at ease following Dora's lead. His very early psychotherapeutic method of firing questions at the patient and steering her in the direction of his own associations often dominated the psychoanalysis.[37] At the start of the treatment, Freud told Dora that he thought the analysis would take about a year for a "complete recovery."

Freud, of course, knew from his brief meeting with Dora two years earlier that she suffered from hysterical symptoms. But now her father emphasized to him her depression and her obsession with an imaginary affair between himself and Mrs. K., an old friend of the family. Dora was insisting, Philipp reported, that he break off all relations between the Bauers and the Ks, whom Dora, after years of close friendship, now hated. Freud appreciated that Philipp's "shrewdness" had showed him vital "points of contact between the circumstances of [Dora's] life and her illness, at all events in its most recent form." Yet not everything Philipp told him appeared consistent. So Freud turned to Dora and asked her to give him the whole story of her life and illness.

It was not long before Dora trusted Freud well enough to tell him of her earliest sexual encounter with Mr. K., in his office when she was thirteen. And soon after that, by dint of many precise details, Dora was able to convince Freud that her father and Mrs. K. were indeed "bound [by] a common love-affair." She even persuaded Freud that her father's refusal either to acknowledge the situation or break off with Mrs. K. showed him to be insincere, selfish, and self-deceptive. "I could not in general dispute Dora's characterization of her father," Freud admitted. "And there was one particular respect in which it was easy to see that her reproaches were justified. . . . She had been handed over to Mr. K. as the price of his tolerating the relations between her father and his wife."[38] Thus, Freud not only came to accept the reality of K.'s proposition at the lake but saw that the man's behavior toward Dora during the preceding two or three years resembled nothing so much as courtship.

Freud recognized that Philipp had brought his daughter to him in the hope that Freud would convince Dora to accept her father's relationship with Mrs. K., get her to stop threatening suicide, and make her act in a pleasanter manner at home. At the same time, he became aware that Dora had her own goals: She wanted Freud to take notice of the injustices that had been done to her, tell her father that the scene by the lake had really taken place, and persuade Philipp to end his love affair. But Freud had his own agenda, distinct from both Philipp's and Dora's. The lack of clear agreement among Philipp, Dora, and Freud on what the treatment was supposed to accomplish made the case problematic from its inception and continued to operate so as to prevent any satisfactory resolution.

Freud's very definite notions of what he wanted to accomplish in Dora's psychoanalysis arose out of his professional concerns in 1900. His primary goal was to rid Dora of her hysterical symptoms, most pointedly the cough and loss of voice, by making her aware of her unconscious fantasies and desires regarding her father and Mr. K. Freud believed Dora's illness had arisen from her still strong and unconscious love for her father and jealousy of her mother—the triangular oedipal conflict Freud declared "a universal event in early childhood"—which in Dora's case had outlived its healthy perimeters.[39] Regardless of what Freud had learned about the actuality of K.'s pursuit of Dora, she remained in his eyes the girl who had suffered from nervous ailments for almost half her lifetime. He wanted to ferret out the etiology of her hysteria and rid her of her physical symptoms. At the turn of the century, this was what Freud believed to be the revolutionary, therapeutic contribution of psychoanalysis.

But besides achieving Dora's cure, Freud hoped to use her case to prove the validity of *The Interpretation of Dreams*. Earlier in the year, he had been criticized in reviews for not providing detailed case material that clearly showed how dream interpretation could remedy a neurosis. Now a splendid opportunity had presented itself in Dora's analysis. Dora reported to Freud two dreams whose interpretation he believed enabled him to clarify her true feelings about Mr. K., her father, and Mrs. K., as well as to explain the origins of her hysterical symptoms. Thus Dora's case could prove incontrovertibly the theories about dreams and neuroses he had set forth in his masterpiece. The original title of the paper he wrote on Dora's treatment was "Dreams and Hysteria." Only later did it become "Fragment of an Analysis of a Case of Hysteria."

Freud's further goal in Dora's treatment was "to subject [certain theoretical] assumptions to a rigorous test." He wished to verify his new theory of instinctual infantile sexuality—that "sexual impulses operated normally in the youngest children without any need for outside stimulation."[40] To support his hypothesis, he wanted to demonstrate that Dora's hysteria had resulted from repressed sexuality. In accordance with this notion, he eventually offered a solution to Dora's predicament that would go the farthest toward normalizing what he saw as a generally unsatisfactory sexual situation: The Ks should get divorced, and Dora and Mr. K. should marry. Such a denouement, he believed, would be the healthiest for the largest possible number of Bauers and Ks involved.

Freud also wanted to demonstrate the deleterious effects of masturbation on mental health since he believed that Dora's illness had begun as a result of her masturbating. While he was revolutionary in his understanding of hysteria, Freud was still an ordinary nineteenth-century physician when it came to knowledge about "self-abuse." He maintained that masturbation was an incomplete sexual discharge and, therefore, damaged the body's sexual physiology through "spinal irritation." "The role played by this addiction [that is, masturbation] in hysteria is enormous," he wrote, also calling it a "specific" cause of neurasthenia, with such symptoms as "fatigue, intracranial pressure, flatulent dyspepsia, constipation, spinal paraesthesias, sexual weakness, etc."[41]

The existence of bisexuality and its application in psychoanalysis was another assumption Freud was eager to establish. As Dora's psychoanalysis progressed, Freud came to believe that the relationship between Dora and Mrs. K. showed the connection between bisexuality and neurosis. This touched on a sensitive personal issue and, at first, made Freud eager to publish his findings rapidly. He believed a question of priority over Fliess was at stake. The matter of bisexuality in human beings was one of the issues that instigated the parting quarrel between Freud and Fliess just two months before Freud began treating Dora. At this final meeting in August 1900, Freud had told Fliess that he had decided that one could not understand neuroses unless one accepted bisexuality as part of the human makeup. Fliess was startled by this pronouncement and reminded Freud that bisexuality had originally been his idea—one at which Freud had scoffed. A week later Freud remembered that Fliess had indeed originated the theory, but it was not until a year later that he actually acknowledged to Fliess that bisexuality was Fliess's discovery and not his.[42] That Freud was anxious to introduce clinically the notion of bisexuality is borne out, moreover, by the abrupt, awkward placement of the material about Dora's homosexuality at the end of the case history.[43]

Freud also found Dora's treatment an appropriate vehicle to enunciate fully for the first time his ideas on the motives for illness in hysteria. Since Dora's symptoms and behavior since age fifteen had had as their goal the breaking up of the relationship between her father and Mrs. K., Freud believed it would be antitherapeutic for Dora in the long run if he advised Philipp to terminate his affair. Freud said he knew that if Philipp agreed to leave Mrs. K. for Dora's sake, Dora would recover. But in that regard Freud argued, "I hoped [Dora's father] would not let himself be persuaded to do this, for then [Dora] would have learned what a powerful weapon she had in her hands, and she would certainly not fail on every future occasion to make use once more of her liability to ill-health." Here Freud was setting out a new formulation about the two kinds of "gain"—primary and secondary—a patient could derive from an illness. The neurosis the patient developed was the "primary gain"; albeit an uncomfortable or disabling symptom, it was the person's unconscious, psychological solution to a mental conflict. The primary gain revolved around the original liability to become ill. The "secondary gain," however, came from a motive for remaining ill, for example, staying ill to "gain" attention. It was this type of gain that Freud sought to prevent Dora from attaining for the sake of her future health. A secondary gain could be deeply self-destructive to her as well as manipulative of those around her.

Freud never achieved his main goal of ridding Dora permanently of her hysterical cough and aphonia because on Monday, December 31, 1900—after barely three months of therapy—Dora suddenly announced to him that this was her last visit. Freud explained her abrupt termination as a transference onto him of the "cruel impulses and revengeful motives" she harbored toward her father and Mr. K. Unfortunately, he confessed, he had not been sufficiently aware of this transference to deal with it in time.

———————

Freud had begun Dora's psychoanalysis with the conviction that given enough time he could cure her of the physical afflictions she had borne for so many years. After she left prematurely, he realized that his overlooking the transference had played a decisive part in her departure. He was not aware, however, that more than theoretical and technical aspects of psychoanalysis were involved in her precipitous leaving. Although Freud had made brilliant discoveries about hysteria and had developed methods to apply these insights therapeutically, his analysis of Dora was still affected by the nineteenth-century medicine of which he was a part. He shared the uncomfortable feeling most contemporary physicians had about their female hysterical patients.

Doctors saw a hysterical woman as a major medical challenge. "You must expect to have your temper, your ingenuity, your nerves tested to a degree that cannot be surpassed even by the greatest surgical operations," the physician L. C. Grey told a class of medical students in 1888. "I maintain that the man who has the nerve and the tact to conquer some of these grave cases of hysteria has the nerve and the tact that will make him equal to the great emergencies of life."[44] Freud, too, after coping with Dora for three months, confessed that "no one who . . . conjures up the most evil of those half-tamed demons that inhabit the human breast, and seeks to wrestle with them, can expect to come through the struggle unscathed."

Toward women who so tested them, doctors were at the very least ambivalent. They wanted to help, their job was to cure, but how could they react when their patients were indeed difficult and exasperating, and when they were being challenged in their authority both as men and physicians? The ambivalence was expressed by Dr. Grey when he urged that the hysterical "patient must be taught day by day . . . by . . . that combination which the French . . . call 'the iron hand beneath the velvet glove.' "[45] So Freud determined that Dora must receive no sense of power from the treatment, even if that meant forgoing a cure. Knowing that if Philipp ended his love affair, that would cure Dora of her recurrent cough and loss of voice, Freud could not urge it. He would not allow Dora to learn "what a powerful weapon she had in her hands."

Accepting the reality that Freud's decision was, in part, culturally determined does not negate the fact that his attempt to prevent Dora from achieving a secondary gain from her illness had a sound psychological basis. Freud's decision had more than one motivation; it was "over-determined," to use his own word for multicausation. Freud—like anyone else—was perfectly capable of using a psychological theory as a rationalization for a conclusion that was congenial to him. In this case advocating the continuation of Philipp's affair was doubly congenial because it touched on his sympathies for Philipp's sexual situation.

Freud, moreover, had a personal fantasy that fed into and therefore strengthened in him the physicians' feeling that they were waging a perilous battle with their hysterical female patients. There is evidence to indicate that Freud felt that women in general were a dangerous foe who held men back professionally. Hence, Freud not only shared his medical colleagues' attitudes about the professional hazards posed by female hysterical patients, but carried within himself a heightened belief in his own, personal vulnerability.

Interpreting one of his dreams ("Autodidasker") in the late 1890s, Freud was reminded of Émile Zola's *The Masterpiece*. In this novel a relationship with a woman interferes with the artist's creative work, and because of a woman the artist "feels compelled to die. . . . [A] series of [Freud's] allusions expresses the common denominator that the consequences of a relationship with a woman has a detrimental effect upon the professional life of a man, culminating in his progressive mental deterioration and ultimately in an agonizing death. If a woman destroys the man in these ways, then she must be dreaded." Analyzing yet another dream ("Self-Dissection"), Freud's association was to Rider Haggard's novel, *The Heart of the World*. A theme in this novel is "that a woman stands in the way of a man's ambitions and ultimately leads him to his destruction. . . . A relationship with a woman is dangerous and even disastrous and only [a sublimated] homosexual relationship . . . is safe."[46] Freud blamed his fiancée, Martha Bernays, for preventing him from making an important scientific discovery—the eye-anesthetic property of cocaine—which he claimed he would have achieved if only he had not rushed off to visit her in Hamburg. Ernest Jones convincingly demonstrates that Freud's accusation against Martha was baseless and was his own neurotic notion.[47] But Freud's feeling of having been professionally cheated did not stop there. Since Martha was poor and had no dowry, he believed he had paid dearly for her love. He had had to sacrifice a career as a research scientist, which had dim remunerative prospects, in order to open a private medical practice so he could support a family.[48]

Beyond the theme of women as destroyers of men's careers, there is evidence of a belief that women per se were dangerous and always "cost" a man something. In the "Autodidasker" dream, Freud felt "concern . . . over the danger of coming to grief over a woman—for that was the kernel of my dream thoughts . . . an example [were] the cases of [Eduard] Lasker and [Ferdinand] Lassalle which made it possible to give a simultaneous picture of the two ways in which this fatal influence can be exercised. '*Cherchez la femme.*'"[49] Freud's associations were to these two German-Jewish politicians, one of whom caught syphilis from a woman and died from degeneration of the spinal cord (*tabes dorsalis*), and the other who was killed in a duel over a woman. One of the main components of a third dream ("Company at table d'hôte"), which Freud had at the same time he was treating Dora, was that he had "always paid dearly for whatever advantage [he had] had from other people [and that he] should like to get some enjoyment without cost." Yet this was not happening. A free cab ride he had gotten the night before reminded him that "a few days earlier I had paid out a considerable sum of money on behalf of a member of my family of whom I am fond. [This was Freud's sister-in-law, Minna.] No wonder, said the dream-thoughts, if this person were to feel grateful to me: love of that sort would not be 'free of cost.'"[50] In short, a relationship with a woman was never an even exchange; the woman always gained something. At stake for the man was his career, money, power, even life.

Without a doubt Freud's determination that Dora should not "win"—either over her father or over him—was quite marked, for he was already dismayed that she was a "young woman of very independent judgement, who had grown accustomed to laugh at the efforts of doctors." Freud had felt the same "discomfiture" about a previous hysterical patient, Miss Elisabeth von R., whose upbringing and attitude had remarkable similarities to Dora's and whom Freud termed "cheeky" and "ill-behaved" when she mocked his inability to relieve her pains.[51]

Thus Freud and his medical contemporaries felt "locked in a power struggle with their hysterical patients. Such women, doctors claimed, used their symptoms as weapons in asserting autonomy in relation to their physician; in continued illness was their victory."[52] Freud accused Dora of leaving treatment deliberately to thwart him: "For how could the patient take a more effective revenge than by demonstrating upon her own person the helplessness and incapacity of the physician?"

Victorian physicians could not but feel acutely the anger hysterical women felt toward them. Freud, after the treatment, recognized that he was the recipient of Dora's accumulated rage at the men in her life. He saw that she had transferred her lifelong "cruel impulses and revengeful motives" toward men onto him. Although Freud became aware of this transference while writing up the case, in his actions during the treatment, he responded like other contemporary physicians. Stung by their patients' anger, disdainful of their female weakness, resentful of their manipulations, often impotent to evoke permanent cures, doctors reacted with hostility. Oliver Wendell Holmes (1809–94), the American physician prominent for his jokes and good humor, was yet powerfully moved to declare that "a hysterical girl is a vampire who sucks the blood of the healthy people around her."[53] By comparison Freud's comment that Dora's behavior in the treatment was at times "intolerable" is a mild one. When Dora suddenly announced her imminent departure from the analysis, Freud made no effort to have her reconsider her abrupt decision. He became quite bitter and bombastic: "Her breaking off so unexpectedly, just when my hopes of a successful termination of the treatment were at their highest and her thus bringing those hopes to nothing—this was an unmistakable act of vengeance on her part."[54]

Dora's putative vengeance had aroused Freud's. Three weeks later, as he wrote up the case, he mulled over his decision to let Dora leave without his first trying to make her remain in treatment. He recognized that she was a girl who longed for affection. Should he have acted as if her staying were important to him? Should he have shown a warm personal interest in her? He shifted uncomfortably: "I do not know," and his explanation was defensive:

> Since in every case a portion of the factors that are encountered under the form of resistance remains unknown, I have always avoided acting a part, and have contented myself with practising the humbler arts of psychology. In spite . . . of every endeavor to be of assistance as a physician, I keep the fact in mind that there must be some limits set to the extent to which psychological influence may be used, and I respect as one of these limits the patient's own will and understanding.

When he learned the next year that Dora had wrung from the Ks full confessions of their true relations with her and her father, Freud was displeased at Dora's acting out.[55] His own revenge was to reject her wish to return to treatment for a facial neuralgia, even though this time she was not dragged in by her father but came of her own free will. He swiftly based his decision not to accept her back into analysis by *"one glance at her face [which] was enough to tell me that she was not in earnest"* (italics supplied). Freud rationalized his punishment of Dora with puzzled musing: "I do not know what kind of help she wanted from me," but promised "to forgive her" for depriving him of "the satisfaction of affording her a far more radical cure of her troubles."[56]

But at least Freud did not physically torture Dora, which is what some of his angry colleagues did to their hysterical patients. "Doctors frequently recommended suffocating hysterical women until their fits stopped, beating them across the face and body with wet towels, ridiculing and exposing them in front of family and friends."[57] One gynecologist trained his patients not to have hysterical attacks by inserting tubes into their rectums after each hysterical episode. They soon learned "self-control." Another gynecologist advocated making "a strong mental impression," such as that made by the surgeon Boerhave, when he threatened hysterical girls with the application of hot irons to their spines.[58] For a while, the famous gynecologist, Alfred Hegar (1830–1914), and his pupils performed ovariectomies in cases of "intractable" hysteria, and the renowned neurologist, Nikolaus Friedreich (1825–82), was at the forefront of a medical cohort who cauterized their patients' clitorises.[59]

Dora received extended courses of electrotherapy and hydrotherapy for perhaps as long as three years. It is impossible to learn how vigorous or drastic they were and if they had educational or punitive aspects. Yet we do know from Wilhelm Erb's and Charles Féré's textbooks that many of her physical treatments were unpleasant, and Freud testified to her increasing scorn for doctors. Hence it is certainly possible—considering her intractable symptoms and increasingly negative attitude toward physicians—that some of her doctors assumed an adversarial relationship with her and relieved some of their frustration through legitimately medical but also forceful and painful therapies.

Yet the practice of "heroic" medicine—as one historian has dubbed medically extreme tactics—cannot be explained solely in terms of male hostility and revenge.[60] Physicians in the mid- and late nineteenth century often resorted to severe or drastic techniques (many of which were theoretically discredited remnants from medicine's prescientific days) because they had nothing else to offer except an admission of ignorance. Such a confession they were loath to make; moreover, it might drive their patients into the waiting arms of numerous quacks. The doctors were desperate to act and practiced heroic medicine on women and men indiscriminately. Male genitals were cauterized to cure venereal disease, and one physician even recommended creating a sore on boys' penises to prevent masturbation.[61]

S. Weir Mitchell (1829–1914), the American neurologist who developed the "rest cure" for women's nervous illnesses, originally used his technique during the Civil War for soldiers suffering from battle fatigue (the notorious "shell shock" of World War I), which he thought of as a purely physical illness. And he regarded his later rest cure as superior to the heroic medicine many of his female patients had previously undergone.[62]

It is true that physicians did not set out deliberately to victimize women, nor did an eager sadist hide in the psyche of every doctor.[63] Yet it is psychologically naive to explain the stubborn persistence of heroic medicine and Weir Mitchell's devotion to his rest cure purely on grounds of internal medical developments. One has only to read Mitchell's own words on why his cure worked to see that there was indeed a power struggle between patient and doctor:

> To lie abed half the day, and sew a little and read a little, and be interesting and excite sympathy, is all very well, but when they were bidden to stay in bed a month, and neither to read, write, nor sew, and to have one nurse— who is not a relative—then rest becomes for some women a rather bitter medicine, and they are glad enough to accept the order to rise and go about when the doctor issues a mandate which has become pleasantly welcome and eagerly looked for.[64]

Thus, a great deal of the medical handling of hysteria was either overtly or covertly punitive. Like Weir Mitchell's enforced rest, Freud's withholding of treatment from Dora when she returned to him for help after fifteen months was masked retribution. Even though Freud was in the avant garde in his discovery of the psychological significance of hysterical symptoms, he could not but help see Dora as an "hysterical woman." An automatic chain of thought and action was thus set in motion. Before Freud ever got to know Dora, he knew she would be manipulative; he was on guard, wary. His hostility was easily aroused, and the weight of convention disposed him to discipline her.

Like other doctors of his era, Freud also, quite traditionally, linked Dora's female physiology and her masturbation to her hysteria. In the nineteenth century, "a woman's emotional states generally, and hysteria in particular, were believed to have the closest ties to her reproductive cycle. . . . Indeed, the first question routinely asked hysterical women was, 'Are your courses regular?' "[65] Freud, though not emphasizing the matter, also commented on Dora's irregular periods. What Freud shared to the fullest with fellow physicians, however, was the belief that masturbation caused hysteria.[66]

Like the witch hunts of the sixteenth and seventeenth centuries, the antionanism campaign of the nineteenth century testifies to the extent to which irrationality dominates human thought and action. Anxiety about change played a role in both events. While the witch hunts primarily reflected the malaise among the lower and rural classes in early modern Europe, the campaign against the "vice of self-abuse" mirrored the uncertainties in the middle classes two centuries later. "The terroristic prophecies, the ingenious mechanical devices and barbarous operations that doctors inflicted on masturbators" they did for reasons very similar to their practice of heroic medicine: their own inability to do much, skepticism from their patients as to whether they could do anything, and their uncertainty of how to appear modern and all-knowing as medicine moved into its new scientific and increasingly effective state.[67] Once physicians finally achieved status as scientific professionals and gained public confidence, they relinquished their fight against masturbation. But, till then, "what made physicians, in company with their patients, so apprehensive about masturbation in the nineteenth century was that it seemed a pointless and prodigal waste of limited and valuable resources . . . it constituted a loss of mastery over the world and oneself. The campaign to eradicate self-abuse was a response to that danger: a way of conserving strength and maintaining control, both highly cherished and maddeningly elusive goals in the nineteenth century."[68]

Freud told Dora that the onset of her illness was due to her masturbating, as was her failure to respond sexually to Mr. K. "Her premature sexual enjoyment," as he styled Dora's masturbation, had made Dora repress her love for K. "instead of surrendering to it." Freud spelled this out: An early history of masturbation is bound to result in one of two behaviors when the person is confronted by "the demands of love in maturity." He or she will either become so promiscuous that sexual activity will "border upon perversity; or there will be a reaction—he will repudiate sexuality, and will at the same time fall ill of a neurosis. [Dora's] constitution and the high level of her intellectual and moral upbringing decided in favour of the latter course." But this was not all. According to Freud, certain of Dora's physical problems and ills over the years could also be traced to masturbation: her bed-wetting, her vaginal discharge, and her gastric pains.[69]

In this vein Freud explained the mechanism of how Dora had fallen ill and why her symptoms continued unabated: "Hysterical symptoms hardly ever appear so long as children are masturbating, but only after-wards, when a period of abstinence has set in; they form a substitute for masturbatory satisfaction, the desire for which continues to persist in the unconscious until another more normal kind of satisfaction appears." In arguing that Dora's symptoms would remain even if she returned to masturbating, Freud shared the nineteenth-century medical assumption that "unfulfilled physiological functions could be pathogenic." The cure for a woman's hysteria was sexual intercourse in marriage; a man's nervous illness could be cured through sexual intercourse in or out of matrimony.[70]

Freud's grasp of Dora's psychology was impressive. But his some-times-brilliant insights were not effectively translated into a successful therapy not only because he overlooked the transference but because of his conventional medical notions about hysterical women. Moreover, "medical" in 1900 almost always meant "male," and this, too, complicated the treatment of hysterical women. As Freud's medical attitudes about hysteria operated on him without his awareness, so did his male, middle-class outlook, with its specific assumptions about the place of women in fin-de-siècle Vienna.

––––––

Stefan Zweig, just one year older than Dora, remembered how he and his high school friends regarded girls: "It seemed to us that walking with the girls was time lost, for in our intellectual arrogance we looked from the start upon the other sex as being mentally inferior, and did not wish to waste our precious hours in inane conversation." Clothing and hair fashions at the time of his adolescence, Zweig recalled, were meant to portray visibly the accepted inherent differences between men and women: "The stronger sex was accentuated over the weaker one in the bearing demanded of each, the man vigorous, chivalrous, and aggressive, the woman shy, timid and on the defensive, the hunter and his prey."[71]

In Viennese society women's lives were decided by their fathers, brothers, and husbands. Freud's younger sister had been learning to play the piano as part of the "accomplishment" that she needed to make a good marriage. When Freud complained that the playing disturbed his studies, her practicing ceased, and the piano was removed from the apartment.[72] Men decided what should be, and girls and women did not generally dispute their right to do so. Indeed, most women as well as men upheld the established order of things.

Her resort to hysteria indicated that Dora was not an overt rebel. When it came to significant decisions regarding her life, she conformed to what was expected of her, though she did so with such ambivalence that she wrecked any chance of personal happiness. Her masochistic conformity was automatically accepted and encouraged by Freud. Regarding her first hysterical illness, her dyspnea, Freud wrote that this was the beginning of her feminine sexual life: She became "girlish for the first time." Although unaware of what was implicit in his description, Freud was equating illness with femininity. Dora had been a tomboy ("a wild creature") and the equal of her brother up to the age of eight; she had been "masculine." Then she developed a nervous asthma. After the illness Dora became "quiet and well-behaved" and fell behind Otto; she was now "feminine."[73] For Freud, Dora had slipped into her more natural role, albeit one filled with sickness and lower achievement. With this interpretation Freud strengthened Dora in a belief that she was fulfilling the feminine ideal. She had, as we know, three close role models on which to pattern a life of illness, her mother, Mrs. K, and her Aunt Malvine.

A conventional girl of Dora's background was expected to marry and to run a household. Although Dora presented Freud with a great deal of evidence that this was precisely what she did not want to do, Freud was unable to respond empathically to any of it. Freud's ideas on the traditional place and role of women were fixed. When his fiancée happened to write to him about John Stuart Mill and his wife, Freud responded with a criticism of Mill's "absurd" position that a married woman was capable of earning as much as her husband. "I dare say we agree," Freud wrote to Martha Bernays, "that housekeeping and the care and education of children claim the whole person and practically rule out any profession; even if simplified conditions relieve the woman of housekeeping, dusting, cleaning, cooking, etc."

Roused by the subject, Freud, at twenty-seven eagerly looking forward to domestic bliss, was eloquent on what awaited him and his beloved:

> It seems a completely unrealistic notion to send women into the struggle for existence in the same way as men. Am I to think of my delicate, sweet girl as a competitor? After all, the encounter could only end by my telling her . . . that I love her, and that I will make every effort to get her out of the competitive role into the quiet, undisturbed activity of my home. It is possible that a different education could suppress all women's delicate qualities . . . with the result that they could earn their living like men. . . . But I believe that all reforming activity, legislation and education, will founder on the fact that long before the age at which a profession

can be established in our society, nature will have appointed woman by her beauty, charm, and goodness, to do something else. No, in this respect, I adhere to the old ways, to my longing for my Martha as she is, and she herself will not want it different; legislation and custom have to grant to women many rights kept from them, but the position of woman cannot be other than what it is: to be an adored sweetheart in youth, and a beloved wife in maturity. [74]

The changes occurring around the turn of the century and the fact that Freud had three daughters did nothing to shake his early outlook. In 1905 Freud was asked to testify on divorce law reform before a non-governmental investigative society. One of the questions put to him was: "Should equality of the sexes be demanded?" Freud responded tersely: "Equality of the sexes is impossible because of their different roles in the process of reproduction."[75] Throughout the decade, at meetings of the Vienna Psychoanalytic Society, Freud maintained his traditionalist views. At a 1908 meeting devoted to "The Natural Position of Women," Freud commented during the discussion: "A woman cannot earn a living and raise children at the same time. Women as a group profit nothing by the modern feminist movement; at best a few individuals profit." After he returned from his 1909 visit to Clark University in Massachusetts, he turned in a negative assessment of American coeducation. He had learned from G. Stanley Hall, Clark's president and a psychologist, that "the girls develop more rapidly than the boys, feel superior to them in everything, and lose their respect for the male sex." Freud added: "In America the father ideal appears to be downgraded, so the American girl cannot muster the illusion that is necessary for marriage."[76]

At no time in his career was Freud prepared to recognize women's sensibilities. Five years before he saw Dora, he treated Elisabeth von R. and already indicated his uneasiness with women who departed from the feminine ideal. At that time, Freud described the twenty-four-year-old Miss von R. as "greatly discontented with being a girl [*sic*]. She was full of ambitious plans. She wanted to study or have a musical training, and she was indignant at the idea of having to sacrifice her inclinations and her freedom of judgement by marriage." This was a "girl" whose "harsher side" was her "cock-sure" nature and her characteristic of "being too positive in her judgements."[77]

Born in 1856, himself from a most traditional background, leading a conforming married life, Freud cannot be blamed for his conventional views. But his lack of empathy with Dora, though understandable, further narrowed her already circumscribed situation. Freud interpreted elements in Dora's second dream as signifying her conviction that "men are all so detestable that I would rather not marry. This is my revenge." But he did not for a moment take her seriously. He assumed Dora would someday marry, and he patronizingly discounted her "more or less serious studies." But a nondomestic vocation or avocation, or a successful psychoanalysis were the only two things that might have rescued Dora from her otherwise inescapable misery. An avocation-turned-career had been the salvation of "Anna O." (Bertha Pappenheim), Josef Breuer's severely hysterical patient, whose "talking" treatment was Freud's inspiration for psychoanalysis. Anna O. never married and became the first German social worker. At the same time that Freud assumed Dora's eventual marriage and motherhood, he openly disparaged Dora's own mother and her domestic role, labeling her as "uncultivated" and "foolish" and afflicted with "housewife's psychosis."

Freud shared most of his contemporaries' notions that when girls and women married, they were to be pliant and compliant wives.[78] These opinions about the roles and aspirations of girls and young women affected Freud's psychoanalysis of Dora. Freud also was comfortable with the incongruities and hypocrisies that were an integral part of his late-Victorian world. He found nothing unusual about the arrangements the Bauers and Ks had worked out for themselves, and even suggested partly formalizing them by having the Ks get a divorce. In this way Dora and K. could marry, Dora could become a real mother to the Ks' children, and—although Freud did not spell this out—Mrs. K. would be freer as Philipp's mistress. Freud also did not consider Mr. K.'s proposal to Dora by the lake to be odd in any way. "Why," Freud wondered, "did [Dora's] refusal take such a brutal form [a slap on the face], as though she were embittered against him? And how could a girl who was in love feel insulted by a proposal which was made in a manner neither tactless nor offensive?" Furthermore, Freud reasoned, Dora certainly had no romantic reason to reject K.; after all, he had met the man and seen that "he was still quite young and of prepossessing appearance."

The Bauers and Ks' involvement and the adults' use of Dora did not shock Freud because he saw the like all around him in his own social circles and heard similar tales from the middle- and upper-middle-class people who were his patients. And he read about them, too. The interfamilial entanglements, lushly breeding quarrels, sickness, deception, and despair, all of it masked by the respectable appearance of two bourgeois families seemingly linked in ordinary friendship, might have been the stuff of a novella or play by Freud's contemporary, Arthur Schnitzler. Schnitzler traveled in some of the same Jewish circles as did the Bauers and the Freuds.[79] He wove many of his stories and plays around themes that dealt with the casual, sexual use of "the sweet young thing" (*das süsse Mädel*) or exposed the frustrations and even desperations of other women, both young and middle-aged, victimized sometimes by their families but most often by their fathers and husbands.[80]

Schnitzler openly acknowledged his dalliances with sweet girls; "bedded and then betrayed" was his own succinct phrase.[81] With psychological acuity, he depicted in his works the unhappy fates of women he had observed or heard about. But, whether his stories stemmed from personal or secondhand experience, his goal was the same: He wanted to portray the reality that underlay upright, bourgeois existence. One story, that of "Miss Else," is startlingly reminiscent of Dora's. Else, at nineteen, is begged by her parents to act agreeably toward an older, wealthy acquaintance of the family. Their aim is to get the man to lend Else's reprobate but outwardly respectable father a large sum of money that will save him from bankruptcy and, therefore, public disgrace. The parents never specify what it is they want Else to do, nor does she imagine to herself any precise act. This very intangibility infuses the story with a malignant air. When the man finally makes his wish known—it is not a request for physical sex but for Else to appear naked before him—Else is plunged into madness and suicide.[82] She has listened to her parents in order to preserve their bourgeois mores, but it is precisely the bourgeois mores that have destroyed her.

Even before he began to treat Dora, Freud recognized that Schnitzler's plays and stories described the same phenomena he was seeing in his office.[83] Afterward in 1906, in a letter to Schnitzler, he made explicit the congruity between Dora's case and the world Schnitzler portrayed: "For many years I have been conscious of the far-reaching conformity existing between your opinions and mine on many psychological and erotic problems; and recently I even found the courage expressly to emphasize this conformity ('Fragment of an Analysis of a Case of Hysteria,' 1905)."[84] In his "Prefatory Remarks" to the case, Freud could have been Schnitzler, although his didactic and condensed language concealed the congruence: "The causes of hysterical disorders are to be found in the intimacies of the patients' psychosexual life . . . hysterical symptoms are the expression of their most secret and repressed wishes . . . the complete elucidation of a case of hysteria is bound to involve the revelation of those intimacies and the betrayal of those secrets."

Mutually recognizing their joint interests, the two men corresponded intermittently but did not meet until late in life.[85] Congratulating Schnitzler on his sixtieth birthday in 1922, Freud confessed:

> I think I have avoided you from a kind of reluctance to meet my double. Not that I am easily inclined to identify myself with another, or that I mean to overlook the difference in talent that separates me from you, but whenever I get deeply absorbed in your beautiful creations I invariably seem to find beneath their poetic surface the very presuppositions, interests, and conclusions which I know to be my own. Your determinism as well as your skepticism—what people call pessimism—your preoccupation with the truths of the unconscious and of the instinctual drives in man, your dissection of the cultural conventions of our society . . . all that moves me with an uncanny feeling of familiarity.[86]

Keenly aware of its harmful effects, Schnitzler and Freud were critical of the middle-class life they saw around them.[87] Naturally, they differed in the medium and language each used to describe the ineluctable outcome. But although they were social critics, they remained an integral part of the society they were condemning and accepted a great deal of its noxiousness as inevitable. Schnitzler's father was a well-to-do doctor, so Schnitzler grew up among the very groups about which he later wrote. Freud, of course, came from a very different background. But by the time Freud began analyzing Dora, he had been treating patients from the wealthy bourgeois world for fourteen years, many of his referrals coming from his friend and mentor Josef Breuer, personal physician to the best Viennese Jewish families. Because of his contacts with these people, and his knowledge of their intimate lives, Freud had developed an acceptance of and even a cynicism about the kinds of labyrinthine relationships he learned about from Dora. It was common practice, for example, for the husbands of wealthy hysterical women, who spent so much of their lives in sickness, openly to take a mistress. One of Freud's patients in the late 1880s and early 1890s was the rich, well-connected, and very troubled Anna von Lieben; she appears in Freud's writings as Mrs. Cäcilie M. About 1890 Cäcilie M.'s husband, Leopold von Lieben, took a mistress, Molly Filtsch, who was eventually accepted by the family circle.[88] In short, Freud knew many families like the Bauers, and it would not normally occur to him that one way to help Dora was to address familial relationships.

In spite of its short duration, Freud's psychoanalysis of Dora was a most complex affair involving strongly held beliefs. As Freud learned Dora's story and sought to evaluate the determinants of her illness, he was heavily influenced by contemporary medical attitudes about hysterical patients, by nineteenth-century views about women, and by late-Victorian middle-class customs and conventions. Yet these are only a portion of the factors that affected his treatment. The state of psychoanalysis in 1900 also played a decisive role.

6

"This Child of Fourteen . . . Entirely and Completely Hysterical"

Dora's psychoanalysis was a doomed affair. It was not at all possible for Freud to have treated Dora successfully in 1900. Medicine knows many such instances, where the necessary technique or the drug is available, but the lack of experience or sophistication on the part of the physician prevents its proper utilization.

Freud's shaky understanding of the fact that Dora was transferring feelings about other people onto him is a revealing perspective on psychoanalysis as it was practiced in its first decade. Just six months before Freud took Dora into treatment, he concluded the analysis of a patient of several years, Mr. E.[1] E. had gotten a great deal better, but not entirely, and Freud had an inkling why. "I am beginning to understand," he wrote to Fliess, "that the apparent endlessness of the treatment is something that occurs regularly and is connected with the transference. . . . Since [E.] had to suffer through all my technical and theoretical errors, I actually think that a future case could be solved in half the time. May the Lord now send the next one."[2] But the Lord sent only two new patients (and one of them lasted just a month) before Dora entered treatment. Freud had little chance to sharpen his knowledge of the transference before she showed up.

While he was treating her, Freud was largely unaware of Dora's conscious or unconscious views of him. He ignored the fact that Dora was

111

aware he personally knew both Mr. K. and her father. But, in Dora's eyes, this acquaintanceship placed Freud on their side, against her. For the adults Dora was closest to—Philipp and both the Ks—had united in denying her "the reality of her experience,"[3] that is, that the scene by the lake had truly taken place. Dora had been living with the anguish of being disbelieved by her father and traduced by the Ks for more than two years, since she was fifteen and a half. Now, at eighteen, she had been turned over, against her will, to a friend of her father's with the words, "Try to bring her to reason."[4] This was a situation in which any therapist would find it extremely difficult to earn a patient's trust and cooperation. Although Freud sensed Dora's suspiciousness and hostility, he was not sensitive to this psychotherapeutic problem. In retrospect Freud recalled that Dora was "constantly comparing me with [her father] consciously, and kept anxiously trying to make sure whether I was being quite straightforward with her, for her father 'always preferred secrecy and roundabout ways.'"

From the very first day Dora began therapy with Freud, he was identified in her mind with her father and Mr. K., both of whom had tried to use her in a sexual way. This linkage actually started in Dora's twelfth year, when K. had brought Philipp to Freud's office for treatment of his syphilitic symptoms. Freud intensified Dora's identification of himself with the other two older men, and, indeed, heightened her fears of adult sexual involvement, by his insistence on discussing sexual matters with her very early in the psychoanalysis.[5] It was never clear to Dora what Freud's motives were for seeing her and what was the basis for his inquiries about her sexual knowledge and thoughts.[6] During the treatment Freud seems to have had a vague sense of her uneasiness, but it never prompted him to a discussion of her feelings about him. The closest Freud got to recognizing Dora's wariness of him was when he interpreted her recurrent dream of her father rescuing her from a house on fire as a sign that she once more felt in danger. This time she felt the threat came not only from Mr. K. but from Freud himself, and it was because of this, Freud told Dora, that she had decided to give up the treatment. Not until Dora had quit the psychoanalysis and Freud was writing up the case for publication did it dawn on him that he had overlooked the feelings Dora had transferred from K. onto him.

Freud's inexperience with the transference was also linked to his failure to recognize that an adolescent has different psychological needs from an adult. The most important adults in Dora's life had not only used her for their own ends, but they then denied using her. When Dora protested such treatment to Freud, he interpreted it as a resistance by which she could avoid admitting the truth about her feelings for Mr. K. and her father. Freud was technically right in this; Dora had loved her father and had spun many romantic fantasies about K. Freud was also correct that getting the adults to admit the truth was not going to effect a permanent cure of Dora's propensity both to express and hide her emotions via hysterical symptoms. But Dora was in need of more than a symptomatic cure.[7]

At eighteen, Dora was in the process of defining her relationship to the adult world. She needed reinforcement of her teenage idealism to ensure the healthy growth of her ego. Adolescents are concerned with truth because they are developing the capacity to give and receive loyalty and faithfulness. Dora was thus exhibiting a very normal preoccupation, akin to her brother's involvement with socialist truth. Otto received encouragement and support from his uncle and to some extent from his father, who allowed him to go to the university instead of the textile institute. Dora's concern with truth received respect neither from her family nor from her psychotherapist. To Dora, Freud's insistence on dealing only with the meanings of her physical symptoms was the equivalent of his denying the existence of problems equally important to her. Erik Erikson speculated that "to call the older generation's infidelities by their name may have been a necessity before she might have been able to commit herself to her own kind of fidelity."[8] Dora's adult life was to prove him right.

Adolescents do not react psychologically as mature adults do when sexual issues are raised. Certainly a girl in 1900 would have been uncomfortable and intimidated by sexual talk from a man the age of her father. Not only was the onset of puberty approximately two years later than at present, but the public discussion of sex and the use of formal anatomical designations was very rare. Dora may have been swept away by Mantegazza's romantic rhapsodies and titillated by his anthropological revelations; she may have had intimate conversations with the "adorable" Mrs. K. But she was neither ready to confront fully the range of sexual behavior nor face frankly the sexual feelings that were aroused—consciously or unconsciously—by direct references to sex. She had demonstrated this when she wrenched herself free from Mr. K.'s embrace in his office and when she slapped his face as soon as she realized he was making her a sexual offer. She expressed her discomfiture again when she abruptly quit the treatment after Freud had interpreted the second dream.

But, unaware of Dora's transference, eager to demonstrate that her hysteria came from repressed sexuality, and seeking to apply his new theory of instinctual infantile sexuality, Freud plunged into sexual discussions with Dora and spared her no detail of her unconscious sexual fantasies and desires as soon as he discovered them. The first occurrence of this kind was his telling Dora that her cough expressed her unconscious fantasy that Mrs. K. was gratifying her father sexually through fellatio. Dora protested having such a thought, but Freud said that later on she "tacitly accepted" his interpretation. When Freud wrote up his thoughts on this subject, he referred to Dora as a girl of nineteen. Distorting her age to make her a year older may have meant that, on some level, Freud had felt uncomfortable in confronting an adolescent so quickly and baldly with a supposition of oral sex that involved her father.

Freud also pointed out to Dora how she continued to demonstrate, unconsciously to be sure, her former masturbatory activities. She had refused to see new doctors, he claimed, because each time she was unconsciously afraid that the physician would unearth her secret—masturbation—by discovering her vaginal discharge or finding out about her childhood bed-wetting. If forced to visit the doctor anyway, she would come away full of contempt for him, supposedly because he had been unable to help her, but actually because he had failed to divine her secret.[9] When questioned, Dora denied remembering ever having masturbated, but when a few days later she came for her session wearing a reticule—a small cloth purse—at her waist, Freud felt triumphant. During the course of the hour, as she lay on the sofa "playing with it—opening it, putting a finger into it, shutting it again," he watched and then carefully explained the significance of this "'symptomatic act.' . . . Dora's reticule, which came apart at the top in the usual way, was nothing but a representation of the genitals, and her playing with it . . . was an . . . unmistakable pantomimic announcement of what she would like to do with them—namely, to masturbate." Dora should realize, Freud informed her, that he had trained himself to detect all kinds of symbolism. Before him, "no mortal [could] keep a secret. If [the patient's] lips are silent, he chatters with his finger-tips; betrayal oozes out of him at every pore."

Most of Freud's sexual discussions with Dora centered on his belief that she loved Mr. K. deeply and had an unconscious desire to have sex with him. The springboard for Freud's contentions was the jewel case in Dora's first dream. One of the presents K. had given Dora was an expensive jewel case *(Schmuckkästchen),* which was also a slang expression for a woman's genitals. "He gave you a jewel-case; so you are to give him your jewel-case," Freud announced. Furthermore, Dora had reported that in the dream "mother wanted to stop and save her jewel-case." Dora's association to this was that her mother had wanted pearl drops to wear in her ears, but her father would not buy them for her. Tying together many things, Freud declared that "wet" (the opposite of "fire" in the dream) and "drops" were important to Dora. She "knew that there was a kind of getting wet involved in sexual intercourse, and that . . . the man presented the woman with something liquid *in the form of drops*. She also knew that the danger lay precisely in that, and that it was her business to protect her genitals from being moistened," since "*Schmuckkästchen*" referred to genitals that are "immaculate and intact." Her mother's jewel case, therefore, had dual meaning for Dora: the temptation to "reciprocate" K.'s love (as her mother had her father's), and the fear of being wet and dirtied like her mother had been by her father's venereal disease.[10]

The second dream gave Freud a further opportunity to indicate to Dora her preoccupation with sexual intercourse or alternatives to it:

> I was walking about in a town which I did not know [Dora reported]. I saw streets and squares which were strange to me. Then I came into a house where I lived, went to my room, and found a letter from Mother lying there. She wrote saying that as I had left home without my parents' knowledge she had not wished to write to me to say that Father was ill. "Now he is dead, and if you like(?) you can come." I then went to the station *["Bahnhof"]* and asked about a hundred times: "Where is the station?" I always got the answer: "Five minutes." I then saw a thick wood before me which I went into, and there I asked a man whom I met. He said to me: "Two and a half [later amended to two] hours more." He offered to accompany me. But I refused and went alone. I saw the station in front of me and could not reach it. At the same time I had the usual feeling of anxiety that one has in dreams when one cannot move forward. Then I was at home. I must have been travelling in the meantime, but I know nothing about that. I walked into the porter's lodge, and enquired for our flat. The maidservant opened the door to me and replied that Mother and the others were already at the cemetery *["Friedhof"]*.[11]

Two of Dora's associations to the dream were that the wood was just like the wood by the shore of the lake where Mr. K. had made his proposition, and that the day before the dream she had seen a painting with a thick wood and nymphs at the Secessionist exhibition.

Bahnhof, literally "railway court," and *Friedhof,* literally "peace court," declared Freud, "striking[ly]" represented a woman's genitals. "With the addition of 'nymphs' visible in the background of a 'thick wood,' no further doubts could be entertained" that a theme in Dora's dream was a fantasy of defloration. Moreover, Dora's attack of appendicitis in Vienna, nine months after the scene by the lake, had enabled her to realize a fantasy of having K.'s child. Her love for K., although unconscious, lived on.[12]

Finally, Freud proposed the following: In reporting her dream, Dora had omitted an essential question that one would have had to ask after entering the porter's lodge, that is, "Does Herr _____ [Bauer] live here?" or "Where does Herr _____ [Bauer] live?"[13] Why had she forgotten to report this "apparently innocent" part of the dream? Because, said Freud, the name "Bauer" was not all that innocent; it was in reality "suggestive" and "improper." Since Freud could not publish the Bauer name, he had to leave out as well from the case history its improper meaning, but there is only one interpretation he could have made to Dora. *Bauer* (peasant) is part of the vulgar phrase *kalter Bauer*, literally "cold peasant," which means ejaculate, usually ejaculate from a nocturnal emission—a "wet dream"—or from masturbation.[14]

The accuracy of Freud's interpretations is not the issue here. Clearly some are convincing, others less so. With some Dora agreed, at many she demurred. What is of utmost importance is their bluntness and timing, the fact that many of them arose from Freud's and not Dora's associations, and that most were told to her after only four to six weeks of treatment—the one about Mrs. K.'s performing fellatio perhaps even sooner.[15] Two classical psychoanalysts have concluded "that the discussion of sex in the analysis had the transference significance of a defloration [which] was . . . elaborated into [an unconscious] transference fantasy of Freud—the purveyor of medical information—forcing his way into [Dora]."[16] Dora's desire to flee from Freud, whose sexual aggressiveness, like K.'s, she may have both feared and welcomed, was adumbrated in the first dream and overlooked at the time by Freud.

———

Freud's blind spots in 1900 included his lack of knowledge about the countertransference—his own reactions to Dora and how they were affecting her psychoanalysis. This shortcoming was due not only to his lack of experience but also to the fact that as the founder of psychoanalysis he had had to analyze himself. While he learned a great deal about his emotions, his self-analysis left inevitable gaps. With respect to Dora, Freud's unrecognized countertransference encompassed vital areas of erotic arousal, identification, discomfort and embarrassment with sexuality, anger, and jealousy.

Freud's midlife sexual discontents bore relevance to aspects of Dora's therapy. Freud concurred with Dora's belief that her father had used her in order to continue his affair with Mrs. K. He described Philipp

Bauer as "one of those men who know how to evade a dilemma by falsifying their judgement upon one of the conflicting alternatives." Yet Freud showed a distinct sympathy with Philipp's sexual situation. He was also an open partisan of Mr. K.'s pursuit of Dora, suggesting that Dora's marrying K. "would have been the only possible solution for all the parties concerned." Freud told Dora he believed that she was in love with K., that fundamentally she had taken K.'s proposal at the lake seriously, and that she hoped K. would continue to press his suit and divorce his wife so Dora could marry him.

There are in the case history frequent references to a man "getting nothing" from his wife. When Philipp consulted Freud about Dora's worsening condition, begging him to "bring her to reason," he told Freud he got nothing out of his wife. In making his speech to Dora by the lake, Mr. K. told Dora he got nothing from *his* wife. In interpreting to Dora her love for K., Freud informed Dora: "So you are ready to give Herr K. what his wife withholds from him." The opposite theme is also portrayed: that a woman can get what she wants from a man. Freud told Dora if she had wanted to marry K., Mrs. K. would have agreed: "Your father's relations with Frau K. . . . made it certain that her consent to a divorce could be obtained; and you can get anything you like out of your father."

The preoccupation with sexually dissatisfied men reflects Freud's own situation in the fall of 1900. He was getting either very little or nothing from his wife and thus empathized with Philipp, a contemporary scarcely three years older. Perhaps he unconsciously envied this "man of not entirely ordinary activity and talents" who, in spite of marital and health obstacles to achieving sexual satisfaction, had worked out solutions to his sexual plight that Freud was either unable or unwilling to adopt. Freud's silence on the pernicious interfamilial relationships in which Dora was enmeshed may be seen as a product of his identification with Dora's father. Freud's sympathy with Philipp is also mirrored in his suggestion that the Ks should get divorced, Philipp and Mrs. K. continue their affair, and Dora marry K., a "scheme . . . by no means . . . impracticable" and the best solution for all concerned. But this was a solution more beneficial to Dora's father than to Dora.[17]

Freud not only identified himself with Philipp Bauer but also with Mr. K. In the same letter—indeed, in the same paragraph—in which Freud informed Fliess he had begun treating Dora, he also told him he was "collecting material for the 'Psychology of Everyday Life.'"[18] In *The Psychopathology of Everyday Life*, which appeared ten months later, in August 1901, Freud recounted an incident of his "accidental" embrace of a young girl at the home of some friends. He related how the girl had "aroused a feeling of pleasure in me which I had long thought was extinct."[19] So, at the time he was seeing Dora, it was quite possible for him to have had a "libidinal involvement" with her and to have been unaware of it.[20] Freud had found Dora to be a girl of "intelligent and engaging looks [and] intellectual precocity." We know that the subject of a sexual relationship between an older man and a younger woman existed in Freud's mind. Freud's finding "incomprehensible" Dora's slapping K., a man twice her age, after she grasped the nature of his proposition by the lake was one more example of the countertransference. To Freud, K. was "still quite young and of prepossessing appearance," and Freud termed the slap a "brutal . . . refusal."

One suspects that Freud's consistent reference to Dora as a year older than she really was lay in his identification with Mr. K. and unconsciously buttressed his suggestion that Dora marry K. It is not only that Freud referred to Dora as being nineteen, although she was not even eighteen when she began the treatment and quit the therapy less than two months after her eighteenth birthday.[21] Freud also wrote she was fourteen when K. kissed her in his office, although she was still thirteen. He said she was sixteen when the scene by the lake occurred, but she was only fifteen.

Freud's failure to be aware of his erotic arousal was also responsible for his viewing Dora's sudden departure from the analysis solely as an act of hostility and revenge and not seeing that she was also fleeing from what she unconsciously perceived as a seduction. Additionally, perhaps his unconscious attraction to the "engaging" young Dora helps to explain why Freud expected her to react with the passion of an adult woman to Mr. K.'s sexual overtures.

Not only did Freud's actions indicate his identification with Philipp Bauer and Mr. K., but the ways in which he expressed himself when writing up the treatment showed his sexual interest in her, his intrusiveness, and his discomfort in discoursing about sexuality. To his readers, a medical audience, Freud was at pains to disavow that the discussions he had with Dora were erotic.

> It is possible for a man to talk to girls and women upon sexual matters of every kind without doing them harm and without bringing suspicion upon himself. . . . The best way of speaking about such things is to be dry and direct. . . . With the exercise of a little caution all that is done is to translate into conscious ideas what was already known in the unconscious. . . . There is never any danger of corrupting an inexperienced girl.

But, as he had explained to Dora, a person's words and actions can have an inner meaning that belie his conscious convictions and statements. Freud was no exception to his own theory.

"I call bodily organs and processes by their technical names," Freud proclaimed, "and I tell these to the patient if they—the names, I mean— happen to be unknown to her. *J'appelle un chat un chat.*" Yet this French phrase was hardly "direct." At the very least, Freud was opting for a roundabout way to make his point as well as choosing substitute, seem-ingly innocuous nouns as replacements for the "technical names" he said he had used. But perhaps even more was involved. *Chat* or *chatte* is also vulgar slang for female genitalia. Freud had taken "a French detour and call[ed] a pussy a pussy."[22] This interpretation holds up well in German since *Junge Katze* (literally "young cat") means young girl in German, and *Kätzchen* is kitten, pussy, or female genitals. If we go back to the French, we find an interesting idiomatic use of *chat* that immediately conjures up Freud's connecting of the supposed fellatio scene between Philipp and Mrs. K. with Dora's hysterical cough and loss of voice. *Avoir un chat dans la gorge* means to have a frog in one's throat, to be hoarse.

Yet Freud was not done with foreign circumlocutions. In the very next paragraph, he argued for the scientific correctness of his sexual discourse with Dora: "No one can undertake the treatment of hysteria until he is convinced of the impossibility of avoiding the mention of sexual subjects. . . . The right attitude is: '*pour faire une omelette il faut casser des oeufs*' [to make an omelet, you have to break eggs]." And where French might be too evocative, he turned to Latin: In Dora's fantasy, she had "pictured to herself a scene of sexual gratification *per os* [orally] between the two people whose love-affair occupied her mind so inces-santly."

Freud's unconscious libidinal countertransference also manifested itself in metaphors of penetration and violation. More than one recent commentator has noted that the very language Freud used to announce the case to Fliess in October 1900 was sexual and intrusive: "It [the past three weeks] has been a lively time and has brought a new patient, an eighteen-year-old girl, a case that has smoothly opened to the existing collection of picklocks."[23] Then, in the preface to the case, Freud argued that in conversing upon sexual questions with a young woman he was "simply claim[ing] for [him]self the rights of a gynaecologist." But a gynecologist, it turns out later in the case discussion, first convinces his patients that his medical examination is an "unavoidable" part of the treatment, and then "does not hesitate to make them submit to uncovering every possible part of their body."[24] By his own metaphor, Freud had admitted to undressing Dora mentally. He also wanted to wrest her secrets from her, yet another defloration. When he came upon Dora one day in the waiting room hastily concealing a letter she had been reading, he demanded that she tell him from whom it came. When Dora refused, Freud insisted. "Freud's eagerness to tear secrets from his patient [contrasted strikingly with his] laborious protestations of innocence. . . . [He was] more like a police inspector interrogating a suspect than like a doctor."[25]

Freud unconsciously wanted to do with Dora what Mr. K. had tried. But consciously he fought these impulses, arguing that by following certain rules it was a simple matter to have sexual conversations with a teenage girl without either becoming aroused or defiling her. He declared that he knew there were certain prurient people who did not believe such detachment was possible, but he dismissed them as beneath his notice. In truth the lascivious interest he attributed to others was in some measure his own. Furthermore, "his harshness and coldness to Dora was [partly an effort to] throw cold water on his own far from cold feelings toward her."[26] And his attempt to fight his identification with K. was one of the reasons he did not note in time Dora's hostile transference from K. onto him.[27]

Freud's conscious innocence of the sexual messages with which he had been bombarding Dora is striking, underscoring once more how unaware Freud was of countertransference in 1900. In writing the postscript to the case, he idly wondered what there had been about him—"the unknown quantity in me"—which might have reminded Dora of Mr. K. The very notion that it was possible to identify a specific countertransference was beyond him: "What this unknown quantity was I *naturally* [italics supplied] cannot tell." But he took a couple of stabs at it: "I suspect that it had to do with money, or with jealousy of another patient." Freud was struggling to discover countertransference, but it would be several years before he did, and even then it would prove difficult to master.

Freud's countertransference was broad, including not only unrecognized libidinal involvement, identifications, and discomfort with frank sexuality, but also anger and jealousy. His anger had three main sources: the ambivalence he, as a physician, had toward hysterical female patients, Dora's abrupt termination at a time when every departing patient was a financial affliction, and the premature ending of a case that was restoring his faith in himself and in the correctness of his theories, as well as providing evidence that his reviewers had underestimated him. These situations spawned a plethora of complaints. Dora, Freud groused, was a difficult patient with a mind of her own who scoffed at the efforts of doctors. During the treatment he had found her behavior insufferable, and he had scars to show from the struggle. He was convinced she had left him to thwart him just when he was on the verge of curing her; this could only have been a vengeful act. In retaliation Freud became vengeful, making no effort to keep Dora in the psychoanalysis either when she abruptly announced her imminent departure or when she returned on her own, with a new physical symptom, asking for his help.

Finally there is the matter of Freud's jealousy, a phenomenon that those who treat adolescents have only recently appreciated in its fullness. A middle-aged therapist may well envy a patient's youth and the vitality and promise it implies. In Freud's day such jealousy would have been tempered when a male therapist treated a girl, because of the inferior status of women, but it would not have been altogether nonexistent. There is also the therapist's envy of young patients who come from wealthy families and whose youth is marked by privilege and ease such as the therapist himself never experienced as a child. This would have been especially operative with Freud, who remembered bitterly his impecunious and debt-ridden youth and his need to rely on friends and mentors in place of his father.

Although Freud came to acknowledge the significance of the countertransference in 1910, it "never loomed large in his mind or in his technical papers."[28] In the beginning his self-analysis may have been responsible for that shortcoming. But as the years went on, bringing with them many competent colleagues with whom he could have discussed cases that were presenting difficulties, Freud still avoided the kind of self-scrutiny that is routinely expected from analysts today. Perhaps the fact that he had founded psychoanalysis and presumed that he understood its byways better than anyone else gave him a false sense of expertise in all areas. Certainly he was surrounded by many worshipful disciples eager to agree and not to contradict. In his role as the grand old man of psychoanalysis and as someone with very decided opinions, it probably did not cross his mind to ask advice. But perhaps more important, he seems to have become convinced fairly early that "recognising actual psychical processes" in one's own self was extremely difficult, if not impossible.[29] An Italian psychoanalyst, Edoardo Weiss, who got to know Freud before World War I and frequently consulted with him about his patients into the 1930s, noted that Freud seldom spoke of the analyst-patient relationship in his writings. Weiss also recalled: "I had the impression that Freud developed strong positive and negative countertransference feelings toward his patients and his pupils."[30]

A great deal is now known about Freud's relationships with patients and followers, and it heavily supports Weiss's recollection. Freud made significant headway in most areas of psychoanalytic thought and technique as the years progressed, but little with countertransference. This truncated development can be traced from the Dora case into his old age. Janet Malcolm has perceptively noted that when Freud gives accounts of his discovery of the transference, he "conveys the idea that it was the erotic importunities of his women patients that caused him to postulate the presence of a universal phenomenon that would explain the behavior he was convinced he had not provoked. Yet from the evidence of the postscript [to the Dora case] one would gather that it was, rather, Freud's [unanalyzed] rage, frustration, and disappointment over Dora's defection that were the fulcrum of his momentous discovery."[31] Even when it came to oedipal matters, which were, after all, Freud's most basic theme, he could overlook his own motivation. When he suggested the Ks get divorced and K. marry Dora, he was proposing a distinctly oedipal solution to Dora's problems, whose danger for Dora's mental health should have been apparent.[32] Freud himself, later discussing Ibsen's fictional character Rebecca West, spelled out how a young woman's displacing an older man's wife brought disaster for the young woman.[33]

Yet Freud continued to evade his own dogmas, seemingly blind to what urged him on. He psychoanalyzed his youngest daughter, Anna, from 1918 to 1921 and then again for a year in 1924. The unconscious psychodynamics present in a father's analyzing his daughter include the father's desire to possess his daughter, thus obstructing her separation from the family and preventing her from establishing an independent heterosexual life. Both Freud and Anna knew that the rules were being transgressed and rarely mentioned the irregular proceedings.[34] When Edoardo Weiss wrote to Freud in 1935 asking his advice about analyzing his son, who had just graduated from high school, Freud's reply was fascinatingly naive and frank:

> Concerning the analysis of your hopeful [of becoming a psychoanalyst] son, that is certainly a ticklish business. With a younger promising brother it might be done more easily. With [my] own daughter I succeeded well. There are special difficulties and doubts with a son.
> Not that I really would warn you against a danger; obviously everything depends upon the two people and their relationship to each other. You know the difficulties. It would not surprise me if you were successful in

spite of them. It is difficult for an outsider to decide. I would not advise you to do it and have no right to forbid it. [35]

Till the end of his days, countertransference issues eluded Freud.

————————

Beyond Freud's inexperience with transference, adolescent psychology, and countertransference lay still other problems of technical unsophistication arising from the embryonic state of psychoanalysis when Philipp Bauer forced his daughter into treatment in the fall of 1900. One quite serious area of difficulty was Freud's attempt to use Dora's treatment as an arena for conducting theoretical research. In so doing, his research interests at times took precedence over the treatment. In all fairness to Freud, it should be noted that conducting research is still a troublesome issue in psychoanalysis today: How can the therapist who is trying to gather clinical data or test a hypothesis do so without affecting the treatment?

As Freud became involved in Dora's therapy, he found to his delight and excitement that the analysis, with its two revealing dreams, was providing confirmation of his theories in *The Interpretation of Dreams*. He was pleased with the progress he was making in the case and was looking forward to publishing it as an answer to his critics. When Dora dropped the bombshell of her departure on him before sufficient time had been devoted to the interpretation of her second dream, he was disappointed and enraged, although he hid his feelings as well as he could from her and never consciously admitted the full extent of his fury to himself. But his words gave him away. He accused Dora of "breaking off . . . just when my hopes of a successful termination of the treatment were at their highest," even though he had told her that the analysis would take about a year, and only three months had elapsed when she walked out.

While analyzing Dora, Freud was also looking for evidence to support his theories of the instinctual basis of infantile and childhood sexuality. He was to publish his new views in *Three Essays on the Theory of Sexuality* (1905d) and in "My Views on the Part Played by Sexuality in the Aetiology of the Neuroses" (1906). His attempt to show that innate sexuality mired in conflict "provides the motive power for every single symptom [of hysteria], and for every single manifestation of a symptom" accounted in part for the large number of sexual interpretations he made to Dora. It also played the dominant role in one of the most startling exegeses of the case, a commentary that has become notorious.

Regarding Mr. K.'s sudden embrace and kissing of Dora when she was thirteen, Freud declared:

> This was surely just the situation to call up a distinct feeling of sexual excitement in a girl of fourteen who had never before been approached. But . . . in this scene . . . the behaviour of this child . . . was already entirely and completely hysterical.
>
> Instead of the genital sensation which would have been felt by a healthy girl in such circumstances, Dora was overcome . . . by disgust [even though the man] was still quite young and of prepossessing appearance.
>
> [Dora] declared that she could still feel upon the upper part of her body the pressure of Herr K.'s embrace. . . . I believe that during the man's passionate embrace she felt not merely his kiss upon her lips but also the pressure of his erect member against her body. This perception was revolting to her; it was dismissed from her memory, repressed, and replaced by the innocent sensation of pressure upon her thorax.

Since Freud's revised theory demanded that a healthy person always have a pleasurable response to any sexual stimuli, he labeled Dora as "already entirely and completely hysterical" when at the age of thirteen she did not respond with mature sexual excitement to K.'s fevered kiss and the sensation of his hard penis against her.

It seems entirely possible that Freud's shift from the seduction hypothesis to a belief in the instinctual basis for childhood sexuality was responsible for his opinion that Dora should have had "a distinct feeling of sexual excitement" in K.'s deserted office. He had reacted quite differently to a case of attempted seduction at an earlier time, when he was advocating the theory that parental or parental surrogates' sexual abuse of children led to hysteria. Seven years before he psychoanalyzed Dora, Freud had very briefly treated Katharina, an eighteen-year-old innkeeper's daughter. Her father had attempted to seduce her when she was fourteen, and when she was sixteen, she saw her father in bed with her cousin. The story has some obvious parallels with Dora's experiences, but when one reads Katharina's case, one finds that Freud reacted sympathetically to Katharina's sexual predicaments, in a manner markedly different from his response to Dora's. In 1895 Freud wrote about "the horror by which a virginal mind is overcome when it is faced for the first time with the world of sexuality." He hoped he had helped Katharina, "whose sexual sensibility had been injured at such an early age."[36] The theory of instinctual infantile sexuality, with its stress on children's inevitable sexual fantasies and the unconscious conflicts arising from their sexual desires, did not lead as easily to compassion when children were prematurely and inappropriately sexually stimulated.[37]

Freud lacked a natural sensitivity or empathy with Dora. In the cases of both Katharina and Dora, Freud's emotions were heavily swayed by his theories. Eventually, when he gained technical sophistication and expertise, he was able to employ the theory of infantile sexuality to treat girls like Dora satisfactorily. But he could not do it instinctively. In 1900, when he told Dora she had been "hysterical" in her reaction to Mr. K.'s kiss, his oldest daughter, Mathilde, was thirteen, the same age Dora had been when K. grabbed her. If Mathilde had felt disgusted under the same circumstances, would Freud have called *her* "hysterical"?

It also seems likely that Freud's abandonment of the seduction theory made him attach less significance to the familial and environmental malignancies in Dora's life: her parents' unhappy marriage, their blind eye to K.'s courtship, K.'s prolonged seductive behavior toward Dora, and K.'s eventual sexual harassment of her, including his sadistic intrusion into the room where she was napping. After 1897 Freud's increasing concentration on intrapsychic conflicts and defenses caused him more and more in practice to regard the family as secondary, although in theory he continued to pay attention to family events. In the Dora case he averred: "We are obliged to pay as much attention in our case histories to the purely human and social circumstances of our patients as to the somatic data and the symptoms of the disorder. Above all, our interest will be directed towards their family circumstances." Many years later, summing up for medical students the variables affecting psychoanalytic therapy, he talked about the decisive role of the patient's family members: "The patient's relatives sometimes betray less interest in his recovering than in his remaining as he is. When, as so often, the neurosis is related to conflicts between members of a family, the healthy party will not hesitate long in choosing between his own interest and the sick party's recovery."[38] But from the viewpoint of Freud's theory, the family had become peripheral: "The external resistances which arise from the patient's circumstances, from his environment, are of small theoretical interest [although they may be] of the greatest practical importance."[39]

Freud's efforts in the treatment to gather theoretical evidence on the role of childhood sexuality in neurosis led him to announce to Dora all his findings, proudly and inexorably, as he deduced them. This bold, intrusive approach frightened her and prompted her to flee from the psychoanalysis before it could do her any substantial good. For example, if she was indeed "in love" with Mr. K., as Freud claimed, many of her feelings and wishes as a child and almost all her current desires regarding this man were unconscious. Much time and carefully phrased questions would be needed before she could face this love. Yet after the first dream, that is, approximately six weeks into the treatment, Freud told her that she was ready to give K. what his wife would not. Freud himself could not yet separate unconscious from conscious reality and could not establish what is necessary to deal with each. If Dora loved K. and yearned for him sexually, it was on an unconscious level, yet Freud talked to her as if she were a grown woman, consciously in love. "The Freud that we meet here is . . . a Freud who is the servant of . . . the demon of interpretation."[40]

Dora's analysis was almost as much dominated by what Freud did not do as by what he did. Perhaps the most important omission was Freud's failure to recognize the fundamental role of anger in psychopathology. In the decade following Dora's analysis, Alfred Adler, one of Freud's earliest followers, insistently called attention to the aggressive impulse, but even then Freud was not ready to stress the independent vitality of such a concept; he was satisfied to subsume human aggressivity under sexuality. Freud himself only came to a full appreciation of the extent and significance of human anger after World War I, when he proposed the death instinct and the existence of an aggressive drive to complement the sexual one.[41]

While treating Dora, he did realize that anger in the form of a desire for revenge played an important role in her psychology, but he never comprehended how prominently unexpressed anger figured in her life and in her production of hysterical symptoms. At the end of the case discussion, Freud referred in a footnote to Dora's desire for revenge against her father, besides that against Mr. K.; the former, Freud commented, was seen in the second dream—her leaving home, her father being ill, her father's death, her lack of sadness at his demise—and in the suicide note she left in a place where her parents would find it. But that was virtually all Freud said, even though almost every significant relationship Dora ever had had ended in angry feelings of betrayal, if resentment or animosity had not suffused the association even earlier.

Closely allied with his lack of adequate recognition of Dora's anger was Freud's failure to confront the fact that she was a Jew surrounded by anti-Semitism. He was acutely aware that anti-Semitism affected his daily life, his career, and his children's prospects. He dreamed about it all the time. Yet in his psychoanalyses of his Jewish patients, he seems not to have dealt with their reactions to anti-Semitism. There is no hint that Freud and Dora talked about her feelings about being Jewish. There is no indication that they discussed the Hilsner case even though it was being tried for the second time at the very moment Dora was being analyzed, prompting boycotts against Jewish-owned shops in Vienna and getting the broadest possible publicity in all manner of publications, including those found in the Freud and Bauer households. Although the early meetings (1906–18) of the Vienna Psychoanalytic Society were devoted to the widest possible range of topics, not a single session focused on the impact of anti-Semitism on Viennese Jews, even though most members of the society were Jewish.[42]

There is a temptation in Dora's case to dismiss any expectation that Freud and Dora, confronting issues of her repressed sexual fantasies, absorbed in her feelings about her family and the Ks, and preoccupied with her incapacitating physical and emotional symptoms, should put yet another item on their crowded agenda. But Dora truly had other pressing grievances besides her father's behavior and Mr. K.'s treacheries. Four and a half years after she quit psychoanalysis, she formally left the Jewish community of Vienna and converted to Christianity, a move not necessitated by either marriage or career. Her brother, a soon-to-be-famous socialist leader, officially remained in the Jewish community his whole life, although many like him took the doctrinal Marxist position of disclaiming their familial religious ties in order to register with the authorities as "without religious affiliation." For Dora being a Jew had been a severe enough trauma that when her first child was born in 1905, she was determined that he not suffer as she and Otto had.

Freud believed his whole life that the progress of psychoanalysis had been retarded because he was a Jew. But when he assessed the implications of being Jewish in an anti-Semitic society, he was content to conclude that such a situation had strengthened his character and made it easier for him to face adversity.[43] His self-analysis and hence his analyses of others could go only so far.[44]

The drawbacks of Freud's self-analysis also appeared in the scant notice Freud gave to Dora's relationship with her mother.[45] Freud himself had avoided any penetrating investigation of his personal relationship with his own mother that was not dogmatically linked to the oedipal triangle.[46] As a result he accepted Dora's and Philipp's condemnation of Käthe on a superficial level and ignored the significance this obsessive, angry woman held for his patient. He took this position in spite of his recognition that Dora closely identified herself with her mother in matters of cleanliness, disease, and mistrusting men, as well as in actions he termed "intolerable." Although Freud was well aware of Dora's strong attraction to Mrs. K., he was not knowledgeable enough to look beyond this to the love, however submerged, Dora must have felt for her mother. At the time Freud was analyzing Dora, he was fascinated by the oedipal conflict, and it was not until many years later that he turned his attention, in any truly meaningful way, to preoedipal relationships. It can even be argued that he never took sufficient notice of the early mother-child relationship, and certainly not of the mother-daughter connection.

One might assert that it is too harsh to demand such comprehensiveness and depth from Freud. After all, in 1900 he was seeking nothing more than a symptomatic cure for Dora—not her happiness, just the removal of her chronic cough, loss of voice, and depression. But why, then, did he cast his psychic net so wide as to bring in the matter of Dora's homosexual love for Mrs. K.? Freud appears to have been fishing for a larger catch, although its full extent will be forever unknown since he never finished Dora's psychoanalysis.

Finally, Dora's analysis was handicapped by Freud's simplistic explanation of anxiety. In 1900 Freud believed that "the dyspnoea and palpitations that occur in hysteria and anxiety neurosis are only detached fragments of the act of copulation." When Dora overheard her parents having intercourse, a "sympathetic excitement" was aroused in her which "made the child's sexuality veer round and . . . replaced her inclination to masturbation by an inclination to anxiety."[47] But even if Dora had stayed in analysis the requisite year, this explanation of anxiety would probably not have done very much for her shortness of breath, if indeed she still suffered from this childhood symptom. Nor would it have sufficed to cure other anxiety symptoms. Freud's early views of anxiety rested on physiological and chemical concepts involving the necessity of discharging sexual excitation in order to remain healthy. If frustration got in the way and damned up the libido, he argued, symptoms would form.[48] Many years later Freud realized that the psychological basis of anxiety was a complex process in which the physical accompaniments of anxiety were actually signals broadcast by the ego to the individual so he or she could avoid a psychologically dangerous situation.[49]

To Freud's inexperience in 1900 must be added his domineering personal style when he believed himself to be in the right. The latter was not a function of his important psychotherapeutic discoveries but a trait he had already exhibited as an adolescent and kept his entire life. Freud not only bombarded Dora with premature interpretations because he as yet did not know any better but also because—with rare exceptions—insistence and confrontation came naturally to him. When he was in college, he dictated to his younger sister what books to read; when engaged to be married, he demanded that his fiancée perform irreligious acts, such as writing on the Sabbath, forcing her to follow his secular preferences rather than those of her Orthodox mother; as a therapist in later years, when his authority was great, he did not hesitate to tell his analysands whom they should marry and when they should divorce.[50] So with Dora in 1900: As Freud became increasingly convinced that she was presenting him with confirmatory evidence of the correctness of his theories, he was forcible and domineering in asserting his views.

Yet Freud's treatment of Dora was not just a compound of psychoanalytic immaturity and dogmatism leading to a dismal end. Although psychoanalysis was new, Freud accomplished some quite positive things with Dora, who was, after all, a difficult and resistant patient. She had not wanted to be treated by him from the very beginning and challenged him throughout the entire analysis. Nevertheless Freud got her to trust him enough so that she told him about Mr. K.'s kiss when she was thirteen. This is something she had never confided in anyone and a burden she had been shouldering alone for more than four years. Freud was also the first person to believe Dora's account of K.'s seduction attempt, which was probably the main reason her suicidal depression eventually lifted. Moreover, Freud was able to achieve some temporary removal of Dora's symptoms. The most recent attack of her cough remitted fairly early in the treatment. Freud speculated that this was due to his relation of her unconscious fantasy of oral sex between Mrs. K. and her father. Four or five weeks after Dora left the analysis, her coughing attacks and loss of voice definitely became less frequent for a while, and her depression ameliorated. By being the first adult to take Dora seriously, Freud gave her the courage to confront the Ks and gain from them an admission of the actual roles each had played in her life. Finally, as a product of the passing of the immediate crisis, Dora was able to marry in 1903. These results must be contrasted with the lack of any benefit Dora derived from electrotherapy and hydrotherapy.

———

Freud's treatment of Dora was a complex affair. His goals differed fundamentally from those of Philipp Bauer, who initiated his daughter's therapy, and from Dora's as well. Freud welcomed the analysis as a vehicle to prove his ideas of infantile sexuality, the relation of masturbation to mental and physical health, and the existence of bisexuality in human beings. Furthermore, he was influenced in ways he did not even recognize by contemporary medical views about hysterical girls and women, by current notions of both the natural and proper roles for women, and by late-Victorian—and perhaps peculiarly Viennese—middle-class attitudes and sensibilities (one thinks again of Schnitzler's stories.)

Psychoanalysis in 1900 was in its earliest days, still a crude instrument even in the hands of its brilliant and insightful founder. The errors Freud made in treating Dora attest both to the shortcomings of his self-analysis and to his lack of therapeutic sophistication. Yet Freud did rid Dora of her depression, temporarily alleviate her worst physical symptoms, and spell out for her the dangers of using illness to bend people to her purpose. He advanced the development of psychoanalysis by coming to understand the powerful nature of the transference. He also offered an often-profound view of the psychology of an unhappy and self-destructive young woman, a victim of the vicissitudes of her social and familial environments.

What remains most striking about Dora's therapy is the vista it affords of an intricately woven doctor-patient relationship. A variety of strong feelings are aroused in a physician by a long-standing or frequently seen patient. Freud's encounter with Dora reveals the many known and unknown agendas a physician can bring to a treatment and the special and deep significances a particular case can assume. This being so, the answer to one critical question will shed further light on Freud's attitude toward Dora as well as the meaning her analysis came to hold for him: Why did Freud give the name "Dora" to Ida Bauer?

7

'Who Else Was There Called Dora?"

During the months Freud was treating Dora and for many weeks afterward, he worked on a long article on psychic determinism, ultimately expanding it into a book—*The Psychopathology of Everyday Life*—that became a best-seller. The work deals primarily with forgetting, slips of the tongue and pen, misreadings, bungled actions, superstitions, and errors. In it Freud argued that *"seemingly unintentional performances prove . . . to have valid motives and [are] determined by motives unknown to consciousness"* (italics in original).[1] Freud illustrated this principle with an explanation of why he had chosen the name Dora for a patient whose case history he had prepared for publication.

"I asked myself," Freud wrote, "who else was there called Dora?" "Dora," he replied, was the name taken by a nursemaid, Rosa, who worked for his younger sister, who was also named Rosa. To prevent confusion in the household, the maid had had to take another name and had chosen "Dora." So Freud, in searching for a name for his young patient, whose real name could not be used publicly, thought of the plight of the nursemaid who could not use *her* name. Moreover, added Freud, a governess (nursemaid) employed by his patient's family had "exercised a decisive influence" on the patient.[2] Thus his seemingly arbitrary choice of the name "Dora" was an illustration of psychic determinism at work.

Freud had had no difficulty or hesitation in dubbing Ida Bauer "Dora." "It might have been expected—and I myself expected—that a whole host of women's names would be at my disposal. Instead, one name and only one occurred to me—the name 'Dora.'"[3] "Dora" was a perfect fit. But can Freud's strong conviction of the aptness of the pseudonym be explained solely by the story he related? "Dora" was just right, but for more reasons than Freud consciously considered.[4]

The subject of nursemaids and governesses alone had much broader significance than Freud admitted. It not only reflected Freud's anger at Dora but pointed to the distinctly secondary position Dora occupied vis-à-vis her own family and the Ks. Dora had actually resolved to quit the psychoanalysis a fortnight before she announced her departure to Freud. He correctly interpreted this decision as analogous to a servant's giving notice. Since she had acted toward him like a servant, he responded in kind by naming her after a servant.[5]

Moreover, Dora's governess, the Ks' nursemaid, and Dora's role as the Ks' baby-sitter all played parts in events that had assaulted her worth as an individual. It had become apparent to Dora that her last governess, whom she had found so agreeable, was in love with her father, and was pleasant to her only when Philipp was at home. When he was away the woman ignored her. As for the Ks' children's nanny, she was a young girl who had been importuned by Mr. K. with the same words he had used with Dora: "I get nothing from my wife." The girl had given in to his entreaties, and there had been a brief affair until K. grew distant. Eventually, seeing that K. had no feelings for her, this nanny had left the family's employ.[6] A day or two before K. had propositioned Dora, she had heard the nursemaid's story and, therefore, recalled it during K.'s lakeside speech, feeling she was being treated no better than a hired servant. Last, for two or three years in her early adolescence, Dora had been devoted to the Ks' two children, a dedication K. had greatly appreciated at the time but that had not ultimately prevented him from betraying her. The theme is clear: Either Dora had been used by servants or had been used as a servant. For Freud to equate her with a nursemaid was only too accurate.[7]

While illuminating, these observations only amplify Freud's own associations. They do not address the question: "Who else was there called Dora?" The answer is, quite an array of young women, none of whom have traditionally had positive images. That there was more than one Dora in Freud's mind should come as no surprise. Conscious acts often represent mental syntheses of many separate unconscious elements. It was Freud himself who posited the principle of overdetermination.

Freud's earliest known acquaintance with a Dora was with the frivolous, empty-headed girl who was David Copperfield's first wife in

Charles Dickens's eponymous, autobiographical novel. Like many Victorians, Freud liked and read a lot of Dickens, and *David Copperfield* was his favorite. His first present to his fiancée, in June 1882, was a copy of this book. Freud enjoyed the work so much because he thought, that of all of Dickens's books, *David Copperfield* had the least-stereotyped characters. He wrote to Martha Bernays that Dickens's other works showed the novelist's "mannerism" of drawing an unreal and "sharp distinction between virtue and vice which doesn't exist in life . . . *Copperfield* has the least of this. The characters are individualized; they are sinful without being abominable."[8]

Steven Marcus has alluded to the negative image of Dickens's Dora—"an incompetent and helpless creature who asks David to call her his 'child-wife.'"[9] But a fuller description of Dora (Spenlow) Copperfield will illustrate the extent to which Ida Bauer may have recalled the fictional Dora to Freud's mind and the low estimation Freud had of both. When David Copperfield meets Dora Spenlow, he is so swept away by her loveliness that he overlooks that fact that she is an impractical, spoiled rich girl. And in spite of all his efforts to change her during the time of their marriage, he never succeeds. She remains an immature young woman who knows nothing of housekeeping and refuses to accept any adult responsibility. She cannot cook, shop, or manage a household. She is neurotic, easily disturbed, and frightened, immediately bursting into tears when confronted with an unhappy fact of life. This is not a suitable girl for a wife, and the reader clearly sees that she is a hindrance to David as he tries to make his way in life. Luckily for David she sickens and dies, leaving him free to marry a supportive and dependable woman he has known all along. Freud's wife Martha was the epitome of a sound manager, so that if Freud named Ida Bauer in part for Dora Copperfield, it suggests he had little sympathy for Ida's rebellion against housework and no use for a hysterical, undisciplined young woman, no matter how attractive or intelligent.

Freud's next brush with a Dora is also revealing of what Ida Bauer aroused and inspired in him. When Freud finished his residency in 1885, he secured a traveling fellowship to study in Paris and Berlin. While in Paris he took as much advantage of its cultural variety as he could afford, and one night he went to the theater to see the famous Sarah Bernhardt. She was acting the lead in a drama, *Théodora,* by the French playwright, Victorien Sardou (1831–1908.) Sardou seems to have been captivated by the syllable "dor" and wrote three plays whose titles incorporated it: *Fédora, Théodora,* and *Thermidor.* Although Freud was bewitched by Bernhardt, he disliked the play and described it as "a pompous trifle, magnificent Byzantine palaces and costumes . . . pageants of armed warriors and so on, but . . . as for characterization, it leaves one completely cold."[10] Theodora was the wife of the sixth-century emperor Justinian and, in Sardou's play, a woman deeply in love with a young, rebellious republican. In the course of the action, she kills her lover's friend in order to prevent her lover from being implicated in a murderous plot, then inadvertently poisons her lover, and is herself put to death by the emperor, who has discovered her infidelity.

Although Freud was not sorry to have seen the great Bernhardt, he suffered through the long evening, finding the seat cramped and the theater excruciatingly hot; the experience ended with a migraine attack. He resolved to go to the theater only rarely in the future. He also caricatured Sardou's dramatic creations, reporting that the playwright "has already written a *Dora* and a *Feodora* [sic] and is said to be busy on a *Thermidora, Ecuadora,* and *Torredora!*" For unknown reasons Freud fastened on "Dora," making Thermidor, Ecuador, and Torredor (actually *toreador*) end with the feminine "dora," and even inventing a play entitled *Dora.* Freud's negative reaction to Sardou's drama and his wretched evening expressed themselves in his disporting with the name "Dora." Perhaps his migraine headache cannot be accounted for strictly by the overheated theater, the uncomfortable seats, and the superficiality of the drama.

There is no certain way of knowing who all the real and imagined Doras of Sardou's dramas represented for Freud, but it is *Théodora* Freud actually saw, so "Dora" here may well have stood for the Empress Theodora, a woman of plebeian origins, who began life as an actress and courtesan. When she married Justinian, he was twice her age, and she was reputed (correctly or not) to have exercised an unusually strong influence over him. She did indisputably speak her mind most independently for a woman. Theodora, "gift from God [or the gods]" in Greek, was renowned for her beauty, intelligence, vindictiveness toward her enemies—she had a network of spies—and for having created a life of imperial pomp. Fortuitously, or perhaps significantly, the empress and Freud's patient shared intelligence, outspokenness, good looks, and an interest in revenge. Moreover, Theodora had contracted a marriage, like the one Freud proposed for his Dora, with a man twice her age.

What Freud actually knew about Theodora is only scantily recorded. Having excelled in Greek in *Gymnasium,* he had to know what her name meant. He also described her to Martha as "Justinian's famous empress, originally a ballet dancer who . . . once appeared in public *toute nue.*"[11] In his life Freud made only one more recorded mention of a naked woman, and that was of his mother. In the early days of his self-analysis, he remembered that "between two and two and a half years [it was actually closer to three and a half] my libido toward *matrem* was awakened, namely, on the occasion of a journey with her from Leipzig to Vienna, during which we must have spent the night together and there must have been an opportunity of seeing her *nudam.*"[12] The psychological import of Dora's name may be considerable indeed.

Six months before Freud began treating Dora, he asked the Lord to send him a new patient on whom he might practice his newfound skills in using the transference.[13] Was Dora a gift from the gods, first presenting him with a publishable case but then withdrawing from the therapy "just when [his] hopes of a successful termination . . . were at their highest?" Gifts from the gods are rarely predictable and trouble-free.

The conclusion that Freud unconsciously thought of Dora as a divine gift has been arrived at in other contexts, making it all the more compelling. "Who," demands Janet Malcolm, "could Dora be but Pandora? The case rattles with boxes."[14] There is a jewelry box in the first dream, which stands for the female genitals, two boxes in the second dream—one the opposite of a key/penis and the other represented by the railroad station—and the reticule, with which Dora symptomatically masturbates. The reticule reminded Freud of the miniature box of sweets another woman patient had carried about. He wrote that it was "like the reticule and the jewel-case . . . once again only a substitute for the shell of Venus, for the female genitals." Boxes were on Freud's mind from the very beginning of the treatment, when he wrote to Fliess about his new patient, "a case that has smoothly opened to the existing collection of picklocks."[15]

Boxes were the female genitals, and Pandora, like Eve, stood for dangerous female sexuality.[16] Theodora, another gift from the gods, had used her sexuality to become empress and, once ensconced, became a powerful ruler, perhaps even over her husband. Did these themes contribute to Freud's migraine attack the night after he saw Sarah Bernhardt? Recall Freud's associations to his dreams of women as dangerous both professionally and personally.[17] Women were a gift that Freud had difficulty accepting. An encounter with a woman was always a power struggle, never an even exchange, and very often the man lost something.[18] Analyzing Dora had been doing battle, forcing Freud "to wrestle with . . . the most evil of those half-tamed demons that inhabit the human breast." These were the very same evils Pandora had loosed on the world when she opened the box given her by Zeus. Dora as Pandora helps explain Freud's antipathy toward his patient. "If Freud's countertransference invested Dora with all the seductiveness and dangerousness of Eve, if he saw her not as the messed-up little Viennese teen-ager she was but as Original Woman, in all her beauty and evil mystery, it is no wonder that he treated her as he did."[19]

But in addition to his sister's nursemaid and to fictional, historical, and mythological Doras, Freud knew a real Dora who was the identical age as Ida Bauer. This was Dora Breuer, the daughter of his former friend and collaborator, Josef Breuer.[20] Both girls had been born in 1882, Dora Breuer on March 11 and Ida Bauer on November 1. Freud thought, however, that Dora Breuer had been born "shortly after" June 1882, thus bringing the two birthdates close together in his mind.[21] This introduces yet another dimension. There is a great deal of evidence to suggest that Freud also named Ida Bauer after Dora Breuer and that Dora's psychoanalysis in 1900 came to signify the tempestuous feelings that still raged in Freud about Josef Breuer, a man who had been like a father and elder brother to him. That the naming of Dora can signify so much—Freud's anger and erotic impulses toward his patient, his more general distrust of women (especially independent-minded, outspoken ones), his ambivalence about the progress and outcome of Dora's treatment, as well as his emotions about a former close friend—indicates the possibly intricate nature of any physician-patient relationship.[22]

Josef Breuer (1842–1925) was a physiologist and highly respected and sought-after Viennese internist who had befriended Freud early in his career and who had coauthored *Studies on Hysteria* (1895). Freud had met Breuer during his medical-school days in the late 1870s, when he worked in a physiological laboratory. The two men—Freud hardly out of his teens—had been drawn to each other by mutual professional and cultural interests, and Freud adopted the affluent and successful Breuer as a father figure. Breuer supported Freud in many tangible and nontangible ways, and Freud was a frequent visitor to the Breuer household, admiring Breuer's wife, Mathilde, almost as much as he did Breuer himself. Breuer contributed significantly to the development of psychoanalysis by confiding in Freud in the early 1880s about his hypnotherapeutic treatment of a young hysterical woman, Anna O., his pseudonym for Bertha Pappenheim (1860–1936), who was a pioneer in German social work as well as a leader in feminist causes and Jewish women's organizations.[23]

It is of importance to Freud's naming of Dora that there were remarkable similarities in the lives of both Breuer's Anna O. and Freud's Dora. Both girls were from upper-middle-class Jewish families, did not get on well with their mothers, had a brother very close in age, doted on and were indulged by their fathers, had fathers with tuberculosis, nursed their fathers, were educated above the usual level for a girl, and presented initially with the same symptom—a hysterical cough. Both also suffered from a facial neuralgia. Moreover, Anna O. and Dora may both have experienced hysterical childbirths; Freud certainly believed this to be true. Finally, in both cases, it was the patient who set the date for the treatment to terminate.

Each case, respectively, was a tumultuous event in the lives of Breuer and Freud, marking or coinciding with substantial milestones in their personal and professional activities. Furthermore, the central features of each case were unrecognized transference and countertransference. In both instances, this culminated in Breuer and Freud's rejecting their patients' requests to be taken back into treatment. In order to see the parallels, a condensed description of Breuer's medical care of Anna O. is helpful.

Josef Breuer was probably Anna O.'s family physician, just as he was the physician to many other well-to-do and prominent Viennese families, Jewish and non-Jewish. Before Anna O.'s parents called on him to treat her, Breuer had already been caring for her father, who was suffering from tuberculosis. Anna O. was nursing her father devotedly, to the detriment of her own health: she became increasingly weak, lost her appetite, and developed a bad cough.[24] Breuer began to treat Anna O. in November 1880 and eventually made a diagnosis of hysteria. As the weeks went by, she developed a variety of symptoms: paralyses, contractions, ocular disturbances, a loss of normal grammatical speech patterns, and dual personalities. Breuer visited her frequently—sometimes once or twice a day—and hypnotized her. She then told him her daydreams, which made her feel better, and she labeled this her "talking cure." The treatment was time-consuming, and Breuer got in the habit of making her his last patient of the day.[25]

Anna O.'s father died on April 5, 1881, which precipitated a severe shock in her, and her symptoms became much worse throughout the remainder of the year. She recognized no one except Breuer, who even had to feed her for a while, and she spoke only English. She became suicidal and could not be kept at home. But under hypnosis many of her florid symptoms were talked away. The treatment came to an end in June 1882, a date she had set in advance—although, as it turned out, she was far from well.[26]

Anna O.'s transference to Breuer was marked. There were times in the treatment when she recognized no one but Breuer, ate only when he fed her, drastically worsened when he had to leave for several days, and would not talk to him until she knew it was indeed he by feeling his hands. In addition, based on information Freud said he got from Breuer, plus his own reconstruction, Freud declared that Anna O. had developed "a condition of 'transference love' " that culminated in a hysterical childbirth. Faced with this event, Breuer "retired in dismay."[27] Whether Freud's description of the transference is totally correct or not, Breuer was not aware of Anna O.'s transference, or, at the most, recognized it only at the dramatic conclusion of the treatment, if Freud's story is accurate. As for Breuer's countertransference, it remained at an unconscious level. Yet there is considerable evidence of its existence.

At the time Breuer began caring for Anna O. he was thirty-eight years old and a highly regarded private practitioner. He was also a *Privatdozent* (a position somewhat akin to that of a modern lecturer or instructor) in internal medicine at the University of Vienna medical school and had ambitions to rise to a professorial rank. He was married and the father of four children.

Anna O. was a well-educated, very intelligent, physically attractive young woman of twenty-one. It is probably significant for the counter-transference that Anna O.'s real name—Bertha—was also the name of Breuer's mother as well as that of his eldest daughter. Breuer's mother had died when she was about twenty-six and Breuer himself was only two or three.[28] He did not remember his mother but knew her tombstone said that she had died "adorned [*im Schmuck*] with youth and beauty."[29] It has been postulated that Bertha Pappenheim's youth and attractiveness may have aroused Breuer's repressed childhood longings for his lost young mother.[30]

Breuer's high regard for Anna O. is apparent in his case history, which begins with an empathic and vivid portrait of an appealing personality, one of whose strongest components was a motherly drive to care for others. He wrote:

> She was markedly intelligent, with an astonishingly quick grasp of things and penetrating intuition. She possessed a powerful intellect which would have been capable of digesting solid mental pabulum. . . . She had great poetic and imaginative gifts. . . . One of her essential traits was sympathetic kindness. Even during her illness she . . . look[ed] after a number of poor, sick people [thus being] able to satisfy a powerful instinct. . . . The element of sexuality was astonishingly undeveloped in her. The patient, whose life became known to me to an extent to which one person's life is seldom known to another, had never been in

love.[31] . . . This girl, who was bubbling over with intellectual vitality, led an extremely monotonous existence in her puritanically minded family.[32]

Within two weeks of being called to treat Anna O., Breuer was seeing her every day. But daily visits to hysterical women were not routine medical practice. Breuer's unusually frequent visits to Anna O. must be seen as part of the countertransference. It is true that Breuer was known as a conscientious and sympathetic physician, yet his involvement with this particular patient was overly intense. Not only was there his attraction to the young Anna O./Bertha, but he was very likely drawn by her upset over her father's illness and, later on, her grief over her father's death. This death could have evoked in Breuer unconscious memories of his own feelings over the losses of his mother[33] and of a younger brother, who had died seven years earlier of tuberculosis, the same disease that killed Anna O.'s father.

The countertransference was further manifest when Anna O. became suicidal about six months after Breuer began seeing her. Breuer did not wish to stop treating her, but he knew she should be hospitalized. The usual way to handle a well-to-do woman would be to send her away to a sanatorium. Breuer compromised. In June 1881, he had her moved to a cottage on the grounds of a nearby sanatorium, but she was not officially listed as a patient and remained under his personal care.[34]

Meanwhile discord had developed between Breuer and his wife over the degree of his involvement with Anna O. Two years later, when Freud learned of these troubles, he wrote to his fiancée, Martha Bernays, who was a friend of Anna O.—the Pappenheim and Bernays families were quite close—that Mathilde Breuer had been jealous of the relationship between her husband and his medically demanding patient.[35] In June 1881, at or right after the time Breuer decided not to send Anna O. away to a hospital or sanatorium, but to keep on treating her, the Breuers conceived the last of their five children—Dora—who was born six years after her next oldest brother.[36] Clearly this was an emotionally difficult time in the individual lives of both Breuer and his wife as well as in their marriage. Many years later, in a letter to the Swiss psychiatrist, Auguste Forel, Breuer confessed: "At that time I learned . . . something of practical importance . . . namely, that it was impossible for a 'general practitioner' to treat a case of that kind without bringing his activities and mode of life completely to an end. I vowed at the time that I would *not* go through such an ordeal again."[37]

Freud recalled Breuer telling him that on the same day his treatment of Anna O. formally concluded, he was called back to her home. He "found her confused and writhing in abdominal cramps. Asked what was wrong with her, she replied: 'Now Dr. B.'s child is coming!' . . . Seized by conventional horror [Breuer] took flight and abandoned the patient to a colleague."[38] If Freud was right about the dramatic event of Anna O.'s hysterical childbirth, we would have to include Breuer's flight from her bedside as another example of countertransference. If the scene never occurred, there were nevertheless some rather remarkable subsequent events.

After a year and a half of treatment, Anna O. remained ill. By March 1882, she had developed, among other symptoms, a facial (trigeminal) neuralgia, and she had become a morphine addict. In June, still further symptoms appeared. Now, at last, she had to be hospitalized. She remained at a Swiss sanatorium for three months, but when she was ready to leave, Breuer refused to take her back as a patient.[39] Although he continued to treat hysterical patients, he never again used the "cathartic" method of treatment he had evolved with Anna O. Breuer's withdrawal both from Anna O. and from his pioneering course of therapy is a further example of his countertransference.[40]

Finally, instances of countertransference can be seen both in Breuer's reluctance to publish the case history—he was pushed to it by Freud—and in the actual account itself. The case, as it appears in *Studies on Hysteria*, contains neither the information that Anna O. was still ill (and indeed had developed new symptoms toward the end of the treatment) nor the fact that she continued to be ill for many years afterward, although the circumstances were well known to Breuer.[41]

Parallels between the Breuer/Anna O. relationship and the Freud/Dora relationship spring immediately to mind. In the three months he saw Dora, Freud had an incomplete awareness of the transference, even though by that time he had already written on the subject. Like Breuer, Freud treated the patient's father before caring for the daughter. While psychoanalyzing Dora, Freud's recognition of her transference was limited to the awareness that she identified him with her father in a negative way, suspecting both men of not being honest and straightforward. But he did not make use of this knowledge in the psychotherapy, just as Breuer had no knowledge that Anna O. had transferred her love for her father onto him, and perhaps also her resentment and anger. For Anna O. had sacrificed every inch of her being to nurse her father, and when she became ill, some of her symptoms were a demand for total care by Breuer. Furthermore, only after the treatment ended did Freud become aware that Dora had also transferred her negative feelings toward Mr. K.

onto him. So Freud, like Breuer, "did not succeed in mastering the transference in good time."

Similarly, the countertransference remained unconscious. Aspects of each case made Breuer and Freud, respectively, loath to publish the history. Breuer did so only because Freud pressured him, and Freud remained ambivalent for four and a half years before submitting his final version of the Dora case. But even by the time each history appeared in print—thirteen years after Breuer's treatment of Anna O., five years after Freud's of Dora—neither man had come to any explicit realization of countertransference. Yet both case histories are replete with evidences of countertransference. In Breuer's case, in addition to the illustrations already cited, perhaps the most telling testimony is his refusal to publish a complete and accurate account of Anna O.'s illness. Freud's counter-transference has been amply detailed—or rather, almost so. One facet remains unexplored. While Freud was treating Dora at the end of 1900 and writing up the case in the early weeks of 1901, Breuer was never far from his mind. Thus still more links the cases of Anna O. and Dora and demonstrates the existence of yet another affective basis for Freud's choice of the name "Dora."

Freud and Breuer had for many years enjoyed a mutually satisfying relationship based on several conscious and unconscious roles: student/mentor; bright, poor "comer"/respected, established patron; younger brother/older brother; and son/father. They also became friends and scientific collaborators. After *Studies on Hysteria* appeared, Breuer made it clear that while he admired Freud and encouraged him in his endeavors, he could not be a wholehearted companion on the paths Freud was determinedly pursuing.[42] Freud resented this professional rejection and allowed a distance and eventually a certain anger to develop.[43] By the time he was treating Dora, the two men were estranged.

Freud's ambivalence toward Breuer can already be seen in his dream of "Irma's injection," which took place over the night of 23–24 July, 1895, at a summer resort, the Villa Bellevue,[44] a bare two months after the appearance of *Studies on Hysteria*. The circumstances surrounding the dream of Irma's injection are an uncanny harbinger of events and feelings occurring five years later when Freud psychoanalyzed Dora. There is a direct line from Irma to Dora based on Freud's anger at Breuer, his acknowledgment of Breuer's experience with Anna O., and his desire that Breuer approve of his work with hysterical patients.[45] The search to understand why Freud's Dora was in part named after Dora Breuer must begin in 1895.

There are significant similarities between the case of Irma (since revealed as Emma Eckstein) and that of Dora. Irma was a young woman, a widow, who was Freud's patient as well as a friend of Freud and his family. There were transference and countertransference problems in the treatment owing to Irma's friendship with the Freuds. In Dora's case, too, some of the transference and countertransference phenomena can be traced to Freud's treatment or acquaintance with various members of Dora's family as well as with Mr. K. Freud wrote of his therapeutic relationship with Irma: "I proposed a solution to the patient which she seemed unwilling to accept. While we were thus at variance, we had broken off the treatment for the summer vacation."[46] Freud called Irma "disobedient" and "recalcitrant to treatment" and wished she had been more like a friend of hers—another woman he knew—who he imagined would have been more cooperative and "told [him] more."[47] Dora shared with Irma what Freud saw as negativism, and he was annoyed at them both.

Now, one day during the summer break of 1895, Freud concluded that a friend, Dr. Oskar Rie, who was his children's pediatrician, a friend of the family, and also acquainted with Irma and Breuer, had hinted that Freud had not done all he should have for Irma. Stung by this seeming reproach, Freud sat down that very night—the night before the dream of Irma's injection—and wrote a copious account of his treatment of Irma, with the intention of giving it to Breuer to justify himself. Freud wanted Breuer's judgment on the case because of his experience with Anna O. "Freud may have felt that of all people Breuer would certainly be the one to understand the kind of problems that *his* patient Irma would have as well as the kind of problems with which the psychotherapist would be confronted in this kind of situation."[48] Indeed, in the dream that night, Freud had the Breuer figure—"Dr. M."—repeat his own "examination" of Irma and confirm it.[49]

As his own interpretation of the dream revealed, Freud also wanted to chastise Breuer for not joining him in his psychological method of treating hysteria. In the dream, Freud had Dr. M. make some nonsensical statement so that he would appear foolish. Freud explained that he "was expressing derision at physicians who are ignorant of hysteria" and also feeling superior to Breuer for not spotting a hysteria in a patient he was treating for tuberculosis (this was Irma's friend, the woman Freud thought would have been a more cooperative patient). In short, as Freud put it: "I had . . . revenged myself in this dream on . . . Dr. M."[50]

Five years later, in 1900, the year Freud treated Dora, he spent his summer vacation in the same place—the Villa Bellevue—where he had

had the dream of Irma's injection. He even recalled the event in letters to Wilhelm Fliess.[51] Then, in October, Dora came to him for treatment, and he began at the same time to collect the examples of psychic determinism—the slips, the misreadings, the forgettings—that were to end up as *The Psychopathology of Everyday Life.* An anecdote concerning Breuer immediately found its way into the section on the forgetting of knowledge. It had been on Freud's mind since May, when he revealingly wrote to Fliess: "I have asked myself why it is that I cannot finish with Breuer, and a recent instance of forgetting provided me with the answer." Freud continued:

> I had promised Miss L. that I would buy her a small iron strongbox in which she could keep her valuables, but I continually forgot about it. Eventually, she reminded me, and I went out shopping for it. I remembered a store, Tanczos, and had the most distinct visual memory of a window in which a small box was to be seen. It must have been somewhere in an easy-to-find location in the inner city. But I was absolutely unable to find this place on my walk. So I resolved to look it up in the telephone book or the register of business firms before my next walk. [Freud walked every day.] But then I forgot about it again on five successive days. Finally I forced myself to remember and looked up the address. And where is the place of this window with the iron box? Brandstätte [Street], across from Breuer, where I must have seen it several thousand times.[52]

In *The Psychopathology of Everyday Life* Freud spelled out his innermost feelings. He had avoided Brandstätte "as if it were forbidden territory" because it was the street of "the M. family" with whom he had once had an "intimate friendship" that had given way to "a total estrangement. . . . The mechanism of forgetting . . . applied . . . to [a] person whom I did not want to think about; and from this latter person it was then transferred to [the location of the Tanczos store.] There was a second connection there, one involving its subject matter, for money played a part among the reasons for my estrangement from the family living in the building."[53]

Money was an issue between Freud and Breuer because Breuer refused to be repaid some money he had lent the young and poor Freud. Freud resented this, seeing it as a way for Breuer to keep him in an inferior position.[54] Moreover, in the same month Freud began seeing Dora, he had the table d'hôte dream, a portion of which he interpreted as dealing with a man to whom he had been in debt. Freud felt he had "paid dearly" for the use of the man's money.[55]

Simultaneously with treating Dora, Freud was recalling his past relationship with Breuer, which obviously involved the case of Anna O. But Freud's dwelling on the old friendship and collaboration does not end with the incidents of the strong-box store and the dream of being in debt. For before Dora came to Freud, and continuing throughout 1900 and even into 1901, Freud had been plunged into rumination on his relationship with Breuer because Breuer was treating Wilhelm Fliess's mother-in-law, who lived in Vienna. Fliess and Freud corresponded for months on the subject. Freud's feelings and reactions at this time have to be seen in the light of his deteriorating relationship with Fliess. This inevitably evoked conscious and unconscious memories of his friendship with Breuer. Freud was now contemplating the ruins of an old emotional tie at the same time as he was involved in the disintegration of a current one. Since Fliess did not agree with Breuer's treatment of his mother-in-law, Freud had the opportunity to vent his strong ambivalence toward Breuer.[56] In a letter to Fliess, Freud let show the deep emotions Breuer still aroused in him, in spite of his disclaimers:

> [You and I] have drawn apart to some extent. . . . So, too, in the judgment of Breuer. I no longer despise him and have not for some time; I have felt his strength. If he is dead as far as you are concerned, then he is still exerting his power posthumously. What is your wife doing other than working out in a dark compulsion the notion that Breuer once planted in her mind when he told her how lucky she was that I did not live in Berlin and could not interfere with her marriage? . . . As to Breuer you are certainly quite right about *the* brother, but I do not share your contempt for friendship between men, probably because I am to a high degree party to it. In my life, as you know, woman has never replaced the comrade, the friend. If Breuer's male inclination were not so odd, so timid, so contradictory—like everything else in his mental and emotional makeup—it would provide a nice example of the accomplishments into which the androphilic current in men can be sublimated.[57]

Finally, this last determinant of Dora's name begins to come into focus. For one thing, Freud had already named two of his daughters after Breuer's relatives. His first daughter, Mathilde, was named after Breuer's wife, and his last daughter, Anna, was named after Breuer's daughter's sister-in-law, who was also Freud's patient. So a precedent had been established. Second, Freud always recognized the very distinctive place of the case of Anna O. in his own professional development. When he wrote his autobiography at sixty-nine, he stressed: "The state of things which [Breuer] had discovered seemed to me to be of so fundamental a nature that I could not believe it could fail to be present in any case of hysteria if it had been proved to occur in a single one."[58] When troubled in 1895 by difficult transference and countertransference conditions in the case of Irma, Freud turned to Breuer—Anna O.'s psychotherapist—for confirmation of his therapeutic procedure. This was already at a time when relations between the two men were strained.

But by 1901 matters between Freud and Breuer—or at least Freud's perception of them—stood so badly, and Freud was so angry, that he could no longer write a case history for Breuer's approbation. Yet it seems entirely likely that he unconsciously wished he could. The case of Dora had great similarities to that of Anna O. Freud, as the evidence indicates, kept thinking about Breuer, even though he did not want to. Freud had derived wide-ranging and intense satisfaction from his friendship with Breuer, and Breuer, as Freud admitted to Fliess, was a man who could "exert . . . his power posthumously." In 1900 Freud was still excited and moved when he received a report that Breuer recognized his theoretical and therapeutic capacities.

Any statement of an individual's motivation without his or her confirmation can arguably be labeled speculation. However, in this instance, there is compelling data to conclude—even without Freud's own participation—that Freud unconsciously wanted Breuer's continued approval, that he was aware of the obvious correspondences between Dora and Anna O., and that these made him feel even more than he had in 1895 that Breuer's scientific desertion was "ridiculous" and "nonsensical."[59] Combining a remembrance of past namings, a wish that a dead friendship were still alive, and an ironic, nose-thumbing gesture, Freud named his patient in part after Breuer's daughter, who was, after all, the same age and had been conceived—as Freud absolutely believed—in connection with marital difficulties brought on by Breuer's treatment of Anna O.

While Freud could consciously admit his anger at Breuer, he could not consciously admit his desire for their continued friendship. Moreover, he could neither face his feelings about surpassing Breuer, who had been like a father to him, nor confront the libidinal attachment that had existed between him and Dora, an attachment like the one he believed had existed between Breuer and Anna O. These were the psychic resistances that prevented his complete understanding of his choice of the name "Dora." Eighteen years earlier, when Freud and Martha Bernays were still engaged, Martha had written to him that she hoped as Freud's wife she would never be in the situation where a patient would be in love with her husband. Whereupon Freud, still living under his father's roof, blithely told her not to worry: "For that to happen one has to be a Breuer."[60]

Freud took four and a half years to make public the case history of Dora, although he wrote it in three weeks. Immediately after he completed the manuscript, in January 1901, it was accepted, sight unseen, by the editors of the *Monatsschrift für Psychiatrie und Neurologie,* who had previously printed two of his papers. Then, for unknown reasons, he submitted the case to another periodical, the *Journal für Psychologie und Neurologie,* whose editor rejected it, presumably on the grounds that it was a violation of medical discretion. In June, Freud sent the manuscript, as promised, to the *Monatsschrift* but soon asked for it back. He then sat on it another four years before finally publishing it in the *Monatsschrift* in 1905.[61] Freud's biographers and other commentators have wondered at the delay and have adduced several possible motivations.[62] Surely one source of Freud's ambivalence toward publishing lay in the welter of associations and emotions Ida Bauer had stirred within him, as reflected in the pseudonym he gave her.

Unconsciously Dora was many things to Freud. She was Dora the servant and childlike wife, over whom he could exercise superiority and a certain amount of control. In this way a threatened physician was able to deal with the challenges presented by an hysterical female patient. She epitomized as well Freud's lack of sympathy for the well-to-do, quasi-functional young women who formed a part of his practice. Dora was also Theodora, from Freud's viewpoint a not-entirely-benevolent gift from the gods. As a woman Theodora had used her sexuality to rise in life and assert herself in marriage so as to share imperial rule with her husband. Such a woman embodied the very dangers Freud feared from all women: They would handicap his professional life. This was based on a fantasy of woman in her vengeful role as destroyer—or certainly emasculator—of men.[63] Such was the Dora who had abruptly left treatment, an action Freud construed as "an unmistakable act of vengeance," carried out in order to deprive him of the therapeutic success he eagerly anticipated. He also interpreted certain elements of Dora's second dream to signify still another kind of vengefulness, believing that her innermost thought was: "Men are all so detestable that I would rather not marry. This is my revenge."

Pandora—yet another Dora—and Theodora were actually quite similar, put on earth by the gods to tempt men. Using or overcome by their sexual and often hysterical nature, women could make life harder and less bearable than it otherwise might have been. Freud himself admitted to Fliess that he did not regard a woman as having the capacity to be a close and trusted ally: "In my life . . . woman has never replaced the comrade, the friend." A woman's sexuality was a dangerous lure and could ultimately be a trap. Freud had been drawn by Dora's youth and attractiveness, had probed her most secret sexual thoughts and feelings, and out of his inexperience had allowed an antitherapeutic sexual tension to develop between them. Finding herself overwhelmed, Dora had bolted. Freud did not understand this and felt betrayed. On a conscious level, he blamed Dora for denying him the professional victory which he had counted on to silence unsympathetic critics. He had depended on a Pandora—an "all-gift"—to rescue him. But like all divine gifts, she nurtured a hidden flaw, and after exciting him, she had failed him.

As it turned out, not only women, but "timid" men like his father and Josef Breuer, had disappointed him. And so Dora was also Dora Breuer, born the very year of Anna O.'s hysterical childbirth and thus conjuring up memories of the young woman whose illness and treatment had provided the inspiration for Freud's development of psychoanalysis. Dora Breuer was the living reminder to Freud that his former mentor and comrade had first supported and guided him but had ultimately deserted and hurt him. Naming Ida Bauer "Dora" allowed Freud to express what he could not admit to himself: his wish for continued closeness with Josef Breuer and his awareness of the erotic parallels between Breuer's relationship with Anna O. and his own with Dora.

Freud's naming of Ida Bauer calls attention to the possible range of physician-patient relationships, with their countertransference components that range from slight and virtually meaningless to intense and hence significant. Yet, revealing as they are, there is a trap in focusing on countertransference elements because of their titillating quality and their ability to arouse feelings of superiority or condemnation in the audience. Poking into the countertransference has an erotic, voyeuristic attraction. So one must remember that in spite of marked personal prejudices and professional shortcomings, Freud did more for Dora, albeit temporarily, than any other physician had accomplished in all the years she had been sick. And with all his biases, misapplications, and clear failures, he nevertheless helped dozens of other girls and women in the years to come as a result of his revolutionary and powerful theory and therapy.

8

"The Realities of Life"

Dora left Freud's office Monday, December 31—
New Year's Eve, 1900—saying good-bye "very warmly," as Freud recalled, and extending to him "the heartiest wishes for the New Year." As
she had predicted, she did not return, although Philipp Bauer dropped in a
few times after the New Year to assure Freud his daughter would be back
since "she was eager for the treatment to continue." Freud, by then wise
to Philipp's tendency to play with the facts, took this news with a grain of
salt. He concluded that Philipp had lost all interest in making Dora come
for therapy since Freud was not following Philipp's injunction to bring
Dora "to reason" on the subject of her father's relationship with Mrs. K.
So within the week Freud began to write up the case for publication,
finishing it Thursday, January 24, 1901.[1] He wrote, as usual, in the after-
dinner hours, late into the night.

The story of Dora—"Fragment of an Analysis of a Case of Hysteria"—begins with some "Prefatory Remarks" that were probably not
composed until four years after Freud wrote the main text—that is, in
1905, when he finally decided to go through with his original intent to
publish it.[2] These opening comments shed some light on Freud's reasons
for delaying publication. Above all he was concerned with the issue of
medical discretion, acknowledging that patients who had revealed the
intimacies of their sexual life as well as their most secret wishes "would
never have spoken if it had occurred to them that their admissions might
possibly be put to scientific uses." But he was publishing, he explained,
because he had a duty toward science to make public any information that
would save persons afflicted with hysteria from future suffering. Besides,
the patient in this case had lived most of her life in a town remote from
Vienna, and he had "taken every precaution" to disguise her identity.

Freud was not only defensive about his disclosure of the case but about his frank discussion of sexual matters with a young woman as well. Cognizant that the case material would shock many in the medical audience, he anticipated his critics with a strong statement of his morality: "It would be the mark of a singular and perverse prurience to suppose that conversations of this kind are a good means of exciting or of gratifying sexual desires." Freud did protest too much.

Freud's fears of professional reaction were not all that had made him vacillate about committing his work to public scrutiny. He lacked emotional support to buoy him up when the critics began their inevitable onslaught. He had been deprived of Breuer's full-hearted encouragement years ago, and his closeness to Fliess was fast waning. In one of his last letters to his old friend he confessed that he had withdrawn the case history "from publication because just a little earlier I had lost my last audience in you."[3] In February 1901, Oscar Rie, Freud's friend and his children's pediatrician, had read the paper and not thought much of it. At that time Freud had disconsolately written to Fliess: "I shall make no further attempt to break through my isolation."[4] And clearly, Freud did not believe this was a work he could profitably share with his Jewish lodge brothers. It was not until the fall of 1902 that a replacement for Fliess and a more suitable audience than B'nai B'rith appeared in the form of a group of four physicians who came to Freud's apartment every Wednesday night to talk psychoanalysis.

In addition Freud was somewhat abashed about how he had treated Dora after she had abruptly announced that she was quitting the analysis. As he thought over in his mind the final session, Philipp's post–New Year's visits, and his own realization that Dora was not going to return, a wave of uneasiness swept over him: "Might I perhaps have kept the girl under my treatment," he ruminated, "if I myself had acted a part, if I had exaggerated the importance to me of her staying on, and had shown a warm personal interest in her—a course which, even after allowing for my position as her physician, would have been tantamount to providing her with a substitute for the affection she longed for? I do not know."

While Freud sat on the case, waiting for the resolution of his contradictory feelings, Dora also tried to bring some order into her life. It was not easy after her many sessions with Freud, and she found herself "all in a muddle" throughout January. Then, miraculously, as it appeared, she began to feel better. Her attacks of aphonia and coughing became less frequent and her depression lifted. In May the Ks' sick daughter, Klara, died at nine years of age from her congenital heart defect, and Dora decided to pay a condolence call on her former friends. They greeted her as if the events of the past three years had never happened. Nonetheless, she used the occasion to confront them with the subjects that were of such importance to her, and she carried the day. Mrs. K. did not deny having an affair with her father, and Mr. K. admitted that he had indeed made her a sexual offer that time by the lake. She then returned home and gave this news to her father. Unfortunately we do not know his reaction.

Essentially Dora remained well and occupied with her studies, lectures, and summer activities for the next five months. But in October she experienced "a violent fright." One day she and Mr. K. accidentally saw each other, right in the middle of a great deal of traffic. K. stopped as if transfixed and was knocked down by a passing carriage. Although Dora realized that he was not seriously injured, she nevertheless lost her voice and began to cough, the entire attack lasting for six weeks. She recovered, however, and her life went forward. Absorbed by her studies, she gave no thought to marrying. The only aftereffect of her former misery seemed to be a slight quiver of emotion when she heard someone speak of her father's affair with Mrs. K.

The year ended uneventfully. Dora was now nineteen. Then— suddenly—in the middle of March 1902, the right side of her face began to ache day and night.[5] She suffered this for two weeks and then went back to Freud, asking for help for her pain. Freud did not take her request for treatment seriously, deciding by "one glance at her face . . . that she was not in earnest." He noted also the "significance" of the fact that she had come to him on April 1—April Fools' Day. He did take the time to listen to the story of her activities over the past fifteen months and briefly interpreted her symptom, pointing out that her facial neuralgia had started just after she read a notice in the newspaper of his promotion from university lecturer to associate professor. He also informed her of the meaning of her pain: It was self-punishment for having slapped Mr. K. in the face and transferring her feelings about him onto Freud. But Freud adamantly refused to take Dora back as a patient, declaring that he did not know what kind of help she wanted from him. Instead he "promised to forgive her for her having deprived [him] of the satisfaction of affording her a far more radical cure for her troubles." Dora left and never saw Freud again.

On the night of 27–28 December, 1900, Dora had dreamed that she met a man in a wood who offered to accompany her. But she had refused him and had gone on alone, just as she had declined her cousin's company in the Dresden art museum.[6] Freud had interpreted these events, along with her sudden withdrawal from the psychoanalysis, to signify her desire not to marry since she found men to be so detestable. Dora herself had informed Freud in April 1902 that "she was absorbed in her work, and had no thoughts of marrying." Yet within the next year and a half, she became engaged and married.

What had happened to change Dora's mind? Did she simply succumb to conventional pressures? Had her parents urged her to wed in spite of her inclinations? Did she experience a romance that momentarily swept all before it? Had she been moved by feelings of wanting a child? There is evidence only to support the latter, although much else probably played a role. Clearly Dora had found great emotional satisfaction in mothering the Ks' two children. Then later, when she had visited the Zwinger, she had remained for two hours in front of the *Sistine Madonna*, "rapt in silent admiration." When Freud had asked her what had drawn her so compellingly, she could only answer with difficulty, but at last said: "The Madonna." Raphael's Madonna is but a girl herself, apparently little older than sixteen.

Because of his insufficient knowledge, Freud had not addressed in the analysis the lack of warm mothering in Dora's life. But he had sensed one of the outcomes of such a situation, Dora's desire to mother a child, and he had easily seen that Dora identified with the adolescent virgin mother in the painting. He even carried this line of thinking to the point of interpreting Dora's attack of appendicitis at sixteen as hysterical (and hence virginal) childbirth, since it had occurred nine months after Mr. K.'s proposition by the lake.[7] In an ancillary consideration of the Madonna as Dora, Freud concluded that "if the analysis had been continued, Dora's maternal longing for a child would probably have been revealed as an obscure though powerful motive in her behaviour." Because of Dora's deep need to be mothered, this longing was indeed powerful, perhaps even strong enough to bring her to marriage. The desire for a child was, therefore—contrary to Freud—not such an obscure emotion if it overrode her strong distrust of men and her fear of the ill-health the married state could bring. Somehow, she had to close her eyes, at least for a while, to the marital examples of her own mother, her favorite aunt, and the temporarily idolized Mrs. K., for all of whom marriage had spawned sickness.

And so on December 6, 1903, Dora married an unsuccessful engineer and composer born in Budapest, who lived in Vienna with his parents in the Leopoldstadt.[8] Freud knew about the marriage and optimistically judged it a healthy step. He based his opinion on the juxtaposition of Dora's two dreams: "Just as the first dream represented her turning away from the man she loved to her father—that is to say, her flight from life into disease—so the second dream announced that she was about to tear herself free from her father and had been reclaimed once more by the realities of life."

The wedding was celebrated in Vienna's fashionable Reform temple located on Seitenstättengasse in the Inner City. Like her mother, Dora married a man nine years older than herself, and like her Aunt Malvine, she chose a man from Hungary. Dora's parents had serious misgivings about her bridegroom, but Otto, true to character, refrained from joining in their negative voices, thus giving the impression—true or not—of solidarity with his sister.[9] He had long before established a posture of philosophical acceptance of family members' actions. Dora's husband went to work for her industrialist father, who was still a wealthy man and continued to indulge his daughter materially. Philipp "once hired an entire orchestra just to provide his son-in-law with the pleasure of hearing his music performed."[10]

After sixteen months of marriage, Dora, then twenty-two years old, gave birth to her first child, a boy.[11] If Dora had indeed married to gratify her maternal longings, her labor and delivery dealt her a grievous blow. After her son was born, she felt she could not undergo the pains of labor again and vowed to have no more children.[12] In more than one way, this was a decisive period in her life. On June 14, 1905, two months after their infant son's birth, Dora and her husband formally left the Jewish community. The following day they were baptized in the Protestant church.[13]

The percentage of Viennese Jews who converted at the turn of the century was higher than that of Jews converting anywhere else in the Austro-Hungarian Empire or even in Europe as a whole, although the actual numbers in Vienna were quite small—four out of every thousand. Yet the ratios were significant. In the ten short years from 1890 to 1900, the number of Viennese Jews who formally renounced their legal Jewish affiliation doubled. The trend was serious because it was overwhelmingly the young who were repudiating Judaism—single men and women in their twenties and thirties.[14]

The urge to convert had strengthened at the turn of the century, as increasingly voluble anti-Semitism roused many Jews to consider their situation. From 1897–1910, the mayor of Vienna, Karl Lueger, vowed to eliminate Jews from public life and had the unwavering support of his Christian constituency. On the heels of Lueger's election came the Hilsner ritual murder trials of 1899 and 1900.[15] In 1901 two Viennese newspapers published as fact the incendiary "Protocols of the Elders of Zion," a putative Jewish plan for world domination that had in fact been concocted by the Russian secret police.[16] The 1907 Austrian national elections, which ushered in universal male suffrage, proved that anti-Semitism was truly rampant. Of the 233 parliamentary seats allotted to the German regions, the anti-Semitic political parties easily secured 131.[17]

Nevertheless, throughout this period, the vast majority of Viennese Jews merely sighed nervously and hoped passively for the best. But a minority responded actively. These prescient few—although not necessarily far-seeing in their solutions—turned to one of three alternatives: socialism, with its promise of universal brotherhood; Zionism, with its nationalistic goal of a Jewish state; and conversion, with its legal erasure of the designation "Jew" and most attendant impediments.

Almost all conversion in Austria owed its occurrence to ramifications of Jewish emancipation; only rarely was religious change a true spiritual act. The actual motives for conversion varied and were reflected in the sectarian allegiances Viennese Jews adopted once they left the Jewish community. (The state required a confessional affiliation.) One-half the converts became Roman Catholic, the dominant Austrian faith. One-quarter chose the Evangelical (Protestant) Church, either Lutheran or Reformed. The last quarter declared themselves *Konfessionslos,* "without religious affiliation," a label akin to the contemporary English term "freethinker."[18] Jews in Vienna generally converted for some combination of reasons: a desire to integrate as completely as possible into the larger society; the lack of any real commitment to Judaism, reflecting a void in formal Jewish education or religious experience; professional advancement, which was available only if one was a Catholic; Jewish self-hatred; the wish to provide one's children with a nonhostile environment; and marriage to a gentile, since interfaith marriage was prohibited. Of all these, only professional advancement and marriage did not apply to Dora and her husband.[19]

Because of their assimilated backgrounds, both Dora and her husband shared the urge for more complete integration into and acceptance by the wider society. Her husband's family, even before they had moved to Vienna, had become as acculturated a part of the Hungarian secular world as the Czech Jews had of the Viennese. In the nineteenth century, the process of Magyarization—preceded by a period of Germanization—had wrought greater assimilation of Hungarian Jews than of Czech Jews. Many Jews not only spoke Hungarian but regarded themselves and were regarded by others as "Magyars of Mosaic persuasion." Hungarian Jews were attracted to the ruling Magyar culture just as Bohemian Jews were drawn by the German cultural orientation.

Indeed, the Hungarian political elite, the aristocratic landowners, actively encouraged Jews to regard themselves as part of the Magyar nation. It was Magyar policy to encourage non-Magyars to become Hungarians since the Magyars were in a minority in a multinational region. The Magyars also wanted to modernize their economy and recognized the usefulness of the Jews in this effort. Hungarian Jews, as a result, became the middle class, there being no indigenous one, and were on their way toward becoming like western European Jewry. After 1867 the Jews in Hungary became first-class citizens, often Magyarized their names—Löwy to Lukács was a common change—and allied themselves with the ruling power. On the eve of World War I, Jews were 25 percent of the population of Budapest and 50 percent of the medical students at the university.[20]

The only thing that stopped the Jews from achieving total assimilation was that they were not accepted socially by the Hungarian gentry and were excluded from the army and bureaucracy. There was also a great deal of crude anti-Jewish feeling among the peasants and artisans, but unlike the authorities in Bohemia and Vienna, the ruling powers worked assiduously to combat popular anti-Semitism, and the Hungarian Catholic and Calvinist churches were not involved in the anti-Semitic movement. So the Jews were a vital and valued part of the Hungarian economy and culture, and Jewish integration into national life was greater only in France, England, and the United States.[21]

Thus Dora and her husband had at least this much in common: They were Jews who lacked a Jewish upbringing and who, since childhood, had been largely assimilated into Western society. Dora had even attended a convent school in Meran. Moreover, they were not in the typical economic groups of converts, nor did they wish to convert for immediately practical reasons. It was unusual for a male Jewish industrialist to convert, and only 9 percent of the female converts had fathers who were industrialists.[22] Neither her husband's career nor Dora's way of life was at stake. He had a job with his wealthy father-in-law and did not have to worry about a civil service or professional position. She was not a poor young woman who wanted to rise through marriage or a working-class woman who simply wanted to marry a Christian man she had met at her job.[23]

Most converts were motivated to a greater or lesser extent by repugnance for their Jewish identity, and such self-deprecation did play a role in Dora's and her husband's conversions. In fin-de-siècle Vienna, Jewish self-hatred manifested itself most commonly in the embarrassment, if not disgust, that westernized Czech and Hungarian Jews felt and even displayed at the noticeable presence of the newly arrived Jews from Galicia, in the eastern part of the empire. These *Ostjuden*—Eastern Jews—were generally poor, religiously observant, Orthodox Jews who were traditional Polish-Jewish dress. Their poverty kept them uncouth, and their non-Western appearance and distinctive Yiddish speech made them highly visible in public places.

Middle-class Western Jews had accepted the Christian majority's judgment that Jewishness was undesirable. In their yearning for integration and acceptance, they did not want to be reminded that they were Jews, and the *Ostjuden* called attention to characteristic preassimilation speech and mannerisms. Once Westernized and secularized, most Jews wanted to erase external indications of their origins.[24]

But self-hatred and the lack of a satisfying Jewish identity were only part of what motivated Dora and her husband to convert to Christianity. Dora was undeniably propelled by her many dissatisfactions with life. She had been mistreated socially as a Jew and a woman, her love for her father and Mrs. K. had been rewarded by their sacrificing her for their own ends, she had been used by Mr. K. as a servant, and she lived in an emotional void created by her angry and compulsive mother. If there had ever been a human being who yearned for acceptance, it was Dora. And while we know little about her husband, he had to have been shocked or even frightened by the mounting and disagreeable official anti-Semitism that was so novel to him and his family in Vienna. Perhaps, also, he had looked for a civil service position in his twenties, before he met Dora, and had been rejected on religious grounds. Yet the weight of these experiences had not caused the newlyweds to forsake the Jewish community immediately after their marriage. It was the birth of their son that pushed the young couple to action.

How often over the centuries did Jews do things *fahr die Kinder*— "for the sake of the children." Historically Jewish parents waged quixotic battles to save their children from life's ordinary, inevitable tolls or felt driven to secure for the new generation what the old had failed to achieve. Frequently Jews nourished the sentiment that their "Jewishness" should survive through the young. But when assimilation caused self-hatred to reach a severe-enough pitch, what Jews most wanted was that the Jewish stamp should be removed from their children.

We know the kind of feeling and thinking that went into Dora and her husband's decision to convert with their infant son, because prominent contemporaries have left us their views on the subject. Theodor Herzl, for example, wrote at age thirty-three:

I myself would never convert, yet I am in favor of conversion. For me the matter is closed, but it bothers me greatly for my son Hans. I ask myself if I have the right to sour and blacken his life as mine has been soured and blackened.

Therefore, one must baptize Jewish boys before they must account for themselves, before they are able to act against it, and before conversion can be construed as a weakness on their part. They must disappear into the crowd. [25]

Herzl's external assimilation and wealth had not compensated in an essential way for his inner feelings of unworthiness. So, too, with Dora. Her wealth, servants, jewelry, clothes, and trips weighed little in the balance when the fact of her Jewishness was on the other side of the scale. And the inferiority she felt as a Jew cannot be separated from what she experienced as a woman in her culture and as a human being who had been used and betrayed by her parents and the Ks. It is also likely that Dora's decision not to raise her son as a Jew reflected an unconscious feeling that any child of hers would be reared in a family atmosphere as different from her own as she could arrange. [26]

Yet for the new racial anti-Semites of the twentieth century, there truly was nothing a Jew could do to gain acceptance. It made no difference if he changed his religion, married a non-Jew, and sent his children to Christian schools. "Racially" he was Jewish, and his children would be Jewish. Heinrich Heine's aphorism about baptism being the admission ticket to European civilization had become outdated.

But in 1905 Jews were only beginning to be aware of the implications of racial anti-Semitism. Making a nominal conversion was regarded by scores of them as an effective solution to the problem of their children's future. For many years their lives were satisfactory, and they were pleased with the external success of their step, annoyed only occasionally by the barriers that remained in their way. Dora was in this group, and in the decade before World War I, she led an outwardly unremarkable middle-class life as a young wife and mother.

Dora's distancing herself from her origins was underscored by her brother's career decision, which likewise took Otto far from his early surroundings. The later lives of both Bauer children stand as an example of the strong motivational force exerted by the confluence of private and public misery. In the cases of Dora and Otto, the conflict and duplicity of their upbringing converged with the disappointment and pain of being

Jewish in a hostile environment to produce determined decisions to forge new identities. Dora and Otto expected a happier life as a result.

During the years Dora pursued her women's lectures and self-studies, married, and settled down to a life of domesticity, Otto, to please his father, took a law degree at the University of Vienna, graduating with high honors. After completing a year's training in the courts to obtain his legal certification—another part of his promise to Philipp—he turned in 1907 to the fulfillment of his adolescent desire—a career as a socialist.[27] At twenty-six, his talents already recognized, Otto became the full-time parliamentary secretary of the Austrian Social Democratic party. Three years earlier, Karl Kautsky (1854–1938), the German socialist, had said of him: "This is how I imagine the young Marx."[28]

Otto's socialist career was brilliantly launched the year after he graduated from the university with the publication of an erudite book on the central problem confronting the Austro-Hungarian monarchy: its continued existence as a multinational state in an era of rabid nationalism. *The Nationalities Question and Social Democracy* (1907) exhibited Otto's broad knowledge of history and his mature sensitivity for politics and psychology.[29] The work set forth the distinctly non-Marxian notion of accepting the cultural diversity of all the various ethnic groups in the empire and granting them cultural-national autonomy. But Otto excluded the Jews from his socialist revisionism. They were the one group he situated tightly within the confines of Marx's antinationalist arguments. There was a perceptible measure of self-hatred in Otto's assessment of the Jews' place in the twentieth century. The Jews were a "historyless" people who had lost their territorial base and had no claim to cultural and national autonomy. European Jews, he declared, were no longer needed to perform the economic tasks they had carried out for centuries, so it was time their visible existence as a distinct people came to an end.

Although Otto advocated separate languages, cultural programs, and educational systems for the ethnic groups of the Habsburg monarchy, he did not believe the Jews should have these institutions. Separate Jewish schools, for example, would perpetuate the "social psychology of a dead epoch" and give Jewish children "a medieval world-view and the life-habits of a Jewish innkeeper." "Maintenance of Jewish identity [would] reinforce the mentality of the Jewish merchant in the worker, and hinder his assimilation into the modern class structure based upon modern industry." Jewish workers should rid themselves of "the inflection of their language, their gestures, their apparel, their customs" in order not to provoke "instinctive dislike" in Christian workers and employers. The answer to "the Jewish problem" lay in intermarriage, "a mixing of Jewish blood with the bloods of the other nations. . . . Only then will the special Jewish misery disappear, and there will be only common proletarian misery, which the Jew will fight and conquer . . . with his Aryan colleagues."[30]

Like Dora, Otto sought, by means he felt available to him, to obliterate the past. He envisioned the Jews merging with the Christian majority so that gradually they would become invisible. That is why he rejected his sister's limited, and to him ineffective, solution of conversion and instead advocated intermarriage. In an article on the limitations of assimilation, he declared: "A great hindrance to assimilation is the difference in race. As soon as the Czech is assimilated into the German nationality his Czech origins are concealed [*verdeckt*]. . . . But it is different in cases where the race of the minority is not similar to that of the majority. Thus, the assimilated Jews are still obviously Jews according to their facial characteristics. Race instincts and race prejudices live on after assimilation."[31] The future of the Jews, therefore, lay in marrying Christians and having non-Jewish children.

But Otto still lived in the present, a very visible Jew. That is why his affiliation with the Austrian Social Democrats became psychologically indispensable to him. The Austro-Marxists were generally middle-class intellectuals reared in and imbued with German culture. They envisioned socialism coming to Austria under the umbrella of the German language and traditions and believed the masses would better themselves through their absorption of German culture.[32] Socialism offered Otto an acceptable way to express his deeply felt German nationalism.[33] The only other effective German nationalist parties in Austria were crudely anti-Semitic, the Liberals being on the wane. But Austro-Marxism provided more than a nationalist haven. It gave Otto Bauer acceptance by a large group, filled the ideological void left by his estrangement from religious and ethnic traditions, and enabled him to renounce the traditions of his Jewish capitalist family without actually breaking with them.

Otto's lifelong pattern of avoiding clear-cut action was reflected in his marriage. When he finally married at the age of thirty-three—after the deaths of his parents—he chose a woman ten years older than himself, Helene Landau, who already had three children.[34] He transgressed his own prescription that Jews should marry Christians—his wife was Jewish—but he married a woman by whom he had no children, thus avoiding placing any new Jews on earth. At forty-five he fell in love with Hilda Schiller-Marmorek, a beautiful married woman, ten years younger, who was also Jewish. Like Helene, Hilda was a committed socialist. Hilda and

Otto talked of divorce ad remarriage to each other, but Otto would not leave his wife.[35] So Otto did not marry his lover or have Jewish children with her. Just like his father in his forties, Otto took an attractive, younger woman as his mistress and remained married to his wife.

Otto temporized in yet another significant way. It was usual for leaders of the Austrian Social Democratic party to abjure their native religion and become *konfessionslos*. But this Otto Bauer never did. He remained on the record books of the Vienna Jewish community and paid its taxes. When challenged by a non-Jewish friend to explain his continued confessional status, he replied that leaving the Jewish community was one thing he just could not do, adding: "You cannot understand that, since no one ever muttered 'dirty Jew' behind your back."[36]

Dora and Otto's parents lived long enough to see their brilliant firstborn cast his lot with a movement pledged to overthrow their way of life and their second child and only grandchild convert to Christianity. Less than a decade afterward, they were both dead. Käthe died first, in August 1912, from cancer of the colon.[37] She was fifty. In the typical way of many widowers, Philipp did not long outlive his wife; he was dead in less than a year from his tuberculosis, the official cause of death being listed as "degeneration of the prostate."[38] Philipp died in July 1913, just a month short of his sixtieth birthday.

In the months before Philipp's death, Dora once more found herself nursing her tubercular father. This time, however, Otto shared in the care.[39] Philipp's failing health seems to have included an organic brain syndrome. This could have been the result of a tubercular meningitis or fever secondary to the tuberculosis. It might even have been a sign of tertiary syphilis. Dora once confided to a physician that before her father died, he "often seemed out of his mind."[40] Dora's "tender attachment" to her father as well as her tendency to somatize her feelings instead of expressing them directly meant that this had to be an exceptionally distressful period for her.

For Otto, however, the deaths of his parents freed him to marry and even provoked him to assess his career and future. Soon after his marriage in 1914, he sought out Freud, who advised him to give up politics and become a teacher or university professor[41], a career better suited to his idealistic temperament than the volatile and hazardous arena of Austrian politics. Otto had already established himself as a charismatic leader of the Social Democrats, an inspiring speaker to its youth, and a dedicated teacher of workers' classes.[42] Moreover, Freud, consistent with his pessimistic and low opinions of human nature, tried to talk Otto out of changing the world, warning him: "Don't try to make people happy, people don't want to be happy."[43]

=========

Although by 1914 neither Dora nor Otto lived around the corner from him, Freud immediately knew who Otto was. He had been keeping track of Dora's life, knew that she had married, and even added a footnote to later editions of the case correcting his mistaken identification of her bridegroom in the original paper. He also may have known about Otto's career, since Otto was a prolific and respected political writer and steady contributor to Socialist party publications.

It is hard to know how Freud felt about seeing this specter of his problematic psychoanalysis of Dora. In many respects Freud, on the eve of World War I, was a different man from the one he had been at the turn of the century. He no longer needed to worry about earning an adequate living to support his large family establishment; patients came to him from all over Europe. He had become the head of an international organization of local psychoanalytic societies, and his time and energies now had to be directed as much, if not more, to administrative and political concerns as to scientific developments and writing.

What had been the unconscious determinants of Freud's feelings and behavior in 1900 seemed in 1914, at least on the surface, to have slackened their hold. Freud was fifty-eight and no longer as driven by his own sexuality as he had been at forty-four.[44] He had replaced his friendships with Breuer and Fliess with a host of other close relationships and was not as dependent on intimates for his sense of worth and professional validity. Although he had just broken with Carl Gustav Jung the preceding year and was hurt, angry, and self-righteous, Freud was not reduced to doubting his own abilities or questioning the existence of a committed readership. And there were several devoted colleagues and followers who were all too happy to pick up the pieces of any broken friendship. Freud's leadership position had significantly altered the nature of all his personal and professional relationships.

Moreover, by 1914, Freud's theories were sufficiently established so that lack of success with a single patient did not carry the same significance as it had when Dora had so severely disappointed him. He had moved far beyond his early emphasis on hysteria and was equally concerned with other forms of psychopathology. He was also rethinking his conception of the mind as well as his instinct theory. The fruits of these preoccupations ripened in the war years and in the 1920s into a series of newly creative as well as revisionist works. Thus Otto's visit may have been no more than an interesting ripple in the daily flow of patients and problems.

Nonetheless it is a distinct possibility that Otto's visit evoked in Freud memories of a long-ago failure and thoughts of the theoretical and technical strides he had made in the intervening time. For it was just in the four previous years that Freud had begun to publish a series of findings that seem directly linked to Dora's treatment.

Freud, in his writings from the period 1910–13, was most impressed by his discovery that the psychoanalyst accomplishes nothing when he precipitously informs a patient of his or her unconscious desires and the links between present illness and past experiences. He admitted his former errors: "It is true that in the earliest days of analytic technique we took an intellectualist view of the situation. We set a high value on the patient's knowledge of what he had forgotten, and in this we made hardly any distinction between our knowledge of it and his." But now Freud knew better and condemned "any line of behavior which would lead us to give the patient a translation of his symptoms as soon as we have guessed it ourselves, or would even lead us to regard it as a special triumph to fling these 'solutions' in his face at the first interview."[45] "Such measures . . . have as much influence on the symptoms of nervous illness as a distribution of [menus] in a time of famine has upon hunger."[46]

Freud acknowledged his past hubris: "What a measure of self-complacency and thoughtlessness must be possessed by anyone who can, on the shortest acquaintance, inform a stranger who is entirely ignorant of all the tenets of analysis that he is attached to his mother by incestuous ties." He understood the price he had paid: "Behaviour of this sort will completely discredit oneself and the treatment in the patient's eyes and will arouse the most violent opposition in him, whether one's guess is true or not. . . . As a rule the therapeutic effect will be nil; but the deterring of the patient from analysis will be final."[47] After long experience Freud was aware of what must precede the psychoanalyst's interpretation: "First, the patient must, through preparation, himself have reached the neighbourhood of what he has repressed, and secondly, he must have formed a sufficient attachment (transference) to the physician for his emotional relationship to him to make a fresh flight impossible. . . . Psycho-analytic intervention, therefore, absolutely requires a fairly long period of contact with the patient. . . . Besides all this," Freud ruefully confessed, "one may sometimes make a wrong surmise."[48]

Freud's papers right before World War I dwelt on the mistakes he had made with Dora. He cautioned new psychoanalysts about the "special difficulties" that will be encountered if the therapist and patient are previously acquainted, if the analyst and the patient's family have a social relationship, and "if [the analyst] behaves like a representative or advocate of some contending party with whom the patient is engaged in a conflict—of his parents, for instance."[49] He even reported briefly that he had "become aware of the 'counter-transference,' which arises in [the physician] as a result of the patient's influence on his unconscious feelings, and [he was] almost inclined to insist that [the analyst] recognize this counter-transference in himself and overcome it. . . . No psychoanalyst goes further than his own complexes and internal resistances permit."[50]

Finally Freud addressed head-on his attempt to use Dora's case to prove that psychoanalysis could cure hysteria through dream interpretation at the same time that he was actually analyzing her. The truth was that "the technique required for [research] opposes that required for [treatment]. It is not a good thing to work on a case scientifically while treatment is proceeding. . . . Cases which are devoted from the first to scientific purposes and are treated accordingly suffer in their outcome; while the most successful cases are those . . . which one . . . meets . . . with an open mind, free from any presuppositions. The correct behavior for an analyst lies . . . in avoiding speculation or brooding over cases while they are in analysis."[51]

In addition to his professional strides as a psychoanalyst, Freud had also taken an important step in his personal maturation. He had come to terms with the fact of his Jewishness and no longer sought to flee from it. Such an accommodation to the onslaught of anti-Semitism in Vienna was made by some Jews—though not the majority—and many of the younger ones then logically gravitated to Zionism.[52] Although remaining totally nonreligious in practice, Freud had begun a journey that, by the time he was fifty, had carried him from shame as a Jew to pride in his ethnic identity.

The first manifestation of change had occurred rather suddenly. In September 1883, Freud had been mortified at the public display of Jews' quarreling and vengefulness at the funeral of his friend Nathan Weiss. Three months later, Freud no longer retreated from his Jewishness. On a train trip to Leipzig, he opened a window to get some fresh air, provoking the annoyance of some passengers in his compartment. While negotiations ensued, a voice from the background shouted: "He's a dirty Jew!" Suddenly what had been a civil discussion turned nasty. One fellow passenger declared that Christians were considerate of other people; maybe Freud should think less of himself. Another threatened a fight. Significantly, Freud wrote to Martha: "Even a year ago I would have been speechless with agitation, but now I am different; I was not in the least frightened of that mob." Freud gave as good as he got and twice summoned the conductor, who remained neutral. Eventually another official intervened and declared that all windows must be closed in the wintertime. Freud had lost and became the object of "jeers, abuses and threats." But he yelled a physical challenge to the ringleader, which abruptly brought the matter to an end. He bragged to Martha:

> I do think I held my own quite well, and used the means at my disposal courageously; in any case I didn't fall to their level. After all, I am no giant, haven't any hackles to show, no lion's teeth to flash, no stentorian roar, my appearance is not even distinguished; all this would have had a lightening effect on that mob, but they must have noticed that I wasn't afraid and I didn't allow this experience to dampen my spirits.[53]

The incident marked a turning point, and by the time Freud was thirty he was consciously proud of his Jewish heritage and had renounced his early German nationalistic identification. While studying in Paris—this was three months after the *Théodora* experience—Freud fell into an introspective mood and began assessing his personality and future professional prospects. He took to a little boasting and confided in Martha: "You know what Breuer told me one evening? . . . He told me he had discovered that hidden under the surface of timidity there lay in me an extremely daring and fearless human being. I had always thought so, but never dared tell anyone. I have often felt as though I had inherited all the defiance and all the passions with which our ancestors defended their Temple and could gladly sacrifice my life for one great moment in history."[54] Perhaps it was "the bit of cocaine" Freud had just taken that emboldened him to confess this secret fantasy to his fiancée;[55] nevertheless, the thought had been with him for a while. Later that night, at a soirée at Charcot's, Freud—again fortified by cocaine—became involved in a political conversation with a French neurologist, who predicted war with Germany. Freud refused to take sides, explaining that he was a Jew, "adhering neither to Germany nor Austria."[56]

These early adult attitudes strengthened and hardened themselves, so by the time Freud was forty he had no doubts about the primacy of his Judaic identity. When in 1897 the Czech-language ordinances were passed, resulting in German and anti-Semitic rioting, and then in the same year Karl Lueger became mayor of Vienna, Freud, still depressed over the death of his father, felt "despised and universally shunned" and joined B'nai B'rith.[57] At the turn of the century, many assimilated Jews, even if not the majority, as a matter of pride purposely remained Jewish or proclaimed their Jewishness; perhaps some of them also recognized the implications of racial anti-Semitism for Jewish assimilation. Heinrich Bermann, the Jewish character in Schnitzler's *Der Weg ins Freie*, spoke for all of them, including Schnitzler: "That's why [as a point of honor] in spite of my complete indifference to every form of religion, I would positively never allow myself to be baptized, even if it were possible—though that is less the case today than ever it was—of escaping once and for all Anti-Semitic bigotry and villainy by a dodge like that."[58] Thus, later, Freud was pleased when his eldest son, Martin, joined Kadimah, a Jewish fraternity.

In the mid-1920s, when Freud had reached the age at which he began to look back on his life, he made strong, unequivocal statements about the primacy of his Jewish allegiance. He told an interviewer: "My language is German. My culture, my attainments are German. I considered myself German intellectually, until I noticed the growth of anti-Semitic prejudice in Germany and German Austria. Since that time, I prefer to call myself a Jew."[59] Additionally, he replied to a correspondent: "I am as remote from the Jewish religion as from all others. . . . On the other hand, I have always had a strong feeling of solidarity with my people and have also fostered it in my children. We have all remained in the Jewish confession."[60] Finally, he struggled to define to B'nai B'rith what bound him to other Jews and why he valued his Jewishness:

> The attraction of Jewry and Jews [was] irresistible—many obscure emotional forces, which were the more powerful the less they could be expressed in words, as well as a clear consciousness of inner identity, the safe privacy of a common mental construction. And beyond this there was a perception that it was to my Jewish nature *alone* [italics supplied] that I owed two characteristics that had become indispensable to me in the difficult course of my life. Because I was a Jew I found myself free from many prejudices which restricted others in the use of their intellect; and as a Jew I was prepared to join the Opposition and to do without agreement with the "compact majority."[61]

While Freud decided to accept his minority status and make a virtue out of necessity, Otto and Dora sought to be part of the majority—though they did so, to be sure, in very different ways. Once Dora was no longer a Jew, she strove for social acceptance at the highest possible level and completely abandoned the intellectual pursuits of her earlier years. Otto's biographer summed up Dora, the young matron, in one trenchant sentence: "She fell into a circle in which external social superficialities and relations with the 'upper ten thousand' (or those who wanted to be) were the most important things."[62] The avant-garde literary and artistic interests of her adolescence turned out to have been temporary, and she decorated her apartment in the style of her parents' generation—"dark, heavily carpeted, typical[ly] Victorian."[63] Like a true Viennese, she regularly attended the opera and joined her musician-husband in seeing to it that their son began his musical education at an early age. At five he began studying the piano with a teacher who was a pupil of Arnold Schönberg.[64] By the age of seven, he happily sat through a performance of *Lohengrin*.[65] Dora poured her hopes into her only child.

Dora's life, like that of every European, was jarred by the outbreak of World War I in August 1914. Just a year after the death of her father, the war spirited away her brother, with whom she had resumed the close relations of their childhood. Within a few months, Otto, who had been decorated for bravery, was a prisoner of the Russians, not to return until September 1917.[66] Dora's husband, at forty-one, was not called up for a year, but in late spring of 1915, he, too, went off.[67] He came back permanently handicapped, having suffered a severe head and ear injury that affected his sense of balance; his memory was also impaired.[68] Coincidentally, in the midst of the war, Philipp's older brother, Karl, the remaining head of the family firm, died of heart failure, leaving the business without effective leadership.[69]

For Freud the war also meant personal agony until his sons in the Austro-Hungarian army finally returned safely. In addition the hostilities caused a breakdown of the communications so necessary to the functioning of the international psychoanalytic organization, and the movement's progress ground to a halt. The war also betokened the loss of Freud's international clientele and a consequent drop in his standard of living. His letters and writings of these years show, not surprisingly, an increased attention to the subject of aggression. The pressures of the time manifested themselves in his altered personal health: The chronic diarrhea he was always battling improved, but he constantly felt tired. Both changes suggest either a change in diet or mild depression, or some combination of the two.

By 1917 Freud, Dora, and their families were sharing the great hardships the war was imposing on all the civilian inhabitants of the Central Powers. Every day they had to cope with scarcities in food and fuel and a steadily mounting inflation, as the government and the population as a whole scrambled to pay for necessities in any possible way. Under these conditions the black market thrived. By the winter of 1917–18, war weariness was immense; civilians and soldiers alike yearned for peace above all.

Although that winter was the first of two starvation winters the Viennese had to endure, Dora was still better off than most. She and her family were able to capitalize on their social contacts and draw on their inherited resources. They spent part of the summer of 1918 on vacation in Bohemia, at the home of a friend of the family, and that fall were able to afford music lessons for their talented son with the president—the first oboist—of the Vienna Philharmonic.[70]

Peace came in November 1918, but instead of marking the beginning of better times, it ushered in three catastrophic years. An episode in Stefan Zweig's life at that time gives a unique preview of the misery and desperation yet to come. Zweig spent the last year of the war in Switzerland, and when the war was over he returned to Austria. At the border he had

> to change [trains] from the spruce, clean Swiss cars into the Austrian. One had but to enter them to become aware beforehand of what had happened to the country. The guards who showed us our seats were haggard, starved and tatterdemalion; they crawled about with torn and shabby uniforms hanging loosely over their stooped shoulders. The leather straps for opening and closing windows had been cut off, for every piece of that material was precious. . . . Whole sections of the [seat] covering [had] been rudely removed by such as needed to have their shoes repaired. . . . Likewise the ashtrays were missing, stolen for the sake of their mite of nickel or copper. . . . That the train moved at all was a miracle. . . . Distances which used to take an hour now required four or five, and when dusk set in we remained in darkness. The electric bulbs had either been smashed or stolen. . . . Everyone held on to his baggage anxiously and hugged his package of provisions close. . . . From the midst of peace I was riding back into the horror of war which I had thought to be over.[71]

Austria had gone from a world power to a third-rate, land-locked small nation. Out of the former Austro-Hungarian Empire, five new countries were created: Czechoslovakia, Yugoslavia, Poland, Austria, and Hungary. Preexisting countries were enlarged at the expense of Austria. The South Tyrol, for example, where Dora had lived from six to seventeen, and where Freud and members of his family had often vacationed, was given to Italy. Austria was deprived of the provinces that had made it an industrial and agricultural force. The Bauer factories were now on foreign soil in Czechoslovakia, and the family lost its wealth.[72]

In Vienna the population subsisted on ersatz bread and coffee or tried to cheer themselves with artificial beer and chocolate. When real bread and potatoes appeared, they were inevitably rotten. Necessities such as milk, meat, soap, fuel, and paper were not to be had. The population donned winter clothing in their apartments to keep warm. In all areas dire shortages were the order of the day. The inflation was severe. Anything edible or useful commanded an enormous and ever-increasing price. The savings of the middle class and the value of real property were wiped out. Dora and Freud's families benefited slightly but mainly lost. The rent on their apartments, set at pre-war prices, was the merest trifle. A medium-size apartment cost its tenant less for the whole year than a dinner, and the government prevented cancellation of leases well into the twenties.[73] But any money saved or salary earned in local currency was worthless. Dora's inheritance virtually disappeared. Only certain foreign currencies had value, so Freud asked for payment of his fees in British, United States, or Swiss money. By 1923 the Austrian currency had completely collapsed.

The very best people took to barter, the Freuds included, so it is highly likely that Dora adapted similarly. Freud gladly took food instead of fees and relied on food packages, money, cigars, and clothing from English and American relatives, wealthy followers, and friends and pupils in Holland and Switzerland. All his old fears and resentments of penury were reawakened.

In sum, from 1918 to 1921 the Viennese dedicated themselves to bare survival. Starvation diets of eight to nine hundred calories were common. It was an ordinary sight to see people scavenging and eating from garbage cans. Infant mortality rose, tuberculosis increased, and many—more women than men—sickened in (and succumbed to) the influenza epidemic of 1918–19, which had not completely abated by 1920. From May to July of 1919, Martha Freud had influenza and pneumonia, with lingering fevers and respiratory symptoms.

Finally, by 1921, the situation began to improve, although Dora had to face the fact that the war had destroyed the industrial base of her family's wealth. Moreover, there were continued hardships from unemployment, and Freud had to support his grown sons, who could not find work. Nevertheless, there were some reasons for optimism. Freud had his practice back,[74] and his international reputation was steadily rising. Dora dreamed of great things from her son and believed that the political prominence of her brother in the new Austrian Republic would prove valuable to her family.

9

"Mad Times"

Dora's and Freud's hopes for the future were sharply tempered by the events of the 1920s. Like many middle-class Viennese who had no love for the antiquated Habsburg dynasty and its class-conscious, inefficient imperial bureaucracy, they were still hardly prepared for the republican, democratic government set up by the new constitution. After seven hundred years of near-absolute rule, the people of Austria had little experience with democracy, and the new republic was also handicapped by the loss of the industrial and agricultural regions that had sustained the imperial government. The logical union of Germany and Austria into one economically viable republic was forbidden by the nervous and punitive Allied peacemakers. There was a brief attempt by the Social Democrats—the Austrian socialists—and the Christian Socials to unify in the face of the great problems confronting the new state, and the two parties put together a coalition government in which the socialists were the stronger. This did not last long. After the Christian Socials emerged with the most votes in October, 1920, the Social Democrats withdrew into opposition, and the Christian Socials governed with the support of the German Nationalists.

An unproductive and dangerous stalemate developed between the two leading parties, which often led to violence on the streets of Vienna. The socialists controlled a Vienna of two million people, the city having been declared a separate province. The Christian Socials controlled the countryside of five million and the national government. The parties viewed each other with suspicion, mistrust, and often outright hatred.

The leaders of the Social Democrats were men like Otto Bauer: moderate, highly intelligent, largely middle-class, and often Jewish—anything but revolutionaries. They had defeated a communist attempt to

168

turn Austria into a soviet republic, and, in order to attract widespread electoral support, they did not adopt an overtly friendly attitude to the Jews. But in the interests of social justice they used the language of the barricades—"class struggle, capitalist exploiters, fight, battle"—which frightened the agricultural classes, much of the urban middle classes, and the upper class.

The Christian Socials, already unnerved by the drastic changes of the postwar period, felt their way of life threatened. In the nationalist climate, they were frustrated by the prohibition against German-Austrian union—as, indeed, was Otto—and drew no distinction between the Austro-Marxists and Russian Bolsheviks. They ranted about defending Western civilization and Germanic Christian values and continually spouted anti-Semitism in order to retain their popularity with the Austrian electorate outside "Red Vienna." They frequently referred to the new state as the *Judenrepublik,* the "Jewish Republic."[1] Egged on against Jewish assimilation by the racists among them, their first postwar manifesto declared: "The corruption and power-mania of Jewish circles, evident in the new state, forces the Christian-Social Party to call on the German-Austrian people for a most severe defensive struggle against the Jewish peril. Recognised as a separate nation, the Jews shall be granted self-determination; they shall never be the masters of the German people."[2]

From the viewpoint of the future ability of Austria to solve its pressing problems within a democratic, constitutional framework, the worst aspect of postwar developments was the establishment by each party of a private army. The Christian Socials had the Heimwehr and Social Democrats had the Schutzbund; the small Austrian National Socialist (Nazi) party also had its own guard. The Austrian Republic was too weak to deal with these paramilitary troops, so the Viennese population not only lived with a stagnant economy and chronic unemployment but in a permanently charged atmosphere of street marches and bloody clashes with whips, beer bottles, and occasionally even guns. Eternal agitation in parliament, pan-Germanic rhetoric, and anti-Semitic demagoguery rounded out the political life of the Austrian Republic.

On July 14, 1927, an obliging Viennese jury acquitted some right-wing, paramilitary toughs who "shot into a socialist crowd, killing a child and an invalid and wounding five others."[3] This proved to be the torch that finally ignited the ill-will and enmity between the Social Democrats and the Christian Socials. On July 15, mob violence and police counterviolence got out of control, and when all was over, there was no hope for Austria's Right and Left ever to coexist again.

Freud was out of town vacationing and heard about the incident second hand. He could only write to his follower, Sandor Ferenczi, that "it is a rotten affair," and to his nephew in England that "bad social and material conditions [exist] in Vienna."[4] If Dora was in the city, she would have been horrified to see rank and file socialists of her brother's party take matters in their own hands and march to the Ringstrasse to protest the jury's verdict. Voting with their feet against the legal pardon of the right-wing culprits, the socialist mob proceeded to set fire to the Palace of Justice. The police on the scene then took matters into their own hands and fired at the demonstrators, killing eighty-nine workers.

Freud, like many other bourgeois Viennese, had no sympathy with either side, in spite of the anti-Semitism of the Christian Socials and the Heimwehr and some very close links between the psychoanalysts and the Social Democrats. Actually, much of the Jewish middle class financially supported the Christian Social and pan-German national governments of the 1920s, viewing their anti-Semitic rhetoric as an essentially meaningless necessity to appease their radical right-wing followers. These Jews regarded the Heimwehr as extremists who would never wield any real power. Middle-class Jews were usually more afraid of the socialists, who they feared would strip them of all they had worked for.[5]

Political excess and economic stagnaton made life in the 1920s unpleasant for Dora. It is true that, having converted, she felt her family was protected from any personal consequences of the Christian Socials' and German Nationalists' anti-Semitism. After all, this was one of the reasons she had left the Jewish community: to gain security for herself and her son. Nevertheless, she, like others, lived amidst violence. There was always the potential of being accidentally involved in street clashes. Gangs of young toughs roamed about, seeking to beat up schoolboys who looked Jewish. Moreover, Dora's economic and social position was not what it had been, and she had to content herself with less. Perhaps it was this latter circumstance that caused her son to explain fifty years later that "a certain psychological and economic severity" which critics had noted in his personality as a musical director was "the direct result of his boyhood. Although the scion of wealth, [he] was raised austerely. Growing up he had next to no money at his disposal. Time after time," Dora's son complained, "[his] parents [had] refused to exercise their considerable influence on [his] behalf."[6] It seems likely that Dora and her husband no longer had the kind of influence their son imagined. But in addition to the public woes Dora shared with other middle-class Viennese, she had her own considerable private misery.

Freud had lost touch with Dora and Otto during the war years and the tumultuous postwar period. But in 1922 he learned from his personal physician, Felix Deutsch (1884–1964), an internist who was analytically oriented, what was going on in Dora's life.[7] Deutsch's portrait of Dora at forty is an eerie evocation of both Käthe Bauer and the adolescent Dora Freud had known. Dora was unhappily married, frustrated in her love life, and unable to enjoy sex. She had premenstrual pains, a vaginal discharge after menstruation, and chronic constipation. She was worried about the colds she occasionally caught, her shortness of breath, and her morning coughing spells—attributing the latter to her excessive smoking. She also suffered from periodic attacks of migraine on the right side of her head. She still walked with the slight limp of her right leg Freud had noticed in 1900. To her various physical sufferings, her husband remained indifferent. Although she was convinced that he had been unfaithful to her, she could not decide if she should divorce him. "She denounced men in general as selfish, demanding, and ungiving."[8]

Dora's son, now seventeen and just graduated from *Gymnasium*, had begun to move away from her and focus his interests outside the home. "He often stayed out late at night and she suspected he had become interested in girls. She always waited, listening, until he came home." She did not know if he would continue with his studies and had little hope that he would follow in the illustrious footsteps of her brother.[9]

Dora was proud of Otto's career. For a while he had been the foreign minister of the new Austrian Republic and was now the ideological leader of the Social Democratic Party. She was extraordinarily fond of Otto and remembered the two of them as always being very close. Otto could be depended upon to visit her when she needed him, and she compared him favorably with her self-centered father, whose unfaithfulness to her mother and affair with Mrs. K. she still thought of with anger.[10]

Felix Deutsch had been called in to see Dora by an ear, nose, and throat specialist who had been treating her for Ménière's syndrome, which had kept her bedridden for some time. She had ringing in the ears, dizziness, and decreased hearing in the right ear, and continual noises in this ear prevented her from sleeping. The referring physician had found no pathology when he had examined Dora's inner ear, nervous system, and vascular system. Since his patient seemed "nervous," he thought a psychiatric examination might be in order. After hearing Dora's history, her complaints about her life, and being proudly told by her that she had been Freud's patient—"a famous case in psychiatric literature," she boasted—Deutsch told Dora that he thought her current symptoms had to do "with her relationship to her son and with her continual listening for his return from his nightly excursions." Dora was receptive to this interpretation and asked Deutsch to return for another consultation.[11]

When Deutsch revisited Dora's home, he found her out of bed; she declared that her dizziness and tinnitus were gone. She thanked him "eloquently" and said she would send for him once more if she got sick; however, she never called again. Shortly after Deutsch's visit, Otto telephoned him several times, "expressing his satisfaction with her speedy recovery. He was greatly concerned about her continual suffering and her discord with . . . her husband. He admitted it was difficult to get along with her because she distrusted people and attempted to turn them against each other." Otto requested an office appointment with Deutsch, "who declined in view of Dora's improvement."[12]

Writing about his contact with Dora, Deutsch remarked on her propensity to use her sensory perceptions in her hysterical symptoms. Freud had already noted her displacements of the senses of taste (her disgust), vision (her looking away from romantically involved couples), and touch (her shifting to her upper body the feeling of Mr. K.'s penis against her). Now Deutsch observed her use of auditory perception in her Ménière's syndrome, which brought to his mind the connection of Dora's childhood dyspnea with overhearing her parents' lovemaking. Deutsch argued that Dora was using her sensory symptoms as a defense to ward off guilty feelings. He also believed that she tried to keep guilt at bay "by an identification with her mother. . . . Dora resembled her not only physically but also in [her] excessive cleanliness. . . . She and her mother saw the dirt not only in their surroundings, but also on and within themselves. Both suffered from genital discharges." Deutsch was tempted to draw the "somewhat fatalistic conclusion . . . that [Dora] could not escape her destiny." However, he qualified this judgment by blaming Dora for her continued illness. Her masochistic and vengeful departure from psychoanalysis had wrecked her future, and Deutsch exonerated Freud for overlooking the transference.[13]

It is safe to assume that this was not the first time illness had plagued Dora since she had last seen Freud. If the anger and disappointment she felt—both at her son's growing up and pulling away from home and at his decision not to pursue a conventional professional career—if these feelings could arouse such debilitating symptoms, one may imagine that other significant life experiences had probably done likewise: her parents' deaths, her brother's wartime imprisonment, her husband's permanent postwar disabilities, the loss of much of her inherited wealth, her own aging. It is known that throughout her life she was repeatedly treated for recurrences of the same conditions she had had as an adolescent: right-sided migraines, coughing spells, and hoarseness.[14] During her adult years, therefore, she must have endured multiple periods of sickness that heightened familial frustrations and tensions in a predictable, cyclical pattern. Her illnesses genuinely but mysteriously tortured her, their chronicity evoked resentment from her husband and son, she was further embittered by her family's lack of sympathy, and they drew away from her all the more. The pyre for the next hysterical attack was laid while the current one smoldered.

Even as Freud absorbed from Deutsch the news of Dora's most recent sickness and its broader implications, a chronic illness was embedding itself in him. While in its final manifestation Freud's sickness was purely physical, it had its roots in neurotic denial. In February 1923 Freud detected what he called a "leukoplastic growth." Leukoplakia is a condition of white, thickened patches on the mucuous membranes of the mouth. It is not an unusual finding in habitual, long-term smokers, which Freud, a smoker since the age of twenty-four, surely was.[15] But it is always a cause for concern. Freud suspected that what he had was no longer a benign leukoplakia, yet he told no one about it for two months. This was not the first time he had discovered something amiss in his mouth. In 1917 he had noticed a painful swelling of the palate, but it had receded uneventfully, for which Freud was most grateful since he knew very well that smoking had caused it.

Freud was psychologically and, most likely, physically addicted to cigars. There were times when he smoked twenty in a day. His father had been a cigar smoker, and for Freud, cigars and the ability to work went hand in hand. He had tried to quit in the 1890s when he was having heart problems, but the longest he managed to abstain was fourteen months.[16] His dependence on cigars was expressed in many letters to Fliess; once he was especially eloquent: "I have not smoked for seven weeks. . . . At first I felt, as expected, outrageously bad. Cardiac symptoms accompanied by mild depression, as well as the horrible misery of abstinence. [These wore off but] left me completely incapable of working, a beaten man. After seven weeks . . . I began smoking again. . . . From the first cigars on, I was able to work and was the master of my mood; prior to that, life was unbearable."[17]

In 1923, after carrying for two months the secret of the growth in his mouth, Freud knew he could no longer ignore it. He did indeed have this "rich man's cancer,"[18] although he and his doctors avoided speaking the truth for several months. The first operation on Freud's jaw and palate took place in April, but the procedure was merely a temporizing one. In October and November, Freud had three more operations in which the cancer was thoroughly excised, and he was fitted with a large prosthesis to replace the parts of his right palate and upper and lower jawbones that had been removed by surgery. After this time he always had trouble eating and talking, and he was usually in pain.

Faced with the full extent of his illness, Freud tried one dubious but understandably alluring cure. In November he underwent a "Steinach rejuvenation," an operation on the testicles—in essence a vasectomy—which was then in vogue as a sexual and health restorative. Eugen Steinach (1861–1944), an endocrinologist, was among the first to discover that the interstitial cells of the testicles produce the male sex hormone. Even before hormones were discovered, Freud had believed they existed and when found would prove to play a significant role in psychopathology. Thus he had a long-standing interest in the role of hormones in bodily processes and followed the relevant research work as it appeared. He knew that Steinach had hypothesized that the surgical tying off of the spermatic ducts would result in a hypertrophy of the sex hormone-producing cells, thus bringing about the "rejuvenation" of the individual. The argument went that since cancer was part of the aging process, making more hormone available to the patient might prevent a recurrence of the disease. Therefore Freud elected to have the procedure, a minor one, done five days after his last cancer operation. [19]

Even under these circumstances, Freud was unable to break his smoking addiction, and as a result, new leukoplakias formed. To deal with these, he endured repeated operations over the years, about thirty in all, and because of the many facial surgeries, gradually became deaf in his right ear. It was impossible to get an entirely satisfactory prosthesis that would do for talking, eating, and smoking, and his life was often a torment. [20] He avoided eating in public and, as his speech was impaired, shunned conferences and public occasions, although in the beginning, he continued to chair the Vienna Psychoanalytic Society's meetings. His youngest daughter, Anna, a fledgling psychoanalyst who never moved from her parents' home, became his nurse. [21] Thus Freud came to be intimately acquainted with the tradition of daughters nursing their fathers, although by this time in his career, his main theoretical interests lay elsewhere.

Freud spent the last several weeks of 1923 recuperating and learning to adjust to his prosthesis—he called it "the monster"—and then went back to seeing patients the day after the New Year. [22] He continued doing analyses and writing papers and books almost until the end of his life, sixteen years later. Indeed, the decades of the twenties and thirties were professionally productive and significant for Freud, in spite of advancing age and chronic problems associated with the management of his mouth disease and various prostheses. His theoretical writings dealt innovatively, although sometimes controversially, with human aggression, ego psychology, the psychology of large groups, the structure of the mind, female psychology, and the role of anxiety. His seventieth birthday in 1926, and succeeding five-year anniversaries in 1931 and 1936, were occasions for world acknowledgment and praise, although he never received the Nobel Prize, which he coveted and many would say he deserved. He had to settle in 1930 for the distinguished Goethe Prize, awarded by the city of Frankfurt.[23] He did not accept it in person but sent Anna with a small speech he had written on Goethe's relation to psychoanalysis and the validity of psychoanalytic biographies of Goethe.[24]

For Dora, too, life went on in spite of personal difficulties. Perhaps it could even be said that for a brief while she found a niche where she fitted in comfortably. In the years between the two world wars, playing and teaching bridge became the center of her life.[25] Bridge, derived from the old game of whist, was developed at the end of the nineteenth century and at first was a game played almost always by men in their clubs or in their country homes. After several years of this exclusivity, at the turn of the century, women began to play, and bridge became a social craze. It became fashionable in Vienna about 1930, and every respectable coffeehouse hired a female bridge teacher. There were also private bridge circles in which a woman bridge master taught middle-class women in their living rooms.[26] It was in this setting that Dora worked, surprisingly together with her old friend, Mrs. K.[27] At least for a while, Dora found a rewarding outlet for her intelligence. She also had something tangible to fill her hours, because by 1930, her son was no longer at home, having secured an assistant director's job with an opera company in Germany.[28]

In 1932 Dora's husband died of coronary disease, which, not unexpectedly, precipitated heart palpitations in Dora; these may also have been related to her cigarette smoking. "She reacted to these sensations with anxiety attacks and fear of death."[29] Frightened, she alarmed those about her as well. Someone who knew Dora at that time told Deutsch that "she utilized [her ailment] to play off friends and relatives against each other." This is a harsh judgment, but that Dora strove for sympathy and indulgence in whatever ways she could get them is not hard to believe.

Unable to express her feelings directly, Dora had been somatizing her unhappiness and unmet wishes at least since she was eight years old. It is understandable, then, that she developed a preoccupation with her body. The vaginal discharge—"catarrh"—she had had ever since childhood particularly bothered her. Identifying with her mother's compulsion for cleanliness as well as with Käthe's efforts to rid herself of her gonorrheal infection, Dora, at some time in her forties, underwent several minor gynecological operations in an attempt to cleanse herself permanently. Moreover, "the inability to 'clean out her bowels', her constipation, remained a problem to the end of her life."[30]

Dora's and Freud's lives in the early and mid-1930s were lived in the shadow of severe economic dislocation and ever-growing political authoritarianism. The Great Depression that began in the fall of 1929 led in Germany, with startling swiftness, to the parliamentary and popular prominence of Adolf Hitler's National Socialists, right next door to the small Austrian Republic. The crash of the American stock market also meant that all the European economies dependent on American investments were in trouble. Yet the events of 1929 and 1930 signaled not a beginning but an intensification of Austria's woes, because the republic had been floundering ever since the socialist rioting and police retaliation of July 15, 1927. From that time forward, the Social Democrats had not been an effective political force, and the Christian Socials hardened their grip on political life. Simultaneously, the Austrian followers of Adolf Hitler began to ape the propagandistic and terrorist tactics of the German Nazis. Under these disintegrating political and economic circumstances, it was only a matter of time before democratic institutions came to an end in Austria.

The Austrian economy could not stand on its own, yet in 1931 the Great Powers thwarted Austria's proposal for a customs union with Germany. Then, later that year, Vienna's largest commercial bank, the Creditanstalt, declared bankruptcy and was saved only by government intervention. Freud gloomily wrote his nephew in Manchester: "Public conditions . . . are going from bad to worse."[31] But Freud's private economic circumstances remained healthy, even though he was no longer practicing full-time. He was being paid in hard foreign currency, and his hourly fee was a steep twenty-five dollars an hour.[32] Dora could not have been in such favorable circumstances, even if she had a small inheritance left. Her work as a bridge teacher brought her not only pleasure but necessary income. She was fortunate that there still were women with some discretionary money for leisure activities, since unemployment was rife throughout the Western world, and Austria was no exception. The chronic 10 percent unemployment of the twenties now almost tripled, until in 1933 Austrian unemployment stood at 27 percent. Luckily, her son, not yet thirty, was employed in Germany and Italy. His achievement was a testimony to his considerable talent and hard-driving habits. But many of the youth in their teens and twenties were out of work, and they responded readily to the lures of the Austrian Nazis.

From 1932 on, the Christian Social chancellor, Engelbert Dollfuss, governed under emergency legislation, circumventing normal governmental arrangements. The democratic republic of Austria was tumbling to its demise. At the annual Socialist Party Congress in November 1932, many delegates felt that if Austrian parliamentary democracy and the gains made in social justice during the twenties were to be saved, this was the time—if ever there was one—for the socialists to use the revolutionary means they had long declared should be implemented in a crisis. But Otto's position at this crucial juncture was "equivocal" and fatalistic; the delegates were confronted with his "indecision and anxiety" regarding a strong socialist stance.[33]

After January 1933, when Hitler came to power in Germany, Dollfuss gained a useful model. On March 7 Dollfuss banned all mass meetings and demonstrations and invoked press censorship. It was clear to the socialists that he intended to eliminate the democratic state, and in several meetings they pondered whether to fight. A week later Dollfuss forcibly prevented the Austrian parliament from convening its session, thus ending democracy with a coup. When all was said and done, the Social Democrats did not resist—although probably by that point their action would have been futile—and the Schutzbund was dissolved by the government at the end of March.[34]

Of Otto and his behavior at that time it has been said that "like Hamlet, he knew what ought to be done; but also like Hamlet, he could not bring himself to do it."[35] Otto himself later recognized that "we shrank back, dismayed, from the battle. . . . We postponed the fight because we wanted to spare the country the disaster of a bloody civil war."[36] From the time Otto was ten, as his play about Napoleon shows, he had been worrying about internecine strife. He had spent his life trying to oblige his relatives, avoid confrontation, and keep the peace at all costs. If such behavior eventually had harmful consequences for himself and others within the family, how much more deadly it was when applied to the political fate of a nation. Yet what choice did he have to be other than who he was? As the bright, insightful firstborn in a dysfunctional family, he had taken upon himself the herculean task of holding that family together, and his preoccupied and self-involved parents had been only too willing to let him assume that role.

In Germany the Nazis established a dictatorship and crushed the opposition. The press was censored, free speech was abolished, opponents were shoved into concentration camps, there was open terrorism, socialists and Jews were fired from government jobs, all other political parties were destroyed, "un-Germanic" books—including Freud's— were publicly burned, and independent organizations of any sort were brought into line with Nazi policies. Freud noted the "mad times" but retained a tempered optimism. He did not think it inevitable "that the Hitler regime will also overwhelm Austria. It is indeed possible, but everyone believes that things here will not reach the height of brutality they have in Germany."[37]

The Austrians, including the Jews, were putting their faith in their chancellor, nicknamed the Millimetternich, a name that not only indicated his five-foot stature but signified their dreams of a time when Austria had dictated to the rest of Europe.[38] The majority of the populace, only too aware of the aggressive intentions of their German neighbor, convinced themselves that their determined chancellor, who believed in Austria's historic mission of defending Christianity against the infidel, would keep Austria independent. Thus they were willing to support him, believing the actions he took would be for the best. On September 11, 1933, at a mass rally of his supporters, Dollfuss announced the end of parliamentary government in Austria and its replacement by an authoritarian corporate state. A London journalist described the scene for his readers:

> It was all very picturesque and depressing at the same time. The Heim- wehr Regiments in their green uniforms were flanked by Tyrolean defence volunteers in their colourful traditional native garb. Hundreds of thousands screamed 'Heil' as the diminutive chancellor in his grey-green uniform of the Kaiserjäger, the Imperial Alpine Regiment, a military cape over his shoulder and a white feather on his cap, traipsed up the speaker's dais.[39]

The Dollfuss regime dressed its soldiers in the old imperial uniforms, and the Austrians allowed themselves the soothing luxury of being trans- ported back in time to glory and safety. Even those middle-class Viennese Jews who had consistently voted for the Social Democrats since the inception of the republic wondered whether the Millimetternich might not really save Austria and revive at least some of the yearned-for Habsburg past. They fortified themselves with the thought that Dollfuss had banned the Nazi party and argued that as long as an individual was not in politics, life would go on pretty much as before. They made some compromises, however, such as accepting discriminatory legislation that segregated Jewish and non-Jewish children in state schools. Also, many "had to join [Dollfuss's] 'Fatherland-Front,' but [convinced themselves it] was such an amorphous political entity, that becoming a member did not involve great issues of conscience."[40] Hundreds of Jews joined and wore the Father-

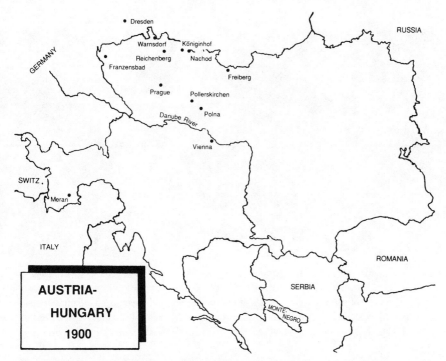

The Austro-Hungarian Empire at the turn of the century, with locations significant in the lives of Dora and Freud. With the exceptions of Meran, Vienna, and Dresden, the places indicated are now in modern Czechoslovakia. *(Drawing by William Decker.)*

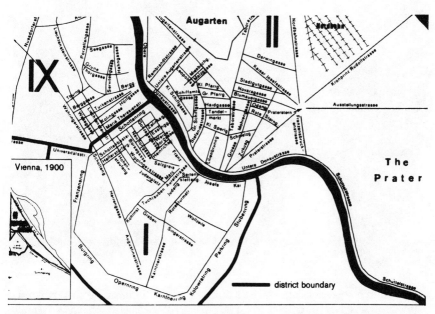

Both Dora and Freud first lived in the suburban and poorer Second District of Vienna before moving to the solidly bourgeois Ninth District. The nearby First District was the fashionable Inner City, encircled by the opulent Ringstrasse where Freud took his daily walk. *(Reprinted from* The Jews of Vienna, 1867–1914: Assimilation and Identity *by Marsha L. Rozenblit by permission of the State University of New York Press.)*

The well-known corner of the Ringstrasse and Kärntnerstrasse in the Inner City, as depicted by Maximilien Lenz in *Sirk-Ecke* in 1900, the year of Freud's psychoanalysis of Dora. The aura of prosperity and respectability exuded by the well-dressed middle-class populace concealed the many social ills and personal torments Freud and his contemporary, Arthur Schnitzler, saw all about them. *(Courtesy Historisches Museum der Stadt Wien.)*

A Jewish street vendor selling ribbons on another corner in the Inner City was emblematic of social strains. Newly arrived Jews, trying to eke out a living, were seen by Viennese artisans and shopkeepers as unwelcome competitors. Thus was born the modern political anti-Semitism that afflicted Dora's and Freud's lives. *(Courtesy Trustees of National Museums of Scotland.)*

Freud in midlife, not long after his psychoanalysis of Dora uncovered the neurosis, physical pain, and life-threatening disease in her world. *(Reproduced by permission of A.W. Freud et al.)*

The entrance to Dora's apartment house, Liechtensteinstrasse 32, in Vienna's middle-class Ninth District, just minutes away from Freud's own residence at Berggasse 19. *(Photograph by Hannah S. Decker.)*

Dora's father, Philipp Bauer, about the time of his marriage at age twenty-nine. He already had the syphilitic infection that was later to bring him to Freud for treatment. *(Courtesy International Instituut voor Sociale Geschiedenis, Amsterdam.)*

Dora at age eight with her brother Otto, age nine. It was at this time that Dora first took ill with a "nervous" shortness of breath and a radical change in personality, going from an active "wild creature" to a "quiet and well-behaved" child. The physical closeness of the two children accurately portrays their life-long attachment. *(Courtesy Verein für Geschichte der Arbeiterbewegung, Vienna.)*

Philipp Bauer, diagnosed with tuberculosis at age thirty-five, moved his entire family in 1888 to Meran (Merano) in the Tyrol. Thus, from age six to seventeen, Dora lived in the artificial environment of a mountain health resort. *(Photograph by Norman Decker.)*

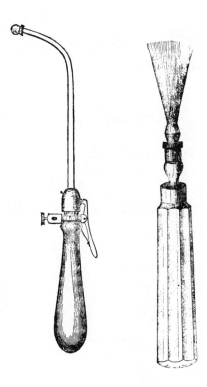

While in Meran, Dora developed health problems of her own. In early adolescence, her stubborn symptoms of cough and loss of voice were treated by neurologists with electrical stimulation to all parts of her body as well as to specific areas. The most extreme treatments she received were from an electric brush and probe inserted in her throat in order to apply electricity directly to her larynx. *(Reprinted from Wilhelm Erb,* Handbook of Electro-Therapeutics, *1883.)*

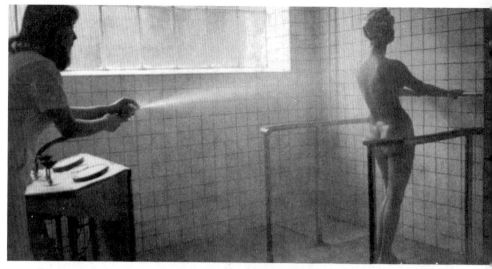

Dora also underwent hydrotherapy for her symptoms. Here a modern-day patient at Františkovy Lázně (Franzensbad), the Bohemian spa visited by Dora and her mother in the 1890s, undergoes the same cold "douche" frequently prescribed a century ago. *(Courtesy Balnea, Czechoslovak Spas and Springs.)*

At the home of her father's mistress, Mrs. K., Dora read popular sex manuals of the day, especially *The Physiology of Love* by Paolo Mantegazza, a well-known Italian anthropologist, physician, and sex reformer. Although the word "physiology" suggests anatomical explanations, in actuality the work extolled a highly romanticized love that had great appeal to a young adolescent, middle-class girl. *(Reprinted from the 1894 English translation.)*

THE

PHYSIOLOGY OF LOVE.

By DR. PAOLO MANTEGAZZA,

Author of "The Physiology of Pleasure." "The Physiology of Sorrow," "The Hygiene of Love." "Pictures of Human Nature," etc., etc.

". . . Questa cara gioia
Sovra la quale ogni virtù si fonda."—DANTE.

". . . This sweet joy
The foundation of every virtue. '—DANTE.

TRANSLATED FROM THE ORIGINAL ITALIAN EDITION.

NEW YORK:
CLEVELAND PUBLISHING COMPANY,
19 UNION SQUARE.

Dora, craving mothering and motherhood, was entranced by the young Madonna in Raphael's *Sistine Madonna* and sat "rapt in silent admiration" before it for two hours. *(Courtesy Gemäldegalerie, Staatliche Kunstsammlungen Dresden.)*

Dora saw Freud in his consulting room six days a week for treatment of her cough and loss of voice. In the course of the psychoanalysis, she related to him the stories of Mr. K.'s attempted seductions. *(Courtesy Edmund Engelman.)*

Bruchstück einer Hysterie-Analyse.

Von

Prof. Dr. SIGM. FREUD

in Wien.

Vorwort.

Wenn ich nach längerer Pause daran gehe, meine in den Jahren 1895 und 1896 aufgestellten Behauptungen über die Pathogenese hysterischer Symptome und die psychischen Vorgänge bei der Hysterie durch ausführliche Mitteilung einer Kranken- und Behandlungsgeschichte zu erhärten, so kann ich mir dieses Vorwort nicht ersparen, welches mein Tun einerseits nach verschiedenen Richtungen rechtfertigen, anderseits die Erwartungen, die es empfangen werden, auf ein billiges Maass zurückführen soll.

Es war sicherlich misslich, dass ich Forschungsergebnisse, und zwar solche von überraschender und wenig einschmeichelnder Art, veröffentlichen musste, denen die Nachprüfung von Seiten der Fachgenossen notwendiger Weise versagt blieb. Es ist aber kaum weniger misslich, wenn ich jetzt beginne, etwas von dem Material dem allgemeinen Urteil zugänglich zu machen, aus dem ich jene Ergebnisse gewonnen hatte. Ich werde dem Vorwurfe

---

The opening lines of Freud's case history of Dora, published five years after Dora's psychoanalysis. Worries about gaining an appreciative audience and concerns with medical discretion led him to withhold the case, even though it had been accepted for publication immediately upon completion. *(Courtesy The New York Academy of Medicine Library.)*

The anti-Semitism Dora had faced as a girl worsened with the passing years, achieving its nadir with the Nazi takeover of Vienna in 1938. Here a streetcar bears a large advertisement for a "special edition" of a vulgar anti-Semitic newspaper with the theme, "Judaism is criminality." *(Courtesy Associated Press/Wide World Photos.)*

land-Front's red-and-white ribbon. The Jews endorsed Dollfuss, and later his successor, in spite of the clerical-fascist nature of the regime, because they appeared to be the only effective barrier against the Nazis. Such loyalty meant determinedly ignoring clerics like the bishop of Linz, who urged his diocese that "it is not only the undisputed right, but the strict and conscientious duty of every devout Christian to fight against [the] harmful [capitalist and Bolshevist] influence of Judaism."[41]

Freud also supported Dollfuss, although the possibility that he might be in personal danger crossed his mind. He considered under what circumstances he would flee Vienna, since he realized that a right-wing dictatorship could be "exceedingly unpleasant for Jews." But he put his trust in international statute. The World War I peace treaties "expressly forbade [discriminatory laws] and the League of Nations would surely step in. 'And as for Austria joining Germany, in which case the Jews would lose all their rights, France and its allies would never allow that.'"[42] Although Dora was startled by events in Germany and worried about her brother, she nevertheless felt that her and her son's baptisms would keep the two of them safe. At any rate, most Jews in Austria expected, at the worst, "a moderate fascism."[43]

Moderate fascism turned out to mean elevating a Heimwehr leader to the vice-chancellorship and crushing the Social Democrats. The government seized its opportunity when socialists in Linz fired on some police who were conducting a search for Schutzbund weapons at a workers' club. The police stormed the building, and on February 12, 1934, the Social Democrats called for a general strike. But Dollfuss was prepared—indeed, eagerly waiting. The army, police, and the Heimwehr controlled the roads into Vienna. Instead of the workers marching into Vienna as they had done in 1927, government soldiers moved out into the working-class suburbs and began systematically shelling the workers' apartments with heavy artillery. Three days of fighting ensued, many hundreds died, and thousands were arrested. When it was all over, the Social Democratic and Communist parties had been outlawed, and socialist leaders who had not escaped were put into concentration camps. A few of those were eventually executed. Otto fled across the border into Czechoslovakia on February 13, and he and other Austrian socialist exiles set up headquarters in Brünn (today Brno).[44] Dora remained alone until her son returned to Vienna later in the year to become an operatic and orchestral conductor.

Freud's attitude toward the brief but bloody civil war is instructive because it was shared by many middle-class Viennese. In a letter to his son Ernst, a week after the insurrection, Freud wrote:

Now of course the victors are heroes and the saviors of sacred order, the others impudent rebels. Had the latter won, however, it wouldn't have been much better, for it would have meant a military invasion of the country [by Hitler]. The government shouldn't be judged too harshly; after all, life under the dictatorship of the proletariat, which was the aim of the so-called leaders, would not have been possible either. Needless to say, the victors will not fail to commit every error. . . . It will not be Dollfuss's fault; he probably won't be able to curb the dangerous fools in the *Heimwehr.*

The future is uncertain; either Austrian fascism or the swastika. In the latter event we shall have to leave; native fascism we are willing to take in our stride up to a certain point; . . . It wouldn't be pleasant, of course; but life in a foreign country is not so pleasant either.[45]

In a letter to the author Arnold Zweig, five days later, Freud reported: "Now [we have] the calm of tension . . . just like waiting in a hotel room for the second shoe to be flung against the wall. It cannot go on like this," he predicted, "something is bound to happen."[46] Freud was right. Five months later, the Nazis attempted a takeover of the Austrian government. It failed, but Dollfuss was killed. In the strange environment of the times, the dead fascist Millimetternich became a patriotic cult hero to most Austrians.[47]

The new chancellor was Kurt von Schuschnigg, a studious, distant thirty-four-year-old lawyer who continued to govern an independent Austria under emergency decrees. But most people recognized that the new regime was only providing a respite before the Nazis tried again. Dora could no longer feel safe. Under a Nazi regime, her and her son's Christian conversions would be undone by the Nazi Nuremberg Laws of 1935 that declared anyone with a single Jewish grandparent to be a Jew. Moreover, she was increasingly alone. She could visit Otto in Czechoslovakia, but he could not visit her or provide the emotional support and physical caretaking she had come to depend on. Her son's career took him out of the city to Salzburg in 1936 and 1937, and to Czechoslovakia in 1937 and briefly in 1938; in addition, he had married and was making a life of his own. If Dora was at all able to distract herself from her bodily concerns in those tense times, it was through pride in the sure progress of her son's career. For a while he was an assistant conductor—along with Georg Solti and Erich Leinsdorf—under Toscanini at the Salzburg Festival, and he remained to teach at the Salzburg Mozarteum.[48]

Austrian independence began to fade unmistakably in July 1936, when Schuschnigg made a pact with Germany in a vain effort to appease Hitler with half measures. The Austrian chancellor secretly agreed to allow the outlawed Austrian Nazi party to go about its business and to take into his cabinet some of the party's leaders. A year and a half later, Hitler became determined to be done with the game. After New Year's Day 1938, the signs in Vienna were unmistakable. George Clare, then eighteen, living not far from Dora and Freud in the Ninth District, remembered vividly:

> Spurred on from Germany, encouraged by the growing confusion of the Austrian authorities, our local Nazis became more restive and aggressive with every passing hour. Petrol and smoke bombs landed in synagogues. . . . Huge swastikas and Nazi slogans appeared on house walls overnight. Mobs of teenage boys and girls roamed the streets molesting anyone who looked the least bit Jewish in their eyes, including, much to the amusement of Vienna's Jews, a party of Italian fascist dignitaries visiting the city. These tightly organised Nazi groups were easily recognisable. They all wore white knee-length socks to show their political affiliation. Sporting the swastika badge was still illegal, but the police could hardly arrest someone because of the color of their socks.[49]

Within a few weeks, the Austrian chancellor accepted Hitler's "invitation" to visit him in Berchtesgaden. Having gotten Schuschnigg on to his own turf, the Führer surrounded him with German generals, forbade the chain-smoking Schuschnigg to light a cigarette, and shouted and threatened dire consequences if the chancellor did not cooperate. Schuschnigg was no match for such coercion and agreed to appoint the Austrian Nazi Artur Seyss-Inquart minister of the interior, with control over the nation's security forces. Freud was reluctant to face the reality of what was just ahead and still thought that Austria could remain independent. He fantasized defenses: "The Catholic Church is very strong and will offer strong resistance. . . . Our Schuschnigg is decent, courageous and a man of character."[50] In fact Schuschnigg did try to resist, calling a national plebiscite on the question of Austrian independence. But Hitler forced him to withdraw it and resign from the chancellorship in favor of Seyss-Inquart, who immediately invited German troops to enter Austria.

Schuschnigg capitulated on March 11, 1938. That night, around 8:00 P.M., George Clare, in his parents' apartment at the corner of Pichlergasse and Nussdorferstrasse, heard

> the sounds of hundreds of men shouting at the top of their voices . . . Still indistinct, still distant, it sounded threatening nonetheless. Those raucous voices grew louder, were coming closer.

I rushed to the window and looked out into [the empty street]. A few moments. Then the first lorry came into sight. It was packed with shouting, screaming men. A huge swastika flag fluttered over their heads. Most of them had swastika armlets on their sleeves, some wore S.A. caps, some even steel helmets. Now we could hear clearly what they were shouting: *"Ein Volk, ein Reich, ein Führer!"* they were chanting in chorus, followed by *"Ju-da verr-rrecke! Ju-da verr-rrecke!"* ("Perish, Judah!") . . . Coming from a thousand throats, screaming it out in the full fury of their hate, as lorry after lorry with frenzied Nazis passed below our window, it is a sound one can never forget.[51]

Not too far away, Dora and Freud, in their apartments, heard the same sounds.

On March 12 German troops crossed the border, and squadron after squadron of Luftwaffe bombers, all in precise formation, flew over Vienna. "City of Frenzy and Fear," was the London *Times* headline. Jews, including Freud, sat close to their radios, hearing the bulletins chronicling the takeover and, the next day, the proclamation of *Anschluss*—union with Germany. On March 14 Hitler entered Vienna.

The *Anschluss* was not just a transfer of power emanating from the German Nazi occupation. It was also an internal takeover of power by the Austrian Nazis and a spontaneous uprising in which the populace acted on feelings of anger and helplessness accumulated throughout decades of unwanted social change and economic and political disruption. As a result there were anti-Semitic depravities such as had rarely been seen in Germany up to that time. The German Nazis themselves soon realized this fact. Six weeks after the *Anschluss*, a writer for the official SS periodical, *Das Schwarze Korps*, noted: "The Viennese have managed to do overnight what we have failed to achieve in the slow-moving, ponderous north up to this day. In Austria, a boycott of the Jews does not need organizing—the people themselves have initiated it."[52]

Even before the German Nazis entered the city, local Nazis and impulsive mobs unconnected with National Socialism began to molest and beat Jews and plunder and destroy business and residential Jewish property. Soon customers of Jewish merchants and wholesalers, and clients of Jewish doctors, dentists, and lawyers, stopped worrying about paying their bills. "For many Viennese the *Anschluss* marked a sort of Jubilee Day, with all debts now erased. Adults entered Jewish-owned toy shops and candy shops with their children and, after allowing the youngsters to pick out what they wanted, left without paying."[53] The police looked the other way.

Jews became an entertainment spectacle. In the Prater, they were forced to dance and adapt humiliating positions for the enjoyment of leisure-time crowds. In the city, as passersby watched closely, Jewish children were made to deface their parents' stores and places of business. The favorite sport on the streets was a "rubbing party." Jews—youth, sex, or age was not a protector—were indiscriminately grabbed up and pushed to a wall or down on a sidewalk and forced to scrub out the Schuschnigg plebiscite slogans. The lucky ones had regular brushes. Many had to use their hands or toothbrushes. Some were given acid to rub bare-handed. The "party" atmosphere was provided by the onlookers, who quickly gathered around the scrubbing Jews to laugh and jeer. Mobs howled: "Work for the Jews, at last the Jews are working! We thank our Führer, he's created work for the Jews!" Lueger's anti-Semitism had borne its full fruit. Hundreds of Jews committed suicide to avoid arrest and maltreatment.[54]

The Catholic primate of Austria, Cardinal Innitzer, wrote a pastoral letter to be read from all pulpits, instructing Catholics to vote for the *Anschluss.* The Nazis therefore did not need to fabricate the official statistic of 99.71 percent approval for union with Germany.[55] Within a month ninety percent of the Viennese wore the swastika, popularly referred to as "the safety pin."[56] The "volcanic outburst" of popular anti-Semitism in Vienna convinced the Jews they must get out of Austria as quickly as possible.

Dora's son had already left.[57] He had been coaching a young American soprano, daughter of an influential lawyer. Right before the *Anschluss,* she had gotten her father to get a visa for her teacher from the secretary of state, Cordell Hull.[58] Dora's son arrived in the Midwest early in 1938 and became the conductor of an opera company. Two years later he married again and in 1941 became a naturalized citizen. Otto remained in Czechoslovakia for several weeks, watching helplessly, assessing his own safety and the future of his host country. In May he wisely concluded that he should leave, and he flew to France.[59]

Freud, because he was famous and had prestigious contacts, was spared the worst excesses, although he by no means escaped harassment and fear.[60] On March 15, three days after the German occupation began, Nazis entered his apartment to conduct a search. His daughter Anna took them to Freud's safe and told them to help themselves. On the same day, the officers of the psychoanalytic publishing house were also searched, and Freud's son Martin, who managed it, was held prisoner for the day. The Nazis left without finding anything damaging, but thereafter frequently recalled Martin to Gestapo headquarters in the Metropole

Hotel for questioning. At first the Germans were not willing to give Freud and his family passports. At this point, influential friends intervened to rescue him: the British psychoanalyst, Ernest Jones, who had friends in high places; Princess Marie Bonaparte of Greece, a longtime friend and follower of Freud; William Bullitt, with whom Freud had written a biography of Woodrow Wilson, and who was then the American ambassador to France; Secretary of State Cordell Hull, who got President Roosevelt to instruct the American ambassador in Berlin to speak to the German authorities there. Even Mussolini is supposed to have put in an official word.

Freud himself was not sure he actually wanted to leave Vienna, and Jones had to spend some time persuading him that the move was necessary. When Freud finally decided he would go to England, it was fortunate he was world renowned. He wanted to take sixteen people with him—family; in-laws; his physician, Max Schur; and Schur's family—and English residence permits were very hard to come by. Still, the exit permits from the Austrian authorities remained an issue, even though the necessary money could be procured. Any lingering doubts Freud possessed about leaving evaporated when the Gestapo returned to search his apartment a week after their first visit. This time they arrested Anna and held her for an entire day. There was a very real chance she could have been tortured or sent to a concentration camp, as was commonly done with Jews and anyone else who was suspect. Once more Freud's fame came into play, and most likely, some strings were pulled to get Anna released.

The Nazis required a large amount of money from Jews who wanted to leave the country. They had invented what seemed an infinite variety of financial demands, documents, and taxes before emigrating Jews could get the proper certificate declaring them "nonobjectionable" (*unbedenkliche*) individuals. For Freud, at this juncture, Marie Bonaparte stepped in and provided whatever funds were needed. Nevertheless the process dragged on and took many weeks.

> The proverbial Austrian sloth was now transformed into state policy and used to harass and offend the Jewish petitioner. Surprises awaited one at every office when, after queueing for hours at the still constant risk of being hijacked from the queue by a passing S.A. or S.S. patrol for a few hours of cleaning their barracks, one finally faced the official one had come to see. In eight cases out of ten one learned then that one had done it all wrong. Back to the starting point and get a chit to another office to get a chit from another official entitling one to talk to the first one. And when one had come back, duly equipped with the required piece of paper, after queueing for

another few hours, needless to say, then this stamp was not right or that document wrong and one started all over again. The inventiveness of the Nazi officials knew no bounds.[61]

Anna did most of the requisite negotiating and endless running of errands for the Freuds.

Just before Freud was finally let go, the SS demanded that he sign a declaration "willingly" confirming that "neither [he] nor [his] family circle ha[d] been troubled" and that Nazi party members had "always behaved in a correct and considerate manner."[62] Some of his family had already left Vienna, starting with his sister-in-law, Minna, on May 5. Freud, Martha, and Anna finally got their certificates of nonoffensiveness on June 2 and on Saturday, June 4, departed for Paris on the Orient Express. They arrived in England, their haven, on June 6, 1938. In fifteen months Freud was dead, killed by a malignancy that was no longer operable.[63]

Out of the approximately 175,000 Jews in Vienna at the time of the *Anschluss,* only 50,000 remained three years later.[64] Among those were four of Freud's sisters, who perished in the Holocaust.[65] Dora managed to emigrate to the United States, but not before she had lived through a hellish year.[66] The Nazis had sealed Dora and Freud in a common fate.

Dora's agony began on May 20, 1938, if not sooner, when the German Nuremberg racial laws of 1935 were introduced into Austria, declaring Dora a Jew and revoking her citizenship and the right to vote.[67] Now she watched in horror as hundreds of prominent Jews were arrested and sent to the Dachau concentration camp in Bavaria. This convinced Dora—if she still had any doubts—that she had to leave Austria. The Gestapo supported a policy of emigration to make Austria *judenrein* (cleansed of Jews), and a systematized organization to facilitate and accelerate this was created by SS Lieutenant Adolf Eichmann in the "Central Office for Jewish Emigration." Eichmann "was laying the foundations for his future career with his activities in Vienna. No one had yet accomplished what he did: to get the largest number of Jews out of a country in the shortest possible time, at the same time increasing the financial tributes demanded from those ready to go."[68]

Dora began the weary trek that all potential Jewish emigrants faced by going to pick up the necessary forms, but she had to do so at a special office for so-called "racial Jews"—that is, Christians or those without religious affiliation who were defined as Jewish according to the Nuremberg Laws. Although the emigration process contained many enervating detours, the basic steps in getting a passport were to procure the correct forms and then clear the police, the economic and financial authorities, and finally, the Gestapo. If the would-be émigrés were successful, they got passports good for a very short while. Along the way they also lost most of their property. If they did not get an immigration visa or certificate from a foreign country in the week or two for which their passports were valid, they had to begin the emigration process all over again, but this time with most of their financial resources gone. Long lines formed outside the consulates of countries the Jews hoped would accept them: Great Britain, the United States, France, Belgium, Holland, and various South American nations. But this was still a period of worldwide economic depression, and most countries had highly restrictive immigration policies. George Clare remembers how "no country wanted Eichmann's Jews."

> It was all epitomised by the World Refugee Conference, held, following the suggestion of . . . the U.S. Secretary of State in Evian in the summer of 1938. There was not a Jew under German dominion who did not look towards that spa with hopeful expectations. The representatives of thirty-two countries assembled there, listened to evidence, conferred and deliberated, talked and considered: and, after a few weeks at Evian, came to the conclusion that they could not—oh, so regrettably—find a place for the Jews anywhere in the world.[69]

It seems most likely that Dora's son was trying to get his mother a visa to enter the United States, or that Otto was working on getting his sister into France, but neither of these goals could be easily accomplished. In the end the United States took only 28,600 Austrian Jews and France 1,600. Great Britain, so much smaller than both, allowed in almost 31,000.

Meanwhile, Dora, now fifty-six, had to dedicate herself to survival. Through various ordinances the Jews were pushed out of the economic life of Vienna, and their pauperization increased rapidly. By July 1938, soup kitchens were serving seventeen times the number of people they had been in February, and thousands of food parcels were being sent to people who were ashamed to line up publicly for meals. Moreover, Jews were being turned out of their apartments at an ever-rising rate, and Christians who wanted to were afraid to take them in. By late October, some of the homeless were living in windowless and doorless barracks without plumbing, in which rats and roaches ran freely.

If Dora met a friend or relative on the street, she dared not stop to talk. The Gestapo arrested Jews conversing in public and brought them to a special Search Office. Each person was interrogated separately, and if their accounts of their conversations did not match down to the smallest detail, they were kept as prisoners. In the midst of this mounting alienation, Dora got shocking news that made her sense of isolation even more acute. Otto, her one caretaker and protector in the world, was dead. He had died of a heart attack in a small Paris hotel room on July 4. If she did get the news of his stately funeral, attended by socialist leaders from all over Europe, with orations by the highest dignitaries, such as Léon Blum, the former French prime minister, she might have drawn a bit of comfort.[70] Nevertheless, since she had developed cardiac palpitations and anxiety attacks on her husband's death from heart disease, the probability is strong that these symptoms returned to plague her now that her brother had died under similar circumstances.

Harassment and persecution were endless. Three weeks after Otto's death, Dora was ordered to line up at night to get a special identity card required of all Jews over fifteen. The card contained her fingerprints and facial photographs; it was modeled after the records kept of criminals. Early in October, the local Nazi party planned a great expulsion of Jews to force them to speed up their emigration efforts. On Yom Kippur Eve— one wonders if such religious observances had taken on any meaning for Dora—SA men entered Jewish apartments and forced the occupants to pack their personal belongings and hand over their keys. The Jews were told they were going on ships or trains that would take them to Palestine. Some were actually put on boats in the Danube Canal. Jewish community officials intervened with the Gestapo, who then declared the exodus a "mistake," and after two days the Jews were allowed to go back home. The entire episode recalls the capricious medieval and early modern expulsions of the Jews. In 1420, Jews had been expelled from the Austrian lands as a result of the Hussite heresy and masses of the poorer ones set adrift in the Danube.[71] As in earlier times, Jewish families again lived in the uncertainty of never knowing what would happen next. Simultaneous with this mock emigration of October, German passports held by Jews were declared void unless they were marked with a red *J*. Anyone in transit without the red stamp was stopped at the borders of countries adjacent or near to Austria and Germany and returned to his or her place of origin.

The *Kristallnacht* of November 9–10, an officially planned rampage throughout all of Germany, reached Vienna as well. There, eight thousand Jews were arrested, four thousand Jewish businesses were closed and sealed, and Jews were turned out of their apartments. The state admitted to 680 suicides, but the actual number was much greater. Gestapo and Nazi party squads, often following denunciations by neighbors, searched through every corner of Jewish apartments, slit open mattresses, destroyed furniture, and took whatever money, jewelry, and silver they could find. Dora, together with other ousted Jews, was jammed into a public building—probably a school or prison—given no food, and forced to do gymnastics. If she slept, she did it standing up. Five thousand Jews were then deported to Dachau.[72] It is not known if Dora was among them.

The next month most of those deported were released, a repetition of the centuries-old, tormenting cycle of expulsion and remission. They returned to gutted apartments and found all Jewish groceries, bakeries, and butcher shops closed. Moreover, along with other Jews, they had lost access to their savings and stocks, and their land was put up for forced sale. In addition they were forbidden to pawn objects made of precious metals or stones, could not own an automobile, and had to surrender their driver's licenses. Finally, henceforth, they were not allowed to enter any public place. Obviously the Jews tried harder than ever to leave, and the Nazis even facilitated their departure in order to solve "the Jewish problem" and to gain funds needed by Germany. But as of January 1939 Dora was still in Vienna.

In February Eichmann raised the stakes, if further encouragement were needed. He demanded five hundred daily registrations for emigration. If they were not forthcoming, he threatened to curtail the release of prisoners from Dachau and Buchenwald. Those who were released were told they would be sent back to the concentration camps unless they left Austria within two weeks. At the same time the Nazis made an effort to gather the remaining Jews, Dora among them, in certain apartment houses. Jews living in "Aryan"-owned apartments were evicted, and Jewish owners had to take in the evicted Jews. By February 1939, one hundred thousand had left Vienna, and conditions for the remaining seventy-five thousand were so cramped that their quarters were barely livable. In March Dora had to register any foreign bonds she may still have had, thus destroying any income she could hope to get when she emigrated or any income she still derived from them in order to live in Vienna. In the same month, a decree made it obligatory for her, along with all other Jewish women, to change her name to Sara. This ordinance took some time to implement, so it was not until April 28 that her name change appeared in the official records.[73] She had to put "Sara" on her stationery and on any name plate. But the most humiliating aspect of the change was that every time she dealt with any person in authority, she had to show her new identity card, even if she were not asked for it.

Then, at last, after a year, Dora's travail came to an end. She had a visa to France.[74] For the final time she procured and filled out the proper forms, paid her emigration and "Jewish" taxes, and gave a power of attorney to a bank for whatever property remained, because by May 1939, all she could take with her were her personal belongings. From France her son was able to bring her to the United States, thereby ending the torment and terror of life in Nazi Austria.

It is likely that Dora did not live with her son in the Midwest and later on the West Coast, where he again went to work with an opera company, but instead resided in New York. By now almost sixty, she lived out the war years unhappily with many of her familiar physical problems. Then her constipation worsened. Did Dora suspect that she was suffering from her mother's mortal illness? Did she avoid seeking medical advice in order not to hear the dread diagnosis? By the time her cancer of the colon was diagnosed, it was too late for a successful operation.[75] Judging by her reactions to previous stressful periods she had endured, it is likely that her anxiety at this juncture was great. In 1945 her son accepted an engagement in New York, probably to be near his mother. Dora died the same year in Manhattan's Mount Sinai Hospital.[76]

Dora and Freud finished out their lives as refugees in foreign lands, sharing at the end the common destiny of the Viennese Jews forced to leave their homes. Their fate underscores the limits of human control, a theme particularly evident in Dora's life. We are all captives of specific, personal circumstances and of wide, impersonal forces; no one evades either neurosis or history. In 1938 it counted not at all that Dora had declared herself a Christian, nor that Freud—although accepting the fact of his Jewish ancestry—had rejected all religious practice and belief. The tide of anti-Semitism lapped at the shores of all Western countries in the early twentieth century, everywhere polluting the lives of Jews, even if only minimally. Where National Socialism held sway, the worst and even the unimaginable transpired. Freud and Dora, temporarily joined as therapist and patient in 1900, were linked together in their final years not only in a way neither had ever considered but under circumstances no one following the course of their lives would have predicted. The fame of the one and the obscurity of the other had ceased to weigh in the balance. That Freud's potential had been realized and Dora's had not no longer mattered. Their uniqueness vanished under the shared imperative of fleeing Vienna.

Epilogue: Dora Redux

From the moment the "Fragment of an Analysis of a Case of Hysteria" appeared in print, it exercised a magnetic attraction on all readers who found Freud's way of thinking congenial. Ernest Jones, a young neurologist in 1905, was immediately captivated and converted into an avid Freudian. "I well remember," he wrote a half century later, "the deep impression the intuition and the close attention to detail displayed in it made on me. Here was a man who not only listened closely to every word his patient spoke but regarded each such utterance as every whit as definite and as in need of correlation as the phenomena of the physical world. At the present day it is hard to convey what an amazing event it was for anyone to take the data of psychology so seriously."[1]

There is no better explanation than Freud's as to why his case histories were so appealing at the turn of the century. "I have not always been a psychotherapist," he commented.

> Like other neuropathologists, I was trained to employ local diagnoses and electro-prognosis, and it still strikes me myself as strange that the case histories I write should read like short stories. . . . I must console myself with the reflection that the nature of the subject is evidently responsible for this, rather than any preference of my own. The fact is that local diagnosis and electrical reactions lead nowhere in the study of hysteria, whereas a detailed description of mental processes such as we are accustomed to find in the works of imaginative writers enables me, with the use of a few psychological formulas, to obtain at least some kind of insight into the course of that affection. Case histories of this kind . . . have [an] advantage over . . . psychiatric ones . . . namely an intimate connection between the story of the patient's sufferings and the symptoms of his illness.[2]

The five case histories Freud wrote before World War I—familiarly known as Dora, Little Hans, the Rat Man, Schreber, and the Wolf Man— eventually achieved their apotheosis as teaching cases for thousands of psychoanalysts in training the world over, who have thus trod in the footsteps of the master, learning from each case, in an immediate and gripping way, the same lessons he once learned.[3] Freud was bold enough to anticipate this pedagogic use of Dora, pointing out in the "Postscript" that the "great merit" of the case was its "unusual clarity which makes it seem so suitable as a first introductory publication." The obvious message that trainees have ever since imbibed from the "Fragment of an Analysis" is that to neglect the transference is to write finis to the treatment.[4] But that is not the only way in which the case is a pioneering vehicle. It contains Freud's first mention of "fixation" as an arrest of psychosexual development and an unhealthy attachment to the point of arrest. The case also displays clinically two subjects that up to then had had only theoretical attention: the importance of the mouth as an erotogenic zone, and bisexuality. Finally, the notion of a primary as well as a secondary gain from emotional illness, the precise way Freud analyzed dreams, element by element, and the powerful role of sexuality in psychological distress are other fundamental points neophytes have never failed to absorb.[5]

In the past decade Dora's case has taken on new dimensions for psychoanalytic candidates who confront not only Freud's genius but his limitations.[6] Professional interest in Dora's treatment is first of all compelled by the extent to which Freud was blind to his own impulses and reactions. While Freud's conscious innocence of his own involvement has already been demonstrated through an analysis of his words and behavior, his inexperience is also thrown into sharp relief by the findings of modern clinical research. Today knowledgeable psychoanalysts and other psychotherapists freely admit, for example, that they may be aroused when a patient talks about sex; they recognize the situation as an occupational hazard.[7] When Freud analyzed Dora he was unaware of this and avowed that it is an easy matter to prevent sexual stimulation of both the therapist and the patient by dry and direct speech. All it took was calling a penis a penis. Because he had to believe what he was doing was scientific and ethical, Freud shoved his sexual arousal out of conscious awareness. Yet his feelings surfaced in a variety of ways, to the detriment of the treatment.

Remarkably, recent findings confirm as typical, in a large number of male psychotherapists, the particular behavior Freud displayed in treating Dora.[8] They recognize that it is common for a male therapist, treating a girl who has been sexually assaulted by a paternal figure, to identify with the abuser and therefore raise questions about the girl's possible complicity in the assault. Frequently the therapist—like Freud—may "be titillated by the victim's story and become sexually involved with her in reality or fantasy."[9]

Moreover, a sophisticated analyst today knows that the therapy of a child or other dependent person can be affected by the attitudes and wishes of the person who foots the bill.[10] Practically speaking, an analyst often serves two masters and has to balance his or her beliefs between what will best help the patient and what a significant family member demands. Like all therapists, Freud faced this problem.[11] He never confronted Philipp Bauer with what Dora had related to him about her father's love affair and Mr. K.'s sexual overtures. In a patriarchal society, Freud was under pressure to please the head of the family, who was not only an authority figure eliciting empathy but was paying his fee as well. Freud tried to work out a solution that would cure Dora of her symptoms while simultaneously accommodating Philipp Bauer, who had after all deposited his daughter in Freud's office with the heartfelt plea to "bring her to reason." Besides its other meanings, Freud's suggestion that the Ks get divorced and Dora marry K. was a satisfying compromise— naturally on an unconscious level—that met Freud's scientific and personal needs.[12]

Throughout his life Freud paid scant attention to countertransference; the term appears in only two papers of his formal writings.[13] Furthermore, he regarded it as a dangerous phenomenon that the analyst must never allow to occur. If the psychoanalyst recognized in him- or herself strong positive or negative feelings toward the patient, that was a sure sign of incompetence and neurosis; the analyst probably should stop practicing the profession and seek his own psychoanalysis. Freud thus created the myth of the perfectly analyzed, totally neutral, utterly objective analyst. Of course, such a person does not exist. But the myth terrorized the first two generations of psychoanalysts into fear and silence. No one was going to admit publicly to the dread countertransference. It was not until the 1950s that the subject began to draw even a small amount of attention in the analytic literature. This departure was owed somewhat to the analysts of the neo-Freudian school, who stressed the importance of social and cultural factors in the development of personality, but even more to those influenced by Melanie Klein and the British school of object relations, who focused on the child's interper-

sonal relationships.[14] In the United States, however, the classical Freudian establishment echoed Freud's original viewpoint well into the 1960s.[15]

Starting abroad in the late 1960s, and then gradually in this country
in the 1970s, countertransference began to be recognized as a normal
phenomenon and even cited as a useful vehicle in psychoanalytic treatment. But this new view was accepted only slowly, and an analyst's
admission that strong emotions had been aroused by the patient could still
draw censure in a public forum.[16] In the past decade, discussing the
countertransference has come into vogue, finally legitimate. Now it is
argued that "a constant, ongoing transference-countertransference interaction is intrinsic to the analytic process. . . . Clinicians must consider
the countertransference as a counterpart of infantile factors in the therapist with which the patient is getting in touch. . . . Treatment success or
failure is a complex issue that stresses the irrational parts of both the
therapist's and the patient's personalities."[17] At last the Dora case can be
taught to psychoanalytic candidates for what it is: a compelling example of
the mutual influence of a patient's and analyst's intense, submerged
feelings.

It is for good reason that psychoanalysts have taken eighty years to
reach this point. To know one's unconscious is arduous and stubborn
work, and it takes bravery to discuss those findings publicly. The daily
process of self-analysis, advocated by Freud, is conscientiously pursued
by only a tiny minority of psychoanalysts.[18] Thus the discovery and
taming of the countertransference continues to exist as one of the major
challenges for therapists—and actually all physicians as well. A recent
study of experienced, board-certified internists showed that even "sea-
soned, highly trained physicians harbor strong emotional reactions that
may affect their physician-patient interactions. . . . Traditional education
and experience do not eradicate [such] reactions." No matter how practiced—their mean age was fifty—these doctors reacted as Freud did to
Dora. They most often responded to the detriment of their patients in
three circumstances: when the patients were disrespectful, critical, or
demeaning; when they expressed anger; and when they interrupted the
conversation, did not listen, or changed the subject.[19] Almost a century
after Dora, the prognosis is still less favorable for patients "of very
independent judgement."

After 1915 Freud published nothing on the subject of the countertransference. Still another area he scanted, after initial exploration, was
the role of the family in human neuroses. This fell by the wayside when he
abandoned the seduction theory of hysteria in favor of the theory of

instinctual infantile sexuality. Today many psychotherapists quite sympathetic to psychoanalysis, as well as a number of analysts themselves, believe Freud's change of focus from the family to the individual and from the environment to innate, organic factors limited the effectiveness of psychoanalysis.[20]

Currently, psychoanalysts who consider the family as a system amenable to scientific study have united family-systems theory with analytic principles. They have noted that Dora was part of a pathological familial interaction whose like they have repeatedly observed and that has produced children with the same symptoms and psychology Dora manifested.[21] Such "dysfunctional" families are scrutinized either from the vantage point of the parents' relationship or from the child's loss of autonomy. Both models explain how Dora emerged from her familial and social environment emotionally crippled.

The first family approach concentrates on Dora's father as a powerful, exciting, attractive figure but also narcissistic, demanding, and exploitative. Dora's mother is seen as a distant, ungiving person who was demanding in her own way. She was the subordinate partner in the marriage but channeled her emotions into preoccupations that gave her some feeling of control of her environment. Philipp and Käthe were unable to satisfy each other's desires and each felt rejected by the other. When Philipp's incessant needs for care were inevitably frustrated by Käthe, he saw her as a bad person, turned away from her, and openly disparaged her. Käthe, dependent on outside confirmation for validation of her worth, defended herself against Philipp's attacks by retreating even further into herself, withdrawing all the more whatever nurturance she had been able to give. Dora and Otto were the victims of the war between their parents and frequently felt in some way responsible for the turmoil in the household. Philipp often turned to Dora for the gratification of many needs, making her into a parent who took care of him as well as seducing her into feeling like his wife. Father and daughter united in demeaning Käthe. Dora's mother, feeling increasingly isolated and beleaguered, tried all the harder to exert whatever household control she could. Sometimes she was able to enlist Otto to her side, strengthening the familial polarization that already existed.

Käthe allowed the intense father-daughter involvement and Dora's domination by Philipp because it relieved her of meeting her husband's expectations. Ever more, Käthe appeared in the family as a cold yet submissive woman, depressed and dreary. In the end Dora identified with her dominant father as a way of mastering her environment, and as an adult tried repeatedly to recreate with other people the same power relationship she had with Philipp, except in reverse. Now she was seductive, manipulative, and exploitative when trying to satisfy her desires. Yet Dora, since she was a girl, also identified with her devalued, victimized, and depressed mother, and at times in her adult life felt and responded as Käthe did.

When manifesting hysterical symptoms, Dora was identifying primarily with her father (and this eventually became her predominant mode of being). Starting when she was twelve, she began to express her various feelings and especially distress about her father's affair and the ambivalent role of Mr. K. in her life. But she did so indirectly, in the covert way the whole Bauer family dealt with her father's affair.[22] At times, however, Dora identified with her mother and got quite depressed. This occurred at the age of fifteen, when her father treated her exactly as he had her mother, refusing to believe her story of the scene by the lake and thus devaluing her just as he had Käthe for many years. Feeling victimized, Dora became depressed and eventually suicidal.

Viewing the Bauer family from the alternative vantage point of Dora's loss of autonomy, one plumbs below the surface of its "orderly, respectable, and conventional" veneer to find "secret obligations. . . and mutually ignored dishonesty." Dora's family was "enmeshed," a term used by family therapists to describe a situation where the autonomy of each person is ignored and the members intrude on each other's "psychological privacy."[23] The children in such families are raised to serve others and gain their approval. One immediately thinks of Dora as a small child, nursing her father; never visiting her friend Mrs. K. when her father was there; taking care of the Ks' small children in order to give her father and his mistress private time together. Dora's sense of worth was especially dependent on affirmation from her father and Mrs. K., and in Meran, a town mainly of transients, she had little other emotional support. That is why the Ks' and her parents' denial of her reality when she was fifteen made her so desperate. Suddenly the vital figures in her life turned against her. Fast on the heels of these losses came Otto's temporary abandonment of her for his own pursuits, and then the death of her treasured Aunt Malvine. Dora in midadolescence was as angry at being bereft of the care she counted on as she had been as a child. Her anger acted not only to perpetuate the cough, aphonia, and hoarseness that had plagued her since she was twelve but to plunge her into an increasingly deepening depression.

Dora's adult character, which many found difficult, stemmed from her parents' rewarding her when she gratified the desires of others and discouraging her when she attempted to act independently and satisfy her own wishes. Lacking emotional warmth from her mother but receiving praise for her flattery and prettiness from her father, Dora unwittingly struck a bargain: She accepted the adults' notice of her intellectual and physical attractiveness as a replacement for the true nurturance a child needs; she was manipulated and learned to manipulate as a substitute for honesty and assertion; and she came to believe that seductiveness is equal to sexuality.[24] Felix Deutsch commented on her "flirtatious manner" with him when he came to evaluate her Ménière's syndrome.[25] In this second family-systems model, there is an obvious correspondence between the way the Bauers dealt with their daughter and the wider society's treatment of women.

At present, when a severely depressed eighteen-year-old is brought for treatment to a psychoanalyst and a family picture like Dora's emerges, the analyst will rarely recommend analysis as the primary treatment modality. The therapist will, to be sure, agree the adolescent needs care, but he or she will also stress the necessity for some form of family therapy, for without that the odds for the young woman's being substantially helped—as long as she lives at home—are small.[26] The family therapy can be marital counseling for the parents combined with separate psychotherapy for the adolescent or psychotherapy for the entire familial unit.[27] But in a case like Dora's, family therapy alone may not be sufficient, since the sexual seduction by the "family friend" requires prompt attention. To some extent Dora received some rudimentary help from Freud along these lines simply because he was the first person to believe her as well as to enlist the trust necessary for her to relate Mr. K.'s initial seduction attempt. But Freud could go no further. His countertransference intervened, the mores of his period led him to see K. as a suitable partner, and his knowledge of certain theoretical and technical matters was not yet developed.

Adolescents must come to terms with their sexuality, grow away from their families, and find social acceptance of their burgeoning adult selves. Freud did not fully understand these crucial developmental tasks in 1900 and was also well on the path to concluding that it was illusory to expect most people to accomplish them satisfactorily.[28] At any rate, he made Dora feel guilty about her sexuality by telling her that her masturbating as a child had caused her to be ill and that the vaginal discharges and gastric pains she was currently suffering could also be traced back to masturbation. Focusing only on her childhood oedipal development, he overlooked the new and distinct traumas of being ousted from her father's sickroom and handed over to Mr. K. when she was twelve. These events had malignant significance for her task of healthy separation from parental figures. When she was fifteen, her identity as a maturing, trustworthy adult was crushed by her parents' refusal to accept her story of K.'s proposition. This was doubly compounded by the Ks' betrayal, especially that of Mrs. K., who for three years had played the role of a warm, giving mother and offered Dora a better adult identification—however flawed— than her own victimized mother could provide. Although brought to Freud against her will, Dora in desperation turned to him for justice and valida- tion. But he was ignorant of their significance and could not supply them.

The "Fragment of an Analysis," writes Janet Malcolm evocatively, "reads like an account of an operation being performed on a fully awake patient."[29] Not only did Freud lack an awareness that adolescents had a specific psychology, but he was pessimistic about the possibility that any individual might achieve normalcy after living through the perilous oedipal stage. In general, in the first four decades of the century, psychoanalysts paid little attention to adolescence because of notions that "personality structure was basically fixed at the resolution of the oedipal stage [c. 6 years], and that significant personality development did not continue beyond that period."[30] In 1957 Anna Freud could still accurately describe adolescent psychology as a "*stepchild* in psychoanalytic theory."[31] In the 1960s, however, adolescence was "discovered," and Erik Erikson was one of the first to use the new understanding to reevaluate Freud's treatment of Dora. As the twentieth century draws to a close, the distinctiveness and longevity of adolescence in the West, the partial success of the feminist movement, and the receptivity of psychoanalysts to the idea of personality change throughout life all mean that a teenage girl with Dora's problems will usually encounter analysts and other psychotherapists responsive to the specific concerns of her age.

Not only was Freud unaware of vital theoretical issues, but he lacked expertise in certain technical areas. He was still ignorant of the special challenges that the termination of an analysis brings. There probably is never an entirely satisfactory way to say good-bye in an intense relation- ship like a psychoanalysis, but modern analysts know the moment has to be prepared for over a period of time. Freud allowed Dora's abrupt departure to the detriment of the therapeutic relationship. Dora actually dealt better with it than Freud. At first she was—understandably—"all in a muddle," but then, temporarily helped by the analysis, her life im- proved. When she developed a new symptom she was able to return to Freud for additional treatment. But Freud would not take her back because he could not forgive her for leaving him—he was that angry.

Moreover, since he had abandoned the seduction theory after applying it for only a few years, Freud had been unable to amass the kind of expertise that would have provided him behavioral guidelines for treating a girl who had been exposed to untoward sexual pressures.[32] In recent years psychotherapists have schooled themselves in the knowledge that the victim of a seduction has "heightened sensitivity to sexual innuendoes [which] will usually enable her to detect such feelings in the therapist, affirming her feelings of shame and guilt." The shame may make her bolt from the therapy even when a trusting relationship has developed. She feels threatened and is suspicious, fearing "a repetition of the betrayal she experienced with her parents" or parental figures. "This basic fear of trust may cause the patient to flee . . . even though things seem to be progressing well. . . . Bitterness toward the mother [or maternal substitute] is likely to emerge. . . . [The] victim may view her mother's behavior as sacrificing her daughter's welfare." The young woman also wants to confront the perpetrators of the assault, "hoping they will accept responsibility [and] acknowledge that they have harmed her. . . . Confronting the family may be therapeutic as it allows the daughter to absolve herself of the guilt."[33] Freud did not even think it appropriate for Dora to seek outside help with Mr. K.'s proposition, arguing that Dora was "under the influence of a morbid craving for revenge. A normal girl [will not tell her parents but] will deal with a [sexual proposal] by herself."

Yet a general assessment of Freud's psychoanalysis of Dora, in light of what she might expect today, does not yield a totally black picture. Hysteria remained one of the most difficult illnesses to cope with in the first half of the twentieth century. The psychoanalyst and family therapist Helm Stierlin recalls that when he was a psychiatric resident in Munich in 1954, hysterical patients were being treated with "painful electrical currents."[34] The fact is that Freud did help Dora.[35] He got her to recognize some of her repressed emotions regarding her father and Mr. K., which led to a temporary amelioration of her hysterical symptoms. In spite of the many demurrals with which Dora countered Freud's interpretations, there is evidence from the treatment that she was moved to significant self-scrutiny.[36] By believing all that she told him about her relationship with K., Freud gave her the courage to confront the Ks. This belated act owed itself to Dora's sheer gut feeling as to what would make her better, but she probably would never have done it without Freud's laying the groundwork.[37] In all likelihood he also saved her from deeper mental illness by acknowledging the reality of her experience. She had entered treatment badly depressed, thinking of suicide, and having begun a dangerous distancing from life through fainting and amnesia.

Nevertheless the psychoanalysis did Dora permanent harm. Freud compounded her father's betrayal by his unconscious exploitation of her. His primary interest in her predicament lay in using her psychoanalysis to support his theories and his reputation; his interest in curing her, though real, was secondary. Furthermore, Freud's sexual intrusion, although again unconscious, mimicked only too well Mr. K.'s and her father's. To whatever extent Dora had come to believe that the adult world was manipulative and scheming before she got onto Freud's couch, the analysis helped to solidify her view.

_____

The present-day study of the Dora case is not confined to psychoanalytic institutes but has become a part of the undergraduate collegiate curriculum as well. "Dora" is used in the classroom to assess society's attitudes toward women and the roles it sanctions for them, to study the commingling of familiar pathology and broad-scale malaise, and to illustrate how a psychological illness simultaneously reflects social imperatives.

For a Jewish woman in fin-de-siècle society, it is hard to tell whether anti-Semitism or misogyny was more ruinous. In truth, Jewish women and girls bore the burden of the two linked. Evidence of this association in the minds of the populace began to surface in Vienna at the start of the twentieth century. Georg von Schönerer, the anti-Semitic pan-Germanist, reviled the feminists who were demanding the vote: "In general, it is unoccupied women who devote themselves to the idiocy of female suffrage, women who have failed in their calling as women or who have no wish to answer it—and Jewesses. They naturally get the support of all the old women of the male sex and of all 'feminists,' that is, those men who are no men."[38] After the founding of the German League Against Women's Emancipation in 1912, its chairman wrote: "The modern feminist movement is, like Social Democracy, an international, foreign body in our national life. Both movements are, considering the great participation of the Jewish element, international in origin and fight, with equal fanaticism, against all fundamentals of the people's life."[39] That there was a link between anti-Semitism and antifeminism is undeniable.[40] Yet a Jewish girl like Dora was not only the object of this precisely tailored malignment but was simultaneously a victim of a general misogyny that was crippling in its breadth and intensity.

In the second half of the nineteenth century, many male literary figures and artists found their antifeminine sentiments confirmed by Darwinian science. Although their ideas were old, these men "saw themselves as standing in the vanguard of a new era of evolutionary progress. Science had proved to them that inequality between men and women, like that among the races, was a simple, inexorable law of nature."[41] The man embodied *Geist* (spirit or intellect), while the woman embodied instinct. Woman was meant to be erotic and uncomplicatedly sexual. The conventional art of the day, which was popularized for the masses through photographs in magazines, so frequently depicted women as scantily clad tree nymphs, dancing or sprawled on the ground, that one would think the woods were truly full of them! The nymphs were "mythologized representatives of women as passively sexual, self-involved creatures," pleasurably lounging, languidly stretching, tempting men to take them.[42] Also portrayed cavorting hand in hand or in groups, the nymphs of the woods and streams sent the "scientific" message that once women escaped from civilized men's rule, they reverted to their wild and sex-crazed nature. "Nymphomania," a "degenerative" condition of certain women with an "abnormal" interest in sexual gratification, first began to be described as a pathological syndrome after 1860. The insatiable nymph had become a medical fact.[43]

Even here misogyny was linked with anti-Semitism. The satyrs and fauns—men who were part animals—with whom the nymphs caroused, were drawn like the caricatured Jews of cartoons: dark, hairy, and with long, curved noses. And Jews shared the label "degenerate" with nymphomaniacs.[44] Dora lived in a society where everything Jewish was degraded, including Jewish men, who were stereotyped as animals and beasts.

There are two ideal places to observe the exact kind of derogation of women that surrounded Dora. One is in the pages of *Die Fackel,* the popular periodical edited by the Jewish—although Jew-hating—satirist Karl Kraus, and the other is at the meetings of the Vienna Psychoanalytic Society. *Die Fackel* regularly found its way into the homes of the Viennese bourgeoisie, especially those who were Jewish. Freud read it faithfully in its early years—before Kraus turned his venom on psychoanalysis—and there is every reason to assume that the Bauers also subscribed to the periodical.

The cynical attitude of the middle class toward women was evident in the lives of Freud's female patients and his own daughters. Marriages were frequently contracted with business and social interests in the foreground.[45] It is even possible, therefore, that Dora's inherited fortune was a strong motivation for the marriage proposal of her unemployed bridegroom, a man her parents did not like. At any rate, a woman could not count on respect from her husband when he had wed her for financial reasons. Two or three years after Dora's wedding in December 1903, Kraus sneered: "Whether a woman rents out her body for hours or for years, whether she sells herself within matrimony or without isn't the government's business."[46]

Kraus did not expect a woman to make rational decisions, think logically, or even be truthful. He assumed she would act dishonestly if bribed with new clothes or the like. And since he took it for granted that she was in an arranged marriage and, therefore, in the regrettable position of being somewhere between "a beast of burden and a sex object," he did not expect her to be faithful to her husband. In one issue of *Die Fackel,* Kraus commented on the case of a woman who was being tried for burning down a house at the instigation of her lover. Kraus did not consider her guilty, "for she certainly could not have been expected to refuse her lover's request." What Kraus called the female's "charming feeblemindedness" was destroyed by the intellectual or emancipated woman. A woman who wrote for the public lost her sexual attraction, and a woman who fought for the equality of women with men represented a "perversion" of womanhood.[47]

This was the hard-edged, sardonic commentary enjoyed by the Bauers' social circle and neighbors, including Freud. Having read a very favorable review in *Die Fackel* of his "Three Essays on the Theory of Sexuality," Freud wrote to Kraus to enlist his sympathy in a dispute Freud was having with his ex-friend Wilhelm Fliess. He began his letter confidently: "That I find my name repeatedly mentioned in the *Fackel* is presumably caused by the fact that your aims and opinions partially coincide with mine."[48] Not only did Freud's and Kraus's views overlap on many subjects, including women, but Kraus's disdain for educated and politically active women was shared by most early members of the Vienna Psychoanalytic Society.[49] It would have been many years before Dora's attempts at self-education could have obtained a sympathetic hearing in Vienna.

In May 1907, the psychoanalyst Fritz Wittels (1880–1950)—only two years older than Dora—published an essay in *Die Fackel* calling attention to the "absurdity" of women becoming physicians. "Hysteria," he concluded, "is the basis for a women's desire to study medicine, just as it is the basis of women's struggle for equal rights. The suppression of 'basic femininity' has obliterated the 'true woman' known in ancient Greece." Wittels's article became the basis for a discussion at the Psychoanalytic Society and was supported by the musicologist Max Graf, the father of the five-year-old boy in Freud's case "Little Hans." Graf argued that women could never make important contributions to medicine because they lacked "suggestive power" and "authority." They should becomes nurses instead, thus fulfilling the mother's role. But Eduard Hitschmann chimed in to disagree with Wittels about female physicians being hysterics, although he did "admit that most female students are ugly and are true amazons (bosomless)."[50] And by 1913 Hitschmann had swung around to Wittels's viewpoint and equated women's studying with neuroses.[51]

In 1908 Wittels presented a paper, "The Natural Position of Women," and began by discussing "the problem of menstruation, which subsumes the problem of femininity." By the end of his talk he was broadly condemning "our accursed present-day culture in which women bemoan the fact that they did not come into the world as men; they try to become men [via the] feminist movement."[52] Freud sided with the twenty-eight-year-old Wittels, echoing his own letter to Martha of a quarter century earlier.

With his traditional views, it is quite understandable that Freud found nothing congenial in Dora's attempts to free herself from Mr. K.'s attentions, postpone marriage, and pursue her intellectual interests. Furthermore, in light of Freud's personal experiences with his wife, one can see why he was not sympathetic to Käthe Bauer's predicament and lacked insight into the dynamics of the Bauer family's pathological constellation. Martha Freud, too, seems to have been a compulsive cleaner. If not so drastic a one as Käthe, she nonetheless resembled her in having an "unremitting" call to domestic duty. Freud took note of Martha's ways immediately following their honeymoon and wrote to his new sister-in-law, Minna Bernays, after four months of marriage: "My wife scolds only when I spill something or leave something lying about in disorder, or when I lead her across a filthy spot on the street. It is generally said that I am henpecked. What should one do against that?"[53] The words might have been Philipp Bauer's as a newlywed.

Freud also quickly learned and, like Philipp, acceded to the fact that the house was his wife's to rule. Martha, for example, was insistent on punctuality. Anna, the Freud's youngest daughter, complained later in life of the household's "obsessive regularity." A granddaughter who frequently ate at the Freuds' remembers that the main meal of the day was always served at 1:00 P.M. precisely. Throughout the Freuds' marriage, Martha retained "firm control" of domestic affairs, and Freud always acquiesced in this, much as Philipp did. In 1920, when Anna wanted to change one of her rooms at home for another, Freud told her it was fine with him, but she had to consult Martha directly. He wrote to Anna while she was on a trip: "I cannot force her, have always let her have her way in the house."[54]

Freud had let Martha have her way, but not without accumulating some resentments along the way. When he was fifty-seven and Martha fifty-two, he wrote:

> It is a well-known fact, and one that has given much ground for complaint, that after women have lost their genital function their character often undergoes a peculiar alteration. They become quarrelsome, vexatious and overbearing, petty and stingy; that is to say, they exhibit typically sadistic and anal-erotic traits which they did not possess earlier, during their period of womanliness. Writers of comedy and satirists have in all ages directed their invectives against the "old dragon" into which the charming girl, the loving wife and the tender mother have been transformed. We can see that this alteration of character corresponds to a regression of sexual life to the pregenital sadistic and anal-erotic stage, in which we have discovered the disposition to obsessional neurosis.[55]

When he was forty-nine, Freud described women as full of "conventional secretiveness and insincerity"; when he was seventy-six, he found "that envy and jealousy play an even greater part in the mental life of women than of men."[56] Perhaps there was some truth to these latter angry generalizations, which could easily have resulted from the repressive circumstances under which middle-aged women in Vienna lived.

To judge from Schnitzler's short stories, middle-aged women were even more victimized than his sweet young things, having been forced early into marriages that were actually business arrangements. Adolescent girls like Käthe Gerber Bauer immediately "became mothers and were presumed fulfilled and finished."[57] Schnitzler portrays these middle-aged women as degraded nonentities, taken for granted; trapped, they exist only to serve others.[58] It is no wonder that Freud had the impression from his psychoanalytic patients that stark differences separated adult men and women. "A man of about thirty," he noted,

> strikes us as a youthful, somewhat unformed individual, whom we expect to make powerful use of the possibilities for development opened up to him by analysis. A woman of the same age, however, often frightens us by her psychical rigidity and unchangeability. Her libido has taken up final positions and seems incapable of exchanging them for others. There are no paths open to further development; it is as though the whole process had already run its course and remains thenceforward insusceptible to influence—as though, indeed, the difficult development to femininity had exhausted the possibilities of the person concerned. As therapists we lament

this state of things, even if we succeed in putting an end to our patient's ailment by doing away with her neurotic conflict.[59]

Freud was half wrong about the reason for his female patients' rigidity and lack of potential for psychic growth—that is, "the difficult development to femininity."[60] But he was accurate in reporting the results of misogyny he saw everyday in his office: the sad spectacle of middle-class women whose future was foreclosed although many of them had lived only half their lives. Confined to narrow roles, demeaned as incapable of significant political and intellectual activity, patronized by their husbands, hearing and reading daily of their own inherent inferiority, unable to bring to consciousness (much less fulfill) many of their desires, they frequently responded by becoming hysterics. Freud may have lamented this situation, but in some part he contributed to it.

As a hysterical woman, Dora evoked Freud's dislike. He complained of her "intolerable behavior" and of the "string of reproaches" she levelled at those she knew. He resented her general condemnation of the medical profession, and once she left his treatment, he would not take her back. Freud's reaction was part of an imbedded cultural phenomenon, and as such did not end with his generation. The hostility of physicians to women with hysteria can be traced right through the twentieth century. In 1924 Oswald Bumke (1877–1950), the psychiatrist who succeeded the world-famous Emil Kraepelin in Munich, attacked women with hysterical motor disorders, the commonly found "invalids" of the nineteenth century. Bumke took aim at "the familiar figure of the 'suffering' lady, who from bed, wheelchair or sofa tortures and tyrannizes over her parents, her husband, her children, and her doctor; she lies in a half-darkened room with cool compresses on her head, surrounded by an entire arsenal of devices for the care of the sick plus the latest novels; although she is not busy, she keeps the servants in an uproar, knows all the gossip, and spends her time in intrigue."[61]

Psychoanalysts did only a little better than Bumke. In 1955 Ernest Jones portrayed Dora as "a disagreeable creature who consistently put revenge before love; it was the same motive that led her to break off the treatment prematurely, and to retain various hysterical symptoms, both bodily and mental." Two years later, Felix Deutsch, who had seen Dora when she was forty, was content to use the words of a mutual acquaintance to sum her up as "'one of the most repulsive hysterics' he had ever met."[62]

As recently as 1975, Didier Anzieu, a French analyst, who hypothesized about the content of Freud's self-analysis, imagined Freud's "counter-oedipal defensive countertransference" stirred up by Dora. This is a scenario not only factually inaccurate, but a stereotypical depiction of the seductive, "sex-crazed" hysterical woman. Here we find Dora, on the make at eighteen, and Freud's reaction to this vamp. According to Anzieu, Freud thought: "Let us not allow ourselves to be led astray, like Breuer, by the incestuous wishes of a young and charming hysteric who has quite some experience in the matter: did she not seduce a friend of her father's, Herr K., a married man the same age [*sic*] as Freud?" Following this introduction, Anzieu relates his own version of Dora's story: "When she was 14, a great friend of the family, Herr K., the husband of her father's supposed [*sic*] mistress, had kissed her on the mouth: hoarseness ensued [*sic*]. When she was 16, the same man, she alleged, made a proposal of marriage [*sic*] . . . in very decent terms [*sic*]. [Freud] tried to get Dora to understand . . . that [K.'s] behaviour had been a rather natural response to the seduction she had been exerting on him."[63]

Anzieu's bias is so clear and so unflattering to Dora that it is hard to imagine a more extreme modern interpretation of her actions. Yet it exists. Writing at the same time as Anzieu, a psychiatrist, Karl Kay Lewin, portrayed Dora as a devious schemer and malevolent deceiver. "One could well imagine such a girl," Lewin observed, "leading men on, frustrating them, and finally destroying them altogether." What other motivation could Dora have had for telling no one of the incident at Mr. K.'s place of business except that "she was leading him on for an eventual denouncement?" Because she wanted Mrs. K. all to herself, Dora had led K. on as a decoy, luring him away from his wife and finally denouncing him for the lecher he was in the hope of permanently destroying his wife's marriage to him. . . . Hell," concluded Lewin decisively if not originally, "hath no fury like a woman scorned."[64]

What was the decisive milestone on Dora's road to an unhappy adulthood? She was not doomed to her lot at the age of six, when her father began confiding in her and using her as a nurse. Certainly, the intimate attachment to her father from six to eight, her mother's emotional withdrawal from the family after Philipp took sick, and Mr. K.'s sudden assault on her in his empty office were events that dictated the inevitability of some emotional dysfunction. Then her father's affair with Mrs. K. heightened the tensions already existing in the family and laid the basis for a deterioration of Dora's situation. Henceforth, Philipp's love affair was the Bauer family's secret which they all shared but pretended did not exist. This silent collusion meant that Philipp lied and the family had to act on Philipp's lies as if they were the truth; that Käthe was outraged and felt further victimized, but never said so; and that the children were party to numerous family scenes that arose from the fact of the affair but never actually dealt with it.[65] The collusion also produced the parents' blindness to K.'s pursuit of Dora.

But the crucial moment for Dora's future mental health came when she was fifteen and told her parents about Mr. K.'s sexual proposal, and her father declared—with her mother's tacit agreement—that she must have imagined the entire episode. Until this point Dora herself had been a willing member of the family conspiracy and an exemplary pupil of late-Victorian middle-class morality as well. After this she would not tolerate the affair and begged her father to end it. The longer Philipp persisted in proclaiming his innocence, the more distraught Dora became, ending by writing a suicide note and sustaining a loss of consciousness accompanied by convulsions and delirium. These dramatic events—no mere garden-variety hysteria—finally moved a "shaken" Philipp to take her to Freud, with the hope that the talented middle-aged physician would "bring her to reason." Although Philipp genuinely cared about his ill daughter, his depositing her in Freud's office was yet another bargain he sought to strike, as he had done with K., using Dora as the coin. One is put in mind of a long-ago king marrying off a daughter for dynastic purposes, or perhaps even a more ordinary man selling his child into bondage. If there had been any chance that Dora would not mature into a manipulator of those close to her, it vanished with the trauma of her father's betrayal.

One particular aspect of the environment that promoted Dora's personal misery was the illness surrounding her. To be sick, to use sickness, to identify with a sick person was a common fate. Dora's most frequent and chronic illnesses were the quite varied hysterias she endured. It is likely that throughout her adult years she experienced other physical maladies that lacked observable pathological changes. Her tendency to somatize was not by itself indicative of severe pathology, but the continual, lengthy, and at times disabling nature of her symptoms signified deep and unremitting psychic distress.

Dora's somatization further illuminates the social aspects of her hysterical symptoms. Why did Dora have the particular physical disturbances that she did? Freud argued that her cough, for example, was a sign of her unconscious belief that Mrs. K. satisfied her father sexually through fellatio.[66] That is what determined Dora's "symptom choice," in the phraseology of modern psychiatry. But this immediately raises a troublesome issue. Cough was one of the most frequent of all hysterical conditions in the nineteenth century. Certainly we cannot conclude that thousands of girls and women coughed because they were picturing to themselves scenes of fellatio. And if that matter is not provocative enough, what is to be made of the fact that hysterical paralyses, like Dora's aphonia and Mrs. K.'s astasia-abasia—the inability to stand and walk—were rare in the West until the start of the nineteenth century? Before that time the most often-occurring hysterical symptoms were ones mimicking epileptic fits.[67]

Judging by its modern universality as well as accounts in ancient Egypt about 1900 B.C., hysteria seems to have existed throughout time.[68] Yet its manifestations have changed markedly from era to era. While the explanation of its protean nature among women is far from definitive, the most frequent hysterical symptoms at any one time are caricatures of the feminine ideal of that period. In the Victorian era, "the restricted female role considered the norm by society actually demanded a heavy price and a compromise that many women could not easily make. Hysteria is the thorn in the rosy picture of soft femininity that was idealized by our Victorian forefathers."[69] The new hysterical symptoms of the nineteenth century—various paralyses, contractures, weaknesses, and difficulties in locomotion—were extreme representations of the ideal of weak, delicate, dependent, and even frankly sick women.

Hysteria is no longer a common occurrence in the late-twentieth-century urban West. But in its place there is a largely female disease whose manifestations correspond to a new feminine ideal: the illness of anorexia nervosa. The anorexic girl—typically starved, exercising to extremes, and perfectionistic in all her activities—is a hyperbolic version of the slim, strong, active, autonomous, accomplished young woman our society admires. Twentieth-century anorexia was seen earlier, but not in the epidemic and severe proportions encountered in middle-class girls of our day.[70] Anorexia is not hysteria in modern dress, but both illnesses are "a dramatic expression of the internal compromise wrought by Western women . . . in their attempt to negotiate their passions in [times] of extraordinary confusion."[71] Both conditions also show the role of the surrounding culture in producing or shaping sickness: The culture reinforces the familial pathology that fosters the condition.

The family of the anorexic girl is often "enmeshed" like that of the hysteric, producing girls eager to please and gain the approval of parents and teachers. The family constellation is similar to that of the hysteric but with important differences. The father is "vain, erratic, and seductive, while the mother is cold, obsessive and self-denying. . . . [But] the mother is not demeaned; rather she is the mainstay and strength of the family. The daughter perceives the mother as a model of perfection that is difficult to emulate."[72] Hysterical and anorexic girls are frequently fearful of maturity and sexuality. The hysteric rejects growing up by keeping alive her oedipal attachment; she succumbs to her body via a plethora of physical symptoms. The anorexic pushes away sexual expression by stern control over her feelings and her body; she diets and exercises endlessly. In each case the girl at first wins approval because she is meeting the social ideal. It is only later in the course of each illness that approval is withdrawn and the girl is found repugnant. The hysteric is overly demanding and often barely functional; the anorexic is unpleasantly skinny and undernourished. One hundred years apart, hysteria and anorexia—two emotional illnesses expressed physically—represent futile and self-damaging exercises in power by women who feel powerless.[73]

———

Freud concluded his discussion of Dora's treatment optimistically. Dora, in marrying, had been able "to tear herself free from her father and had been reclaimed once more by the realities of life." One wonders why Freud imagined a happy ending to Dora's story. Freud himself was generally a pessimist about life's chances for happiness,[74] and little in the case history supports the notion that a cheery future awaited Dora.

Dora failed, in fact, to fulfill the promise that had greeted her birth in the Bauer's new, upscale apartment in the Ninth District. The very intelligence and precocity that had caused her father to turn her into his nurse and trusted intimate bound her to him too tightly, and her mother could offer no counterbalancing warmth that might have given Dora some slack in the paternal silken rope. The outside world, crammed as it was with antifeminism and anti-Semitism, provided no counterweight to this early familial pathology. Aside from her family's money, only negatives ruled Dora's existence. She failed, therefore, to complete the developmental tasks that would have made her a resourceful adult. She was unable to secure a successful identity either as a wife or mother, and she never immersed herself in any significant way in volunteer or charity work that might have been satisfying. In the latter years of her life, she worked briefly, but her job as a bridge mistress did not define her.

In the short time during her later adolescence when she pursued an existence unlinked to marriage, Dora received neither guidance nor encouragement, a normal state of affairs for women at the time. Her aimless and unknowledgeable floundering in the direction of an alternate occupation was bound to lead nowhere. Yet because of her disappointing experiences with men, marriage beckoned her only weakly. Her relationships with her father, Mr. K., and numerous physicians had all ended unsatisfactorily. She was even temporarily estranged from her brother. When she was nineteen and a half years old she told Freud that "she was absorbed in her work and had no thoughts of marrying."

But with the one exception of her confrontation with the Ks after their daughter died, Dora had a history of succumbing to rather than overcoming circumstances. So, although she was at best ambivalent about marriage, Dora wed at twenty-one. In marrying a man who had no job, she chose someone whom she could regard as deficient, thus adding to the determinants which presaged a problematic existence as a wife. After her only child was born, she rapidly shed her Jewish identity and converted to Christianity in the hope that she and her son would have better lives.

One identity Dora did successfully maintain: a career as a permanent patient. She had been well advanced in the development of this behavior before Freud analyzed her, but the publication of her case history when she was twenty-three confirmed her in such a role. Perhaps it was the one thing at which she succeeded. She even came to take a certain pleasure in being designated as a patient. When Felix Deutsch treated her in 1922, she "display[ed] great pride in having been written up as a famous case in psychiatric literature."

Dora had entered on a career of sickness before Freud ever met her. Her parents and the Ks' disavowal of her integrity propelled her even deeper. But it was after she read her case report, that her identity as "patient" was truly sealed. In those pages she learned Freud's elaborate and authoritative theoretical justification of all he had told her and more. Not only was she condemned for the childhood masturbation by which she had supposedly wrought her own ill health. She received confirmation of a situation she had long feared: As a result of her father's venereal disease she was hereditarily ill. Freud had, quite correctly, been careful in the analysis to avoid telling her of his conviction that Philipp's syphilis had affected her constitution. But then in the published history, he displayed his opinion for the whole world to read. "Offspring of [syphilitics are] very specially predisposed to severe neuropsychoses." For Dora there was no escape.

The accounts that come down to us confirm that Dora lived a joyless existence most of her years and often burdened the lives of those close to her. She was tragically a prisoner of her time in every way. Although born into a well-to-do family, this came to weigh little on the scale of life. Her father and her mother became chronically ill, and Dora herself was surrounded by death during her childhood years in Meran. She shared the fate of countless bright Victorian girls and was gradually worn down by the persistent discounting of women in which even her mother and *confidante* played their unwitting parts. At an early age she became deeply enmeshed in tangled sexual relationships between her family and a neighboring one.

Brought to Freud at eighteen, Dora's bad luck pursued her. Although replete with errors of conceptualization, bias, and method, Freud's imaginative casting of her psychopathology was still correct in many respects. With all its shortcomings, the case study remains a tour de force. But Freud's brilliance alone was insufficient to divert Dora from the unhappy path on which she had been set in childhood.

After World War I, Dora, no longer wealthy, watched the goals for which she had lived increasingly elude her. Her husband was unfaithful to her and remained in broken health from his war wounds. He died in 1932, at age fifty-nine, leaving her panicky and suffering from anxiety attacks. At first, it seemed as if her son might end up an unemployed musician like his father. But then his talents were recognized and he received work. Dora could bask in vicarious joy, but only up to a point, because with increasing success, her son distanced himself from her.

Dora and Freud, after going their separate ways in Vienna for more than thirty-five years, became linked again for one final moment as Jewish outcasts. In exile Freud soon died, and within a few years Dora was dead from the same disease that had killed her mother.

Dora's life, like most people's, was not an extraordinary one. She deserves remembrance as a hapless individual, an accidental victim of familial pathology, social mores, historical upheaval—and the timebound limits of scientific knowledge.

Notes to Text

1. "In Spite of Her Reluctance"

1. References to Sigmund Freud's "Fragment of an Analysis of a Case of Hysteria" (1905c), *Standard Edition* (hereafter *SE*) *of the Complete Psychological Works*, vol. 7 (1953), appear in a separate notes section at the end of the text. All volumes of the *SE* referred to throughout were published in London by the Hogarth Press. The original German text appears as "Bruchstück einer Hysterie-Analyse," in *Gesammelte Werke, Fünfter band* (London: Imago Publishing Co. Ltd., 1942), pp. 163–285. I have used the English translation except in those few places where I think it has not captured the true flavor of the German; there I have supplied my own translations.

2. Julius Althaus, *Diseases of the Nervous System. Their Prevalence and Pathology* (London: Smith, Elder, 1877), pp. 248–49; Charles Féré, *Diseases of the Nervous System*, vol. 10 of *Twentieth Century Practice: An International Encyclopedia of Modern Medical Science By Leading Authorities of Europe and America.* (New York: William Wood, 1897), p. 553. For a modern historical summary see Charles Bernheimer, "Introduction: Part One," in *In Dora's Case: Freud-Hysteria-Feminism,* ed. Charles Bernheimer and Claire Kahane (New York: Columbia University Press, 1985), pp. 2–4.

3. Féré, pp. 455–57.

4. Althaus, pp. 251, 254. An example of the former would have been Frau Cäcilie M., a rich, hysterical woman treated by Freud in the late 1880s and early 1890s. See *Studies on Hysteria* (1893–95), *SE*, vol. 2 (1955), pp. 69–70, 103, 176–81.

5. Althaus, p. 256.

6. Charles L. Dana, *Text-Book of Nervous Diseases,* 9th ed. (New York: William Wood, 1920), p. 574.

7. Samuel Wilks, *Lectures on Diseases of the Nervous System* (Philadelphia: Lindsay and Blakiston, 1878), p. 364.

8. Ibid., pp. 365–66.

9. Ibid., pp. 367–69.

10. This theme is explored in chapter 5.

11. Indeed, electricity was thought to have wide efficacy for many diseases. The famous German neurologist, Wilhelm Erb (1840–1921), waxed rhapsodic in an 1882 treatise: "Electricity is an extremely powerful and many sided remedy, and . . . more

211

evident and undoubted curative effects may be attributed to it in diseases of the nervous system than to almost any other remedy. . . . Electricity is valuable in the treatment of neuralgia, anaesthesia, spasms, and paralysis [and] its introduction in therapeutics has caused a more favorable prognosis of many forms of disease . . . The curative effects not infrequently astonish even the experienced physicians by their magical rapidity and completeness." *Handbook of Electro-Therapeutics* (New York: William Wood, 1883), p. 104.

12. Erna Lesky, *The Vienna Medical School of the 19th Century* (Baltimore: Johns Hopkins University Press, 1976), p. 350.

13. Ibid., p. 351; Moritz Benedikt, *Elektrotherapie* (Vienna: Tendler, 1868); Wilks, pp. 465–69.

14. Letter to Carl Koller, October 13, 1886, quoted in *Sigmund Freud: His Life in Pictures and Words* (New York: Harcourt Brace Jovanovich, 1976), p. 126.

15. For an example of Freud's use and opinion of galvanism in 1887 and 1888, see his comments on "Mrs. A." in *The Complete Letters of Sigmund Freud to Wilheim Fliess, 1887–1904,* ed. and trans. Jeffrey M. Masson (Cambridge: Belknap Press, 1985), pp. 16, 18, 21.

As late as 1920, although clearly stating his belief in the superiority of psychotherapy as a treatment, Freud defended the use of electrotherapy in the treatment of battle neuroses. K. R. Eissler, *Freud as an Expert Witness: The Discussion of War Neuroses Between Freud and Wagner-Jauregg* (Madison, Conn.: International Universities Press, 1986).

16. Erb, pp. 121, 293. I have relied very heavily on Erb's manual for the details of the common electrotherapeutic regimens used in Austria at the end of the nineteenth century. Erb was preeminent in the field of electrotherapy, and many German-language physicians depended totally on his advice. His handbook, first published in 1882, appeared in a second edition in 1886 and was also widely translated in the West. Freud, as a novice neurologist, followed Erb's instructions faithfully. Without the slightest doubt, we can be sure Dora's treatments were similar, if not identical, to the ones Erb prescribed or reported on.

17. Even in the absence of her medical records, one may safely conclude that Dora received both general and local electrotherapy. Not only did textbooks advise both, but she had responded unfavorably to all procedures and had been seen by several specialists over the years. In such a refractory case, her physicians were likely to try every possible modality.

18. Erb, p. 55.

19. Ibid., p. 117.

20. Ibid., p. 52.

21. Althaus, p. 361; Charles L. Dana, *Text-Book of Nervous Diseases and Psychiatry,* 6th ed., rev. enl. (New York: William Wood, 1904), p. 522; J. A. Ormerod, *Diseases of the Nervous System* (Philadelphia: P. Blakiston, 1892), p. 320; H. Campbell Thomson, *Diseases of the Nervous System* (New York: Funk and Wagnalls, 1910), pp. 421–22. It is only in the last generation that textbooks of nervous disease like those just cited, with their standard anatomoclinical descriptions of hysterical symptoms, have disappeared. For a late example see James Purves-Stewart, *The Diagnosis of Nervous Diseases,* 7th ed., rev. (St. Louis: C. V. Mosby Co., 1931), p. 250.

22. Erb, p. 222.

23. Féré, p. 574; A. Ross Defendorf, *Clinical Psychiatry. A Textbook for Students and Physicians,* abstracted and adapted from the 6th German ed. (1899) of Emil

Kraepelin's *Lehrbuch der Psychiatrie* (New York: Macmillan, 1904), p. 368; Dana (1920), p. 528; Purves-Stewart, p. 250 (see also 3rd ed. [1911], p. 364); Ormerod, pp. 320, 322; M. Allen Starr, *Synopsis of Lectures Upon Diseases of the Nervous System* (New York: James T. Dougherty, 1904), p. 96; Irving J. Spear, *A Manual of Nervous Diseases* (Philadelphia and London: W. B. Saunders, 1916), pp. 489–91.

24. Erb, p. 131.

25. Ibid., pp. 223–24. Another energetic procedure for hysterical aphonia, which Erb heard had brought success, was galvanization transversely through the mastoid process (the bone behind the ear). This practice, however, produced nystagmus—a rapid, oscillating movement of the eyes accompanied by vertigo and often by nausea or vomiting. While the nystagmus and nausea passed fairly quickly after the treatment ceased, some patients continued to feel dizzy and ill for the rest of the day (ibid., pp. 54, 293–94).

26. Ormerod, p. 320; Purves-Stewart, p. 563; Wilks, p. 378.

27. Erb, p. 265.

28. Ibid., p. 53.

29. Ibid., pp. 237, 243–44, 256–57.

30. Ibid., pp. 55, 341–43.

31. Ibid., p. 292.

32. Féré, p. 566.

33. These did not exist in the office of the average specialist. Freud remarked in his autobiography: "My therapeutic arsenal [for nervous patients in the 1880s] contained only two weapons, electrotherapy and hypnotism, for prescribing a visit to a hydropathic establishment after a single consultation was an inadequate source of income." ("An Autobiographical Study" [1925], *SE*, vol. 20, 1959, p. 16.) However, for long-term patients, from whom he had derived adequate fees; Freud did prescribe hydrotherapy in the 1880s and early 1890s.

34. The average person swims comfortably in water at 80 degrees Fahrenheit.

35. Féré, pp. 570–71.

36. Dana (1920), p. 528; Féré, p. 573; Spear, p. 489.

37. Starr, p. 96.

2.   "The Purely Human and Social Circumstances"

1. This and other similar factual information about Dora and her close relatives comes from the records of the Israelitische Kultusgemeinde Wien (hereafter IKG).

2. A body of nineteenth-century statistical literature attempted to prove the greater mental instability of European Jews, but some of its premises and arguments were flawed. See Richard M. Goodman, *Genetic Disorders Among the Jewish People.* (Baltimore: Johns Hopkins University Press, 1979), pp. 421–27, quoted in Sander L. Gilman, *Jewish Self-Hatred: Anti-Semitism and the Hidden Language of the Jews* (Baltimore and London: Johns Hopkins University Press, 1986), pp. 287–88.

Yet authoritative testimony to the Jewish predisposition to hysteria and neurasthenia (literally, "nerve weakness") came from respected names such as the French neurologist Jean-Martin Charcot and the Austrian forensic psychiatrist and sexual pathologist Richard Krafft-Ebing. See Gilman, pp. 288–89, with whose thesis regarding the incidence of Jewish neuroses I am partially at odds. The task lies in disentangling the accuracy of clinical impressions from the anti-Semitic bias that may have provoked them.

3. See Oppenheim as quoted in Paul Enke's survey of contemporary notions of the etiology of hysteria, *Casuistische Beiträge zur männlichen Hysterie* (Jena: Frommannsche

Hof-Buchdruckerei, 1900); Gomperz's letter to his sister Josephine, Aug. 23, 1886, in Peter J. Swales, "Freud, His Teacher, and the Birth of Psychoanalysis," in *Freud: Appraisals and Reappraisals*, vol. 1, ed. Paul E. Stepansky (Hillsdale, N.J.: Analytic Press, 1986), p. 28. Gomperz wrote: "Looking around our family circle, there are not too many bright points. Nearly everywhere, at the least, irritable and excited nerves—the inheritance of a very old civilized race and of the urban life"; *Minutes of the Vienna Psychoanalytic Society*, ed. Herman Nunberg and Ernst Federn (New York: International Universities Press, Inc., 1962–75). Meetings of Jan. 30, 1907, vol. 1, pp. 94, 98; Nov. 11, 1908, vol. 2, pp. 44–46; Mar. 12, 1913, vol. 4, pp. 178–79. Not surprisingly, the assimilated Jewish psychoanalysts found that neurosis in Jews was greatest among non-Westernized Polish and Russian Jews.

4. "Vital Statistics," *Encyclopedia Judaica* (hereafter *EJ*) (Jerusalem: Keter Publishing House/New York: Macmillan Company, 1972), vol. 16, col. 179; Paul Johnson, *A History of the Jews* (New York: Harper & Row, 1987), p. 356.

5. The psychological literature draws from Gordon W. Allport's classic study arguing for the deleterious effects of religious and racial discrimination. See *The Nature of Prejudice* (Cambridge, Mass.: Addison-Wesley, 1954). One of the most recent psychological studies following this trend is John W. Berry and Uichol Kim, "Acculturation and Mental Health," in *Health and Cross-Cultural Psychology: Toward Applications*, ed. P. R. Dasen, et al., vol. 10, Cross-Cultural Research and Methodological Series (Newbury Park, Calif.: Sage Publications, 1988), pp. 207–36. Sociological studies often refer back to Robert K. Merton, *Social Theory and Social Structure* (New York: Free Press, 1968). See also J. D. McCarthy and W. L. Yancey, "Uncle Tom and Mr. Charlie: Metaphysical Pathos in the Study of Racism and Personal Disorganization," *American Journal of Sociology*, vol. 76 (1971), pp. 648–72; and William T. Liu and Elena S. H. Yu, "Ethnicity, Mental Health, and the Urban Delivery System," in *Urban Ethnicity in the United States: New Immigrants and Old Minorities*, ed. Lionel Maldonado and Joan Moore, vol. 29, Urban Affairs Annual Reviews (Beverly Hills, Calif.: Sage Publications, 1985), pp. 211–47. Two historians, having just completed works on the Jews in Vienna, argue for the psychological importance of the Jews' background and of their "emotionally shattering" lives in fin-de-siècle Vienna. See Steven Beller, *Vienna and the Jews, 1867–1938: A Cultural History* (Cambridge: Cambridge University Press, 1989), pp. 13, 70, 244; and Robert S. Wistrich, *The Jews of Vienna in the Age of Franz Joseph* (Oxford and New York: Oxford University Press, 1989), pp. 541, 558, 602, 608, 610.

6. Significant work has been carried out, especially by Kenneth L. Dion and his associates. Dion's pathbreaking paper with Brian M. Earn (since amplified in other publications) is "The Phenomenology of Being a Target of Prejudice," *Journal of Personality and Social Psychology* 32: 5 (1975), pp. 944–50.

7. For the history of the Jews in medieval and early modern Bohemia see "Bohemia," *EJ*, vol. 4, cols. 1173–77; "Bohemia," Jewish Encyclopedia (hereafter *JE*), vol. 3 (New York: Ktav Publishing House, n. d.), pp. 286–89; Hillel J. Kieval, "Autonomy and Interdependence: The Historical Legacy of Czech Jewry," in *The Precious Legacy*, ed. David Altshuler (New York: Summit Books, 1983, pp. 47–60, 67, 71; Guido Kisch, "Linguistic Conditions Among Czechoslovak Jewry: A Legal-Historical Study," *Historia Judaica* 8 (1946), p. 20; Jonathan I. Israel, *European Jewry in the Age of Mercantilism, 1550–1750* (Oxford: Clarendon Press, 1985), pp. 6, 15, 38–40, 89, 99, 104; "Nachod," *EJ*, vol. 12, col. 749.

8. Special prohibitions and rules as to livelihood and dress, however, applied to Prague Jews. See "Prague," *JE*, vol. 10, p. 164.

9. It should be noted, however, that the compulsory taking of German surnames at the end of the eighteenth century was not a straightforward procedure. On the grounds that the Jews had evaded taxes by not having last names, the emperor assigned the duty of naming them to the War Department. If a Jew refused to select a name, the officers were empowered to force a name on him. This laid the basis for a great deal of corruption, for by citing Jewish resistance, even if none existed, an officer had the power to give a Jew any name, no matter if it were derogatory or nonsensical. But the army officials could also be bribed, either to bestow a merely descriptive place or occupational name or to award poetic names like Goldstein (golden stone—that is, chrysolite), Edelstein (precious stone), Singvogel (songbird), Blumenthal (valley of flowers), and Schönberg (beautiful mountain). See Will S. Monroe, *The Spell of Bohemia* (Boston: L. C. Page, 1910), p. 185; and "Names (Personal)," *JE*, vol. 9, p. 156.

10. "Bohemia," *EJ*, ibid.; Israel, pp. 146–47, 170, 186, 233; Kieval, pp. 75–76, 78, 83; Simon Dubnov, *History of the Jews from Cromwell's Commonwealth to the Napoleonic Era*, vol. 4, translated from the Russian 4th ed., vols. 7, 8 (South Brunswick, N.J.: Thomas Yoseloff, 1971), pp. 18–20, 173, 186; "Prague," *JE*, pp. 162, 164; Ruth Kestenberg-Gladstein, *Neuere Geschichte der Juden in den böhmischen Ländern*, Erster Teil, *Das Zeitalter der Aufklärung, 1780–1830* (Tübingen: J. C. B. Mohr, 1969), p. 99; "Nachod," *EJ*, col. 749.

11. "Bohemia," *EJ*, ibid.; Shmuel Ettinger, "The Modern Period," in *A History of the Jewish People*, ed. H. H. Ben Sasson (London: Weidenfeld and Nicolson, 1976), p. 755; Israel, pp. 239, 248.

12. Dubnov, vol. 4, pp. 187–92; "Familiants Law," *EJ*, vol. 6, cols. 1162–64.

13. The sharp reduction in the number of Jews since 1724 was also a result of the policies of the Empress Maria Theresa (1717–80), who was extremely hostile toward Jews and abruptly dictated their banishment from Bohemia in 1744. Crisis again became the hallmark of Bohemian Jewish life until the empress was prevailed upon by local authorities and foreign diplomats to delay and finally to rescind her order. But the matter was not settled until 1748, and thereafter the Jews payed increased "toleration" money as well as special levies during the Seven Years' War (1756–63.) Maria Theresa did succeed in expelling Jews from certain towns and insisted that all Jews wear a yellow collar on their coats. Prague Jews were singled out for special treatment; men had to attach strips of yellow cloth to the left shoulder of their garments, and women had to wear yellow strips in their hair. "Bohemia," *EJ*, col. 1177; "Bohemia," *JE*, p. 289; Dubnov, vol. 4, pp. 192–97; Ettinger, p. 755; Israel, p. 239; "Prague," *JE*, p. 164.

14. "Bohemia," *EJ*, ibid.; Dubnov, vol. 4, pp. 337, 459; Israel, p. 250. See also Peter G. J. Pulzer, *The Rise of Political Anti-Semitism in Germany and Austria* (New York: John Wiley & Sons, 1964), p. 129. The *Toleranzpatent* began: "Convinced on the one hand of the perniciousness of all religious intolerance, and on the other hand of the great advantage of a true Christian tolerance to religion and the state . . . "

Joseph II's edicts regarding the Jews were part of a wider policy aimed at Germanizing his subject peoples and severely limiting their use of any language other than German. See Kisch, pp. 22–23.

15. "Bohemia," *EJ*, cols. 1177–78; Dubnov, vol. 4, p. 338; Ettinger, p. 756; Kieval, pp. 86–88; Kisch, pp. 22–24; Hans Kohn, "Before 1918 in the Historic Lands," *The Jews of Czechoslovakia: Historical Studies and Surveys*, vol. 1 (Philadelphia: Jewish Publication Society of America, 1968), p. 15; Hugo Stransky, "The Religious Life in the Historic Lands," ibid., p. 342.

16. "Bohemia," *EJ*, col. 1178; Dubnov, vol. 4, pp. 338–39, 460; Ettinger, p. 756; Israel, pp. 250, 252–53, 255; Kieval, p. 85; Kohn, ibid.

17. Dubnov, vol. 4, pp. 337–38, 461; Kieval, p. 86.

18. This, of course, raises questions about the origin of the Bauer surname. The conferring of last names in 1788 could have been an arbitrary or capricious process (see note 9 above).

19. "Artisans," *JE*, vol. 2, pp. 154–56; Pulzer, p. 5; "Occupations," *JE*, vol. 9, pp. 371–73; Arthur Ruppin, *The Jews of Today*, trans. Margery Bentwich (New York: Henry Holt, 1913), pp. 60, 64.

20. Gustav Otruba, "Der Anteil der Juden am Wirtschaftsleben der böhmischen Länder seit dem Beginn der Industrialisierung," in *Die Juden in den böhmischen Ländern* (München, Wien: R. Oldenbourg Verlag, 1983), p. 246; Kestenberg-Gladstein, "The Jews Between Czechs and Germans in the Historic Lands, 1848–1918," *The Jews of Czechoslovakia: Historical Studies and Surveys*, vol. 1 (Philadelphia: Jewish Publication Society of America, 1968), p. 38.

21. Israel, p. 249; Kieval, pp. 88–89; Kisch, pp. 25–27.

22. Dubnov departs somewhat from this general assessment. He reports that although "German culture began to sprout among Jews in Bohemia . . . the people at large still had their devout leaders . . . the rabbis." See vol. 4, pp. 678–80.

23. Ezra Mendelsohn, *The Jews of East Central Europe Between the World Wars* (Bloomington: Indiana University Press, 1983), pp. 133–34; Stransky, p. 342.

24. However, the quota of legal families rose to 10,272 by 1803. See Dubnov, vol. 4, pp. 656, 663–64.

25. Nevertheless, this oath was not as humiliating as the earlier version, which had required a Jew, wearing only a shirt, to stand barefoot on a pigskin. He put his right hand on the Bible and his left over his heart. Then a second Jew called down upon the oath taker the curses contained in the Bible if he should give false testimony. See "Prague," *JE*, p. 162.

26. "Bohemia," *JE*, p. 290; Simon Dubnov, *History of the Jews from the Congress of Vienna to the Emergence of Hitler*, vol. 5, translated from the Russian 4th ed., vols. 9 and 10 (South Brunswick, N.J.: Thomas Yoseloff, 1973), pp. 120–21; see also Dubnov, vol. 4, pp. 663–68; Ettinger, p. 807; Ruth Kestenberg-Gladstein, "Jews Between Czechs and Germans," p. 22.

27. "Bohemia," *EJ*, cols. 1178–79; Dubnov, vol. 4, pp. 494–500; Dubnov, vol. 5, pp. 289–94, 300–303; Ettinger, pp. 809–11; "Familiants Law," *EJ*, col. 1164; Kestenberg-Gladstein, "Jews Between Czechs and Germans," p. 27; Kieval, p. 91; Kisch, pp. 27–28; Kohn, p. 15; Pulzer, pp. 7–8; Erika Weinzierl, "Die Stellung der Juden in Österreich seit dem Staatsgrundgesetz von 1867," *Zeitschrift für die Geschichte der Juden*, (1968), p. 89.

28. There were some Jews, in this era of nationalism, who urged that Bohemian Jews should cast their lot with the Czechs and together work for the formation of an autonomous Czech state. But this was not the path followed by most Jews from the Czech lands, the Bauers and Freuds being typical.

29. Kestenberg-Gladstein, "Jews Between Czechs and Germans," p. 43; Kisch, p. 28; Mendelsohn, p. 133; Ruppin, p. 115.

30. See William M. Johnston, *The Austrian Mind. An Intellectual and Social History, 1848–1938* (Berkeley: University of California Press, 1972), pp. 265–73, for a brief discussion of the demands and manifestations of Czech nationalism in Bohemia.

31. Dubnov, vol. 5, pp. 293–94; Ettinger, pp. 809–10; Kestenberg-Gladstein, "Jews Between Czechs and Germans," pp. 24, 36, 40, 46; Kieval, pp. 92–94; Guido Kisch, *In Search of Freedom. A History of American Jews from Czechoslovakia* (London: Edward Goldston, 1949), pp. 59–60, 62; Pulzer, p. 140; Marsha L. Rozenblit, *The Jews of Vienna, 1867–1914: Assimilation and Identity* (Albany: State University of New York Press, 1983), p.27; Robert S. Wistrich, *Socialism and the Jews: The Dilemmas of Assimilation in Germany and Austria-Hungary* (East Brunswick, N.J.: Associated University Presses, Inc., 1982), p. 188; Michael A. Riff, "Czech Antisemitism and the Jewish Response Before 1914," *Wiener Library Bulletin* 29 (1976), p. 10.

32. Kestenberg-Gladstein, "Jews Between Czechs and Germans," p. 27.

33. Jews in Vienna have a history going back at least to the twelfth century. Their experience there mirrored that of the Bohemian Jews—a saga of settlement and expulsion—the last major expulsion occurring in 1670. After that Jews were allowed to return on a very limited basis.

34. "Vienna," *JE*, vol. 12, p. 434; Dubnov, vol. 4, pp. 184, 658–60, 676–77.

35. Dubnov, vol. 5, pp. 116–18. These figures are in some dispute. Other sources give a much lower number for the illegal residents. See Arieh Tartakower, "Jewish Migratory Movements in Austria in Recent Generations," in *The Jews of Austria*, ed. Josef Fraenkel (London: Vallentine, Mitchell, 1967), p. 286; "Vienna," *EJ*, vol. 16, col. 124; and Wistrich, *Socialism and the Jews*, p. 179. See also note 37 below.

36. The tolerated Jews so prized their designation that they used the term to describe themselves on official documents, calling cards, and tombstones ("Here rests the tolerated Jew _____"). See Dubnov, vol. 5, pp. 119–200.

37. This growth is calculated from the base figure of the legal (tolerated) Jews. There is no absolute consistency among various seemingly reliable sources either about the total population of Vienna or the Jewish population. My figures draw from three sources: Pulzer, p. 10, table 3; "Vienna," *JE*, p. 437; and F. Wilder-Okladek, *The Return Movement of Jews to Austria After the Second World War* (The Hague: Martinus Nijhoff, 1969), p. 122, table D/3. Other sources that may be consulted include John W. Boyer, *Political Radicalism in Late Imperial Vienna: Origins of the Christian Social Movement, 1848–1897* (Chicago and London: University of Chicago Press, 1981), p. 79; Field, p. 60; Arthur J. May, *Vienna in the Age of Franz Josef* (Norman: University of Oklahoma Press, 1966), p. 39; Rozenblit, pp. 15–16; Tartakower, p. 287; Weinzierl, p. 89; Robert S. Wistrich, *Revolutionary Jews from Marx to Trotsky* (London: Harrap, 1976), p. 96. Especially confusing is the wide variety of figures given for the Jewish population in Vienna in the 1850s. Numbers for all of Lower Austria, including Vienna, may be obtained from Ruppin, p. 38, and Wistrich, *Socialism and the Jews*, pp. 178–79. In this latter book, Wistrich unaccountably says the Jewish population in Lower Austria increased only ten times from 1857–1900.

38. Rozenblit, p. 18.

39. Pulzer, p. 10.

40. The designation *Judenstadt* was changed to *Leopoldstadt* by the Viennese authorities in honor of the Austrian Emperor Leopold, who had ordered the Jews to depart.

41. Rozenblit, p. 76.

42. May, pp. 4, 6, 10, 24–28; Peter Vergo, *Vienna 1900: Vienna, Scotland, and the European Avant-Garde* (Edinburgh: Her Majesty's Stationery Office, 1983), p. 15; Freud, *The Interpretation of Dreams* [1900], *SE*, vol. 4 (1958), pp. 192–93; Arthur Schnitzler, *My Youth in Vienna*, trans. Catherine Hutter (New York: Holt, Rinehart and Winston, 1970), p. 292 n.

43. Marianne Krüll, *Freud and His Father* (New York and London: W. W. Norton and Co., 1986), pp. 148–49. In fact, the Freuds first lived in the Third District (immediately across the Danube Canal) for a couple of years before moving to the Second District.

44. Schnitzler, p. 14; Amos Elon, *Herzl* (New York: Holt, Rinehart and Winston, 1975), pp. 32–33, 37.

45. IKG records.

46. Rozenblit, p. 79; May, p. 41; Johnston, p. 102; Krüll, pp. 148–49; Vergo, p. 15; Ernest Jones, *The Life and Work of Sigmund Freud*, vol. 1 (New York: Basic Books, 1953), pp. 15, 17.

47. Rozenblit, p. 84.

48. Ibid., pp. 88–90.

49. Pulzer, p. 22.

50. May, p. 34; David F. Good, *The Economic Rise of the Habsburg Empire, 1750–1914* (Berkeley and Los Angeles: University of California Press, 1984), p. 162.

51. May, pp. 33–34; Dennis B. Klein, *Jewish Origins of the Psychoanalytic Movement* (New York: Praeger, 1981), p. 3. Whatever the Ring proclaimed outwardly, it also had a hidden function—it was built not only to impress but to enable the army to act efficiently in case the workers in the suburbs rioted.

52. See chapter 3 for a further discussion of the Bohemian textile industry and the Bauer family's participation in it.

53. Wistrich, *Socialism and the Jews*, pp. 180, 182. The only non-Jewish major banking house in Vienna was that of the Greek, Sina (H. Tietze, *Die Juden Wiens*, 1933, quoted by Pulzer, p. 11). However, Jewish bankers did not hold political power comparable to their dominant economic position.

54. Peter G. J. Pulzer, "The Development of Political Anti-semitism in Austria," in *The Jews of Austria*, ed. Josef Fraenkel (London: Vallentine, Mitchell, 1967), p. 431.

55. Freud, *The Interpretation of Dreams* [1900], *SE*, vol. 4 (1958), p. 193.

56. Freud, *An Autobiographical Study* [1925], *SE*, vol. 20 (1959), p. 8.

57. Pulzer, *Rise of Political Anti-Semitism*, pp. 12–13. Figures for all Austria for 1903–4 also show very large Jewish student enrollments. Compared with the proportion of Jews in the population, there were four times as many Jewish as Christian university students, the greatest percentage of them studying law. See Ruppin, pp. 130, 132.

58. The remaining 35 percent included artisans (12 percent), professional men (11 percent), industrialists or factory owners (4 percent), factory workers (4 percent), and civil servants (3 percent). These averages are even somewhat conservative because they do not indicate trends over time. So, for example, the percentage of merchants declined from more than one-half in 1870 to one-third in 1910, when business employees rose to more than a third. (Rozenblit, pp. 48–49, 51–52.) The modern economy was claiming the Jews.

    Note, however, that Ivar Oxaal disputes what he says is Rozenblit's implication that Jews had a virtual monopoly of the salaried, clerical, and white-collar jobs and that this was the way Jews rose in society. See "The Jews of Young Hitler's Vienna: Historical and Sociological Aspects," in *Jews, Antisemitism and Culture in Vienna*, ed. Ivar Oxaal et al. (London and New York: Routledge & Kegan Paul, 1987), pp. 34–35, 38.

59. George Clare, *Last Waltz in Vienna: The Rise and Destruction of a Family, 1842–1942.* (New York: Holt, Rinehart and Winston, 1982), pp. 85, 88.

60. Conversion among Jews in fin-de-siècle Vienna must be understood as primarily a social and political phenomenon, rarely an act of religious conscience. The full meaning of conversion is explored in chapter 8.

61. Elon, pp. 85, 99, 134; Kohn, p. 17; May, pp. 48–49; Pulzer, *Rise of Political Anti-Semitism,* p. 13.

62. Clare, pp. 86–87. Kraus tried, in turn, Catholic and Lutheran conversion; neither brought him inner contentment.

63. Pulzer, pp. 13–14.

64. Wilma Abeles Iggers, *Karl Kraus: A Viennese Critic of the Twentieth Century* (The Hague: Martinus Nijhoff, 1967), pp. 171–72.

65. Letter from Freud to Eduard Silberstein, September 18, 1874, quoted in Klein, p. 45.

66. Elon, p. 93; IKG records for Otto Bauer; Rozenblit, p. 7; Schnitzler, pp. 9, 12; May, p. 67; Mendelsohn, p. 135.

67. Martin Freud, "Who Was Freud?" in *The Jews of Austria,* ed. Josef Fraenkel (London: Vallentine, Mitchell, 1967), pp. 203–4.

68. Elon, p. 53; Pulzer, "Development of Political Anti-semitism," p. 431; Silberner, pp. 266, 271.

69. William J. McGrath, *Freud's Discovery of Psychoanalysis: The Politics of Hysteria* (Ithaca, N.Y., and London: Cornell University Press, 1986), p. 160.

70. Letter to Emil Fluss, June 16, 1873, quoted in Klein, p. 47; Freud, *The Interpretation of Dreams* [1900], SE, vol. 4 (1958), p. 196.

71. Elon, p. 167; Pulzer, "Development of Political Anti-semitism," p. 430.

72. Clare, pp. 90–91; Field, p. 64.

73. Stefan Zweig, *The World of Yesterday* (New York: Viking, 1943), p. 103; Elon, p. 179; Martin Freud, p. 207.

74. Elon, pp. 165, 177; Zweig, p. 104.

75. These included Victor Adler, Max Adler (no relation), Wilhelm Ellenbogen, and Rudolf Hilferding. Heinrich Braun, Freud's good friend in high school, with whom he identified for a while, became a socialist leader. And Alfred Adler, Freud's colleague for almost a decade, was also a committed socialist, although not a part of the movement as such.

76. Silberner, pp. 266, 272–73; Wistrich, *Revolutionary Jews* (James Joll's Foreword, Preface), pp. 6–7, 103.

77. Quoted in Elon, p. 40.

78. Rozenblit, pp. 7, 94–95.

79. Martin Freud, p. 204.

80. Jones, vol. 1, p. 329; Klein, pp. 72–77, 87–93; Freud, *The Origins of Psycho-Analysis: Letters to Wilhelm Fliess, Drafts and Notes: 1887–1902,* ed. Marie Bonaparte, Anna Freud, Ernst Kris (New York: Basic Books, 1954), p. 312.

81. From *Der Judenstaat,* trans. Harry Zohn, quoted in Rozenblit, p. 8. The ghetto also existed without. Even riding in a carriage during a trip in Germany, the wealthy Herzl, as a young man, was identified as Jewish by two officer cadets who called him *Saujud* ("Jewish pig") as he passed by. See Elon, p. 121. Freud, in his late twenties, was also "spotted" as a Jew by fellow passengers in a railway car. See Chapter 8.

Nevertheless, Oxaal (pp. 25–29) disputes Rozenblit's argument on the lack of Jewish integration in Viennese society and offers evidence for integrated residential patterns. He also argues that Jews were more Westernized than Rozenblit describes, even those from Galicia.

82. Carl E. Schorske, *Fin-de-Siècle Vienna: Politics and Culture* (New York: Alfred A. Knopf, 1980), p. 5; Pulzer, *Rise of Political Anti-Semitism*, pp. 25–26, 134–35; Klein, p. 6.

83. May, pp. 36–38.

84. Good, pp. 162, 232; May, pp. 34–35; Schnitzler, p. 12; Pulzer, ibid., pp. 135, 144.

85. Good, pp. 232–33; Schorske, p. 5; Pulzer, ibid., p. 138; Boyer, pp. ix–x, 76; Kestenberg-Gladstein, "Jews Between Czechs and Germans," p. 44; Wistrich, *Socialism and the Jews*, p. 209.

86. Klein, p. 7.

87. Julius Braunthal, ed., *Otto Bauer: Eine Auswahl aus seinem Lebenswerk* (Vienna: Wiener Volksbuchhandlung, 1961), p. 9.

88. Kisch, *In Search of Freedom*, p. 66; Boyer, p. 76; Kestenberg-Gladstein, "Jews Between Czechs and Germans," p. 44; Klein, pp. 12–13; Pulzer, *Rise of Political Anti-Semitism*, p. 13.

89. Arthur Schnitzler noted in his autobiography that before the word "anti-Semitism" existed, Jews used their own contemptuous term, *Judenfresser* (Jew gobbler), to refer to a person who openly showed his dislike of Jews. Schnitzler added, however, that he "scarcely felt" anti-Semitism in high school in the 1870s, and that while such antipathy was indeed latent among many, "it did not [yet] play an important role politically or socially." See pp. 7 and 63.

90. The word "anti-Semitism" was devised by a German journalist, Wilhelm Marr, and quickly won wide usage. The term technically could apply to all "Semites" but was used almost exclusively to refer to Jews. There is irony in the fact that the term was also accepted as a descriptive word by Jews, who were as much influenced by racial concepts as everybody else.

91. Nineteenth- and twentieth-century anti-Semitism in Central Europe was a phenomenon of mass voting; "the people" gave anti-Semitism its legitimacy and popularity. As the franchise widened, the liberals were forced to share power with, or relinquish it to, the lower classes. In this way the Jews lost their most reliable support. Because the liberals were outvoted, they could no longer protect the Jews or speak up for them. Austrian economy and society had never been thoroughly liberalized, so an alliance between the ruling classes and the lower middle class—petty officials, tradespeople, lower professionals, artisans—came about and formed the basis for political anti-Semitism. See Pulzer, *Rise of Political Anti-Semitism*, p. 27.

92. Pulzer, "Development of Political Anti-semitism," p. 431; David Abrahamsen, *The Mind and Death of a Genius* (New York: Columbia University Press, 1946), p. 29; Boyer, pp. 80–81, 85–87; Johnson, p. 395; Johnston, p. 27; Oxaal, pp. 33–38; Weinzierl, p. 89. The Viennese artisans and businessmen of the precapitalist world worked a noncompetitive day with "long midday lunches, early closings, and an easy, unrushed labor schedule" (Boyer, p. 81). They were uncomfortably jarred from their traditional ways by the immigrant Jews, who could afford none of these amenities and competed keenly not only with the Viennese but among each other to scratch out a living. The overwhelmed Viennese accused the Jews of "fraudulent" business practices, which may occasionally have occurred but most often were simply noncustomary, determined efforts to succeed.

93. Andrew G. Whiteside, *The Socialism of Fools: Georg Ritter von Schönerer and Austrian Pan-Germanism* (Berkeley: University of California Press, 1975), pp. 79, 81,

309; Pulzer, ibid.; Pulzer, *Rise of Political Anti-Semitism*, pp. 145–46; May, p. 39; Klein, p. 9; Boyer, p. 90.

Actually, the Reform Association united three founts of anti-Semitism: artisanal, anticapitalist, and antimodernist fury; Roman Catholic social theory, critical of the constitutional basis and institutions of liberal society (its representatives wished to recast the nineteenth century along corporate lines so as to return to the social order of medieval times when the church stood supreme;) and German nationalism, which was fast becoming dedicated to "racial purity" and a pan-Germanic nation-state.

94. Whiteside, p. 85.

95. Whiteside, p. 87; Wistrich, *Socialism and the Jews*, p. 190.

96. Schorske, p. 129; Whiteside, p. 120.

97. Schönerer shared the anticapitalist bias of the artisans because he sought to glorify a precapitalist, prebourgeois ideal. He dreamed of an ancient Germania, two thousand years old and "pure." His goal was to restore Germania, bringing together the "true-blooded Teutonic tribes" under his leadership. Frederic Morton, *A Nervous Splendor: Vienna 1888/1889* (New York: Penguin, 1981), p. 73.

98. Boyer, p. 92; Schorske, p. 126; Pulzer, *Rise of Political Anti-Semitism*, p. 151. The three anti-Semitic planks were action against the "moral rottenness" of the press (a goal Schönerer literally pursued in 1888 by breaking into the offices of the liberal *Neues Wiener Tagblatt* with some followers, beating up the staff, and wrecking furniture and typefaces); taxing the rich to free the state from dependence on "money powers"; and compulsory training certificates for artisans, prohibition of house-to-house peddling, and regulation of lawyers' fees.

99. Whiteside, pp. 88–89.

100. Klein, p. 10; Pulzer, *Rise of Political Anti-Semitism*, p. 153; Pulzer, "Development of Political Anti-semitism," p. 432.

101. Schorske, p. 130; Whiteside, pp. 311–12.

102. Whiteside, pp. 311, 313.

103. The 1882 electoral reform increased Viennese voters from 15,385 to 45,695. Obviously this initial extension of the suffrage was hardly radical in a city with a population of three-quarters of a million. But it gave the franchise mainly to anti-Semites whose numbers increased with each successive electoral reform, until they controlled the city government in 1895. See May, p. 39; Pulzer, "Development of Political Anti-semitism," p. 432; Pulzer, *Rise of Political Anti-Semitism*, pp. 154, 174; Wistrich, *Socialism and the Jews*, p. 188.

104. August Rohling, *Der Talmudjude. Zur Beherzigung für Juden und Christen aller Stände* (Münster: Adolph Russell, 1871).

105. Johnston, p. 344; Whiteside, p. 88.

106. Freud, *The Interpretation of Dreams* [1900], *SE*, vol. 4 (1958), pp. 136–37, 196.

107. Wistrich, *Socialism and the Jews*, p. 200. In a dissenting essay, Sigurd Paul Scheichl attempts to differentiate among different types of anti-Jewish sentiments. He argues that not everyone who had anti-Jewish attitudes was an anti-Semite. He limits anti-Semites to hard-core followers of Schönerer and Lueger and does not include intellectuals who were part of the antiliberal backlash or participants in everyday ethnic hostilities. He downplays pre–World War I "antisemitism" compared to that of the 1930s. See "The Contexts and Nuances of Anti-Jewish Language: Were All the 'Antisemites' Antisemites?" in Oxaal et al., pp. 89–110.

108. Boyer, p. 41.

109. Whiteside, p. 307. Arthur Schnitzler, thinking back over those days, wondered if in the future his readers would truly grasp "the importance, spiritually, almost more than politically and socially, that was assigned to the so-called Jewish question." Schnitzler, p. 6.

110. Besides, even if the Jews turned to socialism with the belief that it would create a better world for them, they were mistaken. Schnitzler was mordant on this point: "Who created the liberal movement in Austria? The Jews! By whom were the Jews left in the lurch? . . . spat on like dogs? . . . By the German Nationals! And the same thing will happen in the case of Socialism and Communism. When the soup is served at the table, you will be driven away. It has always been so and always will be so." Quoted in Wistrich, *Socialism and the Jews,* p. 222.

111. Schnitzler, pp. 6–7.

112. An anonymous pamphlet appearing in Berlin in 1886 exhibited this particular genre of attack: "Christians . . . are amazed and pained by the behaviour of Jewish families. There is no exhaustive expression to describe the unseemliness, the offensiveness and the noise . . . which are to be observed in public gardens . . . bathing places, in the streets, on tramways and railway stations, in every province and town." Pulzer, *Rise of Political Anti-Semitism,* p. 26.

113. In his novel *Der Weg ins Freie (The Road into the Open),* Schnitzler had one of his Jewish characters admit: "I will not deny that I am particularly sensitive to the faults of Jews. If a Jew shows bad form in my presence, or behaves in a ridiculous manner, I have often felt so painful a sensation that I should like to sink into the earth." Quoted in Klein, p. 12. In the mid-1880s, Theodor Herzl (1860–1904) was vacationing abroad. From Ostend he reported that the Viennese and Budapest Jews were spoiling the beach, and from Berlin, that "some thirty or forty ugly little Jews and Jewesses" had unfortunately overrun a grande soirée. See Herzl's letters to his parents in 1885, quoted in Elon, p. 69.

114. There is scholarly disagreement on the use of the term as well as the notion of "Jewish self-hatred". The concept entered common usage around the turn of the century and was followed by the actual phrase itself. (For factors in its prehistory see Gilman, pp. 286–93.) The notion was clearly put forth by Otto Weininger in *Geschlecht und Charakter* (Vienna: Braumüller, 1903), and by Fritz Wittels in *Der Taufjude* (Vienna: Breitenstein, 1904). Arnold Zweig, in *Caliban, oder Politik und Leidenschaft: Versuch über die menschlichen Gruppenleidenschaften dargetan am Antisemitismus* (Potsdam: Gustav Kiepenheuer, 1927), p. 199, concretely discussed "the so-called Jewish self-hatred, that specific Austrian form of ego denial." Then in 1930, there appeared a book of biographical sketches with the phrase as its title—Theodor Lessing's *Der jüdische Selbsthass* (Berlin: Jüdischer Verlag). Freud showed his acceptance of the concept, commenting in 1936 on Lessing's volatile life, first as a converted Jew and later as a Zionist: "Don't you think that self-hatred like Theodor Lessing's is an exquisite Jewish phenomenon?" Quoted in Peter Gay, *Freud, Jews and Other Germans: Masters and Victims in Modernist Culture* (New York: Oxford University Press, 1978), p. 195. Kurt Lewin explained the concept psychologically in "Self-Hatred Among Jews," *Contemporary Jewish Record* 4 (1941), pp. 219–32.

Gay, however, takes issue with using the term to cover situations of Western Jews' embarrassment at the Eastern Jews. See *Freud, Jews,* p. 199. Gilman argues that the phrase is not merely descriptive but in itself a form of Jewish self-hatred—that is, Jewish writers have created a particular type of "bad" or "sick" Jew—the Jew who hates himself. Allan Janik goes so far as to deny the existence of Jewish self-hatred based as it is, he claims, on "irrelevant" psychological interpretations of Viennese culture. He believes that the views of individuals like Otto Weininger (see this chapter below) have been falsely reduced to psychopathology rather than being assessed within their "anti-liberal and anti-modernist" context. But Janik's antipsychological bias prejudices his own interpretation. See "Viennese Culture and the Jewish Self-Hatred Hypothesis: A Critique," in Oxaal et al., pp. 75–88. Finally, William O. McCagg attempts, unconvincingly in my opinion, to strip the issue of its emotional component. He declares that rejecting one's origins is an inevitable phenomenon of assimilation and should be seen as "self"-denial as opposed to self-hatred. McCagg asserts that everyone wants to assimilate. "Assimilation is the price most of us are willing to pay for comfort." What else, he queries, could Jews have done, apart from "self"-denial, when they were faced with the challenge of modernization yet had no land and possessed an ancient self that stood in the path of change? See *A History of Habsburg Jews, 1670–1918* (Bloomington and Indianapolis: Indiana University Press, 1989), p. 5.

115. Freud's letter to his friend Emil Fluss, Sept. 18, 1872, quoted in Klein, p. 46.

116. Freud's letter to Martha Bernays, Sept. 16, 1883, in *The Letters of Sigmund Freud*, ed. Ernst L. Freud (New York, Toronto, London: McGraw-Hill, 1964), p. 65.

117. Harry Zohn, *Karl Kraus* (New York: Twayne, 1971), p. 39; Kraus, *Die Fackel*, July 1913, p. 58, quoted in Iggers, p. 189.

118. Iggers, p. 180.

119. For the details of Weininger's unhappy life and summaries of his thought see Abrahamsen, pp. 6–14, 38, 43–47, 54–60, 69, 104, 112, 120–21, 124–32, 144–47, 183–84, 208; Henri F. Ellenberger, *The Discovery of the Unconscious: The History and Evolution of Dynamic Psychiatry* (New York: Basic Books, 1970), pp. 293, 788–89; Gay, *Freud, Jews,* pp. 196–97; Gilman, pp. 244–46, 294, 425 n. 35, 427, n. 63; Johnston, pp. 158–61.

120. "Whoever detests the Jewish disposition detests it first of all in himself; that he could persecute it in others is merely his endeavour to separate himself from Jewishness." Weininger quoted in Gilman, p. 294.

121. Ellenberger, pp. 293, 788–89; Johnston, pp. 160–61.

122. Rosa Mayreder, *A Survey of the Woman Problem*, trans. Herman Scheffauer (New York: G. H. Doran, 1913), p. 110.

3. *"The Family Circle"*

1. Richard J. Evans, *The Feminists: Women's Emancipation Movement in Europe, America and Australasia 1840–1920* (London: Croom Helm/New York: Barnes & Noble, 1977), p. 93.

2. In 1961, Julius Braunthal, an Austrian socialist who wrote at length about Dora's brother, Otto, was unable to find any "documentary traces" of Jakob and Babette or of Philipp's in-laws, the Gerbers. Braunthal assumed that they all emigrated from Bohemia to Vienna since Czech was the "second mother tongue" of both Philipp and his wife. See Julius Braunthal, ed., *Otto Bauer: Eine Auswahl aus seinem Lebenswerk* (Vienna: Wiener Volksbuchhandlung, 1961), p. 9. Other writers about Otto Bauer, into the 1980s, have also failed to discover additional, specific biographical information about his grandparents. Because Otto became a historically important figure, his biographers provide a significant avenue to gaining factual information about Dora and her family.

3. "Bohemia," *JE*, vol. 3, p. 290; Ruth Kestenberg-Gladstein, "The Jews Between Czechs and Germans in the Historic Lands, 1848–1918," *The Jews of Czechoslovakia. Historical Studies and Surveys*, vol. 1 (Philadelphia: Jewish Publication Society of America,

1968), pp. 28–31. A short history of the Humpoletz Jews mentions many Bauers active in the nineteenth century, but Philipp's father, Jakob, is not listed among them. See Adolf Brock, "Geschichte der Juden in Humpolec," in *Die Juden und Judengemeinden Böhmens in Vergangenheit und Gegenwart*, ed. Hugo Gold, vol. 1 (Brünn-Prag: Jüdischer Buch- und Kunstverlag, 1934), pp. 193–96.

4. E. Meynen, ed., *Sudetendeutscher Atlas* (München: Verlag der Arbeitsgemeinschaft zur Wahrung sudetendeutscher Interessen, 1954), pp. 1, 8, 42; *EJ*, vol. 10, col. 104; and *JE*, vol. 6, p. 557.

5. John W. Boyer, *Political Radicalism in Late Imperial Vienna: Origins of the Christian Social Movement, 1848–1897* (Chicago and London: University of Chicago Press, 1981), p. 80. Freud's father, Jacob, was also involved in the textile industry, but on a very elementary level, as a wool trader.

6. Ruth Kestenberg-Gladstein, *Neuere Geschichte der Juden in den böhmischen Ländern*, Erster Teil, *Das Zeitalter der Aufklärung, 1780–1830* (Tübingen: J. C. B. Mohr, 1969), p. 99. Philipp's mother, Babette Mautner, may have been part of those Mautners who were to become so successful in the cloth industry. Israel Mautner established a linen and cotton factory in Prague, in 1827, and the next year the firm of Ellbogen and Mautner in Prossnitz (Prostějov), Moravia began producing men's clothing and uniforms. Austrian Textile Works originated out of the weaving factory of Isaak Mautner and Son in Nachod, where the Bauers came to have a factory. Nachod also boasted the large spinning works of Mautner and Warndorfer. See Gustav Otruba, "Der Anteil der Juden am Wirtschaftsleben der böhmischen Länder seit dem Beginn der Industrialisierung," in *Die Juden in den böhmischen Ländern* (München, Wien: R. Oldenbourg Verlag, 1983), p. 250; "Geschichte der Juden in Nachod," in Gold, p. 412.

7. Braunthal, ed., p. 9.

8. Joseph C. Pick, "The Economy," *The Jews of Czechoslovakia: Historical Studies and Surveys*, vol. 1 (Philadelphia: Jewish Publication Society of America, 1968), pp. 359–60.

9. My sources record only these four children. I do not know if there were others who died young, or even others, in addition, who lived into adulthood.

10. Letter of Otto Bauer to Karl Kautsky, June 20, 1922, in Peter Loewenberg, *Decoding the Past: The Psychohistorical Approach* (Berkeley: University of California Press, 1985), p. 172.

11. Stefan Zweig, *The World of Yesterday* (New York: Viking Press, 1943), pp. 87–88.

12. Zweig, pp. 81–83. There were exceptions. A few of the wealthiest young men could afford to support a mistress, and another few were lucky enough (and envied by their friends) to have an affair with a married woman. However, there was a certain measure of safety with prostitutes, many of whom were licensed by the state and were examined by a physician twice a week. And, Zweig says, they were very available: "It cost a man as little time and trouble to purchase a woman for a quarter of an hour, an hour, or a night, as it did to buy a package of cigarettes or a newspaper."

13. Freud almost fit the stereotype. He was engaged at twenty-six and married at thirty. But he did not have a venereal disease.

14. Braunthal, ed., p. 9.

15. Zweig, p. 8. Steven Beller upholds Zweig's observations about the abstemious, hardworking, "Puritan" Jews from Bohemia and Moravia. See *Vienna and the Jews, 1867–1938: A Cultural History* (Cambridge, New York, Melbourne: Cambridge University Press, 1989), pp. 169–170.

16. Julius Braunthal, *In Search of the Millennium* (London: Victor Gollancz, 1945), p. 75. The Bauers could have afforded to live in a more fashionable neighborhood than the Ninth District. See Marsha L. Rozenblit, *The Jews of Vienna, 1867–1914: Assimilation and Identity* (Albany: State University of New York Press, 1983), pp. 85–90, for the other districts where most factory owners and wealthy industrialists lived.

17. Braunthal, ed., p. 9; Braunthal, *The Millennium*, p. 77; Otto Leichter, *Otto Bauer: Tragödie Oder Triumph* (Wien: Europa Verlag, 1970), p. 22.

18. Leichter, ibid. According to a Jewish rabbinical decision, still in force when the Bauers moved to Meran in 1888, Jews were forbidden to settle in the entire Tyrolean region around Trent (Trento) and Bozen (Bolzano.) The ban went back to 1475, when the Jewish community in Trent was convicted of ritual murder. In response, the rabbis of Italy declared the entire area under *herem*—excommunication. Christian authorities also expelled the Jews from Trent in the fifteenth century, and as late as the eighteenth century they were not even allowed to pass through the town. In spite of these decrees, Jews from Central Europe began to move into Merano around the middle of the nineteenth century, and the region became a favorite vacation and health spa for Austrian Jews. See "Merano," *EJ*, vol. 11, col. 1381, and "Trent," *EJ*, vol. 15, cols. 1374–75.

19. *Encyclopaedia Britannica*, 11th ed., s. v. "Meran."

20. Paul Heyse, *Incurable*, trans. H. W. Eve (London: David Nutt, 1890), pp. 11, 21, 174. Another translation into English is to be found in Paul Heyse, *The Dead Lake and Other Tales*, trans. Mary Wilson (Leipzig: Bernhard Tauchnitz, 1870).

21. Ernest Jones, *The Life and Work of Sigmund Freud* (New York: Basic Books, 1953–57), vol. 1, pp. 334–36; vol. 2, pp. 23, 35; vol. 3, p. 98; Edoardo Weiss, *Sigmund Freud as a Consultant: Recollections of a Pioneer in Psychoanalysis* (New York: Intercontinental Medical Book Corp., 1970), p. 28; Didier Anzieu, *Freud's Self-Analysis*, trans. Peter Graham (Madison, Conn.: International Universities Press, 1986), pp. 528, 542.

22. Arthur Schnitzler, *My Youth in Vienna*, trans. Catherine Hutter (New York: Holt, Rinehart and Winston, 1970), pp. 182–87. Schnitzler may have had scrofula—tuberculosis of the lymphatic glands—which appears mainly in younger people.

Merano continues to thrive as a modern European health resort. A visitor's guide prepared in 1985 touted the baths at the "new Thermal Centre," where one could get "medicinal treatments of all kinds, from radioactive baths to mud-, ozone-, carbonic acid-, or herb-essence-bath, medicinal whole water massage from inhalations to douching and sauna." Cures were offered for "peripheric arterial vasculopathy and phlebopathy (varices), arthro-rheumapathy, senescence ailments, affections of the upper respiratory organs, chronic gynaecological diseases." See *A Guest in Merano* 8: 2 (Summer–Autumn 1985), published by the concierges of Merano.

23. Loewenberg, p. 172.

24. Steven Marcus, "Freud and Dora: Story, History, Case History," in Marcus, *Representations: Essays on Literature and Society* (New York: Random House, 1975), p. 249.

25. Peter J. Swales, "Freud, His Teacher, and the Birth of Psychoanalysis," in *Freud: Appraisals and Reappraisals*, ed., Paul E. Stepansky, vol. 1 (Hillsdale, N.J.: Analytic Press, 1986), pp. 13, 27, 33–36, 43.

26. Anzieu, p. 71.

27. Freud's letter to Wilhelm Fliess, February 4, 1888, in *The Origins of Psycho-Analysis: Letters to Wilhelm Fliess, Drafts and Notes: 1887–1902*, ed. Marie Bonaparte, Anna Freud, Ernst Kris (New York: Basic Books, 1954), p. 55.

28. Sigmund Freud, "An Autobiographical Study" [1925], *SE*, vol. 20 (1959), p. 17.

29. We know Philipp put in long hours on his business because when Otto was an adult, his tireless dedication to his work was said to resemble his father's. One of Otto's close followers wrote that as an adult, Otto generally worked eighteen hours a day. See Leichter, p. 22, and note 15 above.

30. Braunthal, ed., p. 9; Braunthal, *The Millennium*, p. 77.

31. David F. Good, *The Economic Rise of the Habsburg Empire, 1750–1914* (Berkeley and Los Angeles: University of California Press, 1984), p. 20.

32. Otruba, pp. 248, 250; Good, pp. 199, 226–27; Pick, p. 409.

33. Zweig, pp. 5–6.

34. "Nachod," *EJ*, vol. 12, col. 749.

35. "Geschichte der Juden in Nachod," in Gold, p. 412.

36. Meynen, pp. 4, 42; Pick, p. 410; Otruba, pp. 251–52.

37. Otruba, p. 251.

38. Meynen, p. 3; "Geschichte der Juden in Rumburg [includes Jews in Warnsdorf]," in Gold, p. 578.

39. Otruba, p. 250; "Geschichte der Juden in Reichenberg," in Gold, p. 548. The names of the wool dealers who did business in Reichenberg in the years 1702–82, 1850–54, and 1863–65 are all lumped together alphabetically. One "Jacob Bauer"—the name is the same as that of Philipp's father—is listed in the Reichenberg tax rolls as a wool merchant, although the source does not make it clear whether he traded in the eighteenth or nineteenth century.

40. Braunthal, *The Millennium*, p. 77; Braunthal, ed., p. 14.

41. Ezra Mendelsohn, *The Jews of East Central Europe Between the World Wars* (Bloomington: Indiana University Press, 1983), pp. 135–37.

42. "Reichenberg," *JE*, vol. 10, p. 364; "Liberec," *EJ*, vol. 11, cols. 187–88.

43. Arthur J. May, *The Hapsburg Monarchy, 1867–1914* (Cambridge: Harvard University Press, 1960), p. 326; Good, p. 180.

44. German nationalists expressed their opposition in Parliament by preventing the renewal of the *Ausgleich* (the Austro-Hungarian union), and there were massive demonstrations of university students and workers in front of the Vienna City Hall, Parliament, and the Ministry of the Interior. The situation was hardly better inside Parliament. Physical fights broke out among the deputies, and the police had to be called to restore order. See William J. McGrath, *Freud's Discovery of Psychoanalysis: The Politics of Hysteria* (Ithaca, N.Y., and London: Cornell University Press, 1986), pp. 180–81, 232; Carl E. Schorske, *Fin-de-Siècle Vienna: Politics and Culture* (New York: Alfred A. Knopf, 1980), p. 145.

45. Michael A. Riff, "Czech Antisemitism and the Jewish Response Before 1914," *Wiener Library Bulletin* 29 (1976), pp. 11–12.

46. Mark Twain, "Stirring Times in Austria," *Literary Essays*, vol. 22 of *The Writings of Mark Twain* (New York and London: Harper & Brothers, 1899), p. 249.

47. Quoted in Good, pp. 182–83.

48. Braunthal, ed., p. 9. There is a slight possibility that Ludwig Bauer lived permanently in Nachod, as the resident manager of the Bauer factory there. See "Geschichte der Juden in Nachod," in Gold, pp. 412–13.

49. Braunthal, ed., p. 9. Karl Bauer's most famous capitalist predecessor was Friedrich Engels, who first managed and later owned his father's factory in England.

50. Karl died of chronic heart disease during World War I. The Jewish community records note that at his death he was a "man of independent means."

51. The medical term for an illness like Malvine's is "marasmus." It means a progressive wasting away and emaciation without any obvious or ascertainable cause. Malvine may have been anorexic, since Freud diagnosed her as severely neurotic. It is possible she had a serious eating disorder since Dora, who took Malvine as her model, "was a poor eater [and showed a] disinclination for food" ("Fragment," p. 29).

52. Freud's words were at least partly correct. Like Malvine, Dora also married a man from Hungary.

53. This episode appears open to varying interpretations. Arnold Rogow would probably accept Dora's thoughts as indicative of the true state of Philipp's health, because he writes that after Philipp's meningitis, "he was never entirely well." See "A Further Footnote to Freud's 'Fragment of an Analysis of a Case of Hysteria,'" *Journal of the American Psychoanalytic Association* 26 (1978), p. 345. However, Rogow gives no source for this statement. Moreover, Philipp lived thirteen years after Christmas 1900 and did not die of syphilis. Freud interpreted Dora's reaction of pity and worry to the toast as proof of her hostility toward her father. See "Fragment," p. 98. Freud's and my interpretations do not contradict each other, and both may be applicable.

54. *Encyclopaedia Britannica* [hereafter *EB*], s.v. "Dvůr Králové"; Meynen, p. 4, folio 23.

55. It is likely, however, that her father, a brother, or an uncle was Leo Gerber since that is the name of a formal witness to Dora's birth listed in the IKG records. Leo Gerber's address in 1882 was Berggasse 32 (in the Ninth District), the same as Philipp's and Katharina's.

56. Leichter, p. 22.

57. Iwan Bloch, *The Sexual Life of Our Time in its Relation to Modern Civilization*, trans. (from the 6th German ed.) M. Eden Paul (London: Rebman Limited, 1908), p. 367. The latter part of this passage is Bloch's quotation from the 1902 work of a Leipzig gynecologist.

Bloch's (1872–1922) stated intentions in writing his book were to press for sexual reform and better love relations between men and women, which he deemed impossible without the eradication of venereal diseases. See pp. ix–x.

58. *EB*, 1951, s.v. "Franzensbad"; Will S. Monroe, *The Spell of Bohemia* (Boston: L. C. Page, 1910), pp. 187, 418, 431; Meynen, p. 2; Swales, p. 19; Hugo Stransky, "The Religious Life in the Historic Lands," *The Jews of Czechoslovakia: Historical Studies and Surveys*, vol. 1 (Philadelphia: Jewish Publication Society of America, 1968), p. 348; Pick, p. 378.

There was a small, permanent Jewish community in Franzensbad munificently supported by contributions from the many wealthy Jewish visitors. Their largesse paid for a temple, a cemetery, and even a hospital for poor Jews unable to pay for their cures. "Geschichte der Juden in Franzensbad," in Gold, pp. 141–42; "Bohemia," *JE*, vol. 3, p. 290; Meynen, pp. 47–48; Monroe, pp. 10, 418.

59. Joanne Furio, "Czechoslovakia's Opulent Spas," *New York Times*, Nov. 26, 1989, sec. 5, pp. 14, 19; Judith Shulevitz, "A Sampling of Spas," ibid., p. 16.

60. Monroe, pp. 418, 420–23, 429–32; *EB*, s.v. "Franzensbad." The waters and baths at František Lázně are still very popular today, although their efficacy is considered more limited. See note 59 above. Considering the minerals in the springs, which include iron and lithium, one can conjecture that certain anemias and manic-depressive symptoms might benefit, if the mineral levels were high enough. Sodium sulfate (Glauber's salt), a bowel cathartic, is also abundant in the springs, and many people still rate a periodic "cleaning out" highly.

Mud-compresses from spa mud also continue to be valued. A one-pound jar of mud from an Italian spa, sold in this country under the name *Terme di Saturnia,* cost seventy dollars recently. See Linda Wells, "Mirror Images," *New York Times Magazine,* February 21, 1988, p. 76.

61. Monroe, pp. 423, 431; Meynen, pp. 47–49. Freud himself preferred Karlsbad to treat his chronic gastrointestinal ailments, particularly constipation. When he experienced a stomach upset in Vienna, he would take a cold bath and a dose of Karlsbad salts for their laxative effect. This home treatment began at least as early as 1885, when he was twenty-nine. Jones, vol. 2, pp. 4, 59–60, 78, 83, 391, 396; Max Schur, *Freud: Living and Dying* (New York: International Universities Press, 1972), p. 255; *The Letters of Sigmund Freud,* ed., Ernst L. Freud, trans. Tania and James Stern (New York, Toronto, London: McGraw-Hill, 1964), p. 166.

62. Felix Deutsch, "A Footnote to Freud's 'Fragment of an Analysis of a Case of Hysteria,'" *Psychoanalytic Quarterly* 26 (1957), p. 167; Braunthal, ed., p. 9.

63. Leichter, p. 363 n. 6. At the time of the fight over the locked dining room door, Otto was already a university student.

64. Braunthal, ed., ibid.; Leichter, ibid.

65. Deutsch, p. 163. Käthe's constipation was another reason for her going to spas to take the cure.

66. Leichter, p. 23; Braunthal, ed., ibid., p. 10.

67. Deutsch, ibid.

68. IKG records. The *mohel* was one "M. Spitz."

69. Braunthal, ed., p. 9; Loewenberg, p. 192.

70. Braunthal, ed., p. 10; Leichter, pp. 22–23.

71. Braunthal, ed., pp. 10–11; Leichter, pp. 12, 23. Otto's play was found after World War II among some of Dora's belongings, and it was privately printed in 1948 in Vienna, by and for Otto's friends. It can be found in the archives of the Verein für Geschichte der Arbeiterbewegung Wien.

72. *Programm des K.K.-Ober-Gymnasiums in Meran,* courtesy of Dr. Albrecht Hirschmüller. This contradicts the information given by Braunthal, ed., p. 11. However, the primary source from Meran appears more convincing than the secondary information, without a source, given by Braunthal.

73. Perhaps "interrupted" is a better word than "lightened." Stefan Zweig, also born in 1881, remembered (p. 31) that "twice a week we were led into the gymnasium; and there, with the windows carefully closed, we marched stupidly around on the wooden floor, and every step sent the dust high into the air. With that the demands of hygiene had been satisfied and the State had done its 'duty' towards us, so far as *mens sana in corpore sano* was concerned."

74. Braunthal, *The Millennium,* p. 30; Rozenblit, p. 101; Mark E. Blum, *The Austro-Marxists, 1890–1918. A Psychobiographical Study* (Lexington: University Press of Kentucky, 1985), pp. 2, 8; Braunthal, ed., p. 11.

75. Dora attended the school of the *Kloster der Englischen Fräulein* (Convent of the English Sisters). Information courtesy Dr. Albrecht Hirschmüller.

76. Rozenblit, pp. 119–20.

77. Ibid., p. 99; William M. Johnston, *The Austrian Mind. An Intellectual and Social History, 1848–1938* (Berkeley: University of California Press, 1972), pp. 67–68.

78. Braunthal, ed., p. 11; Braunthal, *The Millennium,* p. 78.

79. Braunthal, ed., p. 9; Robert S. Wistrich, *Revolutionary Jews from Marx to Trotsky* (London: Harrap, 1976), p. 96. The springs of Karl's own attraction to socialism

are unknown, but when Otto was in *Gymnasium,* it is entirely likely that this "hypo-chondriacal" man had turned his pessimistic gaze to the fading Austrian liberals and decided that socialism was the only viable political option for a Jew in Austria. Karl was certainly not alone in this conclusion. Freud himself, though he became increasingly pessimistic in the 1890s about the social and political climate, looked neither to socialism nor to Zionism for a solution. It has been argued that the deteriorating political situation nevertheless remained fruitful for Freud since his development of psychoanalysis at just that time had political significance for him and that, even further, his political frustrations fueled his discovery of psychoanalysis. See Schorske and McGrath.

80. Braunthal, *The Millennium,* pp. 108–9.

81. Ibid., pp. 77–78; Braunthal, ed., pp. 11–12, 14.

82. *Yearbook of the Leo Baeck Institute,* vol. 5, p. 266, quoted in Elon, p. 71.

83. Otruba, p. 266; Wistrich, James Joll's Foreword and p. 16.

84. Andrew G. Whiteside, *The Socialism of Fools: Georg Ritter von Schönerer and Austrian Pan-Germanism* (Berkeley: University of California Press, 1975), pp. 54–56, 170, 307.

85. George Clare, *Last Waltz in Vienna: The Rise and Destruction of a Family, 1842–1942* (New York: Holt, Rinehart and Winston, 1982), p. 29; Schnitzler, p. 128.

86. Schnitzler, pp. 296–97.

87. Boyer, p. 90; Martin Freud, "Who Was Freud?" in *The Jews of Austria,* ed. Josef Fraenkel (London: Vallentine, Mitchell, 1967), pp. 206–7; Paul Johnson, *A History of the Jews* (New York: Harper & Row, 1987), p. 397; Johnston, p. 66; Denis B. Klein, *Jewish Origins of the Psychoanalytic Movement* (New York: Praeger, 1981), p. 12; Schnitzler, p. 128; Whiteside, p. 313.

88. Klein, p. 17; Rozenblit, pp. 161, 164; Arthur Ruppin, *The Jews of Today,* trans. Margery Bentwich (New York: Henry Holt and Co., 1913), p. 279.

89. Braunthal, ed., p. 15.

90. Johnston, p. 100; Wistrich, pp. 105–10; Edmund Silberner, "The Jewish Background of Victor and Friedrich Adler," *Yearbook of the Leo Baeck Institute* (1965), vol. 10, p. 271; Peter G. J. Pulzer, *The Rise of Political Anti-Semitism in Germany and Austria* (New York: John Wiley & Sons, 1964), pp. 267–68.

91. Pulzer (p. 269) remarks: "It is a strange commentary on the pre-1914 world that even revolutionary Marxists felt secure in its stability and reasonableness. They consoled themselves with repeating the *mot* . . . that anti-Semitism was 'the Socialism of the dolt' ('*der Sozialismus des dummen Kerls*')."

92. Otto once quoted with approval the remark of Baron Karl von Vogelsang (1818–90), one of the ideological fathers of the Austrian anticapitalist/anti-Semitic move-ment: "If by some miracle all our 1,400,000 Jews were to be taken from us, it would help us very little, for we ourselves have been infected with the Jewish spirit." Robert S. Wistrich, *Socialism and the Jews: The Dilemmas of Assimilation in Germany and Austria-Hungary* (East Brunswick, N.J.: Associated University Presses, 1982), pp. 190–91.

4.   *"Merely a Case of* 'Petite Hystérie'"

1. Josef Breuer and Sigmund Freud, *Studies on Hysteria* [1895], *SE,* vol. 2 (1955), pp. 161–62. One is struck by the use of the masculine pronoun regarding this almost totally female situation.

2. Robert Seidenberg and Evangelos Papathomopoulos, "Daughters Who Tend Their Fathers: A Literary Survey," *The Psychoanalytic Study of Society,* vol. 2 (New York: International Universities Press, 1962), pp. 138, 156, 158.

3. Freud attributed Dora's vaginal discharge to her early masturbation prior to age eight!

4. Although this may have been Dora's fantasy, it was not totally without foundation. While it is hard to come by accurate statistics of the frequency of venereal diseases in late-nineteenth-century Vienna, we do have the anecdotal accounts of Stefan Zweig's, Arthur Schnitzler's, and others' experiences. There are also some statistics for Germany at the turn of the century. One study showed that of the male clerks and merchants in Berlin between the ages of eighteen and twenty-eight, 45 percent at some time had syphilis and 20 percent gonorrhea. Another study for all of Germany estimated that one man in five had contracted syphilis and that gonorrhea averaged at least one attack per man. See Maria Ramas, "Freud's Dora, Dora's Hysteria: The Negation of a Woman's Rebellion," *Feminist Studies* 6: 3 (Fall 1980), pp. 488–89.

5 The fact that Hans Zellenka was born in Meran shows that Jews, excluded from Meran since the fifteenth century, had begun to move into the town after the liberating events of 1848. Mr. K.'s identity was first revealed to me by Peter Loewenberg, a historian and psychoanalyst. It has subsequently been confirmed by other historians of psychoanalysis.

6. Information courtesy of Dr. Albrecht Hirschmüller.

7. The incidence of hysteria has been highest among groups that have little control over their lives, such as soldiers and women. After World War I, when the rate of hysteria had greatly diminished in the West, hysteria was still frequently found there among men who had dangerous jobs and women who were servants and nurses. Laurence Kirmayer, "Culture, Affect and Somatization," Parts 1 and 2, *Transcultural Psychiatric Research Review* 21:3 and 4 (1984), pp. 160–61, 168–69; Bennett Simon, *Mind and Madness in Ancient Greece: The Classical Roots of Modern Psychiatry* (Ithaca and London: Cornell University Press, 1978), pp. 241–42; Edward Shorter, "Paralysis: The Rise and Fall of a 'Hysterical' Symptom," in *Expanding the Past: A Reader in Social History,* ed. Peter N. Stearns (New York and London: New York University Press, 1988), p. 234.

8. The physician and sexologist, Iwan Bloch, listed sixty-four such experts and ranked Mantegazza second only after the renowned Krafft-Ebing. Freud was eleventh on Bloch's list. *The Sexual Life of Our Time in its Relations to Modern Civilization,* trans. (from the 6th German ed.) M. Eden Paul (London: Rebman, 1908), p. 758 n. 1.

9. Spread over time there appeared *The Physiology of Pleasure, The Physiology of Love, The Physiology of Hate, The Physiology of Pain, The Physiology of Woman, The Hygiene of Love,* and *The Hygiene of Beauty.* In related veins there were *Elements of Hygiene, The Physiognomy and Expression of Feelings, Human Ecstasy, The Nervous Century,* and *The Hypocritical Century.*

10. Articles on Mantegazza can be found in the following: *Dizionario Biografico degli Scrittori Contemporanei,* vol. Cav–Del (Firenze: Angelo de Gubernatis, ed., 1879), pp. 679–81; *La Grande Encyclopédie: Inventaire Raisonné des Sciences, des lettres et des arts,* vol. 22 (Paris, 1886–1902), p. 1179; *Brockhaus' Konversations-Lexikon,* 14th ed., vol. 11 (Leipzig, 1894); "Nécrologie," *L'Anthropologie* (1910), vol. 21, pp. 721–22; *Encyclopaedia Britannica,* 11th ed., s.v. "Mantegazza, Paolo" and "Physiognomy"; *Enciclopedia Italiana di Scienze, Lettere ed Arti* (Roma, 1934), vol. 22, pp. 159–60; *Ministri Deputati e Senatori D'Italia dal 1848 al 1922,* vol. 2 (Tosi/Roma: Alberto Malatesta, ed., 1946), p. 146.

11. *Anthropological Studies in the Sexual Relations of Mankind,* unnumbered frontmatter pages.

12. *The Physiology of Love* (New York: Cleveland Publishing Company, 1894), pp. 194–95.

13. Any passage at random will illustrate this. The dedication itself is proof enough: "To the daughters of Eve, that they may teach men that love is not lechery nor the simony of voluptuousness, but a joy that dwells in the highest and holiest regions of the terrestrial paradise, that they may make it the highest prize of virtue, the most glorious conquest of genius, the first force of human progress."

14. *The Physiology of Woman* (Jena, 1893), p. 442, quoted in Bloch, p. 164.

15. For relevant historical discussions see: Alan Krohn, *Hysteria: The Elusive Neurosis*, Psychological Issues Monograph 45/46 (New York: International Universities Press, 1978), especially pp. 174–96; Esther Fischer-Homberger, "Hysterie und Miso-gynie—ein Aspekt der Hysteriegeschichte," *Gesnerus* 26 (1969), pp. 117–27; Marc H. Hollender, "Conversion Hysteria, A Post-Freudian Reinterpretation of 19th Century Psychosocial Data," *Archives of General Psychiatry* 26 (1972), pp. 311–14; Carroll Smith-Rosenberg, "The Hysterical Woman: Sex Roles and Role Conflict in 19th-Century America," *Social Research* 39 (1972), pp. 652–78; Ilza Veith, *Hysteria: The History of a Disease* (Chicago: University of Chicago Press, 1965), pp. 199–212; Ann Douglas Wood, "'The Fashionable Diseases': Women's Complaints and Their Treatment in Nineteenth-Century America," *Journal of Interdisciplinary History* 4 (1973), pp. 25–52.

16. Study of the "feminization" of Victorian society does not invalidate this generalization. Neither does the fact that some women coped admirably with the vicissitudes of daily life. Note, for example, the energetic and very practical Isabella Beeton, whose *Book of Household Management* (1861) depicts a far-from-vulnerable women who obviously wrote for those middle-class women desirous of taking charge of their lives and families. See Ann Douglas, *The Feminization of American Culture* (New York: Avon, 1978); Peter Gay, *Education of the Senses*, vol. 1 of *The Bourgeois Experience* (New York and Oxford: Oxford University Press), 1984, pp. 345–49.

17. See chapter 1, p. 6, and chapter 2, p. 15.

18. Of course, men suffered from hysteria, too. They used their symptoms and evoked the same responses women did. But the medical literature of the day reflects a greater preoccupation with women.

19. Armand Hückel, a German neurologist, in *Münchener medizinische Wochenschrift* (March, 19, 1889), quoted in Shorter, p. 228.

20. Freud's full interpretation of Dora's cough was both single-minded and dazzling. Whether it was true in all details is another matter. Freud found "excessively intense" ("Fragment," p. 54) Dora's preoccupation with her father's relations with Mrs. K.: "Her behaviour obviously went far beyond what would have been appropriate to filial concern. She felt and acted more like a jealous wife. . . . By her ultimatum to her father ('either her or me'), by the scenes she used to make, by the suicidal threat she allowed to be noticed . . . she was clearly putting herself in her mother's place. If we have rightly guessed the nature of the imaginary sexual situation which underlay her cough, in that phantasy she must have been putting herself in Frau K.'s place. She was therefore identifying herself both with the woman her father had once loved and with the woman he loved now. The inference is obvious that . . . she was in love with him" ("Fragment," p. 56).

21. Gay, p. 287.

22. Ibid., pp. 56–67.

23. Gay superbly documents nineteenth-century shams and the contemporary awareness of them. See pp. 404–22. I also address certain aspects of the situation in

Freud in Germany: Revolution and Reaction in Science (New York: International Universities Press, 1977), pp. 4–11.

24. Gay, p. 420. And "even those who espoused doctrinaire purist views on sexuality while keeping a mistress or resorting to prostitutes, were [not] necessarily untroubled frauds. They were, more often than not, at war with themselves. . . . The bourgeois conscience [was] exacting [and] persecuting" (p. 421).

25. Zweig, p. 74.

26. Ibid.

27. Ibid., pp. 77–78. The Victorians were acutely aware of the results. Commented the *Saturday Review:* "The best and most innocent-minded girl of the labouring class knows far more at fifteen than the high-born damsel of twenty-five." Quoted in Gay, *The Tender Passion*, vol. 2 of *The Bourgeois Experience* (1986), p. 405.

28. Zweig, pp. 71–73.

29. Perhaps the daughters of assimilated Viennese Jews lived in two worlds more than did their middle-class Christian counterparts. One such Jewish girl was Käthe Leichter, who went to a secondary school attended by bureaucrats' daughters (*Beamtentöchterschule*). She recalled that her Jewish friends read Oscar Wilde and Arthur Schnitzler, while the officials' daughters read typical "girls' " books. Steven Beller, *Vienna and the Jews, 1867–1938: A Cultural History* (Cambridge, New York, Melbourne: Cambridge University Press, 1989), p. 186.

30. Susan Quinn, *A Mind of Her Own: The Life of Karen Horney* (New York: Summit Books, 1987). The information comes from Horney's own diary.

31. See my chapter 6 below. Another confusing aspect of Dora's daily life was her smoking. Women did not generally smoke, but Dora at fifteen was already a "passionate smoker," taking as her models her father, her brother, and Mr. K. ("Fragment," p. 73.) It is not clear, however, whether her parents knew that she smoked or if she smoked only with the Ks.

32. Getting information from servants was a common path followed by middle-class girls. Emily Lytton, an English girl just seven years older than Dora, recalled: "I was an inquisitive child, especially about the facts of sex, but it never occurred to me to ask my mother any questions on the subject. I pestered the servants with questions, however, and pretended to know more than I did in order to draw them out." *A Blessed Girl: Memories of a Victorian Girlhood, 1887–1896*, quoted in Gay, *Education of the Senses*, p. 281.

33. Freud, "Sexuality in the Aetiology of the Neuroses" [1898], *SE*, vol. 3 (1962), p. 266.

34. Zweig, pp. 78–79.

35. Freud had used the pseudonym of "Mr. K." once before to describe a twenty-four-year-old man who developed an anxiety neurosis after falling in love with a young woman, being sexually excited by her, and then being unable to have any sexual contact with her because she was engaged to someone else. See *The Complete Letters of Sigmund Freud to Wilhelm Fliess, 1887–1904*, ed. and trans. Jeffrey M. Masson (Cambridge: Harvard University Press, 1985), pp. 90–93. The earlier edition of Freud's letters to Fliess *(The Origins of Psycho-Analysis)* gives Mr. K.'s age as twenty-seven (p. 96).

36. One might argue that her last governess and Mrs. K. did encourage her somewhat. But the validity of their influence quickly vanished after Dora learned that both women had been interested in her only as a route to her father's affections.

37. At seventy-six Freud declared that women have "little sense of justice, [are] weaker in their social interests and [have] less capacity for sublimating their instincts than men." "New Introductory Lectures" [1933], *SE,* vol. 22 (1964), p. 134.

38. Recently, Carol Gilligan has intelligently amended Freud's ideas. See *In a Different Voice: Psychological Theory and Women's Development* (Cambridge: Harvard University Press, 1982).

39. In those cases where a girl's growing-up years had been satisfactory and she had, on the whole, received equitable and considerate treatment within the family, she could sublimate whatever grievances she had and injustices she had observed in charity work. This is what Anna O. had done, and it eventually led to a career. Not surprisingly, she never married.

40. One of Freud's chief complaints against Dora, which he repeatedly advanced, was that she had a desire for revenge. See in "Fragment": "her motives for revenge" (p. 100); her actuat[ion] by jealousy and revenge" (p. 106); "you give free rein to your feelings of revenge" (p. 107); "her craving for revenge" (p. 110).

41. IKG records.

42. Marsha L. Rozenblit, *The Jews of Vienna, 1867–1914: Assimilation and Identity* (Albany: State University of New York Press, 1983), pp. 120–22. It must be noted, however, that the demands of Austrian feminists, were far less radical than those of their opposite numbers in Western Europe and the United States because it was against Austrian law for women to join or form political associations. Therefore, no female suffrage society was ever founded. See Richard J. Evans, *The Feminists: Women's Emancipation Movements in Europe, America and Australasia 1840–1920* (London: Croom Helm/New York: Barnes & Noble, 1977), pp. 94, 102.

43. William M. Johnston, *The Austrian Mind. An Intellectual and Social History, 1848–1938* (Berkeley: University of California Press, 1972), p. 71; Arthur J. May, *Vienna in the Age of Franz Josef* (Norman: University of Oklahoma Press, 1966), pp. 51, 121. However, it was only the emperor's *Diktat* that overrode the faculty's resistance to training women physicians. Franz Josef declared that his female Islamic subjects needed women doctors. Women were not admitted to the law faculty until after World War I.

44. Johnston, p. 156; Evans, p. 95.

45. *Minutes of the Vienna Psychoanalytic Society,* vol. 1, *1906–1908,* ed. Herman Nunberg and Ernst Federn (New York: International Universities Press, Inc., 1962), p. 195, and ibid., n. 1. Such marriages, of course, intensified the already inherent superior-inferior relationship between husband and wife and in many cases created psychological distress or even illness for the girl within a few years.

46. John W. Boyer, "Freud, Marriage, and Late Victorian Liberalism," *Journal of Modern History* 50: 1 (March 1978), pp. 89–90.

47. Fifteen years earlier, Freud, too, had been a first-time tourist at the Dresden Art Gallery, although he had spent only an hour there, all told. He went looking for the well-known Madonna, but when he found her his reaction was the opposite of Dora's; he was somewhat disappointed by what he experienced as her mundanity. He reported in a letter to his fiancée: "I have a serious objection to raise. . . . Raphael's Madonna . . . is a girl, say sixteen years old; she gazes out on the world with such a fresh and innocent expression, half against my will she suggested to me a charming, sympathetic nursemaid, not from the celestial world but from ours." *The Letters of Sigmund Freud,* ed. Ernst L. Freud (New York: McGraw-Hill, 1964), p. 82.

48. Carl E. Schorske, *Fin-de-Siècle Vienna: Politics and Culture* (New York: Alfred A. Knopf, 1980), pp. 232, 238.

49. Peter Vergo, *Art in Vienna, 1898–1918: Klimt, Kokoschka, Schiele and Their Contemporaries.* (London: Phaidon Press, 1975), pp. 28, 31; James Shedel, *Art and Society: The New Art Movement in Vienna, 1897–1914* (Palo Alto, Calif.: Sposs, Inc., 1981), pp. 71, 74–75, 77–78.

50. Shedel, pp. 55–57, 59–61, 85–86; Vergo, pp. 15–16, 39; May, p. 108, Schorske, pp. 227–38. "To the horror of the old school, [the Secessionists] exhibited the Impressionists and the Pointillists of Paris, Munch of Norway, Rops of Belgium, and all the other extremists imaginable" (Zweig, p. 44). The Secessionists' motto was "To the Age Its Art, To Art Its Freedom." Anti-Semites who did not like the style of the new school raged at the Jewish involvement.

51. Zweig, pp. 21–22.

52. Schorske, p. 227

53. Ibid., p. 223.

54. Vergo, *Art in Vienna,* p. 62; Vergo, *Vienna 1900: Vienna, Scotland, and the European Avant-Garde.* (Edinburgh: Her Majesty's Stationery Office, 1983), p. 43.

55. Michael A. Riff, "Czech Antisemitism and the Jewish Response Before 1914," *Wiener Library Bulletin* 29 (1976), p. 12.

56. For the origins and history of blood libel see "Blood Libel," *EJ,* vol. 4, cols. 1120–31.

57. František Červinka, "The Hilsner Affair," *Yearbook of the Leo Baeck Institute,* vol. 13, (1968), p. 145.

58. Histories of the Jews in Polna are in "Polna," *EJ,* vol. 13, col. 836, and "Dějiny Židů v Polné," in *Die Juden und Judengemeinden Böhmens in Vergangenheit und Gegenwart,* ed. Hugo Gold (Brünn-Prag: Jüdischer Buch- und Kunstverlag, 1934), pp. 508–11. Červinka discusses the Jews' poor economic condition in the nineteenth century, pp. 143, 145.

59. Červinka, p. 145.

60. "Hilsner Case," *EJ,* vol. 8, col. 496.

61. "Blood Accusation," *JE,* vol. 3, p. 276; Hans Kohn, "Before 1918 in the Historic Lands," *The Jews of Czechoslovakia: Historical Studies and Surveys,* vol. 1 (Philadelphia: Jewish Publication Society of America, 1968), p. 17.

62. Červinka, pp. 150–52; "Nachod," *EJ,* vol. 12, col. 749; "Hilsner Case," *EJ,* col. 496.

63. "Polna Affair," *JE,* vol. 10, p. 117; Johnston, p. 28.

64. "Blood Accusation," *JE,* p. 267.

5.   *"I Do Not Know What Kind of Help She Wanted from Me"*

1. Sigmund Freud, "Heredity and the Aetiology of the Neuroses" [1896], *SE* vol. 3 (1962), p. 151. For the two years before 1896, he had used terms like "psychical analysis," "clinico-psychological analysis," and "psychological analysis." See *SE,* vol. 3, p. 47, n. 1.

2. Ernest Jones, *The Life and Work of Sigmund Freud,* vol. 1 (New York: Basic Books, 1953), pp. 11–12; Peter Gay, *Freud: A Life for Our Time.* (New York and London: W. W. Norton, 1988), pp. 7–8; Henri F. Ellenberger, *The Discovery of the Unconscious* (New York: Basic Books, 1970), p. 428; Max Schur, *Freud: Living and Dying* (New York: International Universities Press, 1972), pp. 20–21; Ronald W. Clark, *Freud: The Man and the Cause* (New York: Random House, 1980), pp. 5–6; Marianne Krüll, *Freud and His Father* (New York and London: W. W. Norton, 1986), p. 103. Even

when I do not give specific attribution, I rely heavily on these six sources for my brief biography of Freud's life. Also vital is Freud's own "Autobiographical Study" [1925], *SE*, vol. 20 (1959), pp. 7–70.

3. Paul C. Vitz, "Sigmund Freud's Attraction to Christianity: Biographical Evidence," *Psychoanalysis and Contemporary Thought* 6 (1983), p. 85.

4. Krüll, p. 93.

5. Gay and Krüll, relying on the research of Josef Sajner, have concluded that the shop was a blacksmith's. Previous biographers (Clark, Ellenberger, Schur) stated that it was a locksmith's.

6. Jones, p. 15; Gay, p. 8; Krüll, pp. 147–51. Didier Anzieu, *Freud's Self-Analysis*, trans. Peter Graham (Madison, Conn.: International Universities Press, 1986), p. 10.

7. Freud's letter to Wilhelm Fliess, Sept. 21, 1897, in *The Complete Letters of Sigmund Freud to Wilhelm Fliess, 1887–1904*, ed. and trans. Jeffrey M. Masson (Cambridge: Belknap Press, 1985), pp. 264–66.

Recent works have questioned the validity of this traditional explanation of Freud's movement away from his seduction theory. Instead they have hypothesized that his renunciation was an unconscious or even conscious device to protect the reputation of either his father or his intimate friend the ear, nose, and throat doctor Wilhelm Fliess. See Krüll's imaginative *Freud and His Father* and Masson's questionable *The Assault on the Truth: Freud's Suppression of the Seduction Theory* (New York: Farrar, Straus and Giroux, 1984). Yet a third interpretation, close to the conventional one but with a different emphasis, is to be found in William J. McGrath's suggestive *Freud's Discovery of Psychoanalysis: The Politics of Hysteria* (Ithaca, N.Y., and London: Cornell University Press, 1986).

8. *The Interpretation of Dreams* [1900], *SE*, vols. 4 and 5 (1958). The book actually appeared in November 1899.

9. "Three Essays on the Theory of Sexuality" [1905d], *SE*, vol. 7 (1953), pp. 130–243.

10. Freud to Fliess, Sept. 14, 1900, in Masson, *Letters*, p. 424.

11. Freud, *The Interpretation of Dreams*, pp. 136–40. See also note 14 below.

12. Dennis B. Klein, *Jewish Origins of the Psychoanalytic Movement* (New York: Praeger Publishers, 1981), p. 72. It may be relevant that Freud joined the B'nai B'rith one week after he wrote to Fliess that his seduction theory of hysteria was incorrect. Freud seemed to be seeking a safe harbor to ride out more than one storm.

13. Freud, "Address to the Society of B'nai B'rith" [1926] (1941), *SE*, vol. 20 (1959), pp. 273–74.

14. Freud, *The Interpretation of Dreams*, pp. 193, 442. Right after the new year, Freud saw Theodor Herzl's play, *The New Ghetto*. His dream that night called to mind "the Jewish problem, concern about the future of one's children, to whom one cannot give a country of their own, concern about educating them in such a way that they can move freely across frontiers."

15. Freud to Fliess, March 11, 1900, in Masson, ibid., p. 404.

16. Freud, "Preface to the Second Edition," *The Interpretation of Dreams*, p. xxvi.

17. Ilse Bry and Alfred H. Rifkin, "Freud and the History of Ideas: Primary Sources, 1886–1910," in *Science and Psychoanalysis*, vol. 5 (New York: Grune & Stratton, 1962), pp. 6–36; Hannah S. Decker, "*The Interpretation of Dreams*: Early Reception by the Educated German Public," *Journal of the History of the Behavioral Sciences*, 11 (1975), pp. 129–41; Decker, *Freud in Germany: Revolution and Reaction in Science, 1893–1907* (New York: International Universities Press, 1977), pp. 104–8, 211–12, 277–92.

18. Freud to Fliess, March 23, 1900, in Masson, ibid., p. 405.

19. Freud to Fliess in ibid. In 1899: Nov. 7, p. 383; Nov. 12, p. 385; Dec. 9, p. 391; Dec. 21, p. 392. In 1900: Jan. 8, p. 394; Jan. 26, p. 396; Mar. 11, pp. 402–3; May 16, p. 414; July 10, p. 422; Oct. 14, p. 427.

20. Freud to Fliess, Jan. 8, 1900, in ibid., p. 394, and March 11, 1900, p. 404.

21. Freud to Fliess, Mar. 23, 1900, in ibid., p. 405; April 25, 1900, p. 410; May 7, 1900, p. 412, and Gay, p. 134.

22. Assessments of Freud's libido, his personal sexual habits, and his attitude about the role of sexual relations in his life can be found in Krüll, pp. 18–20; Gay, pp. 38, 59, 162–64; Jones, vol. 1, pp. 99, 139, 271; vol. 2, pp. 386–87; Paul Roazen, *Freud and His Followers* (New York: New American Library, 1976), pp. 49–55, 62–63, 83–84, 232. See also Freud to Fliess, in Masson, ibid., Aug. 20, 1893, p. 54; Oct. 31, 1897, p. 276; March 11, 1900, p. 404; *The Freud/Jung Letters*, ed. William McGuire (Princeton, N.J.: Princeton University Press, 1974), pp. 443, 456.

The issue of whether Freud's declining and sparse sexual life with his wife was compensated for by an affair with his sister-in-law, Minna Bernays, is discussed intelligently by Roazen and especially Gay (pp. 752–53.) Both men conclude that there is no evidence available at present to confirm any such supposition, and I concur. For the most recent evaluation, see Peter Gay, "Sigmund and Minna? The Biographer as Voyeur," *New York Times Book Review*, January 29, 1989, pp. 1, 43–45. This report on the correspondence between Freud and Minna raises some questions, since a significant block of letters is missing.

23. Freud to Fliess, Dec. 21, 1899, in Masson, ibid., p. 392; In 1900: Jan. 26, p. 396; Feb. 12, p. 399; Feb. 22, p. 400; Apr. 25, p. 411; May 20, p. 415; June 12, pp. 417–18; June 18, p. 419.

24. Freud even referred to himself as a helpless beggar. Freud to Fliess, March 23, 1900, in ibid., p. 406, and May 7, 1900, p. 412. Freud had a masochistic component in his personality, doubtless based on some persistent guilt. It pushed him in a pessimistic direction and even led him to deny positive occurrences in his life, be they professional acclaim or personal success. See Gay, *Freud*, pp. 140, 449, 572.

25. Rome represented to Freud the Semite Hannibal's campaign against the Romans, symbolizing "the tenacity of Jewry and the organization of the Catholic Church." Rome also stood for "other passionate wishes." In a passage on *"disguised* dreams of sexual intercourse with the dreamer's mother,"* Freud gave as an example the oracle given to the Tarquins that "conquest of Rome would fall to that one of them who should first kiss his mother." See Freud, *The Interpretation of Dreams*, pp. 196–97, 398, and 398 n. 1.

26. Freud to Fliess, Mar. 2, 1899, in ibid., p. 347.

27. There was a time when Freud addressed Fliess as "Beloved Friend" and plaintively asked him: "Daimonie [Demon], why don't you write?" (The latter was in a letter of July 24, 1895, in ibid., p. 134.) Freud began writing to Fliess in November 1887 and by 1895 was sending him more than two letters a month. In 1899 Freud wrote forty-four times, but in 1900 twenty-seven, and in 1901 only seventeen.

28. Jones, vol. 1, p. 301.

29. Gay, p. 165.

30. Freud to Fliess, Dec. 6, 1896, in Masson, ibid., p. 214, and May 8, 1901, p. 440; Gay, pp. 170–71.

31. Gay, p. 156.

32. Fritz Wittels and Max Graf quoted in Gay, ibid.

33. Gay, p. 157.

34. Sigmund Freud, *On Dreams* [1901a], *SE*, vol. 5 (1958), pp. 636–37. Mrs. E. L. was a composite female figure representing at least three women to whom Freud was attracted; one of them was probably Dora. See Anzieu, pp. 531, 542–44.

35. On taking notes see Freud, "Recommendations to Physicians Practising Psycho-Analysis" [1912b], *SE*, vol. 12 (1958), pp. 113–14.

36. In the summer of 1899 Freud was still advising patients to shut their eyes so that they could concentrate on self-observation. By 1903 he had stopped giving them that direction, but it was a recent innovation. Therefore it seems likely that Dora was treated during the period when he was still telling patients to close their eyes. See *The Interpretation of Dreams*, p. 101, and "Freud's Psycho-Analytic Procedure" [1904], *SE*, vol. 7 (1953), p. 250.

37. Anzieu, p. 374. Freud did not become expert in the technique of free association for several more years. He was still having trouble with the method when he saw the "Rat Man" in 1907–8, and he reported a "struggle" with the patient. According to the minutes Otto Rank took when Freud presented the case at the Wednesday Psychological Society, Freud announced that "the technique of analysis has changed insofar as the analyst now no longer seeks what is of interest to him, but lets the patient develop his thoughts naturally." Rank then added a revealing footnote: "What we have here for the first time is an account of an analysis carried out successfully according to the free-association method." See Anzieu, p. 375.

38. It is not without meaning for Philipp's character that Freud perceived that Philipp had "handed [Dora] over to [him] for psychotherapeutic treatment" ("Fragment," p. 19).

39. Freud's letter to Fliess, October 15, 1897, in Masson, ibid., p. 272.

40. James Strachey, "Editor's Note" to the *Three Essays on the Theory of Sexuality* [1905], *SE*, vol. 7 (1953), p. 128. See also p. 108.

41. Freud, "Heredity and the Aetiology of the Neuroses" [1896], *SE*, vol. 3 (1962), p. 150, and Freud's letter to Fliess, Dec. 22, 1897, in Masson, ibid., p. 287. In his 1896 paper, Freud labeled "(immoderate) masturbation or spontaneous emissions" as "this pernicious sexual satisfaction," and in his letter to Fliess added: "Doubt arises whether an addiction of this kind is curable, or whether analysis and therapy must come to a halt at this point and content themselves with transforming hysteria into neurasthenia." See also Annie Reich, "The Discussion of 1912 on Masturbation and Our Present-Day Views," in *Psychoanalytic Study of the Child*, vol. 6 (New York: International Universities Press, 1951), p. 81. The Vienna Psychoanalytic Society held many discussions on masturbation in the early years of the twentieth century. Freud's views as well as those of his early followers appear in the *Minutes*. See *Minutes of the Vienna Psychoanalytic Society*, vols. 2–4, 1908–1918, ed. Herman Nunberg and Ernst Federn (New York: International Universities Press, 1967–75). For a summary statement of Freud's thoughts on masturbation in 1910 see vol. 2, pp. 560–63.

42. Freud, *Psychopathology of Everyday Life* [1901], *SE*, vol. 6 (1960), pp. 143–44; Freud's letter to Fliess, August 7, 1901, in Masson, ibid., p. 448.

43. In the fall of 1900, bisexuality lay heavily on Freud's mind. In the same month that he began treating Dora, he had as a patient Hermann Swoboda, whom he convinced of the bisexual disposition of all human beings. See David Abrahamsen, *The Mind and Death of a Genius* (New York: Columbia University Press, 1946), p. 43, and the 1904 correspondence between Freud and Fliess in Masson, ibid., pp. 460–68. All this evidence combined convinces me that Freud inserted the idea of bisexuality into the Dora case to link it early and publicly to psychoanalysis. Frank J. Sulloway, however, interprets Freud's use of

the idea as his attempt to "placate" Fliess in an effort to keep their friendship alive. See *Freud, Biologist of the Mind* (New York: Basic Books, 1979), p. 223.

44. L. C. Grey, "Clinical Lecture," quoted in Carroll Smith-Rosenberg, "The Hysterical Woman: Sex Roles and Role Conflict in 19th-Century America," *Social Research* 39 (1972), p. 675.

45. Ibid.

46. Alexander Grinstein, *On Sigmund Freud's Dreams* (Detroit: Wayne State University Press, 1968), pp. 234, 239–40, 392, 394, 411.

47. Jones, vol. 1, pp. 78–85.

48. Anzieu, p. 546. Freud was jealous of his friend Fliess, who in 1892 had married a woman from a well-to-do Viennese family.

An element of Freud's negative countertransference to Dora may be hidden in his feelings about Fliess's wife. Her name was Ida Bondy, which the name "Ida Bauer" was bound to evoke, and Freud did not like Ida Bondy Fliess, believing her to be jealous of his close friendship with her husband. A decade later, he warned his follower in Berlin, Karl Abraham, against Mrs. Fliess, labeling her a "clever-stupid, malicious, positive hysteric." See Freud's letter to Fliess, Aug. 7, 1901, in Masson, ibid., p. 447, and Freud's letter to Abraham, Feb. 13, 1911, quoted in Gay, p. 182. (This portion of Freud's letter to Abraham was omitted from the published Freud-Abraham correspondence.)

49. Freud, *The Interpretation of Dreams,* pp. 299–300.

50. Freud, "On Dreams" [1901], *SE,* vol. 5 (1958), pp. 638–39, 650, 656. Anzieu, with the musing of a psychoanalyst, carries this theme much further. See his interpretation, p. 546, in which he argues that Freud, feeling deprived, thought of other ways in which one had to pay for women: Every visit to a prostitute must be paid for each, separate time; he could not possess his sister-in-law sexually; and he could not respond to the beautiful young women patients who were in love with him.

51. Josef Breuer and Sigmund Freud, *Studies on Hysteria* [1895], *SE,* vol. 2 (1955), pp. 144–45.

52. Smith-Rosenberg, p. 674.

53. Quoted in Ilza Veith, *Hysteria: The History of a Disease* (Chicago: University of Chicago Press, 1965), p. 216.

54. As Steven Marcus points out, there was nothing "unexpected" about Dora's leaving ("Freud and Dora: Story, History, Case History," in *Representations: Essays on Literature and Society.* [New York: Random House, 1975], p. 304). Freud had recognized about a month into the treatment, after the first dream, that Dora had dreamed this recurrent dream again precisely at this time because she wanted to flee from him. This point is discussed more fully in chapter 6 below.

55. Erik Erikson, "Psychological Reality and Historical Actuality," *Insight and Responsibility* (New York: W. W. Norton, 1964), p. 167.

56. See also Karl Kay Lewin, "Dora Revisited," *The Psychoanalytic Review* 60 (1974), p. 529, and Hyman Muslin and Merton Gill, "Transference in the Dora Case," *Journal of the American Psychoanalytic Association* 26 (1978), p. 325.

57. Smith-Rosenberg, p. 675.

58. Marc H. Hollender, "Conversion Hysteria, a Post-Freudian Reinterpretation of 19th Century Psychosocial Data," *Archives of General Psychiatry* 26 (1972), p. 314.

59. Fielding H. Garrison, *An Introduction to the History of Medicine,* 4th ed. (Philadelphia and London: W. B. Saunders Co., 1929), pp. 512, 603; Veith, p. 210.

60. Regina Morantz, "The Lady and Her Physician," in *Clio's Consciousness Raised: New Perspectives on the History of Women,* ed. Mary S. Hartman and Lois Banner (New

York: Harper & Row, 1974), pp. 38–53, and "The Perils of Feminist History," *Journal of Interdisciplinary History* 4 (1974), pp. 649–60.

61. Morantz, "The Lady and Her Physician," p. 47.

62. Morantz, "The Perils of Feminist History," pp. 652–53. Mitchell's method was based on rest, separation, and special feeding. The patient was isolated in a sanitarium, lay in bed, and had a rich diet. In order to compensate for the effects of rest and fattening food, the patient had daily massage and electrical stimulation. The treatment normally lasted for weeks but could go on for months or years. It became fashionable among the well-to-do and educated. See Veith, pp. 212–20; Ellenberger, p. 244; Franz G. Alexander and Sheldon T. Selesnick, *The History of Psychiatry* (New York: Harper & Row, 1966), p. 159.

63. Barbara Sicherman makes this point in a sophisticated fashion in "The Uses of a Diagnosis: Doctors, Patients, and Neurasthenia," *Journal of the History of Medicine and Allied Sciences* 32 (1977), pp. 33–54.

64. S. Weir Mitchell, *Fat and Blood: And How to Make Them* (Philadelphia: J. B. Lippincott, 1877), p. 41.

65. Smith-Rosenberg, p. 669; See also Hollender, p. 311.

66. Hollender, p. 313; Charles E. Rosenberg, "Sexuality, Class and Role in 19th-Century America," *American Quarterly* 25 (1973), p. 136; Smith-Rosenberg, p. 669.

67. Peter Gay, *The Bourgeois Experience, Victoria to Freud*, vol. 1, *Education of the Senses* (New York and Oxford: Oxford University Press, 1984), pp. 312, 315–16.

68. Ibid., pp. 316–17.

69. About the last, Freud wrote: "It is well known that gastric pains occur especially often in those who masturbate. According to a personal communication made to me by Wilhelm Fliess, it is precisely gastralgias of this character which can be interrupted by an application of cocaine to the 'gastric spot' discovered by him in the nose, and which can be cured by the cauterization of the same spot" ("Fragment," p. 78). Even with much understanding, such statements are hard to explain. Perhaps Gay (p. 295) does best when he comments: "Nervous fears [about masturbation] paralyzed the mental powers of physicians who, in other areas of their expertise, knew better." But one can also comprehend Marcus's totally emotional reaction: "We . . . are in the . . . presence of demented and delusional science" (p. 302).

70. Rosenberg, p. 135. Freud added that if marriage and sexual intercourse did not give a woman the necessary physical satisfaction, "the libido flows back again into its old channel and manifests itself once more in hysterical symptoms." ("Fragment," p. 79).

71. Stefan Zweig, *The World of Yesterday* (New York: Viking, 1943), pp. 57–58, 73.

72. Jones, vol. 1, p. 17.

73. Was this another reference to bisexuality? Freud never said so explicitly.

74. Freud to Martha Bernays, November 15, 1883, in *The Letters of Sigmund Freud*, ed. Ernst L. Freud (New York: McGraw-Hill, 1964), pp. 75–76. Vis-à-vis the earlier discussion on Freud's negative perception of women, note that in this letter Freud describes women's delicate qualities as "powerful."

75. Quoted in John W. Boyer, "Freud, Marriage, and Late Viennese Liberalism: A Commentary from 1905," *Journal of Modern History* 50: 1 (Mar. 1978), p. 92.

76. Nunberg and Federn, *Minutes*, vol. 1, p. 351, and vol. 3, p. 14.

77. Breuer and Freud, *Studies on Hysteria*, p. 140.

78. In 1908 Freud's eldest daughter, Mathilde, twenty years old, was worried that she was unattractive. Freud reassured her on her marriageability: "I know that in reality," he wrote, "it is no longer physical beauty which decides the fate of a girl, but the

impression of her whole personality. [Besides] the more intelligent among young men are sure to know what to look for in a wife—gentleness, cheerfulness, and the talent to make their life easier and more beautiful." Freud's letter to Mathilde Freud, March 19, 1908, in Ernst L. Freud, ibid., p. 272. A year later, Mathilde married a Viennese businessman twelve years her senior.

79. Even before Freud met Schnitzler himself, he was friendly with Schnitzler's brother, Julius, a surgeon. Julius Schnitzler was one of the players in the regular Saturday night card game Freud attended for years. Moreover, when Freud finally decided, in 1923, to seek medical help for the growth in his mouth, he went to see a brother-in-law of Schnitzler's, Marcus Hajek, an ear, nose, and throat specialist with whom he was long acquainted.

80. Sidney Bolkosky, "Arthur Schnitzler and the Fate of Mothers in Vienna," *The Psychoanalytic Review* 23:1 (Spring 1986), pp. 1–15.

81. Frederic Morton, "Foreword," in Arthur Schnitzler, *My Youth in Vienna*, trans. Catherine Hutter (New York: Holt, Rinehart and Winston, 1970), p. xi; Bolkosky, p. 4.

82. Arthur Schnitzler, "Fräulein Else," *Viennese Novelettes* (New York: Simon & Schuster, 1931), pp. 123–200.

83. Freud's letter to Fliess, March 19, 1899, in reference to Schnitzler's play *Paracelsus*, in Masson, *Complete Letters*, p. 348. Jones (vol. 1, p. 346) mistakenly gives the date as 1898 and errs as well in writing that Freud read Schnitzler's play. Actually Freud saw the play.

84. Freud to Schnitzler, May 8, 1906, six months after the publication of the Dora case, quoted in Ernst L. Freud, ibid., p. 251.

85. Sigmund Freud, "Briefe an Arthur Schnitzler" (with notes by Henry Schnitzler), *Die neue Rundschau* 66:1 (1955), pp. 96–98.

86. Freud to Schnitzler, May 14, 1922, in ibid., p. 339.

87. For two of Freud's critiques of his society see "Sexuality in the Aetiology of the Neuroses" [1898], *SE*, vol. 3 (1962), pp. 263–85 and "'Civilized' Sexual Morality and Modern Nervous Illness" [1908], *SE*, vol. 9 (1959), pp. 181–204.

88. Peter J. Swales, "Freud, His Teacher, and the Birth of Psychoanalysis," in *Freud: Appraisals and Reappraisals*, ed. Paul E. Stepansky, vol. 1 (Hillsdale, N.J.: Analytic Press, 1986), pp. 48, 51.

Cäcilie M. was twelve years younger than her husband. The frequency of such marriages, in which women married so heavily for reasons of personal economic security and the financial interests of the extended family, partly accounts for the high incidence of emotional illness among middle- and upper-middle-class women.

6.   *"This Child of Fourteen . . . Entirely and Completely Hysterical"*

1. According to Freud's letters to Fliess, E. had been in analysis since at least 1896, and maybe even since 1895. See *The Origins of Psycho-Analysis. Letters to Wilhelm Fliess, Drafts and Notes: 1887–1902*, ed. Marie Bonaparte, Anna Freud, Ernst Kris; trans. Eric Mosbacher and James Strachey (New York: Basic Books, 1954), p. 131 n. 1.

2. Freud's letter to Fliess, April 16, 1900, in *The Complete Letters of Sigmund Freud to Wilhelm Fliess, 1887–1904*, ed. and trans. Jeffrey M. Masson (Cambridge: Belknap Press, 1985), p. 409.

3. Steven Marcus, "Freud and Dora: Story, History, Case History," *Representations: Essays on Literature and Society* (New York: Random House, 1975), p. 256.

4. See also Hyman Muslin and Merton Gill, "Transference in the Dora Case," *Journal of the American Psychoanalytic Association* 26 (1978), pp. 314–15.

5. It is even possible that Dora worried that this man, who took up sexual subjects with her, might betray her like Mrs. K., who had also encouraged Dora's sexual interests only to use the fact of Dora's knowledge against her.

6. Robert Langs, "The Misalliance Dimension in Freud's Case Histories: I. The Case of Dora," *International Journal of Psychoanalytic Psychotherapy* 5 (1976), p. 313.

7. Erik Erikson, "Psychological Reality and Historical Actuality," *Insight and Responsibility* (New York: W. W. Norton, 1964), pp. 169–74. See also Philip Rieff's comments, which deal with this issue from another perspective, in *Freud, The Mind of the Moralist* (New York: Viking Press, 1959), pp. 81–84, and in *Fellow Teachers* (New York: Harper & Row, 1973), pp. 84–86.

8. Erikson, p. 174.

9. This interpretation spoke volumes, of course, for the pride with which Freud regarded himself and for the power which it now gave him over Dora. He alone had divined her secret.

10. See also the discussion of Dora's associations to and Freud's interpretation of Dora's first dream in Phillip McCaffrey, *Freud and Dora: The Artful Dream* (New Brunswick, N.J.: Rutgers University Press, 1984), pp. 43–45.

11. See McCaffrey's expanded narrative of Dora's second dream, pp. 20–21.

12. McCaffrey is critical of Freud's analysis of the separate elements in Dora's second dream, and he attempts to make aesthetic and literary sense of the manifest content of the dream as an interrelated whole. See McCaffrey's argument on pp. 39, 77, 127, 139.

13. In the published case history, naturally, Freud omitted the name "Bauer" and wrote only "Herr _____."

14. I am much indebted to Dr. Reinhold A. Aman, editor of *Maledicta: The International Journal of Verbal Aggression,* who confirmed my deduction with great care and scholarship. Through him I also learned of the following useful reference: Herbert Moller, "Wet Dreams and the Ejaculate," *Maledicta* 4 (1980), pp. 249–51. I am grateful, too, to Professor Claus Reschke of the German Department at the University of Houston who shared his knowledge with me.

    The English "come" is an equivalent, although drab in comparison to the style of "cold peasant."

15. Two additional interpretations may not have been actually told to Dora, but they appear in the published case. One arose from Dora's reporting on the second day after she had the first dream that she had smelled smoke each time she awoke from the dream. Freud took this addendum to apply to himself. He pointed out that Mr. K. and Philipp Bauer smoked, as did he. Dora had been kissed by K. Therefore the meaning of smelling the smoke was that Dora wanted a kiss from Freud. ("Fragment," pp. 73–74.) The second interpretation was that of Dora's unconscious homosexual attraction to Mrs. K. ("Fragment," pp. 60–63, 105 n. 2.)

16. Muslin and Gill, p. 322.

17. And perhaps even a design colored by Freud's dislike of Mrs. K., whom he compared to Medea ("Fragment," p. 61), the sorceress who betrayed her father, plotted the death of her brother, killed her husband's second wife, and murdered her children.

18. Letter of October 14, 1900, in Masson, ibid., p. 427.

19. Freud, *The Psychopathology of Everyday Life* [1901], *SE,* vol. 6 (1960), pp. 175–76.

20. Muslin and Gill, p. 324 ff.

21. When Freud made some revisions in the case for its republication in 1924, he amended "nineteen" to "nearly nineteen"—a grudging and hardly accurate correction.

22. Jane Gallop, "Keys to Dora," in *In Dora's Case: Freud—Hysteria—Feminism,* ed Charles Bernheimer and Claire Kahane (New York: Columbia University Press, 1985), p. 209.

Almost simultaneously with writing up Dora's case, Freud addressed this very subject of an author's circumlocutions: "A clear and unambiguous manner of writing shows us that here the author is at one with himself; where we find a forced and involved expression . . . we may recognize the intervention of an insufficiently worked-out, complicating thought [or] of an internal conflict." *The Psychopathology of Everyday Life,* pp. 100–101.

23. Letter of October 14, 1900, in Masson, ibid., p. 427.

24. Madelon Sprengnether, "Enforcing Oedipus: Freud and Dora," in *In Dora's Case,* pp. 261–63.

Here Freud raised the issue of Dora's submitting to his sexual conversation. We must note that there were many times in the course of the analysis when Dora objected to Freud's interpretations about sexual matters. But Freud stuck to his guns (!) because he was intent on proving a theory and ended up, like Philipp Bauer and Mr. K., using Dora sexually.

25. Janet Malcolm, *Psychoanalysis: The Impossible Profession* (New York: Vintage Books, 1982), pp. 73, 98. Malcolm colorfully imagines Freud saying "to poor Dora . . . 'I know about you. I know your dirty little secrets. . . . Admit that you masturbated when you were five.'"

26. Ibid., p. 100.

27. Recall the dream about Mrs E. L., which Freud had around the time he started treating Dora. In the dream he removed E. L.'s hand from his knee. She protested: "But you've always had such beautiful eyes." If Didier Anzieu is correct that E. L. partly represented Dora, the dream reveals that Freud had projected his sexual aggressiveness onto E. L. And if Freud was right that looking is a civilized substitute for touching, then the E. L./Dora figure was justified in insisting that it was Freud who had made the advance.

28. Peter Gay, *Freud: A Life for Our Time* (New York, London: W. W. Norton, 1988), p. 254.

29. Freud's letter to Ernest Jones, September 22, 1912, quoted in Gay.

30. Edoardo Weiss, *Sigmund Freud as a Consultant: Recollections of a Pioneer in Psychoanalysis* (New York: Intercontinental Medical Book Corporation, 1970), p. 12.

31. Malcolm, p. 94.

32. Marcus, p. 305.

33. Freud, "Some Character-Types Met With in Psycho-Analytic Work" [1916], *SE,* vol. 14 (1957), pp. 324–31.

34. Gay, pp. 435, 439–40.

35. Weiss, pp. 80–81.

36. Josef Breuer and Sigmund Freud, *Studies on Hysteria* [1893–95], *SE,* vol. 2 (1955), pp. 127, 133. See also Freud's letter to Fliess, August 20, 1893 in Masson, ibid., p. 54, and Masson's note 5, p. 55, as well as Gerhard Fichtner und Albrecht Hirschmüller, "Freuds 'Katharina'—Hintergrund, Entstehungsgeschichte und Bedeutung einer frühen psychoanalytischen Krankengeschichte," *Psyche* 39 (1985), pp. 220–40. This latter article contains an historical reconstruction of Katharina's family life and social milieu and indicates the role of this case in the theoretical and technical development of psycho-analysis. For very complete biographical information on Katharina see Peter J. Swales,

"Freud, Katharina, and the First 'Wild Analysis'," in *Freud Appraisals and Reappraisals: Contributions to Freud Studies,* vol. 3, ed. Paul E. Stepansky (Hillsdale, N.J.: Analytic Press, 1988), pp. 81–164.

37. In 1893 even Freud's technique was softer and less insistent when it came to sexual matters. We can observe his gentler demeanor when he talked to Katharina about the sensation she felt when her father tried to force himself on her: " 'Tell me just one thing more [Freud said]. You're a grown-up girl now and know all sorts of things. . . . ' 'Yes, now I am [Katharina replied].' 'Tell me just one more thing. What part of his body was it that you felt that night?' But she gave me no more definite answer. She smiled in an embarrassed way. . . . Her facial expression seemed to me to be saying that she supposed that I was right in my conjecture. But I could penetrate no further." *Studies on Hysteria,* pp. 131–32.

38. Freud, *Introductory Lectures on Psycho-Analysis* [1916–17], *SE,* vol. 16 (1963), p. 459.

39. Ibid., pp. 458–59. For the thrust of the above observations, I am indebted to Helm Stierlin, "The Dynamics of Owning and Disowning: Psychoanalytic and Family Perspectives," *Family Process* 15: 3 (Sept. 1976), p. 281.

40. Marcus, p. 300.

41. Freud, "Beyond the Pleasure Principle" [1920], *SE,* vol. 18 (1955), pp. 7–64. Before this work, Freud discussed anger in terms of "sadism" (or "cruelty"), which he defined as a component of the sexual instincts. This concept was first spelled out in *Three Essays on the Theory of Sexuality,* 1905.

42. *Minutes of the Vienna Psychoanalytic Society,* vols. 1–4, ed. Herman Nunberg and Ernst Federn (New York: International Universities Press, Inc., 1962–75).

43. Freud, "An Autobiographical Study" [1925], *SE,* vol. 20 (1959), p. 9. Freud advised a Jewish friend not to have his young son baptized because remaining Jewish would strengthen the boy's character.

44. Freud even had a disinclination to apply psychoanalysis to the origins of anti-Semitism: "With regard to anti-semitism," he wrote to Arnold Zweig in 1927, "I don't really want to search for explanations; I feel a strong inclination to surrender to my affects in this matter and find myself confirmed in my wholly non-scientific belief that mankind on the average and taken by and large are a wretched lot." *The Letters of Sigmund Freud and Arnold Zweig,* ed. Ernst L. Freud, trans. Elaine and William Robson-Scott (New York: Harcourt, Brace & World, 1970), p. 3. However, three years later Freud did address the reasons for anti-Semitism in *Civilization and Its Discontents* and, responding to Hitler's dramatic consolidation of power, wrote *Moses and Monotheism* (1938) in part to explain "why [the Jew] has drawn upon himself this undying hatred." Freud to Zweig, Sept. 30, 1934, in *The Letters of Sigmund Freud,* ed. Ernst L. Freud, trans. Tania and James Stern (New York, Toronto, London: McGraw-Hill, 1964), p. 421.

45. Karl Kay Lewin, "Dora Revisited," *The Psychoanalytic Review* 60 (1974), p. 519 ff; Muslin and Gill, p. 317.

46. Harry T. Hardin, "On the Vicissitudes of Freud's Early Mothering. I: Early Environment and Loss; II: Alienation From his Biological Mother; III: Freiberg, Screen Memories, and Loss," *Psychoanalytic Quarterly* 56 (1987), pp. 628–44; vol. 57 (1988), pp. 72–86 and 209–23.

47. Freud spelled out his thinking as follows: "[At eight years of age] when [Dora's] father was away and the child, devotedly in love with him, was wishing him back, she must have reproduced in the form of an attack of asthma the impression she had received [from her parents' intercourse]. She had preserved in her memory the event which had

occasioned the first onset of the symptom, and we can conjecture from it the nature of the train of thought, charged with anxiety, which had accompanied the attack [of dyspnea]. The first attack had come on after she had over-exerted herself on an expedition in the mountains, so that she had probably been really a little out of breath. To this was added the thought that her father was forbidden to climb mountains and was not allowed to over-exert himself, because he suffered from shortness of breath; then came the recollection of how much he had exerted himself with her mother that night, and the question whether it might have done him harm; next came concern whether *she* might not have over-exerted herself in masturbating—an act which, like the other, led to a sexual orgasm accompanied by slight dyspnoea—and finally came a return of the dyspnoea in an intensified form as a symptom" ("Fragment," p. 80).

One must note Freud's fantasy of a seven- or eight-year-old girl's masturbating to orgasm and breathlessness, like an adult. While there is a wide variability in young girls' masturbation, adult physiological experiences and dyspnea are not common features. In his writings up to 1900, Freud indicated no specific knowledge of little girls' masturbation, and Dora denied to him that she had ever masturbated; so he certainly got no information from her. But his theory of infantile sexuality called for the potential existence of full-fledged sexuality in young children.

48. Freud, "Types of Onset of Neurosis" [1912a], *SE*, vol. 12 (1958), pp. 231–33, 235–37.

49. Freud, "Inhibitions, Symptoms, and Anxiety" [1926], *SE*, vol. 20 (1959), p. 138.

50. Anna Freud Bernays quoted in Ernest Jones, *The Life and Work of Sigmund Freud*, vol. 1 (New York: Basic Books, 1953), p. 20; Freud's letter to Martha Bernays referred to in ibid., p. 116. There are many instances of Freud's interfering in the personal lives of colleagues, disciples, and analysands. One of the most flagrant was in the case of the American psychoanalyst Horace Frink. See Lavinia Edmunds, "His Master's Choice," *Johns Hopkins Magazine* 40: 2 (April 1988), pp. 40–49.

7.   "Who Else Was There Called Dora?"

1. Freud, *The Psychopathology of Everyday Life* [1901], *SE*, vol. 6 (1960), p. 239.

2. Ibid., p. 241.

3. Ibid., pp. 240–41.

4. We have returned to the land of self-analyses, with their unavoidable shortcomings. As an old man, Freud at last came to this conclusion: "In self-analysis the danger of incompleteness is particularly great. One is too soon satisfied with a part explanation, behind which resistance may easily be keeping back something that is more important perhaps." "The Subtleties of a Faulty Action" [1935], *SE*, vol. 22 (1964), p. 234.

5. Suzanne Gearhart, "The Scene of Psychoanalysis," in *In Dora's Case*, ed. Charles Bernheimer and Claire Kahane (New York: Columbia University Press, 1985), p. 121.

6. Madelon Sprengnether, "Enforcing Oedipus: Freud and Dora," in ibid., p. 256.

7. Uncannily, or perhaps in a dramatic instance of overdetermination, Freud told Martha after he had seen the Sistine Madonna that she reminded him of "a charming, sympathetic nursemaid." Seventeen years later, he wrote in the case history: "The '*Madonna*' was obviously Dora herself" (p. 104 n. 2). See Freud's letter of Dec. 20, 1883, in *The Letters of Sigmund Freud*, ed. Ernst L. Freud (New York: McGraw-Hill, 1964), p. 82.

8. Ernest Jones, *The Life and Work of Sigmund Freud*, vol. 1 (New York: Basic Books, 1953), pp. 104, 174.

9. Steven Marcus, "Freud and Dora: Story, History, Case History," in *Representations: Essays on Literature and Society* (New York: Random House, 1975), p. 309 n. 26.

10. Freud's letter to Martha Bernays, Nov. 8, 1885, in Ernst L. Freud, ibid., p. 179. Adumbrating his later psychoanalytic interests, Freud was already gripped by the complex, realistic characters of *David Copperfield* and repelled by the stereotypic personalities in *Théodora*.

11. Ibid.

12. Freud's letter to Fliess, Oct. 3, 1897, in *The Complete Letters of Sigmund Freud to Wilhelm Fliess, 1887–1904*, ed. and trans. Jeffrey M. Masson (Cambridge: Belknap Press, 1985), p. 268.

13. See chapter 6 above, p. 111.

14. Janet Malcolm, *Psychoanalysis: The Impossible Profession* (New York: Vintage Books, 1982), pp. 96, 167–68 n. 5.

Pandora was the ancient Greek's Eve. According to their legends, she was the first mortal woman to appear after the divine brothers, Prometheus and Epimetheus, had repopulated the earth with men and animals.

Zeus, king of the gods and ruler of the universe, became angry with human beings for accepting Prometheus's stolen gift of fire and for sacrificing to the gods the scraps and entrails of animals instead of the best portions. He punished the humans by sending to earth a beautiful woman, modeled in the likeness of Aphrodite, on whom all the gods had bestowed gifts: a human voice, intelligence, beauty, attractive dress, jewels, cunning, and the abilities to flatter and seduce. Zeus's gifts to this woman were curiosity and a sealed box (actually a jar), which he warned her never to open. Her name was Pandora ("all-gift") because she carried gifts from all the gods.

When Pandora arrived on earth, she was presented to Epimetheus, who married her even though Prometheus had warned him never to accept a gift from Zeus. Thus Pandora came to live on earth. Eventually she became unhappy because of her curiosity over what was in the box. So she opened it, and all manner of evils, diseases, and troubles flew out, hitherto unknown to mortals. Horrified, she clapped the lid back on, just in time to keep hope from escaping as well. So did Zeus revenge himself on mankind.

15. Freud's letter of Oct. 14, 1900, in Masson, ibid., p. 427.

16. Sprengnether, p. 271.

17. See chapter 5 above, pp. 99–100.

18. Sprengnether, p. 275 n. 21.

19. Malcolm, p. 97.

20. Historical information on Josef Breuer is in Albrecht Hirschmüller, *Physiologie und Psychoanalyse im Leben und Werk Josef Breuers* (Bern: Verlag Hans Huber, 1978); Henri F. Ellenberger, *The Discovery of the Unconscious: The History and Evolution of Dynamic Psychiatry* (New York: Basic Books, 1970); George H. Pollock, "The Possible Significance of Childhood Object Loss in the Josef Breuer–Bertha Pappenheim (Anna O.)–Sigmund Freud Relationship, I. Josef Breuer," *Journal of the American Psychoanalytic Association* 16 (1968), pp. 711–39 (reprinted in John E. Gedo and George H. Pollock, eds., *Freud: The Fusion of Science and Humanism. The Intellectual History of Psychoanalysis*, Psychological Issues, Monograph 34/35 [New York: International Universities Press, 1976], pp. 133–63). There are errors in Pollock's article, so it must be used in conjunction with Hirschmüller or Ellenberger; and Arnold Rogow, "A Further Footnote to

Freud's 'Fragment of an Analysis of a Case of Hysteria,'" *Journal of the American Psychoanalytic Association* 26 (1978), pp. 330–56.

21. Freud's letter to Stefan Zweig, June 2, 1932, in Ernst L. Freud, ibid., p. 413.

22. Freud did change his mind about some professional women, much later in his life. Beginning in his late fifties, he often valued their presence in the psychoanalytic movement.

23. In addition to Hirschmüller, see Jones, vol. 1, pp. 222–23, and Peter Gay, *Freud: A Life for Our Time* (New York and London: W. W. Norton, 1988), pp. 32–33, 63–64.

24. Most of the information about Anna O. and her family comes from Hirschmüller, Ellenberger, *Discovery of the Unconscious,* and Ellenberger, "The Story of 'Anna O.': A Critical Review with New Data," *Journal of the History of the Behavioral Sciences* 8 (1972), pp. 267–79.

25. Didier Anzieu, *Freud's Self-Analysis,* trans. Peter Graham (Madison, Conn.: International Universities Press, 1986), p. 57.

26. Ellenberger, *Discovery of the Unconscious,* p. 482.

27. Freud, "An Autobiographical Study" [1925], *SE,* vol. 20 (1959), p. 26; Jones, vol. 1, pp. 224–25; Ernst L. Freud, ibid., p. 413. Ellenberger and Hirschmüller have corrected certain factual inaccuracies in Freud's and Jones's accounts.

28. Breuer's mother's exact date of death is unknown, and extant sources are in conflict over Josef's age when she died.

29. Hirschmüller, p. 22.

30. Pollock, p. 723.

31. Except, that is, with her father. In a contemporary report, referring Anna O. to a medical colleague, Breuer observed that she found "compensation" for the monotony of her personal life in her "passionate love for her father, who spoils her." "Krankengeschichte Bertha Pappenheim," in Hirschmüller, p. 349.

32. Josef Breuer and Sigmund Freud, *Studies on Hysteria* [1893–95], *SE,* vol. 2 (1955), pp. 21–22.

33. Pollock, pp. 718, 723–24.

34. Hirschmüller, pp. 142–43.

35. Freud to Martha Bernays, Oct. 31, 1883, quoted in Jones, vol. 1, pp. 224–25; Peter J. Swales, "Freud, His Teacher, and the Birth of Psychoanalysis," in *Freud Appraisals and Reappraisals: Contributions to Freud Studies,* ed. Paul E. Stepansky, vol. 1 (Hillsdale, N.J.: Analytic Press, 1986), p. 41. Bertha Pappenheim's father became Martha Bernays's legal guardian on the death of Martha's father in 1879. See also Freud's letter to Martha, July 13, 1883, in Ernst L. Freud, ibid., p. 41. On July 12 Freud had stayed late at the Breuers' and talked with his friend about "strange case histories [including] your friend Bertha Pappenheim." Breuer told Freud "a number of . . . personal and very intimate . . . things about his wife and children and asked me to repeat what he had said only 'after you are married to Martha.'"

36. Was this late arrival viewed by the Breuers as a *Gottesgeschenk,* a gift from God?

37. Paul F. Cranefield, "Josef Breuer's Evaluation of His Contributions to Psychoanalysis," *International Journal of Psychoanalysis* 39 (1958), p. 319.

38. Freud's letter to Stefan Zweig, June 2, 1932, in Ernst L. Freud, ibid., p. 413. Freud told Zweig that as a grown woman, Dora Breuer had asked her father if Anna O.'s "transference love" and Breuer's subsequent panic were true. According to Freud, Breuer confirmed the truth of these circumstances.

39. Hirschmüller, pp. 175, 377.

40. It is possible that the same factors that created Breuer's fascination with Anna O.'s case eventually repelled him. "The Anna O. relationship was threatening on several counts: the dangerous revival of repressed oedipal conflicts [yearning for his mother, Bertha], of repressed mourning for the dead mother, and of ambivalent feelings toward his [younger] brother" (Pollock, p. 725). Breuer's mother had died at or after the birth of this brother (the same one who later died of tuberculosis).

41. As early as her stay at the Swiss sanatorium, Anna O. experienced some relapses. She had periods again of being unable to speak, understand, or read German. She continued to suffer pain and had spells of amnesia. She recorded, however, that really bad times of anxiety and crying only occurred when she was overcome by the fear that she would lose her German tongue permanently. See "Bericht Bertha Pappenheims über ihre Krankheit," written in September 1882 and quoted in Hirschmüller, pp. 369–70.

42. Hirschmüller, pp. 203 f., 225 f.

43. Jones, vol. 1, pp. 253–55.

44. Freud, *The Interpretation of Dreams* [1900], *SE*, vol. 4 (1958), pp. 106–21.

45. Didier Anzieu even argues that Freud's self-analysis began with the Irma dream in 1895 and ended with the "table d'hôte" dream in 1900. See chapter 5 above and this chapter below, p. 143. Anzieu, a French psychoanalyst and biographer of Freud's early career, finds two common themes uniting Freud's dreams of this period: Freud's patients and his sexual wishes and thoughts. See Anzieu, p. 569.

46. Freud, *The Interpretation of Dreams*, p. 106.

47. Ibid., pp. 110–15 passim.

48. Alexander Grinstein, *On Sigmund Freud's Dreams* (Detroit: Wayne State University Press, 1968), p. 31.

49. Freud, *The Interpretation of Dreams*, p. 107.

50. Ibid., p. 115.

51. Freud's letters of June 12 and June 18, 1900, in Masson, ibid., pp. 417, 419.

52. Freud's letter of May 20, 1900, in ibid., pp. 415–16.

53. *The Psychopathology of Everyday Life*, pp. 137–38. In the letter to Fliess, Freud said Breuer lived across the street from the store. In *The Psychopathology of Everyday Life* he wrote that Breuer's apartment was in the same building as the store.

54. Jones, vol. 1, pp. 160–61, 255–56.

55. Freud, *On Dreams* [1901], *SE*, vol. 6 (1960), pp. 638–39.

56. Max Schur, *Freud: Living and Dying* (New York: International Universities Press, 1972), p. 210.

57. Freud's letter, Aug. 7, 1901, in Masson, ibid., p. 447.

Although the incidents of looking for the strongbox store, dreaming of an old debt, and being caught up in the issue of Fliess's mother-in-law's medical care provide the strongest evidence of the significance Breuer still held for Freud, there were relevant lesser events. In May 1900, five months before Dora appeared, Freud was finally able to help a patient Breuer had repeatedly referred to him for treatment over the preceding four years. Freud gleefully reported to Fliess: "She told me that when she confessed her extraordinary improvement to Breuer, he clapped his hands and exclaimed again and again, 'So he is right after all!' . . . Why did he for years proclaim that I was wrong? . . . I do not want to deprive you of the news of my little triumph" (letter of May 16, 1900, p. 414). Then, while Freud was either seeing Dora or writing up the case, Breuer, in the face of Freud's reluctance, urged him to deliver a lecture before the Philosophical Society, and Freud agreed to do so (letter of Feb. 15, 1900, p. 437).

58. Freud, *An Autobiographical Study*, p. 21.

59. Freud, *The Interpretation of Dreams,* pp. 113, 114.

60. Jones, vol. 1, p. 225.

61. Jones, *The Life and Work of Sigmund Freud,* vol. 2 (New York: Basic Books, 1955), pp. 255–56; Gay, pp. 246–47. Jones speculates on Freud's possible motivations in submitting the case to two different journals and then not publishing it at all for four years. Gay also ponders the reasons for the long delay but is both more complete and perceptive in his conjectures.

62. See chapter 8 below, pp. 148–49.

63. One suspects that such a fantasy had deep roots in Freud's relationship with his mother, which early on was problematic, containing significant elements of separation, loss, and alienation. Freud idealized his mother, as she did him, but their relationship was never an emotionally warm one. See Harry T. Hardin, "On the Vicissitudes of Freud's Early Mothering. I. Early Environment and Loss," *The Psychoanalytic Quarterly* 56:4 (1987), especially pp. 628–31, 636–42; "II: Alienation from His Biological Mother," ibid., 57:1 (1988), pp. 72–85.

8.   *"The Realities of Life"*

1. Freud's letter of Jan. 25, 1901, in *The Complete Letters of Sigmund Freud to Wilhelm Fliess, 1887–1904,* ed. and trans. Jeffrey M. Masson (Cambridge: Belknap Press, 1985), p. 433.

2. There is much evidence that Freud wrote or at the very least considerably revised the preface a long time after he originally completed Dora's case history: (1) In justifying publication, he noted that he waited "four whole years" and postponed publication until there had been a major change in Dora's life. (2) He mentioned having six or eight patients a day; this was not his situation in 1900–1901. (3) He noted that he had written the case while his recollection of the material "was still fresh and was heightened by my interest in its publication." (4) He referred to *The Interpretation of Dreams* (1900) as if it had been written several years previously.

3. Freud's letter of Mar. 11, 1902, in Masson, ibid., p. 456.

4. Freud's letter of Mar. 3, 1901, in ibid., p. 438. Dr. Rie was the same man who had criticized Freud's treatment of their mutual friend, Emma Eckstein ("Irma"), in July 1895. See chapter 7 above.

5. A facial neuralgia was a ubiquitous hysterical symptom at the turn of the century and one with which Freud was quite familiar. One of the patients written about in *Studies on Hysteria,* Frau Cäcilie M. (Anna von Lieben), suffered for years from a severe facial neuralgia that appeared suddenly two or three times a year and lasted five to ten days at a time. Placing her under hypnosis, Freud traced the pain back to a remark her husband had made, which she experienced as a bitter insult and said felt like a slap in the face.

6. See chapter 6, p. 115, and chapter 4, p. 83 above.

7. This interpretation has been challenged recently by two English critics. See Anthony Stadlen, "Was Dora wel ziek?" *Vrij Nederland.* 44 (November 2, 1985), pp. 27–31, and H. J. Eysenck, *Decline and Fall of the Freudian Empire* (New York: Viking 1985), pp. 165–67.

8. IKG records; Arnold Rogow, "A Further Footnote to Freud's 'Fragment of an Analysis of a Case of Hysteria,' " *Journal of the American Psychoanalytic Association* 26 (1978), p. 341; letter from Kurt R. Eissler, M.D., former secretary of the Freud Archive, to me, Feb. 19, 1983; letter from Dr. Eissler to Edward D. Joseph, M.D., former president of the American Psychoanalytic Association, Dec. 31, 1982; Julius Braunthal,

ed., *Otto Bauer: Eine Auswahl aus seinem Lebenswerk* (Vienna: Wiener Volks-buchhandlung, 1961), p. 9; *In Dora's Case: Freud—Hysteria—Feminism*, ed. Charles Bernheimer and Claire Kahane (New York: Columbia University Press, 1985), p. 33. While the name of Dora's husband is known to me, I have decided to withhold it from publication to protect the privacy of Dora's daughter-in-law and grandchildren.

9. Otto Leichter, *Otto Bauer: Tragödie oder Triumph* (Wien: Europa Verlag, 1970), p. 23.

10. *In Dora's Case,* p. 33.

11. All information about Dora's son, here and throughout, is based on published accounts. I am not stating the actual sources in order to preserve the privacy of family members.

12. Felix Deutsch, "A Footnote to Freud's 'Fragment of an Analysis of a Case of Hysteria,' " *Psychoanalytic Quarterly* 26 (1957), p. 161 (reprinted in *In Dora's Case,* p. 37).

13. IKG records. At the time of their conversion to Christianity, Dora and her husband lived in the Ninth District at Althauplatz 4–6, not far from Dora's parents, who had moved to Porzellangasse 8.

14. Marsha L. Rozenblit, *The Jews of Vienna, 1867–1914: Assimilation and Identity* (Albany: State University of New York Press, 1983), pp. 128, 132, 136; Edward Timms, *Karl Kraus, Apocalyptic Satirist: Culture and Catastrophe in Habsburg Vienna* (New Haven and London: Yale University Press, 1986), p. 242; Arthur Ruppin, *The Jews of Today,* trans. Margery Bentwich (New York: Henry Holt and Co., 1913), pp. 186, 190. In Vienna in 1900, 559 of 146,926 Jews converted. (These figures do not include children under seven, whose religion automatically changed with that of their parents.) The Viennese Jewish community reacted strongly against even these small numbers, the Zionists going so far as to publish in one of their newspapers periodic "lists of shame" with the names of the apostates.

15. Captain Alfred Dreyfus was court-martialed and found guilty twice, in 1894 and in 1899. He was not declared innocent until 1906.

16. Norman Cohn, *Warrant for Genocide: The Myth of the Jewish World-Conspiracy and the Protocols of the Elders of Zion* (Chico, Calif.: Scholars Press, 1981), p. 38.

17. Peter G. J. Pulzer, *The Rise of Political Anti-Semitism in Germany and Austria.* (New York: John Wiley & Sons, 1964), p. 211.

18. Rozenblit, p. 136.

19. Gustav Mahler, of course, presents a good example of the first category. He converted to Catholicism in 1897 in order to become director of the Vienna Court Opera, a government post. In the second category were mainly young women of the working and lower-middle classes who converted to marry Christian men. Paul Johnson, *A History of the Jews* (New York: Harper & Row, 1987), p. 9; Rozenblit, pp. 133, 137, 139.

20. Anti-Semites referred to Budapest as "Judapest."

21. Ezra Mendelsohn, *The Jews of East Central Europe Between the World Wars* (Bloomington: Indiana University Press, 1983), pp. 87–93.

22. Rozenblit, pp. 138–39.

23. Ibid., pp. 136, 139. Eighty-one percent of all converts were unmarried, and of the women converts, 64 percent were artisans (mainly seamstresses, dressmakers, and milliners), unskilled workers, or servants.

24. With anti-Semitism unabating and even growing, their Jewishness continued to haunt many Jews into the twentieth century. As late as 1926, the writer George Clare, then a boy of six, enraged his banker-father by calling him in public, *tahteh,* the Yiddish for

"papa." The elder Clare (the name was Klaar, in those pre-Nazi days), slapped him full in the face and urgently said: "Don't you ever dare to call me *Tate,* never, you hear, never!" George Clare, *Last Waltz in Vienna. The Rise and Destruction of a Family, 1842–1942* (New York: Holt, Rinehart and Winston, 1982), p. 85.

25. Herzl's letter of 1893 to the Viennese Society to Combat Anti-Semitism, quoted in Amos Elon, *Herzl* (New York: Holt, Rinehart and Winston, 1975), pp. 114–15. Herzl had already partly paved the way for his son's conversion by not having him circumcised when he was born in 1891. But at the time Herzl wrote this letter, his son was two and still a Jew. Herzl was obviously having trouble following his own advice. See Elon, p. 93.

Others of Jewish descent who did not want Jewish children were Victor Adler, the physician who founded the Austrian Socialist party, and Louis Friedmann, a good-looking, athletic friend of Arthur Schnitzler's. See Robert S. Wistrich, *Revolutionary Jews from Marx to Trotsky* (London: Harrap, 1976), p. 100, and Arthur Schnitzler, *My Youth in Vienna,* trans. Catherine Hutter (New York: Holt, Rinehart and Winston, 1970), p. 174; Elon, p. 69.

26. Dora's second dream graphically showed that she felt deserted by and alienated from her family. Her mother has withdrawn from her and her father is dead. (Perhaps her father has died because of her uncompromising anger—a death wish?—in response to his betrayal. See Samuel Slipp, "Interpersonal Factors in Hysteria: Freud's Seduction Theory and the Case of Dora," *Journal of the American Academy of Psychoanalysis* 5 (1977), p. 371.) At any rate, Dora cannot turn to her mother, who is cold and distant.

27. Braunthal, ed., pp. 11, 14, 19; Leichter, p. 10. Otto's biographer, Julius Braunthal, used the exact same phrase in referring to Otto's compliance with his father's wishes as he did when he wrote about Otto's toleration of his mother's housekeeping: Otto acted "in order to avoid vexing his father."

28. Wistrich, p. 115.

29. *Die Nationalitätenfrage und die Sozialdemokratie.* Not only the socialists but all of intellectual and political Vienna were impressed by the learning, logic, and clarity of Otto's scholarly book, which he had written in his last year at the university. See Ernst Winkler, "Der grosse Otto Bauer," in Otto Bauer, *Einführung in die Volkswirtschaftslehre* (Wien: Wiener Volksbuchhandlung, 1955), copy in the archives of the Verein für Geschichte der Arbeiterbewegung Wien, catalog No. B1, box 19, file 39.

30. Otto Bauer, "The National Autonomy of the Jews," in *The Nationalities Question and Social Democracy,* quoted in Robert S. Wistrich, *Socialism and the Jews: The Dilemmas of Assimilation in Germany and Austria-Hungary* (East Brunswick, N.J.: Associated University Presses, 1982), pp. 339–40; Mark E. Blum, *The Austro-Marxists, 1890–1918: A Psychobiographical Study* (Lexington: University Press of Kentucky, 1985), p. 94; Peter Loewenberg, *Decoding the Past: The Psychohistorical Approach* (Berkeley: University of California Press, 1985), p. 166. The discussion of Otto's views of the future of European Jewry also draws on Loewenberg, pp. 164–66.

31. Bauer, "Die Bedingungen der Nationalen Assimilation," *Der Kampf* 5 (March 1912), quoted in Blum, p. 98.

32. Adler, who belonged to a German nationalist club in his university days, wrote to Karl Kautsky: "As Germans [both men had been born in Prague], we may not care very much whether the Czechs learn German, but as social democrats, we must positively desire it." Adler's letter to Kautsky, Aug. 21, 1886, quoted in Wistrich, *Revolutionary Jews,* p. 103.

That this view contradicted the Austro-Marxists' plan of cultural autonomy for the nationalities was probably not even apparent to them, so strong was their conviction of the evident superiority of German culture.

33. In a pamphlet published the same year as his book, Otto argued that socialism would bring Kant, Marx, and Goethe to the workers and peasants. Bauer, *Deutschtum und Sozialdemokratie*, quoted in Blum, pp. 94–95.

34. Leichter, p. 24. Did Otto wait until both parents died in order to avoid "vexing" them by a marriage they would have found unsuitable? Dora herself made it clear that she opposed Otto's marriage, and she never became close to her sister-in-law. Rogow, p. 349 n. 15.

35. Loewenberg, p. 195. Otto was the eternal compromiser, always looking for a way to smooth things over without provoking confrontation or a split—even if problems were left unresolved. At a divided Socialist party conference in 1927, Otto urged his colleagues, above all, to unify: "It is a hundred times better to go the wrong way united— for errors can be corrected—than to split in search of the right way." Charles A. Gulick, *Austria from Habsburg to Hitler*, vol. 1 (Berkeley and Los Angeles: University of California Press, 1948), p. 694.

Lenin, ever the revolutionary, called Otto "an educated fool." Quoted in Frank Field, *The Last Days of Mankind: Karl Kraus and His Vienna* (London: MacMillan/New York: St. Martin's Press, 1967), p. 171.

36. Ernst Fischer, quoted in Loewenberg, p. 163.

37. IKG records. Other sources, e.g., the "Biographical Note" in *In Dora's Case*, p. 33, state that Käthe died of tuberculosis, presumably contracted from her husband. But the IKG records, seemingly correct in other aspects of Käthe's biography, give the cause of death as *Neubildung des Dickdarmes*, literally "new growth in the colon." In 1912, it was still possible to have abdominal tuberculosis. But since cancer, until recently, has usually been referred to reluctantly or euphemistically ("a long illness"), and since Dora also died of colon cancer, it seems likely that carcinoma was Käthe's fatal illness. This does not rule out, of course, her having tuberculosis—Deutsch, p. 162, records that Käthe had spent time in a sanitarium for treatment of tuberculosis—but she probably died of cancer.

38. IKG records.

39. Braunthal, ed., p. 10.

40. Deutsch p. 162.

41. Viktor Reimann, *Zu Gross für Österreich: Seipel und Bauer im Kampf um die Erste Republik*. (Wien-Frankfurt-Zürich: Verlag Fritz Molden, 1968), p. 257.

42. Julius Braunthal, *In Search of the Millennium*. (London: Victor Gollancz, 1945), pp. 72–75, 80–81, 230; Reimann, pp. 257, 371; Loewenberg, pp. 168, 196–98. Braunthal, an admiring pupil and later colleague of Otto's asserted: "I have never heard before or since an orator of his vigour. . . . His eloquence was rapid and flowed from a source of grandeur and extraordinary knowledge. . . . He possessed, indeed, the rare gift of making complicated things simple. . . . He did not use any notes, and he never paused in his speech. . . . Otto Bauer's orations were spoken essays" (pp. 72–73).

43. Leichter, p. 371 n. 13. Because of his view that human nature was instinctive and not likely to be changed fundamentally by environmental manipulation, Freud believed that socialist and communist efforts to reform human society could not succeed.

It is possible that the newly married Otto went to see Freud about a more intimate matter than his career development but, as a reserved person (and a good bourgeois), was appropriately reticent in discussing the primary reason for his consultation. This surmise is somewhat borne out by reports that Otto actually saw Freud twice, once before his marriage, and again on a later occasion, when Freud advised him not to go into politics and recommended a psychoanalysis. See Rogow, p. 352 n. 20.

44. Which is not to say, in spite of the early waning of his sexuality, that Freud was not still a sexual being in 1914. In July 1915, he recorded a dream he had about his wife and then his association to it: The dream had "to do with successful coitus Wednesday morning." Peter Gay, *Freud: A Life for Our Time* (New York, London: W. W. Norton, 1988), p. 163.

45. Freud, "On Beginning the Treatment" [1913b], *SE*, vol. 12 (1958), pp. 140–41.

46. Freud, "'Wild' Psycho-Analysis" [1910b], *SE*, vol. 11 (1957), p. 225.

47. Freud, "On Beginning the Treatment," p. 140.

48. Freud, "'Wild' Psycho-Analysis," p. 226.

49. Freud, "On Beginning the Treatment," pp. 125, 140 n. 1. Even before publishing Dora's case history, Freud had realized that "analytic psychotherapy is not a process . . . applicable to people . . . who submit to it only because they are forced to by the authority of relatives." See "On Psychotherapy" [1905a], *SE*, vol. 7 (1953), pp. 263–64.

50. Freud, "The Future Prospects of Psycho-Analytic Therapy" [1910a], *SE*, vol. 11 (1957), pp. 144–45.

51. Freud, "Recommendations to Physicians Practising Psycho-Analysis" [1912b], *S.E.*, vol. 12 (1958), p. 114.

52. See, however, Peter Loewenberg, "A Hidden Zionist Theme in Freud's 'My Son, the Myops . . . ' Dream, *Journal of the History of Ideas* 31 (1970), pp. 129–32.

53. Freud's letter to Martha Bernays, Dec. 16, 1883, in *The Letters of Sigmund Freud*, ed. Ernst L. Freud (New York, Toronto, London: McGraw-Hill, 1964), pp. 78–79.

54. Freud's letter of Feb. 2, 1886, in ibid., p. 202.

55. Ibid., p. 201. Having discovered the exhilarating effects of cocaine in 1884 and published a medical article advocating its use, Freud continued to take cocaine occasionally for many years, not stopping until about 1896. See Freud's letter to Fliess, Oct. 26, 1896, in Masson, ibid., p. 201.

56. Ibid., p. 203. However, this strong declaration was not without ambivalence. Freud admitted to Martha: "Such conversations are always embarrassing to me, for I feel stirring within me something German which I long ago decided to suppress."

57. Freud, "Address to the Society of B'nai B'rith" [1926] (1941), *SE*, vol. 20 (1959), p. 273.

58. Quoted in Rozenblit, p. 144.

59. Interview in 1926 with George Sylvester Viereck, originally published in 1927 and quoted in Gay, *Freud*, p. 448.

60. Freud's letter of Jan 27, 1925, quoted in Peter Gay, *A Godless Jew: Freud, Atheism, and the Making of Psychoanalysis* (New Haven and London: Yale University Press, 1987), p. 122.

61. Freud, "Address to the Society of B'nai B'rith," pp. 273–74.

62. Leichter, p. 23.

63. Published article about Dora's son.

64. Published interview with Dora's son.

65. Published article about Dora's son.

66. Gerhard Botz, "Otto Bauer im Ersten Weltkrieg: Anmerkungen zum Brief Otto Bauers an Helene Bauer vom 6. Dezember 1914," *Zukunft* (July 1978), pp. 32, 34. Article

in the archives of the Verein für Geschichte der Arbeiterbewegung Wien, catalog No. B1, box 19.

67. Published article about Dora's son.
68. "Biographical Note," *In Dora's Case*, p. 34.
69. IKG records.
70. Published interview with Dora's son.
71. Stefan Zweig, *The World of Yesterday* (New York: Viking, 1943), pp. 285–86.
72. Leichter, p. 25.
73. Zweig, p. 292.
74. Gay, *Freud*, p. 387.

9. *"Mad Times"*

1. George Clare, *Last Waltz in Vienna: The Rise and Destruction of a Family, 1842–1942* (New York: Holt, Rinehart and Winston, 1982), p. 95; Peter G. J. Pulzer, *The Rise of Political Anti-Semitism in Germany and Austria* (New York: John Wiley & Sons, 1964), p. 317.
2. Pulzer, p. 318.
3. Peter Loewenberg, *Decoding the Past: The Psychohistorical Approach* (Berkeley: University of California Press, 1985), p. 173; Clare, pp. 98–100. There is some discrepancy between Loewenberg's and Clare's accounts of the original incident.
4. Peter Gay, *Freud. A Life for Our Time* (New York, London: W. W. Norton 1988), p. 589.
5. Pulzer, p. 320.
6. Published article about Dora's son.
7. In 1957 Deutsch, reading in Ernest Jones's biography that Dora had died, published an account of his contact with her. Written thirty-five years after he had seen Dora, his paper is replete with factual errors. The obvious ones are easily corrected by anyone familiar with Dora's case and life. There may yet be other distortions in Deutsch's account, but they must stand unless new material comes to light.
8. Felix Deutsch, "A Footnote to Freud's 'Fragment of an Analysis of a Case of Hysteria,'" *Psychoanalytic Quarterly* 26 (1957), pp. 161–63.
9. Ibid. Dora's son did enter the university in 1923 but left without getting a degree in order to pursue his promising career as a conductor. At the same time that he was attending the university, he was enrolled in the Vienna State Academy of Music.
10. Deutsch, p. 161. Dora's perception of her warm relationship with Otto seems borne out by the fact that as an adult, Otto always had a large picture of Dora in his room, prominently displayed. Loewenberg, p. 192.
11. Ibid., pp. 161–63.
12. Ibid., p. 163.
13. Ibid., pp. 164–66. Deutsch's paper is an uncritical paean to Freud and, as we shall see, a brutal assessment of Dora.
14. Ibid., pp. 166–67.
15. Gay, p. 169.
16. Freud's letter of June 17, 1895, in *The Complete Letters of Sigmund Freud to Wilhelm Fliess: 1887–1904,* ed. and trans. Jeffrey M. Masson (Cambridge: Belknap Press, 1985), p. 132. The following letters chronicle Freud's fight to give up smoking: In 1893: Oct. 18, Nov. 27, Dec. 11; in 1894: June 22, late June, July 14; in 1895: June 17, Oct. 16, Nov. 8; in 1896: Dec. 4.

17. Freud's letter of June 22, 1894, in ibid., p. 84. In 1930 Freud wrote to Lou Andreas-Salomé that smoking had served him "as protection and weapon in the combat with life." Quoted in Gay, p. 573.

18. In Vienna cancer of the mouth from smoking was mainly a disease of men in their sixties and seventies who had enough money to support their expensive habit. Usually death from the cancer occurred within two years of its diagnosis. See Sharon Romm, *The Unwelcome Intruder: Freud's Struggle with Cancer.* (New York: Praeger, 1983), pp. 37–38.

19. Max Schur, *Freud: Living and Dying* (New York: International Universities Press, 1972), p. 363 n. 12.

20. Ibid., pp. 363–64; Gay, p. 427.

21. Since Freud had analyzed Anna for three years—a most unorthodox procedure—their relationship was very close, and it is not surprising that she never married. She followed most eminently in her father's professional footsteps.

22. Schur, p. 366; Ernest Jones, *The Life and Work of Sigmund Freud,* vol. 3 (New York: Basic Books, 1957), p. 99.

23. Freud was the fourth recipient of the prize. The first three were the poet Stefan George; the musician and medical missionary Albert Schweitzer; and the philosophical writer Leopold Ziegler. The prize was 10,000 German marks, at that time worth $2,500 (today about $25,000). See "Goethe-Preis, 1930," *SE,* vol. 21 (1961), p. 206.

24. Freud, "Address Delivered in the Goethe House at Frankfurt," ibid., pp. 208–12.

25. Otto Leichter, *Otto Bauer: Tragödie oder Triumph* (Wien: Europa Verlag, 1970), p. 23.

26. Clare, p. 52.

27. Personal interview with Professor Peter Loewenberg, May 1982.

28. Published interview with Dora's son.

29. Deutsch, p. 167.

30. Ibid.

31. Freud's letter to Samuel Freud, Dec. 1, 1931, quoted in Gay, p. 590.

32. Gay, p. 590.

33. Anson Rabinbach, *The Crisis of Austrian Socialism: From Red Vienna to Civil War, 1927–1934* (Chicago: University of Chicago Press, 1983), pp. 83–84.

34. Ibid., pp. 88–91.

35. Eric J. Hobsbawm, quoted in ibid., p. 91.

36. Otto Bauer, *Der Aufstand der oesterreichischen Arbeiter* (Prague 1934), p. 25, quoted in ibid.

37. Freud's letters to Lou Andreas-Salomé, May 14, 1933, and to Sandor Ferenczi, Apr. 2, 1933, quoted in Gay, pp. 592, 593.

38. Clare, p. 124.

39. G. E. R. Gedye of the London *Daily Telegraph,* quoted in ibid., p. 126.

40. Clare, p. 128; Frank Field, *The Last Days of Mankind: Karl Kraus and His Vienna* (London: MacMillan/New York: St. Martin's Press, 1967), pp. 61, 72.

41. Pulzer, p. 321.

42. Gay, p. 593; Freud's letter to Ernest Jones, Apr. 7, 1933, quoted in ibid.

43. Freud's letter to Oskar Pfister, Feb. 27, 1934, quoted in ibid., p. 594.

44. Clare, pp. 128–31; Loewenberg, pp. 186–87; Zweig, pp. 382–87. For an account of the Austrian civil war, see Rabinbach, pp. 181–215.

45. Freud's letter to Ernst Freud, Feb. 20, 1934, in *The Letters of Sigmund Freud,* ed. Ernst L. Freud, trans. Tania and James Stern (New York: McGraw-Hill, 1964), pp. 419–20.

46. Freud's letter to Arnold Zweig, Feb. 25, 1934, in *The Letters of Sigmund Freud and Arnold Zweig,* ed. Ernst L. Freud, trans. Elaine and William Robson-Scott (New York: Harcourt, Brace & World, 1970), p. 65.

47. Clare, pp. 131–32.

48. Published article about Dora's son.

49. Clare, pp. 159–60.

50. Freud's letter to Ernst Freud, Feb. 22, 1938, quoted in Gay, pp. 617–18.

51. Clare, p. 177.

52. George E. Berkley, *Vienna and Its Jews: The Tragedy of Success, 1880s–1980s* (Cambridge, Mass., and Lanham, Md.: Abt Books and Madison Books, 1988), p. 306.

53. Ibid., p. 329.

54. Clare, pp. 186–88, 190; Field, p. 236; Norman Bentwich, "The Destruction of the Jewish Community in Austria, 1938–1942," in *The Jews of Austria: Essays on Their Life, History and Destruction,* ed. Josef Fraenkel (London: Vallentine, Mitchell, 1967), pp. 467–68; Gerhard Botz, "The Jews of Vienna from the *Anschluss* to the Holocaust," in *Jews, Antisemitism and Culture in Vienna,* ed. Ivar Oxaal et al. (London and New York: Routledge & Kegan Paul, 1987), p. 188.

55. Herbert Rosenkranz, "The Anschluss and the Tragedy of Austrian Jewry, 1938–1945," in Fraenkel, ibid., p. 483.

56. Clare, p. 199.

57. He left without his wife. The sources do not indicate whether he was separated, divorced, or whether, by some chance, a widower.

58. Published article about Dora's son.

59. Loewenberg, p. 187.

60. The account that follows is based on Jones, vol. 3, pp. 218–28; Gay, pp. 622–29; Schur, pp. 495–502; Ronald W. Clark, *Freud: The Man and the Cause* (New York: Random House, 1980), pp. 504–13. Each source has information not found in the others. Some further details, including information about the flight from Vienna of Freud's brother, Alexander, and about Freud's four sisters who did not leave, can be found in Harald Leupold-Löwenthal, "Die Vertreibung der Familie Freud 1938," *Sigmund Freud House Bulletin* 12: 2 (Winter 1988), pp. 1–11.

61. Clare, pp. 205–06.

62. A famous story must now be put to rest. Ernest Jones, in his biography, reported that Freud had daringly added a sentence to the statement demanded of him: "I can heartily recommend the Gestapo to anyone" (vol. 3, p. 226). The original document has now surfaced. It is shorter and less dramatic than the one quoted by Jones and, soberly and realistically, contains no dashing addendum. A copy of the document signed by Freud was found in the papers of Freud's lawyer, Dr. Alfred Indra. See "A Sale in Vienna: Witz Against Legend?", *Journal of the International Association for the History of Psychoanalysis,* English edition, 8 (Autumn 1989), pp. 13–14.

63. Freud's actual death occurred through euthanasia. His physician, Max Schur, acting on a previous agreement with Freud, and then with the approval of Anna, injected him with an overdose of morphine. Gay calls this final episode a "stoic suicide." See pp. 650–51, 739–40.

64. All figures must be rough; the sources disagree on precise numbers. See Bentwich, pp. 474, 476, and Rosenkranz, pp. 513–14.

65. Gay, p. 649 n.

66. The last pre–World War II reference to Dora in the IKG records is dated May 3, 1939.

67. This account of Dora's travail is heavily based on information in Rosenkranz, pp. 487–503.

68. Clare, p. 206.

69. Ibid.

70. Loewenberg, p. 188.

71. Ivar Oxaal, "The Jews of Young Hitler's Vienna: Historical and Sociological Aspects," in Ivar Oxaal et al., ibid., pp. 16–17.

72. The accuracy of all these figures is hard to establish. Recently, the research of Gerhard Botz has somewhat lowered them, from 8,000 to 6,500 arrested and from 5,000 to 3,700 interned in Dachau.

73. IKG records. Botz, disagreeing with Rosenkranz, claims that the name-change legislation occurred in August 1938.

74. Deutsch, p. 166.

75. Ibid., p. 167.

76. Personal interview with Professor Peter Loewenberg, May 1982.

Epilogue: Dora Redux

1. Ernest Jones, *The Life and Work of Sigmund Freud,* vol. 2 (New York: Basic Books, 1955), p. 257.

2. Josef Breuer and Sigmund Freud, *Studies on Hysteria* [1893–95], *SE,* vol. 2 (1955), pp. 160–61. There were physicians, of course, who were hostile to Freud because they believed that he and his riveting narratives were dangerous for psychiatry as a scientific subject. Two especially strong condemnations of the Dora case came from Oswald Bumke in *Schmidts Jahrbücher* 289 (1906), pp. 168–69, and Walther Spielmeyer in *Zentralblatt für Nervenheilkunde und Psychiatrie* 29 (1906), pp. 322–24. Spielmeyer inventively used the expression "mental masturbation" to describe Freud's work.

3. Strictly speaking, "Schreber" was not a true case but Freud's once-removed analysis of the man's memoirs. Freud used Schreber's book as a vehicle to present his newest ideas about paranoia, homosexuality, and psychosis.

4. Freud had somewhat discussed transference in *Studies on Hysteria,* pp. 301–4; *The Interpretation of Dreams* [1900], *SE,* vol. 4, p. 200, and vol. 5, p. 562 n.; and *The Psychopathology of Everyday Life* [1901], *SE,* vol. 6, p. 172. But in Dora's case, he defined transference fully for the first time and clearly showed how it played an essential role in psychoanalytic therapy.

5. Freud could not have preached this last lesson more didactically (or dogmatically) than he did in the "Postscript": "Sexuality does not simply intervene, like a *deus ex machina,* on one single occasion [but] it provides the motive power for every single symptom, and for every single manifestation of a symptom. The symptoms of [hysteria] are nothing else than *the patient's sexual activity.* . . . I can only repeat over and over again . . . that sexuality is the key to the problem of the psychoneuroses and of the neuroses in general. No one who disdains the key will ever be able to unlock the door" (p. 115).

6. For almost sixty years after it was published, the Dora case attracted little special scrutiny. Attention began to focus on it following a 1962 paper by the psychoanalyst Erik Erikson on adolescents' "identity" and their psychological needs. Erikson's paper

proved to be catalytic and timely as Western preoccupations with family systems, adolescence, and "identity crisis" mushroomed in the late 1960s and early 1970s. These coincided with the rise of the feminist movement, whose own concerns about Dora's treatment were partially echoed and given wide and elegantly written circulation by the literary critic, Steven Marcus. After Marcus's article, the floodgates opened and have not since closed. Simultaneous interest by psychoanalysts finally alert to the crucial issue of the countertransference, feminists, historians of psychoanalysis, and literary and philosophic critics have kept the waters roiling. For a review of the Dora literature see Jerry L. Jennings, "The Revival of 'Dora': Advances in Psychoanalytic Theory and Technique," *Journal of the American Psychoanalytic Association* 34: 3(1986), pp. 607–35.

7. Janet Malcolm, *Psychoanalysis: The Impossible Profession* (New York: Vintage, 1982), p. 99.

8. Lisa Swanson and Mary Kay Biaggio, "Therapeutic Perspectives on Father-Daughter Incest," *The American Journal of Psychiatry* 142: 6 (June 1985), pp. 667–74.

9. Ibid., p. 672.

10. L. Z. Vogel, "The Case of Elise Gomperz," *American Journal of Psychoanalysis* 46: 3 (1986), pp. 231, 235–37.

11. In 1895 Freud recounted an episode early in his career in treating "a lively and gifted girl who had suffered for eighteen months from severe disturbances of her power of walking." He had hypnotized her while her father, a physician, was in the room, and asked her to relate "what emotion had preceded the onset of her illness. . . . At this she gave way to the extent of letting fall a single significant phrase; but she had hardly said a word before she stopped, and her old father . . . began to sob bitterly. Naturally I pressed my investigation no further; but I never saw the patient again." The delicate wording of this dramatic moment suggests an incestuous event in the patient's past and shows Freud's decision not to place her father in a compromising light, even though that meant forfeiting the opportunity to help her. Breuer and Freud, *Studies on Hysteria*, pp. 100–101.

12. From a poor background and still barely making ends meet, Freud would have found it difficult in 1900 to resist the demands of the often-wealthy men who employed him as doctor for their families. Vogel suggests that in the 1890s, Freud tailored his treatment of his hysterical patient, Elise Gomperz, to satisfy the wishes of her well-to-do and important husband, the scholar Theodor Gomperz. But it is likely that as Freud grew in status and self-esteem he was able eventually to ignore the pressure to please a patient's family.

13. "The Future Prospects of Psycho-Analytic Therapy" [1910], *SE*, vol. 11, pp. 144–45, and "Observations on Transference-Love" [1915], *SE*, vol. 12, p. 160, (1957 and 1958).

14. Jennings, pp. 624–26.

15. Peter L. Giovacchini, *Countertransference Triumphs and Catastrophes* (Northvale, N.J., and London: Jason Aronson, 1989), p. 15; Theodore J. Jacobs, "Countertransference Resistance and the Process of Self Analysis," paper presented to the Houston-Galveston Psychoanalytic Society, February 8, 1989, p. 2.

16. Comments by George Kochis to Jacobs' paper, reporting criticism of the discussion of countertransference at a meeting of child psychoanalysts in 1978.

17. Giovacchini, pp. ix, 3. Also see Michael J. Tansey and Walter F. Burke, *Understanding Countertransference: From Projective Identification to Empathy* (Hillsdale, N.J.: Analytic Press), 1989 and Peter Buckley, "Fifty Years After Freud: Dora, the Rat Man, and the Wolf-Man," *American Journal of Psychiatry* 146: 11 (Nov. 1989), pp. 1396–97.

18. Jacobs, pp. 2, 15.

19. Robert C. Smith and George H. Zimny, "Physicians' Emotional Reactions to Patients," *Psychosomatics* 29: 4 (Fall 1988), pp. 392–97.

20. See, for example, Theodore Lidz and Stephen Fleck, *Schizophrenia and the Family,* 2nd ed. (New York: International Universities Press, 1985), pp. 444, 446; Helm Stierlin, "The Dynamics of Owning and Disowning: Psychoanalytic and Family Perspectives, *Family Process* 15:3 (Sept. 1976), pp. 281–82, 286–87.

21. Samuel Slipp, "Interpersonal Factors in Hysteria: Freud's Seduction Theory and the Case of Dora," *Journal of the American Academy of Psychoanalysis* 5: 3 (1977), pp. 364–73; Theodore Lidz, Stephen Fleck, and Alice R. Cornelison, *Schizophrenia and the Family* (New York: International Universities Press, 1965), pp. 425–26.

22. Just as earlier, when she was eight, Dora had identified with her tubercular father and developed shortness of breath when her father left Meran for the first time in two years to go off to his factories. Dora, feeling angry and deserted, did not express these feelings openly but took a roundabout route to give vent to them, copying the devious way emotional issues were handled in her family.

23. Jules R. Bemporad et al., "Hysteria, Anorexia and the Culture of Self-Denial," *Psychiatry* 51: 1 (Feb. 1988), p. 98.

24. Ibid.

25. Felix Deutsch, "A Footnote to Freud's 'Fragment of an Analysis of a Case of Hysteria'," *Psychoanalytic Quarterly* 26 (1957), p. 162.

26. Helm Stierlin, *Psychoanalysis and Family Therapy: Selected Papers* (New York: Jason Aronson, 1987).

27. Ibid., chapters 7–9, 11–15.

28. By the time of World War I, he was telling medical students that "from [puberty] onwards, the human individual has to devote himself to the great task of detaching himself from his parents, [yet] it is remarkable how seldom [this is] dealt with in an ideal manner— that is, in one which is correct both psychologically and socially." *Introductory Lectures on Psychoanalysis* [1916–17], *SE,* vol. 16 (1963), p. 337.

29. Janet Malcolm, "Reflections: J'appelle un chat un chat," *The New Yorker,* April 20, 1987, p. 97.

30. Jennings, p. 630.

31. Anna Freud quoted in ibid., p. 629.

32. Of course, because of his theory of instinctual infantile sexuality, he assumed Dora unconsciously wanted K.'s overtures. Freud firmly believed K.'s proposal at the lake was the beginning of a sincere offer of marriage, and that in her heart, Dora knew this to be the case ("Fragment," pp. 95, 107–8, 108 n. 2.)

33. Swanson and Biaggio, p. 673. Although this last has to be recognized as an ideal. The molester will often continue to deny any involvement when confronted, which may further exacerbate the situation.

34. Stierlin, *Psychoanalysis,* p. 10.

35. Even a leading feminist critic of the case concurs. See Maria Ramas, "Freud's Dora, Dora's Hysteria: The Negation of a Woman's Rebellion," *Feminist Studies* 6: 3 (Fall 1980), pp. 476–77.

36. By the final week of the analysis, Dora was "raising a number of questions about the connection between some of her actions and the motives which presumably underlay them. One of these questions was: 'Why did I say nothing about the scene by the lake for some days after it had happened?' Her second question was: 'Why did I then suddenly tell my parents about it?'" ("Fragment," p. 95).

37. It was also, truth must be told, a slightly sadistic action, since Dora chose the occasion of the Ks' daughter's death to speak her mind. One imagines the Ks in mourning, taken aback by Dora's forthrightness and lacking the fortitude to lie.

38. Schönerer in the *Alldeutsches Tagblatt,* Jan. 1907, quoted in Peter G. J. Pulzer, *The Rise of Political Anti-Semitism in Germany and Austria* (New York: John Wiley & Sons, 1964), p. 222.

39. Ludwig Langemann, who was also editor of the league's journal, quoted in ibid.

40. Sandor Gilman concludes that "the linkage of misogyny and anti-Semitism during the latter half of the nineteenth century is not random. For as both Jews and women become more visible on the horizon of European consciousness through their articulated demands for emancipation, both legal and cultural, a natural association takes place." *Jewish Self-Hatred: Anti-Semitism and the Hidden Language of the Jews* (Baltimore and London: Johns Hopkins University Press, 1986), p. 244.

41. Bram Dijkstra, *Idols of Perversity: Fantasies of Feminine Evil in Fin-de-Siècle Culture* (New York and Oxford: Oxford University Press, 1986), p. vii; Cynthia Eagle Russett, *Sexual Science: The Victorian Construction of Womanhood* (Cambridge: Harvard University Press, 1989).

42. Dijkstra, pp. 96–100; Wilma Abeles Iggers, *Karl Kraus: A Viennese Critic of the Twentieth Century* (The Hague: Martinus Nijhoff, 1967), p. 159.

43. Dijkstra, pp. 244–45, 248, 249–50. Krafft-Ebing defined nymphomania in *Psychopathia Sexualis* as a form of "psychical degeneration" in which a woman readily gets excited just by seeing a man and has an insatiable appetite for sex. Not surprisingly, the authorities found that masturbation was a common cause of nymphomania.

44. Dijkstra, pp. 275, 277.

45. All one needs for confirmation of this fact is to read the marriage advertisements in the Viennese newspapers of the period.

46. Karl Kraus, about 1905–7, quoted in Iggers, p. 155.

47. Kraus quoted in ibid., pp. 160–61. The term "total woman," recently used in this country to signify a woman who concentrates, above all, on being sexually attractive for her man, was already used by Kraus almost a century ago (the *Vollweib*). Truly a magician with words, Kraus seems to have had a talent for minting phrases decades ahead of their widespread use. In addition to "total woman," he coined "sex object" (*Lustobjekt*).

48. Freud's letter to Kraus, Jan. 12, 1906, in *The Letters of Sigmund Freud,* ed. Ernst L. Freud, trans. Tania and James Stern (New York, Toronto, London: McGraw-Hill, 1964), pp. 249–50.

49. These men were also Dora's neighbors. More than half the members in 1906–7 lived either in the Inner City (First District) abutting the Alsergrund (Ninth District) or in the Alsergrund itself. See *Minutes of the Vienna Psychoanalytic Society,* vols. 1–4, *1906–1918,* ed. Herman Nunberg and Ernst Federn (New York: International Universities Press, 1962–75) vol. 1, pp. 1, 6.

50. Meeting of May 3, 1907, in ibid., vol. 1, pp. 195–98.

51. Meeting of Feb. 26, 1913, in ibid., vol. 4, p. 170.

52. Meeting of Mar. 11, 1908, in ibid., vol. 1, pp. 347, 350–51. This time, Hitschmann found nothing sympathetic in Wittels's arguments, labeling menstruation as "insignificant" for the society's discussion and Wittels's views "as the fantasy of a youthful reactionary." Hitschmann was not the only one to defend women against Wittels. Alfred Adler, who three years later left the society, did as did a guest from Prague, Christian von Ehrenfels. See pp. 83, 91.

53. Peter Gay, *Freud: A Life for Our Time* (New York and London: W. W. Norton 1988), p. 59; Freud's letter to Minna Bernays, Jan. 1887, quoted in Peter Gay, "Sigmund and Minna? The Biographer as Voyeur," *New York Times Book Review,* Jan. 29, 1989, p. 44.

54. Recollection of Sophie Freud Loewenstein published in the *Houston Post*; Gay, *Freud,* pp. 59, 428 n.

55. Freud, "The Disposition to Obsessional Neurosis: A Contribution to the Problem of Choice of Neurosis" [1913a], *SE,* vol. 12 (1958), pp. 323–24.

56. Freud, "Three Essays on the Theory of Sexuality" [1905d], *SE,* vol. 7 (1953), p. 151; Freud, "New Introductory Lectures on Psycho-Analysis" ([1932] 1933), *SE,* vol. 22 (1964), p. 125.

57. In Schnitzler's stories, such as "Beatrice" or "Frau Bertha Garlan," we see an "oppressive and labyrinthine" society of frustrated women who suffer ennui as they struggle with their sexual fantasies. They may realize that "bourgeois respectability is a lie," but if they have an extramarital relationship, the men treat them as children or objects that can easily be discarded; meanwhile, their husbands lie, pretend, and mask reality before their very eyes. Sidney Bolkosky, "Arthur Schnitzler and the Fate of Mothers in Vienna," *Psychoanalytic Review* 73: 1 (Spring 1986), p. 13.

58. Ibid., pp. 2, 5, 8, 11.

59. Freud, "New Introductory Lectures," pp. 134–35.

60. Freud meant two things by this: (1) "With the change to femininity, the clitoris should wholly or in part hand over its sensitivity, and at the same time its importance, to the vagina" (ibid., p. 118); (2) the girl must surrender her first love object, her mother, and replace it with her father. (The boy starts out with and keeps his mother as his first love object and, therefore, need not make this transfer.)

61. Bumke in the second (1924) edition of his *Lehrbuch der Geisteskrankheiten,* p. 452, quoted in Edward Shorter, "Paralysis: The Rise and Fall of a 'Hysterical' Symptom," in *Expanding the Past: A Reader in Social History,* ed. Peter N. Stearns (New York and London: New York University Press, 1988), p. 229.

62. Jones, p. 256; Deutsch, p. 167.

63. Didier Anzieu, *Freud's Self-Analysis,* trans. Peter Graham (Madison, Conn.: International Universities Press, 1986 [originally published 1975]), pp. 544–45.

64. Karl Kay Lewin, "Dora Revisited," *Psychoanalytic Review* 60 (1974), pp. 521–22.

65. An example of this was Philipp and Käthe's "great dispute about a piece of jewellery" when Dora was fourteen. Dora reported to Freud that her mother "wanted to be given a particular thing—pearl drops to wear in her ears. But Father does not like that kind of thing, and he brought her a bracelet instead of the drops. She was furious, and told him that as he had spent so much money on a present she did not like he had better just give it to some one else" ("Fragment," pp. 68–69).

66. "The conclusion was inevitable," Freud stated with his usual air of certitude, "that with her spasmodic cough, which, as is usual, was referred for its exciting stimulus to a tickling in her throat, she pictured to herself a scene of sexual gratification *per os* [orally] between the two people whose love-affair occupied her mind so incessantly" ("Fragment," p. 48).

67. Shorter, pp. 215–16, 218–19, 222.

68. Ilza Veith, *Hysteria: The History of a Disease* (Chicago and London: University of Chicago Press, 1965), pp. 1–7.

69. Bemporad et al., pp. 96–97.

70. The disorder was first described in 1868 and given the name "anorexia nervosa" in 1874.

71. S. Orbach quoted in Bemporad et al., p. 96.

72. Bemporad et al., pp. 99–100.

73. Joan Jacobs Brumberg has documented the attempt of anorexic girls and women to exercise control over their lives via their intake of food. See *Fasting Girls: The Emergence of Anorexia Nervosa as a Modern Disease*. (Cambridge, Mass., and London: Harvard University Press, 1988). One should also note the pioneering work along these lines of the psychoanalyst Hilde Bruch.

74. Most individuals, he thought, were doomed to neurosis because of the inevitable clash between their instinctual needs and the demands of society. Freud saw no way out of this dilemma, believing people needed civilization. Society took its inevitable toll, and the most psychoanalysis could do was convert neurotic misery into ordinary unhappiness. Freud's lengthiest disquisition on the impossibility of human happiness is his *Civilization and Its Discontents* (1930), published when he was seventy-four. But long before he was embittered by sickness and other of life's buffets, he was deeply convinced that the unavoidable thwarting of instinctual needs made neurosis ubiquitous.

Notes to Freud's Case History, "Fragment of an Analysis of a Case of Hysteria"

Note: The page numbers on the left refer to this volume. The right column lists the relevant phrase and page number(s) in the *Standard Edition,* volume 7.

1. *"In Spite of Her Reluctance"*

2. *"The Purely Human and Social Circumstances"*

3. *"The Family Circle"*

4. *"Merely a Case of* 'Petite Hystérie' "

5.   *"I Do Not Know What Kind of Help She Wanted from Me"*

p. 94   "material under observation": 9
p. 94   left the room: 10
p. 94   "more connected form": 10
p. 94   "very few places": 12–13
p. 95   a "complete recovery": 119
p. 95   "most recent form": 24–25
p. 95   life and illness: 16
p. 95   "a common love-affair": 32
p. 95   "and his wife . . . ": 34
p. 96   its healthy perimeters: 55–57
p. 96   "a rigorous test": 31
p. 96   Mr. K. should marry: 108
p. 96   of her masturbating: 76
p. 97   "liability to ill-health": 42
p. 97   from an illness: 42–46
p. 98   "and revengeful motives": 120
p. 98   "the struggle unscathed": 109
p. 99   "in her hands": 42
p. 100   "efforts of doctors": 22
p. 101   "of the physician?": 120
p. 101   "and revengeful motives": 120
p. 101   at times "intolerable": 75
p. 101   "on her part": 109
p. 101   "will and understanding": 109
p. 102   *"not in earnest"*: 120, 121
p. 102   "of her troubles": 122
p. 104   Dora's irregular periods: 101
p. 104   to her masturbating: 76
p. 104   "surrendering to it" 87
p. 104   "the latter course": 88
p. 104   her gastric pains: 74, 76, 78
p. 105   "of satisfaction appears . . . ": 79
p. 106   was now "feminine": 82*n*.1
p. 108   "is my revenge": 120
p. 108   "less serious studies": 23
p. 108   with "housewife's psychosis": 20
p. 108   "tactless nor offensive?": 38*n*.2
p. 108   "of prepossessing appearance": 29*n*.3
p. 109   "of those secrets": 7–8

6.   *"This Child of Fourteen . . . Entirely and Completely Hysterical"*

p. 112   " 'and roundabout ways' ": 118
p. 112   give up the treatment: 70*n*.2, 93
p. 113   and her father: 35
p. 114   "accepted" his interpretation: 48
p. 114   girl of nineteen: 51
p. 114   divine her secret: 78

7.   *"Who Else Was There Called Dora?"*

p. 141   "in good time": 118
p. 146   "is my revenge": 120

8.   *"The Realities of Life"*

p. 148   goodbye "very warmly": 109
p. 148   "treatment to continue": 109
p. 148   "to scientific uses": 8
p. 149   "gratifying sexual desires": 9
p. 149   "do not know": 109
p. 149   "muddle" throughout January: 121
p. 150   to her father: 121
p. 150   "a violent fright": 121
p. 150   "not in earnest": 120–121
p. 150   "for her troubles": 122
p. 150   be so detestable: 120
p. 151   "thoughts of marrying": 121
p. 151   said: "The Madonna": 96
p. 151   by the lake: 100–104
p. 151   "in her behaviour": 104*n.*2
p. 152   "realities of life": 122
p. 160   the original paper: 122*n.*2

9.   *"Mad Times"*

p. 171   in Dora's life: 14

Epilogue: Dora Redux

p. 191   "first introductory publication": 118
p. 193   "very independent judgement": 22
p. 198   "[proposal] by herself": 95
p. 204   those she knew: 35–36, 38, 75
p. 206   convulsions and delirium: 23*n.*2
p. 206   sexually through fellatio: 47–48
p. 209   "thoughts of marrying": 121
p. 209   "to severe neuropsychoses": 75

Bibliography

Abrahamsen, David. *The Mind and Death of a Genius.* New York: Columbia University Press, 1946.

Alexander, Franz G., and Selesnick, Sheldon T. *The History of Psychiatry.* New York: Harper & Row, 1966.

Allport, Gordon W. *The Nature of Prejudice.* Cambridge, Mass.: Addison-Wesley, 1954.

Althaus, Julius. *Diseases of the Nervous System: Their Prevalence and Pathology.* London: Smith, Elder, 1877.

Anzieu, Didier. *Freud's Self-Analysis.* (1975). Trans. Peter Graham. Madison, Conn.: International Universities Press, 1986.

Barea, Ilsa. *Vienna.* New York: Alfred A. Knopf, 1966.

Bauer, Otto. *Die Nationalitätenfrage und die Socialdemokratie.* Vienna: Wiener Volksbuchhandlung, 1907.

Beller, Steven. *Vienna and the Jews, 1867–1938: A Cultural History.* Cambridge: Cambridge University Press, 1989.

Bemporad, Jules R., et al. "Hysteria, Anorexia and the Culture of Self-Denial." *Psychiatry* 51:1 (Feb. 1988), pp. 96–102.

Benedikt, Moritz. *Elektrotherapie.* Vienna: Tendler, 1868.

Bentwich, Norman. "The Destruction of the Jewish Community in Austria 1938–1942." In *The Jews of Austria: Essays on Their Life, History and Destruction,* edited by Josef Fraenkel, pp. 467–78. London: Vallentine, Mitchell, 1967.

Berkley, George E. *Vienna and Its Jews: The Tragedy of Success, 1880s–1980s.* Cambridge, Mass., and Lanham, Md.: Abt Books and Madison Books, 1988.

Bernheimer, Charles, and Kahane, Claire, eds. *In Dora's Case: Freud-Hysteria-Feminism.* New York: Columbia University Press, 1985.

Berry, John W., and Kim Uichol. "Acculturation and Mental Health." In

Health and Cross-Cultural Psychology: Toward Applications. Cross-Cultural Research and Methodological Series, vol. 10, edited by P. R. Dasen, et al., pp. 207–36. Newbury Park, Calif.: Sage Publications, 1988.

Bloch, Iwan. *The Sexual Life of Our Time in its Relations to Modern Civiliazation.* Translated from the 6th German ed. by M. Eden Paul. London: Rebman, 1908.

Blos, Peter. "The Epigenesis of the Adult Neurosis." *The Psychoanalytic Study of the Child,* vol. 27, pp. 106–34. New York: Quadrangle Books, 1972.

Blum, Mark E. *The Austro-Marxists, 1890–1918: A Psychobiographical Study.* Lexington: University Press of Kentucky, 1985.

Bolkosky, Sidney. "Arthur Schnitzler and the Fate of Mothers in Vienna." *Psychoanalytic Review* 73:1 (Spring 1986), pp. 1–15.

Botz, Gerhard. "The Jews of Vienna from the *Anschluss* to the Holocaust." In *Jews, Antisemitism and Culture in Vienna,* edited by Ivar Oxaal, et al., pp. 185–204. London and New York: Routledge & Kegan Paul, 1987.

————. "Otto Bauer im Ersten Weltkrieg: Anmerkungen zum Brief Otto Bauers an Helene Bauer vom 6. Dezember 1914." *Zukunft* (July 1978), pp. 32–36.

Boyer, John W. "Freud, Marriage, and Late Victorian Liberalism." *Journal of Modern History* 50:1 (Mar. 1978), pp. 72–102.

————. *Political Radicalism in Late Imperial Vienna: Origins of the Christian Social Movement, 1848–1897.* Chicago and London: University of Chicago Press, 1981.

Braunthal, Julius, ed. *Otto Bauer: Eine Auswahl aus seinem Lebenswerk.* Vienna: Wiener Volksbuchhandlung, 1961.

————. *In Search of the Millennium.* London: Victor Gollancz, 1945.

Breuer, Josef, and Freud, Sigmund. *Studies on Hysteria* (1893–95). *Standard Edition of the Complete Psychological Works of Sigmund Freud,* vol. 2. London: Hogarth Press, 1955.

Brock, Adolf. "Geschichte der Juden in Humpolec." In *Die Juden und Judengemeinden Böhmens in Vergangenheit und Gegenwart,* edited by Hugo Gold, vol. 1, pp. 193–96. Brünn-Prag: Jüdischer Buch- und Kunstverlag, 1934.

Brumberg, Joan Jacobs. *Fasting Girls: The Emergence of Anorexia Nervosa as a Modern Disease.* Cambridge, Mass., and London: Harvard University Press, 1988.

Bry, Ilse, and Rifkin, Alfred H. "Freud and the History of Ideas: Primary Sources, 1886–1910." *Science and Psychoanalysis,* vol. 5, pp. 6–36. New York: Grune & Stratton, 1962.

Buckley, Peter. "Fifty Years After Freud: Dora, the Rat Man, and the Wolf-Man." *American Journal of Psychiatry* 146:11 (Nov. 1989), pp. 1394–1403.

Bumke, Oswald. Review of Freud's "Bruchstück einer Hysterie-Analyse." *Schmidts Jahrbücher* 289 (1906), pp. 168–69.

Červinka, František. "The Hilsner Affair." *Yearbook of the Leo Baeck Institute,* vol. 13 (1968), pp. 142–57.

Clare, George. *Last Waltz in Vienna: The Rise and Destruction of a Family, 1842–1942.* New York: Holt, Rinehart and Winston, 1982.

Clark, Ronald W. *Freud: The Man and the Cause.* New York: Random House, 1980.

Cohn, Norman. *Warrant for Genocide: The Myth of the Jewish World-Conspiracy and the Protocols of the Elders of Zion.* 1969. Reprint. Chico, Calif.: Scholars Press, 1981.

Cranefield, Paul F. "Josef Breuer's Evaluation of His Contributions to Psychoanalysis." *International Journal of Psychoanalysis* 39 (1958), pp. 319–22.

Dagan, Avigdor. "The Press." *The Jews of Czechoslovakia: Historical Studies and Surveys,* vol. 1, pp. 523–31. Philadelphia: Jewish Publication Society of America, 1968.

Dana, Charles L. *Text-Book of Nervous Diseases.* 9th ed. New York: William Wood, 1920.

––––––. *Text-Book of Nervous Diseases and Psychiatry.* 6th ed., rev. and enl. New York: William Wood, 1904.

Decker, Hannah S. "The Interpretation of Dreams: Early Reception by the Educated German Public." *Journal of the History of the Behavioral Sciences* 11 (1975), pp. 129–41.

––––––. *Freud in Germany: Revolution and Reaction in Science, 1893–1907.* New York: International Universities Press, 1977.

Defendorf, A. Ross. *Clinical Psychiatry: A Textbook for Students and Physicians.* Abstracted and adapted from the 6th German ed. (1899) of Emil Kraepelin's *Lehrbuch der Psychiatrie.* New York: Macmillan, 1904.

"Dějiny Židů v Polné" in *Die Juden und Judengemeinden Böhmens in Vergangenheit und Gegenwart,* edited by Hugo Gold, pp. 508–11. Brünn-Prag: Jüdischer Buch- und Kunstverlag, 1934.

Deutsch, Felix. "A Footnote to Freud's 'Fragment of an Analysis of a Case of Hysteria,'" *Psychoanalytic Quarterly* 26 (1957), pp. 159–67.

Dijkstra, Bram. *Idols of Perversity: Fantasies of Feminine Evil in Fin-de-Siècle Culture.* New York and Oxford: Oxford University Press, 1986.

Dion, Kenneth L., and Earn, Brian M. "The Phenomenology of Being a Target of Prejudice." *Journal of Personality and Social Psychology* 23:5 (1975), pp. 944–50.

Douglas, Ann. *The Feminization of American Culture.* New York: Avon, 1978.

Dubnov, Simon. *History of the Jews: From Cromwell's Commonwealth to the Napoleonic Era,* vol. 4. Translated by Moshe Spiegel from the Russian 4th definitive rev. ed., vols. 7 and 8. South Brunswick, N.J.: Thomas Yoseloff, 1971.

————. *History of the Jews From the Congress of Vienna to the Emergence of Hitler,* vol. 5. Translated from the Russian 4th ed., vols. 9 and 10. South Brunswick, N. J.: Thomas Yoseloff, 1973.

"Dvůr Králové." *Encyclopaedia Britannica,* vol. 7. 1951.

Edmunds, Lavinia. "His Master's Choice." *Johns Hopkins Magazine,* 40:2 (Apr. 1988), pp. 40–49.

Eissler, K. R. *Freud as an Expert Witness: The Discussion of War Neuroses Between Freud and Wagner-Jauregg.* Madison, Conn.: International Universities Press, 1986.

Ellenberger, Henri F. *The Discovery of the Unconscious: The History and Evolution of Dynamic Psychiatry.* New York: Basic Books, 1970.

————. "The Story of 'Anna O.': A Critical Review with New Data." *Journal of the History of the Behavioral Sciences* 8 (1972), pp. 267–79.

Elon, Amos. *Herzl.* New York: Holt, Rinehart and Winston, 1975.

Encyclopedia Judaica, vols. 4, 6, 10, 11, 12, 13, 14, 15, 16. Jerusalem: Keter Publishing House/New York: Macmillan, 1972.

Enke, Paul. *Casuistische Beiträge zur männlichen Hysterie.* Jena: Frommannsche Hof-Buchdruckerei, 1900.

Erb, Wilhelm. *Handbook of Electro-Therapeutics,* trans. L. Putzel. New York: William Wood, 1883.

Erikson, Erik. "Psychological Reality and Historical Actuality." *Insight and Responsibility.* New York: W. W. Norton, 1964.

Ettinger, Shmuel. "The Modern Period." In *A History of the Jewish People,* edited by H. H. Ben Sasson, pp. 727–1096. London: Weidenfeld and Nicolson, 1976.

Evans, Richard J. *The Feminists: Women's Emancipation Movements in Europe, America and Australasia 1840–1920.* London: Croom Helm/New York: Barnes & Noble, 1977.

Eysenck, H. J. *Decline and Fall of the Freudian Empire.* New York: Viking, 1985.

Féré, Charles. *Diseases of the Nervous System.* Vol. 10 of *Twentieth Century Practice: An International Encyclopedia of Modern Medical Science by Leading Authorities of Europe and America.* New York: William Wood, 1897.

Die Fackel (herausgegeben von Karl Kraus). 2:59, 61 (Nov.–Dec. 1900).

Fichtner, Gerhard, and Hirschmüller, Albrecht. "Freuds 'Katharina'—Hintergrund, Entstehungsgeschichte und Bedeutung einer frühen psychoanalytischen Krankengeschichte." *Psyche* 39 (1985), pp. 220–40.

Field, Frank. *The Last Days of Mankind: Karl Kraus and his Vienna.* London: MacMillan/New York: St. Martin's Press, 1967.

"A Fine Romance: Freud and Dora." *Diacritics, A Review of Contemporary Criticism* 13: 1 (Spring 1983); see "A Dora Bibliography," pp. 81–84.

Fischer-Homburger, Esther. "Hysterie und Misogynie—ein Aspekt der Hysteriegeschichte" *Gesneruse* 26 (1969), pp. 117–27.

"Franzensbad." *Encyclopaedia Britannica,* vol. 9. 1951.

Freud, Ernst; Freud, Lucie; Grubrich-Simitis, Ilse, eds. *Sigmund Freud: His Life in Pictures and Words.* Translated by Christine Trollope. New York: Harcourt Brace Jovanovich, 1976.

Freud, Martin. "Who Was Freud?" In *The Jews of Austria,* edited by Josef Fraenkel, pp. 197–211. London: Vallentine, Mitchell, 1967.

Freud, Sigmund. "Heredity and the Aetiology of the Neuroses" (1896). *Standard Edition of the Complete Psychological Works,* vol. 3, pp. 143–56. London: Hogarth Press, 1962.

———*The Interpretation of Dreams* (1900). *Standard Edition,* vols. 4 and 5. London: Hogarth Press, 1958.

———. "On Dreams" (1901a). *Standard Edition,* vol. 5. London: Hogarth Press, 1958.

———. *The Psychopathology of Everyday Life* (1901b). *Standard Edition,* vol. 6. London: Hogarth Press, 1960.

———. "Freud's Psycho-Analytic Procedure" (1904). *Standard Edition,* vol. 7, pp. 245–54. London: Hogarth Press, 1953.

———. "On Psychotherapy" (1905a). *Standard Edition,* vol. 7, pp. 257–68. London: Hogarth Press, 1953.

———. "Bruchstück einer Hysterie-Analyse" (1905b). *Gesammelte Werke,* Fünfter Band, pp. 163–285. London: Imago Publishing, 1942.

———. "Fragment of an Analysis of a Case of Hysteria" (1905c). *Standard Edition,* vol. 7, pp. 7–122. London: Hogarth Press, 1953.

———. "Three Essays on the Theory of Sexuality" (1905d). *Standard Edition,* vol. 7, pp. 130–243. London: Hogarth Press, 1953.

———. "My Views on the Part Played by Sexuality in the Aetiology of the Neuroses" (1906), *Standard Edition,* vol. 7, pp. 271–79. London: Hogarth Press, 1953.

———. "The Future Prospects of Psycho-Analytic Therapy" (1910a). *Standard Edition,* vol. 11, pp. 141–51. London: Hogarth Press, 1957.

———. "'Wild' Psycho-Analysis" (1910b). *Standard Edition,* vol. 11, pp. 233–34. London: Hogarth Press, 1957.

———. "Types of Onset of Neurosis," (1912a). *Standard Edition,* vol. 12, pp. 231–38. London: Hogarth Press, 1958.

———. "Recommendations to Physicians Practising Psycho-Analysis" (1912b). *Standard Edition,* vol. 12, pp. 111–20. London: Hogarth Press, 1958.

———. "The Disposition to Obsessional Neurosis" (1913a). *Standard Edition,* vol. 12, pp. 317–26. London: Hogarth Press, 1958.

————. "On Beginning the Treatment" (1913b). *Standard Edition*, vol. 12, pp. 123–44. London: Hogarth Press, 1958.

————. "Observations on Transference-Love" (1915). *Standard Edition*, vol. 12, pp. 159–71. London: Hogarth Press, 1958.

————. "Some Character-Types Met With in Psycho-Analytic Work" (1916). *Standard Edition*, vol. 14, pp. 311–33. London: Hogarth Press, 1957.

————. *Introductory Lectures on Psycho-Analysis* (1916–17). *Standard Edition*, vols. 15 and 16. London: Hogarth Press, 1963.

————. "Beyond the Pleasure Principle" (1920). *Standard Edition*, vol. 18, pp. 7–64. London: Hogarth Press, 1955.

————. "An Autobiographical Study" (1925). *Standard Edition*, vol. 20, pp. 7–74. London: Hogarth Press, 1959.

————. "Inhibitions, Symptoms, and Anxiety" (1926). *Standard Edition*, vol. 20, pp. 87–172. London: Hogarth Press, 1959.

————. "Address Delivered in the Goethe House at Frankfurt" (1930). *Standard Edition*, vol. 21, pp. 208–12. London: Hogarth Press, 1961.

————. *New Introductory Lectures on Psycho-Analysis* [1932](1933). *Standard Edition*, vol. 22, pp. 5–182. London: Hogarth Press, 1964.

————. "The Subtleties of a Faulty Action" (1935). *Standard Edition*, vol. 22, pp. 233–35. London: Hogarth Press, 1964.

————. "Address to the Society of B'nai B'rith" [1926] (1941). *Standard Edition*, vol. 20, pp. 273–74. London: Hogarth Press, 1959.

————. "Briefe an Arthur Schnitzler." With notes by Henry Schnitzler. *Die neue Rundschau* 66:1 (1955), pp. 95–106.

————. *The Complete Letters of Sigmund Freud to Wilhelm Fliess, 1887–1904.* Edited and translated by Jeffrey M. Masson. Cambridge, Mass., and London: Belknap Press, 1985.

————. *The Letters of Sigmund Freud.* Edited by Ernst L. Freud; translated by Tania and James Stern. New York, Toronto, London: McGraw-Hill, 1964.

————. *The Letters of Sigmund Freud and Arnold Zweig.* Edited by Ernst L. Freud; translated by Elaine and William Robson-Scott. New York: Harcourt, Brace & World, 1970.

————. *The Origins of Psycho-Analysis: Letters to Wilhelm Fliess, Drafts and Notes: 1887–1902.* Edited by Marie Bonaparte, Anna Freud, and Ernst Kris; translated by Eric Mosbacher and James Strachey. New York: Basic Books, 1954.

The Freud/Jung Letters. Edited by William McGuire. Princeton, N. J.: Princeton University Press, 1974.

"The Freudian Ship." Recollection of Sophie Freud Loewenstein. *Houston Post.*

Furio, Joanne. "Czechoslovakia's Opulent Spas." *New York Times,* sec. 5, Nov. 26, 1989, pp. 14, 19.

Garrison, Fielding H. *An Introduction to the History of Medicine*. 4th ed. Philadelphia and London: W. B. Saunders, 1929.

Gay, Peter. *The Bourgeois Experience: Victoria to Freud*. Vol, 1. *Education of the Senses;* vol. 2, *The Tender Passion*. New York and Oxford: Oxford University Press, 1984 and 1986.

———. *Freud. A Life for Our Time*. New York and London: W. W. Norton, 1988.

———. *Freud, Jews and Other Germans: Masters and Victims in Modernist Culture*. New York: Oxford University Press, 1978.

———. *A Godless Jew: Freud, Atheism and the Making of Psychoanalysis*. New Haven and London: Yale University Press, 1987.

———. "Sigmund and Minna? The Biographer as Voyeur." *New York Times Book Review*, January 29, 1989, pp. 1, 43–45.

"Geschichte der Juden in Nachod." In *Die Juden und Judengemeinden Böhmens in Vergangenheit und Gegenwart*, edited by Hugo Gold, vol. 1, pp. 412–13. Brünn-Prag: Jüdischer Buch- und Kunstverlag, 1934.

"Geschichte der Juden in Reichenberg." In *Die Juden und Judengemeinden Böhmens in Vergangenheit und Gegenwart*, edited by Hugo Gold, vol. 1, pp. 529–69. Brünn-Prag: Jüdischer Buch- und Kunstverlag, 1934.

"Geschichte der Juden in Rumburg [includes Jews in Warnsdorf]." In *Die Juden und Judengemeinden Böhmens in Vergangenheit und Gegenwart*, edited by Hugo Gold, vol. 1, p. 578. Brünn-Prag: Jüdischer Buch- und Kunstverlag, 1934.

Gilligan, Carol. *In A Different Voice: Psychological Theory and Women's Development*. Cambridge: Harvard University Press, 1982.

Gilman, Sander L. *Jewish Self-Hatred: Anti-Semitism and the Hidden Language of the Jews*. Baltimore and London: Johns Hopkins University Press, 1986.

Giovacchini, Peter L. *Countertransference Triumphs and Catastrophes*. Northvale, N.J., and London: Jason Aronson, 1989.

Glenn, Jules. "Freud, Dora, and the Maid: A Study of Countertransference." *Journal of the American Psychoanalytic Association* 34: 3 (1986), pp. 591–606.

Good, David, F. *The Economic Rise of the Habsburg Empire, 1750–1914*. Berkeley and Los Angeles: University of California Press, 1984.

Grinstein, Alexander. *On Sigmund Freud's Dreams*. Detroit: Wayne State University Press, 1968.

A Guest in Merano 8: 2 (Summer–Autumn 1985). Concierges of Merano.

Gulick, Charles A. *Austria from Habsburg to Hitler*, vol. 1. Berkeley and Los Angeles: University of California Press, 1948.

Hardin, Harry T. "On the Vicissitudes of Freud's Early Mothering. I: Early Environment and Loss; II: Alienation From his Biological Mother; III:

Freiberg, Screen Memories, and Loss." *Psychoanalytic Quarterly* 56 (1987), pp. 628–44; 57 (1988), pp. 72–86, 209–23.

Heyse, Paul. *Incurable*. Translated by H. W. Eve. London: David Nutt, 1890.

Hirschmüller, Albrecht. *Physiologie und Psychoanalyse im Leben und Werk Josef Breuers*. Bern: Hans Huber, 1978.

Hollender, Marc H. "Conversion Hysteria: A Post-Freudian Reinterpretation of 19th Century Psychosocial Data." *Archives of General Psychiatry* 26 (1972), pp. 311–14.

Iggers, Wilma Abeles. *Karl Kraus: A Viennese Critic of the Twentieth Century*. The Hague: Martinus Nijhoff, 1967.

Israel, Jonathan I. *European Jewry in the Age of Mercantilism, 1550–1750*. Oxford: Clarendon Press, 1985.

Israelitische Kultusgemeinde Wien, Records.

Jacobs, Theodore J. "Countertransference Resistance and the Process of Self-Analysis." Paper presented to the Houston-Galveston Psychoanalytic Society, February 8, 1989.

Janik, Allan. "Viennese Culture and the Jewish Self-Hatred Hypothesis: A Critique." In *Jews, Antisemitism and Culture in Vienna*, edited by Ivar Oxaal et al., pp. 75–88. London and New York: Routledge & Kegan Paul, 1987.

Jennings, Jerry L. "The Revival of 'Dora': Advances in Psychoanalytic Theory and Technique. *Journal of the American Psychoanalytic Association* 34: 3 (1986), pp. 607–35.

Jewish Encyclopedia, vols. 2, 3, 6, 9, 10, 12. New York: Ktav Publishing House, n.d. (about 1900).

Johnson, Paul. *A History of the Jews*. New York: Harper & Row, 1987.

Johnston, William M. *The Austrian Mind: An Intellectual and Social History, 1848–1938*. Berkeley: University of California Press, 1972.

Jones, Ernest. *The Life and Work of Sigmund Freud*, vols. 1–3. New York: Basic Books, 1953–57.

Kestenberg-Gladstein, Ruth. "The Jews Between Czechs and Germans in the Historic Lands, 1848–1918." *The Jews of Czechoslovakia: Historical Studies and Surveys*, vol. 1, pp. 21–71. Philadelphia: Jewish Publication Society of America, 1968.

————. *Neuere Geschichte der Juden in den böhmischen Ländern*, Erster Teil, *Das Zeitalter der Aufklärung, 1780–1830*. Tübingen: J. C. B. Mohr, 1969.

Kieval, Hillel J. "Autonomy and Interdependence: The Historical Legacy of Czech Jewry," pp. 46–109. In *The Precious Legacy*, edited by David Altshuler. New York: Summit Books, 1983.

Kisch, Guido. *In Search of Freedom: A History of American Jews from Czechoslovakia*. London: Edward Goldston & Son, 1949.

_____. "Linguistic Conditions Among Czechoslovak Jewry: A Legal-Historical Study." *Historia Judaica* 8 (1946), pp. 19–32.

Klein, Dennis B. *Jewish Origins of the Psychoanalytic Movement.* New York: Praeger, 1981.

Kohn, Hans. "Before 1918 in the Historic Lands." *The Jews of Czechoslovakia: Historical Studies and Surveys,* vol. 1, pp. 12–20. Philadelphia: Jewish Publication Society of America, 1968.

Krohn, Alan. *Hysteria: The Elusive Neurosis.* Psychological Issues Monograph 45/46. New York: International Universities Press, 1978.

Krüll, Marianne. *Freud and His Father.* New York and London: W. W. Norton, 1986.

Langs, Robert. "The Misalliance Dimension in Freud's Case Histories: I. The Case of Dora." *International Journal of Psychoanalytic Psychotherapy* 5 (1976), pp. 301–17.

Leichter, Otto. *Otto Bauer: Tragödie oder Triumph.* Wien: Europa Verlag, 1970.

Lesky, Erna. *The Vienna Medical School of the 19th Century.* Baltimore: Johns Hopkins University Press, 1976.

Lessing, Theodor. *Der jüdische Selbsthass.* Berlin: Jüdischer Verlag, 1930.

Leupold-Löwenthal, Harald. "Die Vertreibung der Familie Freud 1938." *Sigmund Freud House Bulletin* 12: 2 (Winter 1988), pp. 1–11.

Lewin, Karl K. "Dora Revisited." *The Psychoanalytic Review* 60 (1974), pp. 519–32.

Lewin, Kurt. "Self-Hatred Among Jews" (1941). In *Resolving Social Conflicts: Selected Papers on Group Dynamics.* New York: Harper & Brothers, 1948.

"Liberec." *Encyclopaedia Britannica,* vol. 13. 1951.

Lidz, Theodore; Fleck, Stephen; and Cornelison, Alice R. *Schizophrenia and the Family.* New York: International Universities Press, 1965.

Lidz, Theodore, and Fleck, Stephen. *Schizophrenia and the Family.* 2nd ed. New York: International Universities Press, 1985.

Liu, William T., and Yu Elena S. H. "Ethnicity, Mental Health, and the Urban Delivery System." In *Urban Ethnicity in the United States: New Immigrants and Old Minorities,* vol. 29, Urban Affairs Annual Review, edited by Lionel Maldonado and Joan Moore, pp. 211–47. Beverly Hills, Calif.: Sage Publications, 1985.

Loewenberg, Peter. *Decoding the Past: The Psychohistorical Approach.* Berkeley, Los Angeles, and London: University of California Press, 1984.

_____. "A Hidden Zionist Theme in Freud's 'My Son, the Myops . . . 'Dream." *Journal of the History of Ideas* 31 (1970), pp. 129–32.

Mahoney, Patrick J. *On Defining Freud's Discourse.* New Haven and London: Yale University Press, 1989.

Malcolm, Janet. *Psychoanalysis: The Impossible Profession.* New York: Vintage, 1982.

―――. "Reflections: J'appelle un chat un chat." *The New Yorker,* April 20, 1987, pp. 84–102.

Mantegazza, Paolo. *Anthropological Studies in the Sexual Relations of Mankind.* New York: Falstaff Press, 1937.

―――. *The Physiology of Love.* New York: Cleveland Publishing Co., 1894.

"Mantegazza, Paolo." *Brockhaus' Konversations-Lexikon,* vol. 11, 14th ed., Leipzig: 1894.

"Mantegazza, Paolo." *Dizionario Biografico degli Scrittori Contemporanei,* vol. Cav-Del. Firenze: Angelo de Gubernatis, 1879.

"Mantegazza, Paolo." *Enciclopedia Italiana di Scienze, Lettere ed Arti,* vol. 22. Roma: 1934.

"Mantegazza, Paolo." *Encyclopaedia Britannica,* vol. 17. 11th ed.

"Mantegazza, Paolo." *La Grande Encyclopédie: Inventaire Raisonné des Sciences, des lettres et des arts,* vol. 22. Paris: 1886–1902.

"Mantegazza, Paolo." *Ministri Deputati e Senatori d'Italia dal 1848 al 1922,* vol. 2, ed. Alberto Malatesta. Roma: Tosi, 1946.

"Mantegazza, Paolo." In "Nécrologie." *L'Anthropologie,* vol. 21. Paris: Masson, 1910.

Marcus, Steven. "Freud and Dora: Story, History, Case History." In *Representations: Essays on Literature and Society,* pp. 247–310. New York: Random House, 1975.

Masson, Jeffrey M. *The Assault on the Truth: Freud's Suppression of the Seduction Theory.* New York: Farrar, Straus and Giroux, 1984.

May, Arthur J. *The Habsburg Monarchy, 1867–1914.* Cambridge: Harvard University Press, 1960.

―――. *Vienna in the Age of Franz Josef.* Norman: University of Oklahoma Press, 1966.

Mayreder, Rosa. *A Survey of the Woman Problem.* Translated by Herman Scheffauer. New York: G. H. Doran, 1913.

McCaffrey, Phillip. *Freud and Dora: The Artful Dream.* New Brunswick, N.J.: Rutgers University Press, 1984.

McCagg, William O. *A History of Habsburg Jews: 1670–1918.* Bloomington and Indianapolis: Indiana University Press, 1989.

McCarthy, J. D., and Yancey, W. L. "Uncle Tom and Mr. Charlie: Metaphysical Pathos in the Study of Racism and Personal Disorganization." *American Journal of Sociology* 76 (1971), pp. 648–72.

McGrath, William J. *Freud's Discovery of Psychoanalysis: The Politics of Hysteria.* Ithaca, N.Y., and London: Cornell University Press, 1986.

Mendel, Emanuel. "Über Hysterie beim männlichen Geschlecht." *Berliner Klinische Wochenschrift* 21 (1884), pp. 314–17, 330–31, 347–48.

Mendelsohn, Ezra. *The Jews of East Central Europe Between the World Wars.* Bloomington: Indiana University Press, 1983.

Merton, Robert K. *Social Theory and Social Structure.* New York: Free Press, 1968.

"Meran." *Encyclopaedia Britannica,* Vol. 18, 11th ed.

Meynen, E., ed. *Sudetendeutscher Atlas.* München: Verlag der Arbeitsgemeinschaft zur Wahrung sudetendeutscher Interessen, 1954.

Mitchell, S. Weir. *Fat and Blood: And How to Make Them.* Philadelphia: J. B. Lippincott, 1877.

Moller, Herbert. "Wet Dreams and the Ejaculate." *Maledicta* 4 (1980), pp. 249–51.

Monroe, Will S. *The Spell of Bohemia.* Boston: L. C. Page, 1910.

Morantz, Regina. "The Lady and Her Physician." In *Clio's Consciousness Raised: New Perspectives on the History of Women,* edited by Mary S. Hartman and Lois Banner, pp. 38–53. New York: Harper & Row, 1974.

————. "The Perils of Feminist History." *Journal of Interdisciplinary History* 4 (1974), pp. 649–60.

Morton, Frederic. *A Nervous Splendor: Vienna 1888/1889.* New York: Penguin, 1981.

Muslin, Hyman, and Gill, Merton. "Transference in the Dora Case." *Journal of the American Psychoanalytic Association* 26 (1978), p. 311–28.

Nunberg, Herman, and Federn, Ernst, eds. *Minutes of the Vienna Psychoanalytic Society,* vols. 1–4. New York: International Universities Press, 1962–75.

Ormerod, J. A. *Diseases of the Nervous System.* Philadelphia: Blakiston, 1892.

Otruba, Gustav. "Der Anteil der Juden am Wirtschaftsleben der böhmischen Länder seit dem Beginn der Industrialisierung." *Die Juden in den böhmischen Ländern,* pp. 209–68. München, Wien: R. Oldenbourg, 1983.

Oxaal, Ivar. "The Jews of Young Hitler's Vienna: Historical and Sociological Aspects." In *Jews, Antisemitism and Culture in Vienna,* edited by Ivar Oxaal et al., pp. 11–38. London and New York: Routledge & Kegan Paul, 1987.

Pick, Joseph C. "The Economy" *The Jews of Czechoslovakia: Historical Studies and Surveys,* vol. 1, pp. 359–408. Philadelphia: Jewish Publication Society of America, 1968.

Pollock, George H. "The Possible Significance of Childhood Object Loss in the Josef Breuer–Bertha Pappenheim (Anna O.)–Sigmund Freud Relationship. I. Josef Breuer." *Journal of the American Psychoanalytic Association* 16 (1968), pp. 711–39.

Pulzer, Peter G. J. "The Development of Political Anti-semitism in Austria." *The Jews of Austria*, pp. 428–43. London: Vallentine, Mitchell, 1967.

————. *The Rise of Political Anti-Semitism in Germany and Austria*. New York: John Wiley & Sons, 1964.

Purves-Stewart, James. *The Diagnosis of Nervous Diseases*. 7th ed., rev. St. Louis: C. V. Mosby, 1931.

Quinn, Susan. *A Mind of Her Own: The Life of Karen Horney*. New York: Summit Books, 1987.

Rabinbach, Anson. *The Crisis of Austrian Socialism: From Red Vienna to Civil War, 1927–1934*. Chicago: University of Chicago Press, 1983.

Ramas, Maria. "Freud's Dora, Dora's Hysteria: The Negation of a Woman's Rebellion." *Feminist Studies* 6:3 (Fall 1980), pp. 472–510.

Reich, Annie. "The Discussion of 1912 on Masturbation and Our Present-Day Views." *Psychoanalytic Study of the Child*, vol. 6, pp. 80–94. New York: International Universities Press, 1951.

Reimann, Viktor. *Zu Gross für Österreich: Seipel und Bauer im Kampf um die Erste Republik*. Wien-Frankfurt-Zürich: Verlag Fritz Molden, 1968.

Reiser, Lynn Whisnant. "Topsy—Living and Dying: A Footnote to History." *Psychoanalytic Quarterly* 56:4 (Oct. 1987), pp. 667–88.

Rieff, Philip. *Fellow Teachers*. New York: Harper & Row, 1973.

————. *Freud: The Mind of the Moralist*. New York: Viking, 1959.

Riff, Michael A. "Czech Antisemitism and the Jewish Response Before 1914." *Wiener Library Bulletin* 29 (1976), pp. 8–20.

Roazen, Paul. *Freud and His Followers*. New York: New American Library, 1976.

Rogow, Arnold A. "A Further Footnote to Freud's 'Fragment of an Analysis of a Case of Hysteria.'" *Journal of the American Psychoanalytic Association* 26 (1978), pp. 330–56.

Rohling, August. *Der Talmudjude. Zur Beherzigung für Juden und Christen aller Stände*. Münster: Adolph Russell, 1871.

Romm, Sharon. *The Unwelcome Intruder: Freud's Struggle with Cancer*. New York: Praeger, 1983.

Rosenberg, Charles. "Sexuality, Class and Role in 19th-Century America." *American Quarterly* 25 (1973), pp. 131–53.

Rosenkranz, Herbert. "The Anschluss and the Tragedy of Austrian Jewry, 1938–1945." In *The Jews of Austria. Essays on Their Life, History and Destruction*, edited by Josef Fraenkel, pp. 479–545. London: Vallentine, Mitchell, 1967.

Rozenblit, Marsha L. *The Jews of Vienna, 1867–1914: Assimilation and Identity*. Albany: State University of New York Press, 1983.

Ruppin, Arthur. *The Jews of Today.* Translated by Margery Bentwich. New York: Henry Holt, 1913.

Russett, Cynthia Eagle. *Sexual Science: The Victorian Construction of Womanhood.* Cambridge: Harvard University Press, 1989.

"A Sale in Vienna. Witz Against Legend?" *Journal of the International Association for the History of Psychoanalysis* (English ed.), 8 (Autumn 1989), pp. 13–14.

Scheichl, Paul. "The Contexts and Nuances of Anti-Jewish Language: Were All the 'Antisemites' Antisemites?" In *Jews, Antisemitism and Culture in Vienna,* edited by Ivar Oxaal et al., pp. 89–110. London and New York: Routledge & Kegan Paul, 1987.

Schnitzler, Arthur. "Fräulein Else," *Viennese Novelettes.* New York: Simon & Schuster, 1931.

———. *My Youth in Vienna.* Translated by Catherine Hutter. New York: Holt, Rinehart and Winston, 1970.

Schorske, Carl E. *Fin-de-Siècle Vienna: Politics and Culture.* New York: Alfred A. Knopf, 1980.

Schur, Max. *Freud: Living and Dying.* New York: International Universities Press, 1972.

Shulevitz, Judith. "A Sampling of Spas." *New York Times,* sec. 5, November 26, 1989, p. 16.

Seidenberg, Robert, and Papathomopoulos, Evangelos. "Daughters Who Tend Their Fathers: A Literary Survey." *Psychoanalytic Study of Society,* vol. 2, pp. 135–60. New York: International Universities Press, 1962.

Shedel, James. *Art and Society: The New Art Movement in Vienna, 1897–1914.* Palo Alto, Calif.: Sposs, 1981.

Shorter, Edward. "Paralysis: The Rise and Fall of a 'Hysterical' Symptom." In *Expanding the Past: A Reader in Social History,* edited by Peter N. Stearns, pp. 215–48. New York and London: New York University Press, 1988.

Sicherman, Barbara. "The Uses of a Diagnosis: Doctors, Patients, and Neurasthenia." *Journal of the History of Medicine and Allied Sciences* 32 (1977), pp. 33–54.

Silberner, Edmund. "The Jewish Background of Victor and Friedrich Adler." *Yearbook of the Leo Baeck Institute,* vol. 10 (1965), pp. 266–76.

Slipp, Samuel. "Interpersonal Factors: Freud's Seduction Theory and the Case of Dora." *Journal of the American Academy of Psychoanalysis* 5 (1977), pp. 359–76.

Smith, Robert C., and Zimny, George H. "Physicians' Emotional Reactions to Patients." *Psychosomatics* 29:4 (Fall 1988), pp. 392–97.

Smith-Rosenberg, Carroll. "The Hysterical Woman: Sex Roles and Role Conflict in 19th-Century America." *Social Research* 39 (1972), pp. 652–78.

Smith-Rosenberg, Carroll, and Rosenberg, Charles. "The Female Animal: Medical and Biological Views of Woman and Her Role in Nineteenth-Century America" *Journal of American History* 60 (1973), pp. 332–56.

Spear, Irving J. *A Manual of Nervous Diseases.* Philadelphia and London: W. B. Saunders, 1916.

Spiegel, Rose. "Freud and the Women in His World." *Journal of the American Academy of Psychoanalysis* 5 (1977), pp. 377–402.

Spielmeyer, Walther. Review of Freud's "Bruchstück einer Hysterie-Analyse." *Zentralblatt für Nervenheilkunde und Psychiatrie* 29 (1906), pp. 322–24.

Stadlen, Anthony. "Was Dora wel ziek?" *Vrij Nederland* 44 (Nov. 2, 1985), pp. 27–31.

Starr, Allen M. *Synopsis of Lectures Upon Diseases of the Nervous System.* New York: James T. Dougherty, 1904.

Stetson, Charlotte Perkins. "The Yellow Wall-paper" *New England Magazine* 5 (Jan. 1982).

Stierlin, Helm. "The Dynamics of Owning and Disowning: Psychoanalytic and Family Perspectives." *Family Process* 15:3 (Sept. 1976), pp. 277–88.

———. *Psychoanalysis and Family Therapy: Selected Papers.* New York: Jason Aronson, 1987.

Strachey, James. "Editor's Note" to "Three Essays on the Theory of Sexuality" (1905). *Standard Edition*, vol. 7. London: Hogarth Press, 1953.

———. "Goethe-Preis, 1930." *Standard Edition*, vol. 21. London: Hogarth Press, 1961.

Stransky, Hugo. "The Religious Life in the Historic Lands." *The Jews of Czechoslovakia: Historical Studies and Surveys*, vol. 1, pp. 330–57. Philadelphia: Jewish Publication Society of America, 1968.

Sulloway, Frank J. *Freud, Biologist of the Mind.* New York: Basic Books, 1979.

Swales, Peter J. "Freud, His Teachers, and the Birth of Psychoanalysis." In *Freud: Appraisals and Reappraisals*, vol. 1, edited by Paul E. Stepansky, pp. 3–82. Hillsdale, N.J.: Analytic Press, 1986.

———. "Freud, Katharina, and the First 'Wild Analysis.'" In *Freud: Appraisals and Reappraisals*, vol. 3, edited by Paul E. Stepansky, pp. 80–164. Hillsdale, N.J.: The Analytic Press, 1988.

Swanson, Lisa, and Biaggio, Mary Kay. "Therapeutic Perspectives on Father-Daughter Incest." *American Journal of Psychiatry* 142:6 (June 1985), pp. 667–74.

Tansey, Michael J., and Burke, Walter F. *Understanding Countertransference: From Projective Identification to Empathy.* Hillsdale, N.J.: Analytic Press, 1989.

Tartakower, Arieh. "Jewish Migratory Movements in Austria in Recent Generations." In *The Jews of Austria*, edited by Josef Fraenkel, pp. 285–310. London: Vallentine, Mitchell, 1967.

Thomson, H. Campbell. *Diseases of the Nervous System.* New York: Funk and Wagnalls, 1910.

Timms, Edward. *Karl Kraus, Apocalyptic Satirist: Culture and Catastrophe in Habsburg Vienna.* New Haven and London: Yale University Press, 1986.

Tur-Sinai, N. H. "Viennese Jewry." In *The Jews of Austria,* edited by Josef Fraenkel, pp. 311–18. London: Vallentine, Mitchell, 1967.

Twain, Mark. "Stirring Times in Austria." *Literary Essays.* Vol. 22 of *The Writings of Mark Twain,* pp. 200–249. New York and London: Harper & Brothers, 1899.

Veith, Ilza. *Hysteria: The History of a Disease.* Chicago: University of Chicago Press, 1965.

Vergo, Peter. *Art in Vienna, 1898–1918: Klimt, Kokoschka, Schiele and their Contemporaries.* London: Phaidon Press, 1975.

――――――. *Vienna 1900: Vienna, Scotland, and the European Avant-Garde.* Edinburgh: Her Majesty's Stationery Office, 1983.

Vitz, Paul C. "Sigmund Freud's Attraction to Christianity: Biographical Evidence." *Psychoanalysis and Contemporary Thought* 6 (1983), pp. 73–183.

Vogel, L. Z. "The Case of Elise Gomperz." *American Journal of Psychoanalysis* 46:3 (1986), pp. 230–38.

Weininger, Otto. *Geschlecht und Charakter.* Vienna: Braumüller, 1903.

Weinzierl, Erika. "Die Stellung der Juden in Österreich seit dem Staatsgrundgesetz von 1867." *Zeitschrift für die Geschichte der Juden.* (1968), pp. 89–96.

Weiss, Edoardo. *Sigmund Freud as a Consultant: Recollections of a Pioneer in Psychoanalysis.* New York: International Medical Book Corp., 1970.

Wells, Linda. "Mirror Images." *New York Times Magazine,* Feb. 21, 1988, p. 76.

Whiteside, Andrew G. *The Socialism of Fools: Georg Ritter von Schönerer and Austrian Pan-Germanism.* Berkeley: University of California Press, 1975.

Wilder-Okladek, F. *The Return Movement of Jews to Austria After the Second World War.* The Hague: Martinus Nijhoff, 1969.

Wilks, Samuel. *Lectures on Diseases of the Nervous System.* Philadelphia: Lindsay and Blakiston, 1878.

Winkler, Ernst. "Der grosse Otto Bauer." In Otto Bauer, *Einführung in die Volkswirtschaftslehre.* Wien: Wiener Volksbuchhandlung, 1955.

Wistrich, Robert S. *The Jews of Vienna in the Age of Franz Josef.* Oxford and New York: Oxford University Press, 1989.

――――――. *Revolutionary Jews from Marx to Trotsky.* London: Harrap, 1976.

――――――. *Socialism and the Jews. The Dilemma of Assimilation in Germany and Austria-Hungary.* East Brunswick, N. J.: Associated University Presses, 1982.

Wittels, Fritz. *Der Taufjude.* Vienna: Breitenstein, 1904.

Wood, Ann Douglas. "'The Fashionable Diseases': Women's Complaints and Their Treatment in Nineteenth-Century America." *Journal of Interdisciplinary History* 4 (1973), pp. 25–52.

Zohn, Harry. *Karl Kraus.* New York: Twayne, 1971.

————. "Participation in German Literature." *The Jews of Czechoslovakia. Historical Studies and Surveys.* vol. 1, pp. 468–522. Philadelphia: Jewish Publication Society of America, 1968.

Zweig, Arnold. *Caliban, oder Politik und Leidenschaft: Versuch über die menschlichen Gruppenleidenschaften dargetan am Antisemitismus.* Potsdam: Gustav Kiepenheuer, 1927.

Zweig, Stefan. *The World of Yesterday.* New York: Viking, 1943.

Index

Haggard, Rider, 99
Hajek, Marcus, 240*n*79
Hall, G. Stanley, 107
Handbook of Electrotherapy (Erb), 8
Hartmann, Ludo Moritz, 59
Haskalah, 18
Headache of hysteria, 11
Heart of the World, The (Haggard), 99
Hegar, Alfred, 102
Heimwehr, 169, 170, 179
Heine, Heinrich, 156
Herem (excommunication), 225*n*18
"Heroic" medicine, 102–3
Herzl, Theodor, 23, 27, 28, 29, 30,
    31, 155–56, 235*n*14, 250*n*25
Hilsner, Leopold, 84–85, 126, 152
History of the Jewish People (Graetz),
    31
Hitler, Adolf, 25, 35, 176–85
Hitschmann, Edward, 202
Holmes, Oliver Wendell, 101
Holocaust, 185
Hormones, 174
Horney, Karen, 74
Housewife psychosis, 54
Hrůzová, Anežka, 84
Hull, Cordell, 183, 184
Humpoletz (Humpolec) Jewish com-
    munity (Bohemia), 42
Hungarian Jews, 153–54
Hungary, 166
Hussite heresy (1420), 187
Hydrotherapy, 8, 12–13, 70, 89,
    102, 129
Hypnosis, 2, 8, 89
Hysteria; *see also* "Anna O."
    (Bertha Pappenheim); "Dora"
    (Ida Bauer)
  anorexia nervosa as 20th-century
    equivalent of, 207–8
  earliest accounts, 207
  Greek source of word, 1
  groups historically prone to, 1, 2,
    6–7, 63–64, 71, 230*n*7

  headache of, 11
  as hereditary, 6–7
  masturbation and, 96–97, 103–4
  among men, 230*n*7, 231*n*18
  19th-century etiology, 6–7, 207
  physical symptoms, 1, 5–6, 207
  retention hysteria, 63–64
  seduction theory of, 89–90, 124,
    125, 193–94, 198, 235*n*7,
    265*n*5
  sexuality as motive power in, 123
  social component, 71
  somatization and, 66, 71
  treatments, 1, 2
    electrotherapy, 2, 8–12, 70,
      89, 102, 129, 198, 211*n*11,
      213
    hydrotherapy, 8, 12–13, 70,
      89, 102, 129
    19-century attitudes and, 7,
      98–99, 100–101, 102, 103,
      110, 129, 204–5
  uterine theory of, 1, 6

Ibsen, Henrik, 27, 122
Infantile sexuality, theory of, 90, 96,
    114, 123–26, 129, 160, 194,
    244*n*47, 258*n*32
Inflation of the 1920s, 167
Innitzer, Cardinal, 183
Intermarriage, 157–58
Interpretation of Dreams, The
    (Freud), 90, 91, 96, 123
"Irma" (Emma Eckstein), 141–43

Jealousy in countertransference,
    120, 121
Jellinek, Adolf, 33
Jewish Enlightenment (*Haskalah*), 18
Jewish State, The (Der Judenstaat)
    (Herzl), 30
"Jewish" tax, 184, 188
Jews; *see also* Anti-Semitism; Bohe-
    mian Jews; Zionism